Introduction to Hospitality Operations

An Indispensable Guide to the Industry

2nd edition

Peter Jones

continuum
LONDON • NEW YORK

Continuum

The Tower Building   370 Lexington Avenue
11 York Road   New York
London SE1 7NX   NY 10017-6503

www.continuumbooks.com

Originally published as *Management of Food Service Operations* in 1994.
Published as *Introduction to Hospitality Operations* in 2001.
This edition published 2002.

British Library Cataloguing-in-Publication Data
A catalogue record for this book is available from the British Library.

ISBN: 0-8264-6078-X (hardback) 0-8264-6077-1 (paperback)

Typeset by YHT Ltd, London
Printed and bound in Great Britain by Biddles Ltd, Guildford and King's Lynn

This book is dedicated to Cliff Goodwin
A fine colleague, a dear friend and a magnificent golfer

Introduction to Hospitality Operations

Related titles

Food Purchasing and Preparation – R. Briggs
Front Office Operations – J. Huyton and S. Baker
Hospitality Operations – S. Ball, P. Jones, D. Kirk and A. Lockwood
Hospitality and Catering: A Closer Look – U. Jones and S. Newton
Sales and Service for the Wine Professional – B. K. Julyan

CONTENTS

LIST OF FIGURES

LIST OF TABLES

ABOUT THE EDITOR

The Editor, **Prof. Peter Jones**, is IFCA Chair of Production and Operations Management in the School of Management at the University of Surrey. Prior to this he was the Forte Professor of Hotel Management at Surrey and the former Associate Dean of the University of Brighton Business School. Since 1981 he has published eight textbooks, as author or editor, and contributed numerous chapters to other texts. In his new role at Surrey, as the 'world's first professor of airline catering', he is applying his expertise and interest in operations management to the flight-catering industry.

CONTRIBUTORS

In preparing this new edition I have been greatly assisted by **Hannah Brown**, who has diligently sought out new data to bring the book up-to-date. Hannah will shortly graduate from the University of Surrey.

The first edition of this book was published in 1996 as an edited text. However, none of the former contributors have been involved in this new edition, but I would like to acknowledge their original contribution.

Since 1996 many have moved on to advance their careers, but this list identifies their institution at the time they contributed their chapter.

Steven Goss-Turner, University of Brighton	The Accommodation Sector Business and Conference Hotels
Angela Roper, Oxford Brookes University	Resort Hotels
Warwick Clifton and Keith Johnson, Huddersfield University	Budget Hotels
Alison Morrison, Strathclyde University	Guest Houses and Small Hotels
Judith Brown, Cheltenham & Gloucester	Hospital Hotel Services and Residential Care
Michael Deakin, Cheltenham & Gloucester	Hostels and Halls of Residence
Hadyn Ingram, Bournemouth University	Licensed Trade Foodservice
Stephen Ball, Huddersfield University	Fast Food
Cliff Goodwin, University of Brighton	Employee Feeding
Nigel Hemmington, Cheltenham & Gloucester	Welfare Catering
David Kirk and Trevor Laffin, Queen Margaret College	Travel Catering

Sadly, in 2001 Cliff Goodwin died. This fourth edition is dedicated to his memory.

Peter Jones, January 2002

PREFACE

This text takes an introductory look at the hospitality industry from a 'macro' perspective. That is to say, it considers sectors of the industry by looking at markets, demand and supply, location, brands, operations and products. Many readers will be familiar with some sectors, such as pubs and restaurants, because they have frequented them as customers. However there are a wide range of sectors that they may be entirely unfamiliar with, some of which are extremely significant, such as employee feeding, welfare, and the different types of hotel operations.

In editing the fourth edition of this text, I have tried to continue writing in an easy-to-read style, to present the information straightforwardly, and to illustrate ideas with practical examples. The book is organized in much the same way as the first edition was, with chapters about each sector of the industry. As far as possible each chapter has been updated with new statistics about the size and scale of the sector, the major operators and brands, and current issues and future trends. The dynamic nature of the industry is captured by identifying how major chains in many sectors have grown in the last five years through merger and acquisition activity. Some of the photographic illustrations have also been updated. There are new sections on a wide range of topics, such as disintermediation, boutique hotels, the better hospital food initiative, micro-footprinting, 'blur', the UK's diamond hotel rating scheme, the internet, and residential care homes. In addtion, each chapter now suggests websites and activities that will help underpin learning in that chapter.

One major change since 1996 is that there is now available another introductory text, *Hospitality Operating Systems*, also published by Continuum (Ball *et al.*, 2002) that takes a very different approach – a 'micro' perspective. This companion volume looks in detail at the different operating systems that are used with the various sectors of the industry discussed in this book. Systems such as front office, housekeeping, bars, production kitchens, and dining rooms.

Many things have changed since I began my career as a hospitality educator. The hospitality industry has become more international, major chains have begun to dominate the industry, new technology has transformed processes, and demand has continued to grow. Likewise UK higher education now attracts many more international students, educates more people from a wider range of backgrounds, and uses new technology to do this. But some things never change – the energy and enthusiasm, the commitment and dedication, the humour and goodwill of colleagues, both in industry and in education. Horst Schulze, CEO of Ritz Carlton Hotels, addressing an audience at a conference about quality management, once said, 'You are quality people. And I love quality people.' You said it Horst!

Peter Jones, January 2002

CHAPTER 1

The hospitality industry

INTRODUCTION

The term hospitality has emerged as the way hoteliers and caterers would like their industry to be perceived. It conveys an image that reflects the tradition of service that goes back over many centuries to the earliest days of inn-keeping. Thus in 1987, the Hotel, Catering and Institutional Management Association – the industry's professional association – changed the name of its journal to *Hospitality*. Likewise in 1991, the British Hoteliers, Restaurateurs and Caterers Association – the UK industry's main trade association – changed its name to the British Hospitality Association. The term has also been adopted by educators, so that most, if not all, universities and colleges now offer courses in hospitality management.

In essence, hospitality is made up two distinct services – the provision of overnight accommodation for people staying away from home, and the provision of sustenance for people eating away from home or not preparing their own meals. Both of these services meet very basic human needs – the need to sleep and the need to eat. It is perhaps because these two things are so fundamental to human existence, that many people, especially in the UK, consider the industry to be straightforward and unsophisticated. Hence a great many people enter the business as small hoteliers, licensees, guesthouse owners and restaurateurs without any previous experience of the industry. A recent study of best practice (Jones, 2001) in small and medium enterprises (SMEs) in the hospitality industry highlighted this. A consultant is reported as saying – '... for many, it's a way of life'. Another suggested, 'Non-professionals come in [to the industry] for a whole range of reasons ... and think of the hospitality sector, whether it's a small restaurant, a guest house, a small hotel or even a pub, they think they bring their life skills to that particular job and can run it successfully'. Likewise the owner of a twenty bedroom hotel and bar/restaurant in Oxfordshire stated, 'Nobody goes into an airport and says "I can fly this!". Everybody, 98 per cent of the population, walks into a pub or hotel and says "It's a piece of cake. I could do this!"'.

Often these entrepreneurs are not as successful as they thought they would be. Indeed the hospitality industry has one of the highest level of bankruptcies of any industry in the UK. The situation in the early 1990s was so bad, that firms of accountants (acting as receivers) owned more hotels than the largest hotel chains in the UK. The prevalence of many small operators also tends to reinforce the argument that quality standards in the industry are poor. Their lack of expertise leads to low standards, and their lack of success leads to little or no investment in their businesses. This also contributes to the industry's image problem. In

1

recognition of this, the UK government launched in 2001 a 'Profit through Productivity' initiative, designed to improve the competitiveness of the UK hospitality industry. Aimed at SMEs, this programme has three steps. The first is a benchmarking index, which will enable small operators to evaluate their performance against industry standards. The second provides a range of interventions designed to help develop the business – a 'best practice club', master class seminars, better business kits, and a helpline. The final step is a recognition programme allowing the operator to receive external accreditation of their business improvement either through Hospitality Assured (a national quality benchmarking scheme, sponsored by HCIMA) or some other business excellence scheme.

Despite low performance by SMEs, the industry has changed significantly over the last twenty years. In the earlier editions of this text, it was argued (Jones, 1988) that this was due largely to the impact of ideas and concepts developed in the USA. Probably a more significant factor, related to American influences, has been the growth of large chains. Throughout the 1980s, there had been the consistent growth of hospitality companies across all sectors of the industry. For instance, roadside dining saw the development of two very strong brands in Little Chef and Happy Eater, along with numerous other smaller operators. On every high street, or in every shopping centre, there were quick-service restaurant chains such as Kentucky Fried Chicken, Burger King and MacDonalds. The large brewers significantly altered their policies towards their licensed premises, developing managed retail outlets rather than tenanted houses. Hotel chains developed strongly branded properties, such as Forte's Travelodge and the Stakis Court hotels. Contract foodservice also saw the emergence of three large companies – Sutcliffes, Gardner Merchant and Compass – who also greatly increased their branding. These large chains transformed the hospitality industry because they introduced more professionalism to the business than ever before. Their size, and hence their financial and manpower resources, enabled them to adopt the highest possible standards and increased competition motivated them to deliver these standards.

In the 1990s this trend has continued with the big firms getting even larger through merger and acquisition. In 1999, over 6000 pubs changed hands. Allied Domecq sold its pub estate to Punch Taverns and major catering companies, such as Scottish & Newcastle, Whitbread and Bass have also reduced their pub businesses to concentrate on other activities. For example Bass disposed of its brewing activities in 2000 in order to concentrate on leisure activities and to expand internationally. Hotel chains have continued to change hands and consolidate. Granada purchased and then disposed of Forte Hotels, with all of the Granada Post House chain becoming Holiday Inns. Greenalls plc changed its name to De Vere Group in February 2000 and sold its pub and restaurant division making space for hotels, leisure and fitness. In 1999, Accor UK Economy Hotels Ltd network grew by 22 per cent as a result of its acquisition of the US chain Redroof Ltd. In May 2000 Marriott International and Hyatt Corporation revealed plans to merge their US hotel supplies-buying businesses, providing all the goods and services needed by the hospitality industry. *Keynote (2000a)* reports that 'there has been a high level of consolidation in the hotels market since the late 1990s and although opportunities for major takeovers are now limited, takeovers will remain an attractive option for some of the very large groups'. In foodservice, Granada Hospitality merged with Compass.

In this chapter, the hospitality industry is defined. The historical background and development of the industry is then described, prior to identifying the current size and scale of the industry in the mid 1990s. The different industry-wide organizations are then identified and their role discussed. This leads into an explanation of what is meant by operations and what trends have influenced the design of operations in the industry. The chapter concludes with an outline of the future of the industry.

DEFINING THE INDUSTRY

In order to describe, discuss and analyse the hospitality industry, it is first necessary to define the industry. This is not as simple as at first might be thought. Different sources, such as government agencies, market intelligence consultants, and other experts, use different criteria for defining the industry. A good starting point is the Standard Industrial Classification, since it is the official government source of data about the industry.

Standard Industrial Classification (SIC)

The Standard Industrial Classification (SIC) was begun in 1948 in an attempt to provide uniform statistical records of industrial growth and activity. It defined the hotel and catering industry, under the 1968 classification, as 'Establishments (whether or not licensed for the sale of intoxicating liquors) providing meals, light refreshments, drink or accommodation'. The classification was subsequently revised in 1980. It comprises 'divisions' made up of broad groups of economic activity. Within each division, individual industries are known as 'classes', which are then subdivided into sectors or 'groups'. Groups can further be subdivided by 'activity'. Most of the hospitality industry is classified in division 6 'Services', class 66 'Hotels and Catering', and further subdivided into six groups. However some activities are included in division 9 'Other Services'. The SIC is illustrated in Table 1.1.

There are, however, some problems with the SIC approach, notably with regard to industrial catering. The classification only includes those operations undertaken by specialist catering contractors. So the turnover and employment of staff in catering units operated by business firms is measured under the main activity of the firm. For instance, petroleum or electronics companies may run their own catering operations, but this would not be included under SIC activity 6640. In addition, the classification tends to be based around the UK's approach to licensing premises, either with regard to health and safety or the sale of alcohol. Whilst this makes classification and data collection relatively easy, licensing arrangement may not be the best way to understand and analyse the industry. There is further discussion of how to define and analyse the the two main sectors of the industry – the accommodation sector and foodservice sector – later in this chapter.

Hospitality Training Foundation (HtF)

The Hospitality Training Foundation (HtF) was originally the Hotel and Catering

Table 1.1 *The Standard Industrial Classification of the hospitality industry*

Division 6 Class	Group	Services Activity	
66			Hotels and catering
	661		Restaurants, snack bars, cafes and other eating places
		6611	Eating places supplying food for consumption on the premises
			a. Licensed places
			b. Unlicensed places
		6612	Take-away food shops
	662	6620	Public houses and bars
	663	6630	Night clubs and licensed clubs
	664	6640	Canteens and messes
			a. Catering contractors
			b. Other canteens and messes
	665	6650	Hotel trade
			a. Licensed premises
			b. Unlicensed premises
	667	6670	Other tourist or short-stay accommodation
			a. Camping and caravan sites
			b. Holiday camps
			c. Other tourist or short-stay accommodation not elsewhere specified
Division 9		**Other services**	
		9310	Catering services ancillary to higher education institutions
		9320	Catering services ancillary to schools
		9330	Catering services ancillary to educational and vocational training not elsewhere specified
		9510	Convalescent and rest homes with medical care
		9611	Social and residential homes

Training Board. It continues to engage in independent research into the industry. Its annual research report was previously entitled *Catering and hospitality industry – key facts and figures*, but is now called the *Labour Market Intelligence Report*. This report illustrates the extent to which more than one source is needed in order to identify all the 'key facts', and that these sources vary quite widely. It tends to use the SIC definitions of sectors for the 'commercial sectors', i.e. hotels, restaurants, pubs and bars; but has to draw up its own definitions for the 'catering services sectors', i.e. education, travel, medical, retail distribution. In identifying the size of these sectors, by number of establishments, it cites a number of different sources including the British Tourist Authority (BTA), Home Office, British Hospitality Association (BHA) and Business Monitor, before stating its own estimates of numbers. For instance, according to the BTA there were 27,712 hotels in the UK in 1994, whereas the HtF cited 52,600. In view of the comprehensive review of sources conducted by the HtF, most of the data about the industry cited in this chapter will be derived from their 1999 report.

THE ORIGINS AND DEVELOPMENT OF THE UK HOSPITALITY INDUSTRY

In order to understand the industry and the different sectors that make it up, it is insightful to review how the industry has developed in the UK. The impetus to the growth of hotels, and subsequently the modern hospitality industry, was provided by the railways. The profitable companies began to invest in large comfortable hotels generally located near the main railway stations, and by 1902 there were 70 major hotels owned and controlled by them. This stimulated hotel building by other companies in city centres and at seaside resorts, and the result was a transformation from relatively poor culinary standards of the old coaching inns to the highest and most sophisticated standards of cuisine. The lead was taken by D'Oyly Carte, who brought over Cesar Ritz, and the man whom Ritz himself described as 'certainly the best chef in the world, he surpasses all the other chefs I have ever met', Georges Escoffier. Escoffier was responsible for creating many classical dishes, perfecting the partie system and influencing greatly the organization of kitchen practice. Eating out in such establishments was, at that time, very formal. Customers were expected to wear evening dress and women were seldom seen in public restaurants. Ritz was largely responsible for breaking down this formality and grill rooms 'emerged from the desire of American tourists to avoid the dining ceremonial each night' (Taylor and Bush, 1974).

At the other end of the scale, two companies emerged to provide eating out of a better quality for the masses – the Aerated Bread Co. and J. Lyons. Their immediate popularity was due largely to women, who could not frequent taverns or fashionable restaurants unless escorted. Although they began as tea shops, they began to serve more substantial meals and to establish national chains of restaurants around the country. What is more significant is the fact that they were far more profitable businesses than the hotels.

The development of the motor car revitalized a sector of the hospitality industry that had declined during the railway age, namely smaller hotels and inns. Many such establishments had become public houses, selling only alcoholic beverages and neglecting the provision of food or accommodation. By 1900, the public-house sector had been considerably affected by government legislation during the nineteenth century, such as the Sale of Food and Drugs Act 1875 and numerous licensing Acts. The restriction on the number of licences issued had the direct result of influencing the brewers to invest in the retail trade and in effect cause the start of the tied-house system. The growing influence of large brewing companies also led to a gradual transition from the old tavern and ale house into the splendid Victorian public house. None the less, standards of public-house operations were not immediately improved by the expanding brewing companies, who effectively kept new entrants out and forced low-profit margins upon their tenants, as a result of which beer, in particular, was often adulterated or diluted. So bad was this state of affairs that Earl Grey began the Public House Trust Company in 1903, which was to become the Trust Houses hotel chain. The company bought up free houses and redeveloped the art of innkeeping by offering commission to the company's managers on the sale of food and accommodation but not on liquor sales. The motor car ensured that Trust Houses and other burgeoning hotel companies were to become very successful.

The First World War, 1914–18, interrupted the development of the industry and severely limited food service in particular, due to the imposition of restrictions, regulations and towards the end of the war, rationing. The greatest impact was in the field of industrial catering, which hitherto had been virtually non-existent. Feeding millions of service personnel and eventually, the whole population compelled the government to consider a nation's dietary requirements. This led to the government pressing employers to recognize the importance of adequate nutrition for the workers. By the end of the war, the number of industrial canteens had increased tenfold to nearly 1000, supplying nearly a million meals a day. It is sad to reflect that, immediately after the war, industry failed to maintain these catering facilities so that it was not until the emergence of the Welfare State and the effect of another world war that industrial feeding developed more fully.

Another effect of the First World War was to raise the expectations of the population. This is not to say that haute cuisine was introduced to the general public. Although popular catering in the ABC and Lyons style became smarter and more hygienic, it remained basically simple fare – for the masses it was tea shops during the year and the landlady's cooking at the seaside on holiday. So, in the 1930s, a new type of catering establishment emerged in this sector. Between 1935 and 1937, nearly 100 milk bars opened around the country and although they originally only sold milk products and ice creams, many of them moved into the main stream of popular catering.

Despite the Depression years of the 1930s, overall the inter-war years were good ones for the hospitality industry. After rationing ended, there was a growth among all except the lowest social class in the popularity of eating out. Restaurant sales were boosted by the Licensing Act 1921, which allowed drinks to be served after 11 pm if accompanying meals. London, or at least Soho, saw the growth in Chinese and Indian restaurants, so that for the first time there was an alternative to the expensive French cuisine of top-class establishments or the British fare of the popular catering units. Slowly too, the more enlightened employers were recognizing the value of canteens and their contribution to job satisfaction and productivity. Public houses built in the period were more spacious and more comfortable than ever before, while rural inns found they were increasingly popular with cyclists and motorists. An increasing number of roadside hotels began to concentrate on providing good, well-cooked food, with a reasonably good wine list. Finally, for the first time in peacetime, the government began to concern itself with the nutritional needs of the population and the foundation of school meals was laid by the introduction in 1934 of the 'Milk in Schools Scheme'.

In many respects, the impact of the Second World War was similar to that which had ended only twenty years previously, except that business was further devastated by destruction due to bombing, as well as the disruption caused by rationing food and requisitioning premises. Thus, whilst the luxury hotel and restaurant trade declined, there was a tremendous increase in mass feeding. Professor Medlik (1978) writes that 'probably the most important development of the war was the emergence of communal feeding on an unprecedented scale', while 'industrial catering developed beyond recognition'. But unlike after the First World War, the expansion in these sectors did not decline at the end of the Second World War. The election of a Labour Government resulted in the development of institutional catering in schools and hospitals within the framework of the Welfare State, and the sheer number of industrial and staff canteens, some 25,000 by 1945, ensured that catering for employees would continue. From this, industrial catering contractors developed during the 1950s, such as Bateman's, Sutcliffes and Midland.

The fact that people were now being catered for at work introduced many to the eating-out experience for the first time. Furthermore, the 1950s and 1960s saw a real improvement in living standards and a narrowing of the gap between the expenditure of the richest and the poorest sections of the population. At the same time, the working week gradually became shorter with a consequent increase in leisure time and holidays. The availability of cheap mass travel abroad has widened the horizons of most Britons and dietary trends show that we drink more milk and coffee and consume more poultry, eggs, vegetables and fruit than before 1939.

This did not mean that everyone could afford the luxury of an extensive à la carte menu served in sophisticated surroundings. Frank Berni recognized the need for the simpler meal experience in a pleasant atmosphere and developed the concept of a steak house, which filled a gap in the market between public houses and popular catering units. This latter sector has always had to keep pace with the changing tastes of the public and developments in the industry. Since the milk bars of the 1930s, there have been innumerable variations on the popular catering theme – Kardomah cafés, Golden Eggs, Wimpy and espresso coffee shops predominated in the 1960s and 1970s. The last in this long line of changing images and products is the fast-food operation. Speciality or concept restaurants too have expanded, due to the growth of our multi-racial society and membership of the EEC, so that in large cities and towns the national cuisine of many European and Far Eastern countries may be experienced. As Taylor and Bush (1974) say, 'changes in the last 30 years have indeed been immense, whichever facet of catering (sic) one examines'.

SIZE AND SCALE OF THE UK HOSPITALITY INDUSTRY

As previously mentioned, the size and scale of the industry is very difficult to measure accurately due to problems of definition and data collection. Thus the figures from one source, such as the HtF may be quite different from those from a market research organization such as Marketpower. In order to avoid contradictory data, this section of the report mainly cites the HtF *Research Report 1999*, which in turn draws on a number of sources.

The industry continues to be a major employer in the economy, as illustrated in Table 1.2. The industry in the UK employs over 1.8 million people, representing 8 per cent of the working population. The HtF *Research Report* identifies a 2 per cent decline in employment levels between 1992 and 1998, which is a good performance by the industry in view of the economic conditions in which it was operating. Pubs, bars and clubs are the major employer with 399,000 employees, followed by restaurants and then hotels with contract catering employing 150,000. The remaining 740,000 employees work in the 'hospitality service' sector which covers organizations whose primary aim is not to provide hospitality, i.e. prisons, hospitals and schools. Total employment in the industry can be broken down by job category, mode of employment and gender. In 1992, according to the Labour Force Survey, 17 per cent of the workforce were in management positions, 29 per

Table 1.2 *Employment in the hospitality industry*

	1992	1998
Hotels	300,000	259,000
Restaurants	291,000	332,000
Pubs, bars and clubs	468,000	399,000
Contract catering	113,000	150,000
Industrial*	87,000	95,000
Education*	178,000	159,000
Medical*	342,000	231,000
Travel*	26,000	9,000
Self-employed	165,000	127,000
Other sectors*	191,500	123,000
(includes recreation/cultural, retail distribution, and public administration.)		
TOTAL INDUSTRY	2,370,000	1,880,000

* Data for these sectors includes 500,000 domestics i.e. cleaning staff, and housekeepers
Source: HtF *Research Report (1999)* citing data from *British Hospitality: Trends and Statistics (1999)*

cent in housekeeping and cleaning services, 28 per cent in food preparation and cooking, and 14 per cent in food and drink service. Less than 1 per cent were employed as hotel receptionists or porters. By 2000, there had been a decline to 13 per cent of the workforce being in management positions, a slight decrease to 27 per cent in housekeeping and cleaning services, an increase of 2 per cent to 30 per cent in food preparation and cooking and a major increase of 24 per cent in food and drink service. Just under 2 per cent, which is still relatively low, were employed as hotel receptionists and porters. Employment in the industry tends to be part-time, with 63 per cent of those employed in this category. In general, part-time employment is greater in the not-for-profit sectors. Finally, in 1998, 71 per cent of the workforce was female, this is partly due to the increasing numbers of part-time positions that females prefer especially in the not-for-profit sectors. However, there were some job categories that were biased heavily towards one gender. For instance, according to the Labour Force Survey, 91 per cent of housekeepers are female, whereas 100 per cent of hotel porters are male. Amongst managers, the gender balance is almost equal, except in the licensed trade, where males predominate.

The number of establishments in the hospitality industry that operate in the commercial sector is illustrated in Table 1.3. Of the total establishments, 60 per cent are owned or operated by self-employed people, especially in the hotel sector (70 per cent of hotels). Most of these establishments (85 per cent) are small, employing ten employees or less, making up only 36 per cent of the workforce. Only in the hotel sector is there a significant proportion of establishments (6 per cent) employing more than 25 people, which now makes up two-thirds of the workforce. Between 1984 and 1991 there had been a 5 per cent growth in the total number of hospitality establishments. But different sectors experienced different

Table 1.3 *Establishment in the commercial sectors of the hospitality industry*

	1991	1998
Hotels	52,200	48,730
Restaurants*	46,981	44,420
Pubs and bars, and Clubs	93,200	87,435
Contract catering	19,200	18,151
TOTAL	211,581	198,736

* VAT registered only
Source: HtF *Research Report (1999)*, citing data from *British Hospitality: Trends and Statistics (1999)*

levels of growth or decline. The number of restaurants grew by 14 per cent in this seven-year period, contract catering by 10 per cent and pubs and bars by 5 per cent. However, the number of hotels fell by nearly 9 per cent and clubs by 5 per cent. A different trend is evident during the 1990s. Between 1994 and 1999 the total number of establishments in the commercial sector fell from 211,581 to 198,736. But nearly all of this decline was in the pub sector, although quick-service restaurants also showed a decline. The number of hotels and restaurants remained almost unchanged during this period. In the same period, trends in the not-for-profit sector continued. The total number of outlets remained at about 88,000, but the number of employee feeding outlets fell, health care increased, and education remained static *(Foodservice Intelligence, 2000)*.

In 1981 a total of 3.13 billion meals were consumed away from home in the commercial sector (restaurants, fast food, pubs, hotels and leisure) of the foodservice industry *(Foodservice Intelligence, 2000)*. By 1999 this had increased by 36 per cent to 4.92 billion. The most significant growth was foodservice in pubs which more than doubled in this period to 1.14 billion meals. This contrasts with the not-for-profit sector of the industry (employee feeding, health care, education and other service), which saw a decline of 9 per cent from 3.88 billion to 3.53 billion meals over the same period. The value of food sales also increased. In the commercial sector sales in 1981 were valued (in 1999 prices) at £13,497 million rising to £19,966 million by 1999 – an increase of 48 per cent *(Foodservice Intelligence, 2000)*. In 1981 the average spend on a meal was £4.30 (in 1999 prices), by 1999 it was £4.05. Clearly one of the ways this industry sector has grown is through the supply of high value, low cost meals – assisted by the general lower cost of food in the UK. In the not-for-profit sector, the value of food sales in 1981 was £2,455 million and in 1999 £2,149 million. The spend per head in this sector is considerably lower than the commercial sector, often due to subsidies of various kinds. In 1981 it was 63 pence and in 1999 just 60 pence.

Table 1.4 *Sales turnover in the commercial sectors of the hospitality industry (£million)*

	1991	1998
Hotels/residential	6,406	9,400
Restaurants/cafes	3,841	7,246
Fast food/take aways	4,264	6,784
Pubs and bars	10,447	
Clubs	2,877	
Contract catering	2,175	2,651
Holiday camps/caravans	1,115	1,460
TOTAL	31,125	27,541

Source: HtF *Research Report 1999*, citing data from *Business Monitor SDA 28*

ORGANIZATIONS IN THE HOSPITALITY INDUSTRY

In considering hospitality, we can identify a large number and variety of organizations involved in the industry. The growth of such organizations is a result of the following factors:

- The structure of the industry which continues to have very many small, individually-owned units, in spite of the growth of large companies.

- The industry is heterogeneous – split up into many different, identifiable sectors, each with its own specific needs.

- Geographically, the industry is widespread, with some types of operation concentrated around population centres, although this is not essential for all types.

- The industry is a very large employer and offers a wide range of job opportunities and employment categories.

The HCIMA's *Hospitality Yearbook 2001* has a UK directory totalling 208 different organizations associated with the industry in one way or another. These include trade unions (e.g. the GMB, Transport and General Workers' Union); trade associations (e.g. European Foodservice Equipment Distributors' Association, British Hospitality Association, International Flight Catering Association); non-industry specific professional associations (e.g. the Institute of Management Consultancy, Chartered Society of Designers); advisory bodies (e.g. British Nutrition Foundation, Flour Advisory Bureau, Royal Society of Health); research agencies (e.g. Leatherhead Food Research Association); consumer bodies; statutory bodies and government departments (e.g. Department for Employment and Education, Department of Trade and Industry, Health and Safety Executive); educational and awarding bodies (e.g. Edexcel Foundation, Qualifications and Curriculum Authority); and others (Guild of Food Writers, British Sandwich Association, National Carpet Cleaners' Association, Microwave Association).

There are broadly two types of organization: voluntary ones, for either individuals or organizations, and government and quasi-government agencies, directly relating to the hospitality industry.

Voluntary organizations for individuals

The Hotel and Catering International Management Association (HCIMA) is the professional body for the mainstream of the industry. Its membership exceeds 20,000 and comprises fellows, members, licentiates, students and associates. The association sees its main priority as establishing recognition of the association in order to influence developments in the industry and to provide better job opportunities for its members. In this respect, it provides advisory services for members, maintains a central library, publishes a monthly magazine called *Hospitality*, and employs officers specializing in employment, careers and technical aspects. The HCIMA is also closely involved in discussions concerning catering education at all levels and runs its own full-time and part-time courses leading to association membership, which is recognized as a management qualification.

In addition to this industry-wide association for managers, there are also sector specific management associations. These include the National Association of Licensed House Managers, Hospital Caterers' Association, Local Authority Caterers' Association, and Catering Managers' Association.

As well as management associations, there are a number of associations for the professional groups in the hospitality workforce. These include United Kingdom Bartenders' Guild, United Kingdom Housekeepers' Association, Craft Guild of Chefs, Court of Master Sommeliers, and the Federation of Bakers.

Voluntary organizations by sector

The British Hospitality Association is a typical trade association – a voluntary, non-profit-making body formed by independent firms to protect and advance their common interests. Its mission is to 'take the initiative to ensure that the views of the British hospitality industry are strongly represented to the UK government and to policy makers in the UK and internationally, in order to ensure its members' businesses can flourish'. To achieve this, it offers a range of services and benefits, has a strong Parliamentary lobby, discusses legislation affecting the industry with government departments, offers advice on recruitment and training of staff, and provides information services to its members through publications or from its specialists. In 1999 there were 25,000 establishments in membership: nearly every major hotel group, independent hotels, restaurants, clubs, contract catering companies, motorway service operators and a large number of local hotel associations.

The Brewers' Society, too, is a trade association involved in sponsoring scientific research into brewing, improving trading relations, discussing with government changes in licensing law, which resulted from the Monopolies Commission report, and liaising with other national and international brewing organizations. Of particular interest is the society's annual report on trends in the sale and consumption of alcoholic beverages in the UK.

Other trade associations include International Flight Catering Association, Restaurant Association and Catering Equipment Manufacturers' Association.

Governmental and quasi-governmental agencies

The Hospitality Training Foundation (HfT) is now a non-governmental agency. It was originally set up as the Hotel and Catering Training Industry Board (HCITB) under the Industrial Training Act 1964 and intended to ensure a trained workforce, secure an improvement in the quality and efficiency of industrial training and share the cost of training more evenly among firms. It was funded by a levy of the 1500 or so largest employers, as defined by the size of their payroll. Those employers who systematically met their own training needs were exempt from the levy, while the money over was spent as specific grants to encourage training in particular areas or as key grants to the smaller, non-leviable employers. It operated mainly by training on-the-job instructors within the firms themselves, by providing regional training centres to undertake specific training of personnel and by offering advice and aid through their staff of training advisors. By 1986 nearly 20 per cent of its income was derived from commercial activities. Such activities included operating a wide range of training courses, the small business start-up programme, an extensive open-learning initiative, video and print publications, and consultancy. In 1992, the Board was closed and the Hotel Catering and Traning Company formed to operate as an entirely commercial agency, using former HCTB funds in order to continue a research role for the industry. Funding comes from a combination of commercial activities, government funded projects, sponsorship and the support of Corporate Patrons. Since 1997 the HtF has been designated as the National Training Organisation (NTO) for the hospitality industry. This status means it is recognized by government as the voice of hospitality employers on all aspects of education, training and qualifications.

Supporting the hospitality industry, there are a number of tourism organizations in the UK. The British Tourist Authority (BTA) is predominantly concerned with the development and promotion of tourism to Britain, whilst regional Tourism Boards are active encouraging British residents to holiday within the UK. BTA is funded by grant-in-aid from the Department of Culture, Media and Sport. Funding for 2000/01 was £37 million, whilst partnership support from airlines, hotels, car rental companies, local authorities and others increases marketing resources by some £15 million each year. Created in 1999, the English Tourism Council (ETC) is the strategic body for tourism in England. It receives government funding of £10 million a year. The ETC's job is to take up issues, provide a focus, develop standards, give policy advice, undertake research and offer the latest intelligence about the tourism market to both government and industry. It is guided by the principles set out in *Tomorrow's Tourism*, the government's tourism strategy document. In addition, there are ten Regional Tourist Boards (RTB) in England. Their role is to promote the sustainable development and effective operation of tourism in the regions, in partnership with local authorities, the industry and regional development agencies. The RTB's key functions are marketing, business development and support, quality assurance, policy development and lobbying. They are funded by their own commercial activities, the English Tourism Council, local authorities and their membership and partners within the tourism industry. There are separate national tourist boards (NTB) for Wales, Scotland and Northern Ireland.

HOSPITALITY OPERATIONS

So far this chapter has looked at the hospitality industry and the sectors that make it up. But this text is also concerned with hospitality operations. It will focus on how organizations go about delivering their product/service to the consumer. At this point it is therefore necessary to differentiate between accommodation and foodservice, because essentially they are different kinds of operation. Johnston (1998) has proposed the concept of three main types of operation – product processing operations; customer processing operations; and information processing operations. In reality most activities are a combination of all three – product, customer and information – albeit in different proportions. This concept is useful in understanding the difference between accommodation and foodservice. An accommodation operation is predominantly a customer processing operation, with very little product (i.e. room servicing) and information processing (i.e. reservations, check-in and billing). Whereas a foodservice operation is a product processing operation (i.e. the meal), with a significant element of customer processing (i.e. the 'meal experience'), and limited information processing.

A simple definition of accommodation services is the provision of facilities for an overnight stay. Likewise foodservice can be simply defined as the provision of food and drink ready for consumption away from the home or not prepared in the home. This, however, fails to differentiate the foodservice industry – which provides 'meals' – from the retailing industry – which provides 'food'. Medlik (1978) recognized this problem and defined a catering (sic) establishment in these terms:

1. The goods sold are usually consumed on the premises.

2. The buyer is able to determine the quantity of the goods purchased in a retail shop, but in a catering unit the caterer determines quantity, i.e. portion size.

3. The caterer also determines quality as in most cases the customer orders the meal without seeing it before the order is placed.

4. The caterer is a processor of materials as well as a retailer of goods.

5. In general, the caterer holds less stock and there is a shorter time between receipt of raw materials to point of sale than most retailers.

However developments in the industry now make it much more difficult to distinguish between foodservice and retail, and also to distinguish between operations within the hospitality industry. In the world of the internet and e-commerce this phenomenon is referred to by Davis and Meyer (1998) as 'blur'. They suggest that e-commerce makes it difficult to distinguish between buyers and sellers, products and services, prices and costs. This is a result of speed, connectivity and intangibles. How does 'blur' manifest itself in hospitality? For instance are concepts like All Bar One, TGI Fridays and so on, bars that serve food or restaurants that serve a lot of drinks? Is Prêt a Manger a sandwich bar or a fast-food outlet? Is there any difference between an automatic vending machine selling cans of soft drinks in a shopping centre and one dispensing them in paper cups in a cafeteria? Is the former 'retailing' but the latter 'catering'? If a single cook–chill facility can produce chilled meals for hotel banqueting, employee feeding in offices, and airline meals, in what industry sector should it be located? These are all examples of 'blur', but in hospitality these examples occur for different reasons to those given by Davis and Meyer. The examples show that it is occurring in this industry at the boundary between one form of foodservice and another, where technology is used in a variety of contexts, and when customers do not distinguish between meal occasions.

One way to understand accommodation and foodservice operations, and tackle the issue of blur, is to consider them as 'systems'. A detailed analysis of operational systems is provided in the companion volume to this text – *Hospitality Operating Systems* (Ball *et al.* 2002). Kirk (1995) warns that systems theory has some shortcomings and that its terminology is not always correctly used nor its ideas properly applied. Nonetheless, experience suggests that operations analysis is greatly helped by systems modelling or 'flow process charting'. Systems theory proposes four key elements of any system – inputs, processes, outputs, and feedback. A key feature of most such systems is that they are made up of a number of processes carried out 'back-of-house', i.e. out of sight of the customer; and other processes performed 'front-of-house', i.e. with the customer's involvement. In the hospitality industry, typical back-of-house processes include materials storage, food production, laundry, bedroom cleaning, and so on; whereas front-of-house operations include guest reception, restaurant service, bar operations, and lounges. This can be illustrated in Figure 1.1.

Figure 1.1 *General systems model of hospitality operations*

If an accommodation operation is systems modelled in this way, as a customer-processing operation, it is possible to identify a 'core system', which is based around the provision of a space in which to sleep, along with a number of sub-systems or 'ancillary services' which may or may not be offered, according to the nature of the service, i.e. hostel, hotel, hospital, etc. Such services might include laundry, meals, drinks, business services (telephone, fax, etc.), and leisure services (fitness centres, swimming pools, etc.). This can be modelled as in Figure 1.2

Foodservice, when modelled as a system, largely focuses on aspects of the product processing operation. Jones and Huelin (1990) propose that there is a maximum of ten stages in the foodservice process, but that these can be combined in different ways, with some of the stages being eliminated. These alternative configurations reflect the different kinds of foodservice operation that have been devised to meet different customer needs. This is illustrated in Figure 1.3.

In modelling the complex, real world in this way, it should be made clear that

CORE SYSTEM

Figure 1.2 *Systems model of accommodation operations*

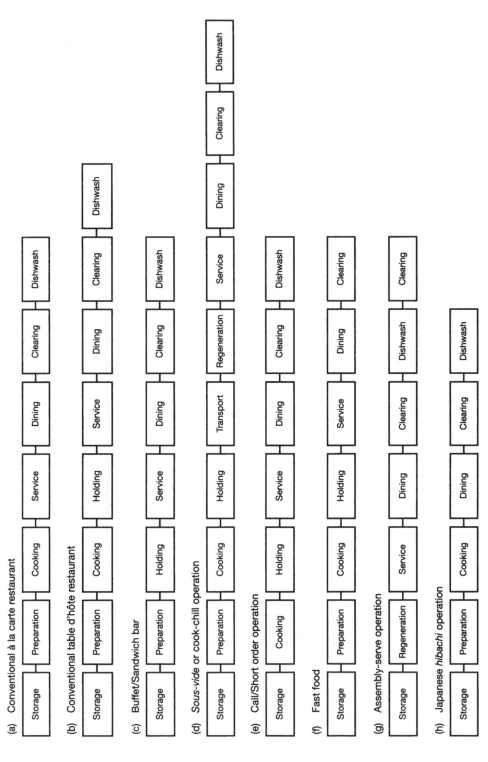

Figure 1.3 *Systems model of foodservice operations*

(a) Conventional à la carte restaurant

Storage — Preparation — Cooking — Service — Dining — Clearing — Dishwash

(b) Conventional table d'hôte restaurant

Storage — Preparation — Cooking — Holding — Service — Dining — Clearing — Dishwash

(c) Buffet/Sandwich bar

Storage — Preparation — Holding — Service — Dining — Clearing — Dishwash

(d) Sous-vide or cook-chill operation

Storage — Preparation — Cooking — Holding — Transport — Regeneration — Service — Dining — Clearing — Dishwash

(e) Call/Short order operation

Storage — Cooking — Holding — Service — Dining — Clearing — Dishwash

(f) Fast food

Storage — Preparation — Cooking — Holding — Service — Dining — Clearing

(g) Assembly-serve operation

Storage — Regeneration — Service — Dining — Clearing — Dishwash — Clearing

(h) Japanese hibachi operation

Storage — Preparation — Cooking — Dining — Clearing — Dishwash these systems diagrams (or flow process charts) are considerable simplifications. In addition, Pickworth (1988) suggests that systems can either be 'multi-faceted', i.e. serve a variety of functions, or 'dedicated', i.e. perform a single function. A good example of a multi-faceted system is a hotel kitchen which produces food not only for the restaurant but also for floor service, banqueting and lounge service. Likewise fast-food restaurants are adding take-out windows and home delivery provision to their operation. Good examples of dedicated service delivery systems would be a sandwich bar, a pub bar, or a hotel laundry. Each of these is designed to serve one purpose and one purpose only.

TRENDS IN OPERATIONS' DESIGN

A fundamental principle of operations management is to reduce complexity, as this adds to costs, threatens quality, and creates inefficiency. Indeed Thompson (1967) has stated that the ideal operation is one in which 'a single kind of product [is produced] at a continuous rate and as if inputs flowed continuously at a steady rate and with specified quality'. More recently, Schmenner and Swink (1998) have proposed the theory of smooth and even flow. It is therefore not surprising that a clear trend in the hospitality industry has been to develop operations that reduce complexity by reducing the number of systems within one operation. In the accommodation sector this has seen the emergence of motels, budget hotels and even 'capsule hotels' in Japan. Likewise over the last thirty years, there has been a trend to move away from multi-faceted service delivery systems towards dedicated ones. In the foodservice industry, many of the recent developments in restaurant chains, cook–chill and sous-vide correspond with this aim.

Jones (1988) has proposed that there have been three major ways in which hospitality operations have developed over the last twenty years, adding a further two in 1999. These five trends are production lining; decoupling; increased customer participation; micro foot-printing; and dual use.

1. *Production-line approach* It has been suggested (Levitt, 1976) that the total system might be looked at as a production line. Thus traditional 'craft-based' kitchen and restaurant operations can be turned into batch-process or mass-production systems. This technocratization of service can be achieved by using 'hard' technologies, such as automatic-vending machines, or 'soft' technologies, which focus on the people and systems in operation. This approach has largely been adopted by the foodservice industry. Because accommodation provision is largely a consumer processing operation, it is difficult to introduce new technology into the system.

2. *Decouple* Chase (1981) has suggested the idea of isolating the technical core of the service business so that efficiency could be improved in the non-contact part of the provision. This is most suited to the service industries he describes as 'low-contact', since the approach suggests that the technical core can then by set up to operate continuously irrespective of short-term changes in customer demand. Cook–chill and sous-vide food production enables such decoupling (see also Figure 1.3).

3. *Increased consumer participation* Another trend investigated involves greater levels of consumer participation in the service experience, both in terms of self-selection and self-service. So approaches to increasing consumer participation might include family-style or self-help salad bars in restaurants, and automated check-in to budget hotels.

4. *Micro foot-printing* Jones (1999) identifies that foodservice operations are being designed much smaller, so that they can be located in 'host environments' that until recently have been too small for catering. One UK chain – Sunnyside UP – was specifically designed in this way, and most of the major international fast-food chains have also developed smaller unit sizes, sometimes as carts or kiosks. This means that foodservice can now be carried out in cinemas, supermarkets, petrol-filling stations, and so on.

5. *Dual use* Another development has been to use the same infrastructure or building for more than one operation. For instance, a single building on London's South Bank houses both a Marriott Hotel and a Travel Inn (both operated by Whitbread Hotels). Accor have built a hotel in Paris that also has two hotels in it. Many roadside restaurants are also dual use with both a Little Chef and Burger King operation in the same unit.

Figure 1.4 *Japanese* hibachi *restaurant.*
Source: Benihana

FUTURE OF THE HOSPITALITY INDUSTRY

In 1996 it was identified (Jones, 1996) that a number of factors would significantly affect the industry in the future. Many of these continue to apply to the 2000s.

The impact of legislation has been significant throughout the 1990s. In 1998 the National Minimum Wage Act established minimum rates of pay for all workers, and the Part-Time Workers' Regulations in 2000 gave part-time workers the same rights as full-timers. Both affected the industry significantly. The European Union and European-wide legislation is also having an impact, such as the Human Rights Act. The Health and Safety at Work Act 1974 was updated through a set of six new regulations in an effort to conform to a European standard. In the public sector, European Union legislation on procurement had a significant impact on materials purchased by universities, local authorities and other public sector hospitality providers. Likewise the European Council agreed the Unfair Contract Terms Directive which affects contractual relationships between hospitality providers and their customers. Finally, there was the long awaited EC Food Hygiene Directive. Its implementation has meant a revision of UK hygiene laws and new guidelines on effective practice. The BHA is concerned that in addition to the recently set up UK Food Standards Agency, there may also be a European Food Authority, further adding to regulation.

The BTA has argued that government does not recognize the difference between the hospitality industry and other industries when creating such new legislation, especially in the area of employment. In particular the industry has a high proportion of small- and medium-size enterprises and employs a very large number of part-time workers. For example, it is claimed that the volume of essential regulatory guidance for small firms has now grown to 1500 pages. Likewise the Part-Time Workers' Regulation, which came into force in July 2000, prevents employers from treating part-time workers differently than full-time workers. It gives part-time workers the same rights in relation to areas such as holiday entitlement, maternity leave, pay and pensions. This has had large implications on the hospitality industry as there are an estimated 6 million part-time employees in the UK and the financial impact, as a result from the regulations is estimated at £23.4 million per annum.

A second trend has been the 'privatization' of public-sector catering, which dramatically altered the nature of catering in these areas, irrespective of whether it was contracted out or retained in-house. In the late 1990s the concept of compulsory competitive tendering was replaced by a 'best value scheme', emphasizing quality rather than cost as a key element of awarding public sector contracts. This issue is now less one concerned with public services, but is tied up with the whole concept of outsourcing. It is no longer assumed that all the activities of a firm will be managed and operated by employees of that firm. So some hotel chains have contracted out cleaning services to cleaning companies. Likewise some hotel restaurants are leased to restaurateurs or operated on a franchise agreement. In flight catering, very few airlines continue to operate their own production kitchens, preferring to outsource to specialist flight caterers.

A third factor has been the growth of health awareness and the trend towards a more healthy diet. This has been recognized by all sectors. This was illustrated by Wimpy's introduction of their wholemeal bun, major campaigns by many local education authorities, the growth of salad bars in steak-house chains, and so on. However, the change in the British diet is far less dramatic than that in the USA, where low-calorie, low-cholesterol and low-sodium items are found on many menus. This reluctance to change may reflect the natural conservatism of the UK population, or it may be a result of the farming lobby in the British Isles, in particular the meat and milk producers, effectively damping down interest in more healthy foods. A number of agencies have responded to the influence of these vested interests. In 1987 there was a £2 million, government-sponsored campaign called 'Look after you Heart'. In 1994, the government was continuing to try to change the hearts and minds (and hence the health) of the population through yet another campaign. An increase in consumers in favour of healthy eating has caused many restaurants to change their menus to cater for consumers' wants. For instance, MacDonalds now offers salad as a healthy option with their burger. In 1999, the first organic fast-food café selling organic sandwiches, juices and coffee opened in North London.

A fourth factor is food health scares. A higher awareness of food contamination and allergies has caused considerable chaos and a decrease in consumer confidence in the food industry. Throughout the years there have been food scares concerning rice, nuts, salmonella in eggs and BSE in beef to name a few, which have severely damaged the reputation of certain foods. In 2000 and 2001 the most recent and most damaging food scare occurred. Foot and mouth spread very quickly around the UK and then eventually on to Europe. It resulted in the slaughter of thousands of cows and sheep across the country. This event not only affected the foodservice industry but also hotels, as the volume of incoming tourists declined substantially and fewer people visited the countryside. The BTA estimates the industry lost £1.5 billion as a result of this.

A fifth factor is the technological advances made in preserving raw or semi-prepared foodstuffs, and finished, ready-for-consumption meal products. The two most innovative techniques are the irradiation of raw materials and sous-vide techniques for finished dishes. Meanwhile, cook–chill has been widely adopted across many sectors. Whilst technology will continue to have an impact, the type of technology in the late 1990s will be very different. Rather than large-scale production technology, the greatest impact will be from information technology. This will not be so much as a result of the introduction of new hardware, but through the development of new software systems. Such systems will greatly simplify reporting procedures, forecasting, inventory control, staff scheduling, energy management, and other complex information processing activities within hospitality operations. Recently, there have been developments in internet services for home delivery and take-away food. In June 1999 Sandwich Online, an independent catering operation, offered online ordering aimed at office workers who were unable to leave the office during their lunch break. Domino's Pizza have also launched an interactive television ordering service and have introduced its online ordering service for take-aways.

The role of suppliers also altered in the late 1980s. A growing trend was the development of cash-and-carry chains aimed specifically at the foodservice market, such as Bookers. In 1999 it operated 176 branches with an annual sales turnover of £3.4 billion. Wholesalers and distributors have also increased in size. In 1987 there were five wholesalers with a catering turnover of over £30 million. By 2000, Brake Brothers' turnover alone was £35.5 million, an 18 per cent increase on 1998. There is also a tendency for caterers to expect a 'one-drop' service, i.e. a supply of the full range of commodities from one supplier in order to reduce delivery frequency, ordering complexity and invoice administration. In the 1990s the major trend has been the level of supplier involvement with their customers. Large companies provide business advice, supply equipment, have nutritional advisory services, and even dispense legal advice. Many of them are large international companies, with many different specialist divisions.

A seventh issue is political stability. The hospitality industry has always had to cope with political situations around the world, that result in the decrease in travellers going to a particular country at certain times. For instance, foot and mouth in the UK and the ongoing delicate political situation in Northern Ireland remains a cause of concern for many people. However, the attacks on New York's World Trade Centre of 11 September 2001 are potentially the most serious to affect the industry since the end of the Second World War. It may prove to be the catalyst to deepen and worsen a slowdown in the global economy. The hospitality industry has clearly suffered with consumer confidence deteriorating, resulting in air travel falling by 40 per cent and the possibility of massive job losses. However, the hospitality industry is large and will survive and continue to grow, confidence will be restored and the continuing need for business people to travel will help boost the market.

Finally, in nearly every segment of the industry there have been mergers and acquisitions leading to higher levels of industry concentration, i.e. a relatively small number of large firms with greater market share. As a result of this the industry is almost certainly likely to become very much more competitive in the future, as these firms seek sustained growth in a relatively stable market.

SUMMARY

This chapter has introduced the hospitality industry and its two main sectors – accommodation and foodservice. It has further defined and subdivided the industry based on the Standard Industrial Classification. The origins and historical development of the UK industry has been explored, identifying the role that government, entrepreneurs and firms have had in creating the industry that we see today. The size and scale of the industry make it one of the largest and most significant industries in the UK, employing nearly 2 million people. As a large and complex industry there are many organizations involved, including voluntary organizations for both individuals and sectors, as well as governmental or quasi-governmental bodies.

The chapter also analysed hospitality operations, separately analysing accommodation systems and foodservice systems. Both of these have been affected by five trends in design – production-lining, decoupling, self-service, micro-footprinting and dual usage. The industry is highly dynamic and is affected by a number of ongoing issues in relation to legislation, outsourcing, health awareness, food contamination, technology, supply chain management, political stability, and industry concentration. All of these will be further explored in the remaining chapters of this book, which look at each part of the industry in some detail.

FURTHER STUDY

Brotherton, R. (2000) *An Introduction to the UK Hospitality Industry: A Comparative Approach*, Butterworth Heinemann: Oxford.

www.britishtouristauthority.org

www.bha-online.org.uk

www.htf.org.uk

www.hcima.org

QUESTIONS

1. Select five hospitality operations found in the area where you study or live. Identify the type of operation they are based on as in Figure 1.2 for hotels or Figure 1.3 for foodservice operations.

2. Examine how the markets these operations serve and their location reflect the type of operation they are.

PART 1

THE ACCOMMODATION INDUSTRY

CHAPTER 2

The accommodation sector

INTRODUCTION

The demand for accommodation as part of an overall experience in hospitality has developed dramatically for those travelling, whether for leisure or business, ever since people had the desire, need and capability, to stay away from home. Such a rapid growth has been fundamentally linked to transport systems and the technological advances of the last 150 years. From the train to the car and the jet aeroplane, travel on an ever-greater scale has become possible. Add to this the increasingly complex patterns of business and trade, and the relatively enhanced wealth and disposable income of the industrialized economies, and this amounts to a massive international demand for hospitality and accommodation.

Demand has a tremendously varied nature and subset of components. The basic division between business and pleasure travellers may in turn be fragmented into a whole series of markets, users with differing needs, all dependent on factors such as availability, price, location and facilities. The accommodation industry began small, with inns and taverns, bed and breakfast and private hotels, and this is still a significant sector of the business. In many countries, such as the UK and France, the industry is still dominated in numerical units by small enterprises, often individually owned and operated. In 2000, Keynote estimated that the UK hotel market was made up of approximately 60,000 businesses offering hotel accommodation, with a turnover of £11 billion. A minority of the UK hotel accommodation is made up of the larger and predominantly international hotel chains such as Holiday Inn and Marriott. The majority are guest houses and privately owned hotels, with less than 50 letting bedrooms, at bed and breakfast rates of £30 per person per night. Contrast this type of operation and demand with a 5-star rated London establishment of perhaps 300 bedrooms with a room rate of £300 for a single room per night, breakfast not included. The accommodation aspect of the hospitality industry is as broad and all-encompassing as this, a circumstance which makes it all the more fascinating.

WHO STAYS AWAY FROM HOME AND WHY?

The types of customer served by the accommodation sector may be broadly divided into those people engaged in travelling on business or recreation, and those people not engaged in travel but who are staying away from home on a temporary basis, such as students in hostels and patients in hospitals. There may also be an overlap of reasons why people are staying away from home. For instance, some business trips involve attending a conference and are followed by a holiday. Broadly speaking, the travellers are served by the commercial hotels chains, and the non-travelling customers by the not-for-profit sector. Table 2.1 illustrates sources of demand by certain categories of individual and by continental and overall dimension. It is instructive to compare the relative percentages of business travellers, tourists and, in this study, the conference delegates. It illustrates the state of the market for different parts of the world, and indicates the forms of accommodation development that need to be developed by the international players.

Table 2.1 *Sources of demand for hotel accommodation 1997 (%)*

Purpose of visit	Worldwide	Africa and Middle East	Asia	North America	Europe
Government officials	2.2	4.6	2.1	5.0	1.0
Business travellers	28.5	39.5	35.7	21.3	26.1
Leisure travellers	34.1	19.5	27.8	42.9	37.6
Tour groups	17.7	18.6	17.9	10.7	18.6
Conference participants	10.1	3.6	5.9	11.8	11.2
Others	7.4	14.2	10.6	8.3	5.5

Source: Horwath International and Smith Travel Research (1998)

In the commercial hotel sector, hotel guests can be divided into two main sources geographically, from domestic and foreign markets of origin. In 2000, there were just over 25 million overseas visitors to the UK (BHA, 2000). This compares with UK residents who took 106 million holidays of one night or more, along with 24 million overnight business trips, and a further 1.26 billion day trips. It is therefore not surprising that the spending of £16.3 billion by overseas visitors to the UK is considerably less than the £58.8 billion spent by UK residents.

There are also two main sources of hotel guest from a distribution viewpoint, direct or through intermediaries in the travel industry. A report by the BTA in 1988 revealed that all hotel reservations were made directly by clients or through travel agents and tour operators. Just over ten years later the trend has changed and two new innovative ways have been introduced to assist clients in reserving a hotel bedroom. At present, only 4.9 per cent of hotel bookings around the world are being made through the internet, however it is estimated that within three years this number would have trebled to over 15 per cent. The accountancy firm KPMG have also estimated that 90 per cent of hotels are now able to provide confirmation to guests making reservations online. A second way for businessmen and women to book a hotel room is by using a booking agency: this trend has grown rapidly over the past few years. The Hotel Booking Agents' Association (HBAA) was formed in 1997 with just four members. There are now 36 members that are booking more than three million rooms and servicing clients who spend £400 million on hotel reservations each year. Another continuing way of making a hotel reservation is through the burgeoning number of central reservations systems. This latter method has led to billions of pounds of investment by the large international chains as they try to bind their clients, both direct customers and travel agents, into making a series of reservations through one computerized reservation centre.

It is now necessary to look at the major demand sources in a little more detail. Clearly, the more specific market sector chapters that follow will concentrate more closely on the relationship between the market segment and the accommodation provision for that segment.

Business travellers

The purposes of business travel and the subsequent need for accommodation may be summarized as the need for company management to attend meetings, undertake sales visits, to attend conferences or conventions, to attend trade exhibitions and training or management development courses. According to the Keynote Report (2000a), 64 per cent of all such travellers stay in hotels. For the larger properties in the main cities and commercial areas, this business is crucial. It fills midweek rooms out of holiday times, it is often at a high rate and volume, and therefore highly profitable. The London-based Granada Group plc (now merged with Compass) claimed that 50 per cent of all their business at their Heritage chain was generated from this market, and that the proportion of US guests had increased 'fourfold' since 1996. In terms of client type, this market is split into corporate (firms sending their employees out on business) and consumer (individual business travellers) sectors, with the corporate sector accounting for the bulk of sales.

Corporate business travel frequently entails firms negotiating special corporate rates with particular hotel chains, usually by guaranteeing a minimum number of bednights per annum. Corporate employees are therefore directed to stay in hotels belonging to that chain. But what are the priorities for the individual business traveller, who can choose their hotel, in selecting a particular property? A major survey of business people has itemized their key decision-making factors. Location and its convenience was predictably high on the list of priorities, as well as transport schedules and the overall comfort of the accommodation, summarized as 'a business setting in comfortable surroundings'. This business setting must include efficient and sufficient business facilities: the office away from home. Many respondents, from both the USA and the UK desired 'corporate and recreational facilities', meaning the most up-to-date business centre, with all required modern communications technology, and a fully equipped leisure centre, on site and readily available for relaxation periods. Other important factors were staff attitude, and the ambience and decor of the property, with a concentration on room furnishings and facilities, notably features such as direct-dial telephone, desk space and lighting, and trouser presses.

Major hotel companies fully recognize both the rate and volume advantages of business travellers and are adapting accommodation to meet the growing needs of this market for which competition is so intense. One such example is the mid-sized British group Friendly Hotels. In 1992 this company's research showed that senior managers preferred to conduct business meetings in their own lounge rather than in public areas. In some of their hotels in highly commercial locations, they have built suites, 'so that the lounge area can double up as a temporary office or boardroom, with fax and work desk'. These suites contain many of the features required by today's business people – colour teletext TV, Internet link, radio, in-room videos and/or satellite channels, phone, tea and coffee-making facilities and welcome drink, trouser press, minibar, hair dryer, and personal toiletries, with a kitchenette equipped with refrigerator and microwave. Other companies have endorsed their increasing segmentation of the business market by offering executive floors to the higher spending senior management, often termed 'Clubs', where there are dedicated executive lounges, with permanent staff to arrange all business needs and to offer special facilities such as fast check-in and check-out and immediate onward reservations to other hotels within the group. The Tower Thistle Hotel in London in 1993 opened just such an executive floor, known as the 'City Club', with the stated aim of being a more attractive venue for high level executives, especially 'if we could create a smaller hotel inside the hotel'.

A growing trend, for the industry, is all-suite hotels which comprise not only space for a bedroom and bathroom, but also 'living' and kitchen space. This type of hotel is particularly attractive to the business traveller as it becomes a 'home from home', it also gives a business traveller enough room to be able to work and hold meetings in the hotel suite. Accor have developed a brand called Suitehotel. Each 30-square-metre suite can be rearranged throughout the day for work, organizing meetings, resting or meals. Suitehotel also offers quality self-service catering, a business area in the lobby allowing guests to use a computer, send faxes and surf the web free of charge and a fitness centre open 24 hours a day. Like many low-cost and budget properties, prepayment on check-in simplifies check-out procedures. Another example of this concept is the more upmarket Benjamin, situated in Manhattan with 209 suites each taking more than $300 a night. The Benjamin opened last year as a family owned business, it currently has nine suite-only properties.

Another developing business travel opportunity emanates from the aforementioned demographic trends and the increasing number of women in senior positions. Companies are attempting to offer women a superior product and service tailored to their specific needs. It is estimated in the USA that 45 per cent of all business travellers are female. Hotel bookings service Expotel have embarked on a Woman Aware Campaign as a result of which 40 per cent of its bookings are made for female business travellers. The Conrad International has introduced a series of measures to afford greater personal security and comfort. For example, it offers all en-suite rooms with large desk and business facilities so that meetings could be held in private and lifts that are operable only by a key given to registered guests. On the comfort front, other hotels have ensured that rooms have full-length mirrors, skirt hangers in wardrobes, and hairdryers that are placed near a mirror. Lone females are never given a ground-floor room (unless requested), corridors are permanently lit, and receptionists are discreet when giving out room number details. However, some hotel companies and indeed many female executives themselves prefer to have the standard product and service, including many of the above features, rather than be singled out.

Another source of demand connected to the business world is conferences and seminars that can be key revenue-generating events for hotels, the longer the event the more fully the hotel facilities can be used, such as food and beverages. Many firms use incentive travel as a motivational tool for its successful employees as rewards for excellent performance, particularly where targets have been met, notably within the sales departments. The total value of the business market to the accommodation industry has been estimated at £4.9 billion. Furthermore this business is expected to increase at perhaps 3.5 per cent per year until the year 2004. Much will depend on the economy, inflation, national taxation policies and other environmental factors that affect business confidence and behaviour.

Recreational travellers

According to the Keynote Report, 2000a, about 36 per cent of total worldwide demand for accommodation is leisure-oriented. A vast market, it is the rival of business travel in many parts of the globe, as previously illustrated by Table 2.1. Yet the tourist market has features which set it apart from the business sector. It is far more price-sensitive, or price-elastic, as tourists are paying from their own pockets, not from a company travel budget. It is also highly sensitive to economic conditions, both in the country of origin and the country of destination, and is greatly affected by political circumstances such as terrorism and civil unrest. Individually, recreational travellers are subject to the leisure time and disposable income available, as well as basic necessities and considerations such as transportation, weather prospects, and even the status or image of a destination.

Goodall (1991) discusses the factors which affect a person's choice of holiday, relating to the 'push' and 'pull' influences: 'A distinction should be made between the role of motivations which PUSH a holiday-maker into a decision and the attraction exercised by holiday images which PULL the holiday-maker towards a particular holiday and destination.' The 'push' factors include an individual's specific motivations, goals and personal preferences: in other words, their criteria for what they want to get out of a holiday. The'pull' factors are tied up with the images of the destination and the products and services it has to offer. This will include perceptions about the level of hospitality, the quality of hotel accommodation, and other 'perceived attributes' like climate, scenery, history and culture. Accommodation and hospitality is a vital component of this scenario, and companies and individual businesses must play a leading role in projecting the appropriate image, and becoming strongly associated with the all-important attraction element of a recreational travel location.

The accommodation industry must also be aware of the amount of time available for recreational travel their many and various potential markets may possess. There are tremendous differences across national boundaries with regard to working hours and holiday entitlements. For instance, according to research by the Union Bank of Switzerland, the average worker in a European city, such as Brussels or London, works around 1700 hours in a year, compared with over 2000 hours in the Far East. Likewise, a worker in Amsterdam, on average, has nearly 35 vacation days each year, whereas in Hong Kong the average is only eight.

One more source of accommodation demand connected to the individual traveller rather than the business community is that of 'personal travel'. Consultants Horwath International rate this as high as 9 per cent of worldwide demand. The reasons for this form of travel are normally concerned with visiting friends and relatives, job seeking, house hunting and regrettably unfortunate circumstances such as serious illness or funerals. This market is stable, though the trips are often unavoidable, and it is another price-elastic demand as the cost is nearly always borne by the traveller. Many accommodation outlets have constructed special rates for this type of travel, particularly the visiting friends and relatives sector, known within hotel reservations departments as the VFR (visiting friends and relatives rate) rate. Christmas and New Year, and other occasions of family celebrations, are notable VFR periods, and many hoteliers believe this is an untapped source of income as it has been estimated that only 25 per cent of people visiting family or friends actually stay in hotels.

Institutional residential demand

As well as demand from business and leisure travellers, a very large number of people stay overnight away from home in 'institutions'. Such institutions include hospitals, prisons, residential care facilities, university and college hostels, YMCA, YWCA, and accommodation related to outward-bound training courses. For instance, the National Health Service in the UK provides accommodation for a variety of people. In 2001, there were 107,956 bedspaces for acute patients, 9767 beds for maternity care, and 27, 838 for geriatric patients (www.doh.gov.uk). In all there were 186,091 bedspaces in the NHS. There are over 100 UK academic institutions offering accommodation to students during term time and to conference delegates and visitors during holidays. A consortium of these universities and colleges has over 144,000 bedspaces available, of which 52 per cent have ensuite facilities. The Youth Hostel Association of England and Wales (YHA) has 230 hostels. They provide low-cost, budget accommodation for people of all ages. A typical YHA hostel might have some 2–4 bedded rooms, some sleeping 6–8 persons and 'dormitories' sleeping 10 or more. Facilities might include common rooms, self-catering kitchen, showers, drying room, cycle store and garden.

THE NATURE OF THE ACCOMMODATION EXPERIENCE

In the past the need was for the simplest form of overnight accommodation, as the term 'bed and breakfast' implies. For many people, the very thought of staying away from home was an unusual and intimidating prospect. It was also seen as a luxury and a significant aspect of an individual's development and maturity. However, across all markets, especially within the last 50 years, consumers have demanded more and more sophisticated accommodation and services. More travel, and tourist holidays overseas, has increased the expectation of hotel, hostel and even hospital users. Accommodation consisting of little other than the bed itself has been augmented by washing facilities, from washstands, to hand basins, to bathrooms; by comfort facilities, from bedside tables to armchairs to suites; and by entertainment facilities, from radio to television to in-house video.

All parts of the hotel industry in particular are striving to improve their amenities and invest in better products and services, from ensuite bathrooms to leisure equipment and business-oriented technology. Increasingly they are having to respond to the demands of their markets, which seek choice and quality as well as affordable prices. Small hotels and guest houses, often at seaside resorts, now proudly boast private bathrooms, sauna and solarium, even a swimming pool and mini-gymnasium. Hotel chains and other multi-unit organizations have attempted to reach all sectors of the accommodation market, from so-called budget hotels, to mid-priced commercially oriented properties, and to top-of-the-range exclusive and internationally renowned outlets. These are illustrated in Figures 2.1, 2.2 and 2.3.

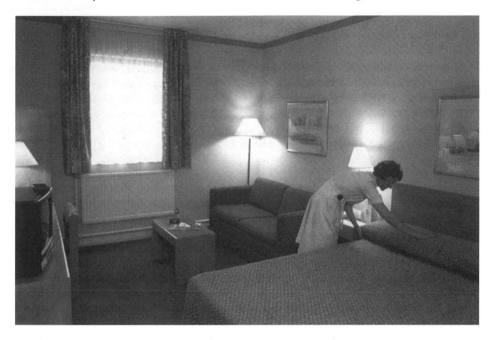

Figure 2.1 *Typical budget hotel bedroom*
Source: Marriott Hotels

These developments in accommodation have been triggered by the needs of the customer. The principal markets for accommodation, the leisure traveller and the business traveller, need some duplicate facilities but also some crucially differing services. The person or family on holiday needs a home from home, with furnishings and service that enhance comfort and indulgence. The business person or conference delegate needs an office away from home, with all the administrative and technological communication resources that enhance efficiency and purpose. Everyone expects high quality and value for money.

FACTORS INFLUENCING ACCOMMODATION PROVISION

The provision of overnight accommodation is greatly influenced by the economics of both developed and developing nations. The commercial sector is particularly susceptible to changes in the social and economic environment of its customers and markets, and these various factors need to be understood. With regard to the industry's place in the wider issue of economic development, it is useful to consider a model constructed by Kleinwort Benson Securities (1991) referred to as a structural theory of hotel business demand, and therefore assessing the relationship between an economy and the demand for accommodation by business travellers and companies. This theory identifies three phases in an economy's growth which in turn exert a varying influence on the demand for hotel accommodation.

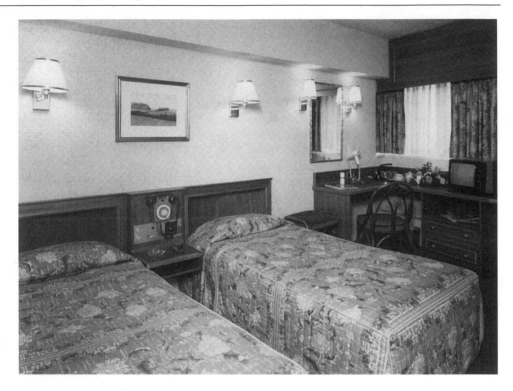

Figure 2.2 *Typical mid-price hotel bedroom*
Source: Mount Charlotte Thistle

The first phase is an economy where activity is predominantly manufacturing, and business people need hotels for overnight stays only, during trips to different areas of the country to sell and promote the products. These clients tend to be middle-ranking executives from single-unit companies and the demand is neither consistent nor particularly lucrative. Phase two is when the service industry begins to assume dominance, as in the UK during the 1980s. Companies within this sector tend to develop into multi-unit concerns, as personified by retail, banking and other consumer-based services. Such an economy boosts the demand for hotel accommodation, often directly associated with corporate gatherings such as sales meetings and training courses. Phase three shows demand stabilizing and any growth is at a much slower rate. Organizations are now developing their own corporate centres and regional networks which may reduce the need for employees to be increasingly away from home.

All accommodation businesses should also be aware of wider socio-economic changes that in time fundamentally affect the environment and the demand for residential outlets. In particular it is important to draw attention to demographics; that is, the structure and profile of populations, and the concept of disposable income, the amount of money people actually have available to them to spend or invest. With regard to the former, the UK must recognize that it has an ageing population, as do most western economies, including the US and the EU (excepting Portugal and the Republic of Ireland). The number of people over pensionable age in the UK is projected to exceed 16 million by the year 2031, more than double the number in 1961. This equates economically to 46 people of pensionable age for

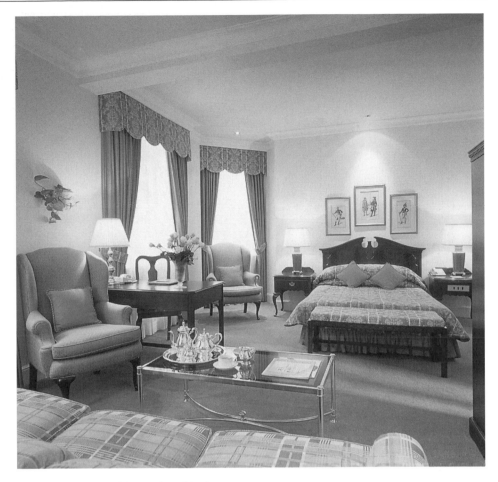

Figure 2.3 *Typical luxury hotel bedroom*
Source: Crowne Plaza

every 100 of working age, also about double the 1961 figures. It is for national governments to consider the implications of these statistics regarding economic activity, social policies and taxation. For the hospitality and accommodation sector there are other potential outcomes to review.

The industry must realize the changing profile of its markets, its consumers, and indeed its workforce. The effects of lower birth-rates from the 1970s, and rapidly improving life expectancy, are having considerable longer-term impact upon the developed countries' populations. As a result, there is an ever-larger group of the population in the age band from 25 years to 44 years. People in this bracket are often young professionals, middle and senior managers at the height of their business careers. They are often two-income families, using hotels and travel for pleasure as well as business, 'broadening personal experience'. They tend to be relatively affluent, status conscious and particularly aware of brand names, a situation not lost on many of today's market leaders. Population changes and changing work patterns are also contributing to more and more women in the workforce, many at senior management levels as more women return from maternity leave or delay starting a family until well into their thirties.

The ageing population is most notable at the age of 45 years and beyond, an age band often now termed by marketing managers as the third age. Apart from living longer, older people are generally healthier than previous generations, and more active, and many now have the time and the disposable income to commit more expenditure on leisure. Further, this age group tends to want more comfortable, full-service accommodation facilities. Statistics have also revealed that they are more likely to stay at home for holidays, whereas the 25-to-44-age-band members are most likely to go abroad. Other demographically influenced factors to be considered are the steady, ever-present demand for the family holiday, the increasing number of single female business travellers, and the larger number of people desiring and being able to afford short breaks and activity holidays.

The Social Trends report of 1994 also clearly indicates that disposable income is generally increasing within the UK. It reports that disposable income per capita is now 80 per cent higher than in 1971. Its analysis of household expenditure shows not only significant rises in spending on catering specifically, but that income and time devoted to leisure, recreation and entertainment have soared. In 1966, 7 per cent of the UK population took two or more holidays. In 1992 that figure had risen to 24 per cent, and in the same year, expenditure on leisure represented 17 per cent of the household budget. This trend has continued.

SIZE AND SCOPE OF THE ACCOMMODATION SECTOR

However the increase in demand for leisure and business accommodation has been international, with a resultant development in competition, especially for the multi-unit, global organizations. It is these companies that have become the innovators and developers of the essential facets of the hospitality experience. Many of these firms have emanated from the USA, the UK and France. Kleinwort Benson Securities illustrated this fact graphically in their Fifth Annual Review (1991) of stock market quoted companies in the hotel industry. Around 83 per cent of the quoted hotel rooms in the world are controlled from these countries. Examples of such organizations are the Marriott Corporation from the USA, Six Continents from the UK, and Accor from France. In all these cases, such companies have been national first and international second.

As a result we have an increasingly complex and inter-linked industry, with many brand names and business concepts. For many years Holiday Inn was part of Bass, the UK brewing giant. In 2000 Bass Brewers, along with the brand name, was divested and the company was renamed Six Continents, focusing on lodging and hospitality retailing. It now includes in its portfolio of hotel brands Inter-Continental (purchased in 1998), Crowne Plaza, Holiday Inn (which in the UK includes nearly all of the former Forte Posthouse chain purchased from Granada in 2001), Express by Holiday Inn, and Staybridge Suites (www.sixcontinents.com). Likewise the famous Hilton brand is also owned (outside the USA) by Ladbrokes, the betting and gaming firm. At the time it was acquired by the group in 1987 for $1,070 million, Hilton International owned or managed 92 hotels. It now operates 379 hotels in 70 countries. In 1997, the group announced the signing of a worldwide alliance with Hilton Hotels Corporation, the owner of the Hilton name within the USA, that reunited the Hilton Hotel brand for the first time since 1964.

Under the terms of the alliance, Hilton Hotels Corporation and Hilton International are cooperating on sales and marketing, loyalty programmes, central reservation systems and other operational matters. In 1999, the group completed the acquisition of Stakis plc, which added 54 hotels in the UK and Ireland to its portfolio, together with 68 Living Well health clubs. In 2001 the group acquired Scandic Hotels.

In addition to these major global brands, the UK has several other large chains. Whitbread has 300 hotels in the UK, operating the Travel Inn budget chain and Marriott Hotels on franchise from Marriott International. In 2000, Thistle Hotels operated 60 properties, Jarvis Hotels (now rebranded as Ramada) also 60 hotels and Queens Moat Houses operated 51 units (Keynote, 2000). Smaller chains include McDonalds Hotels, the Premier Lodge brand now owned by Scottish & Newcaste, Millennium & Copthorne Hotels, and De Vere Hotels.

This fast international development in hospitality accommodation has led to a range of types of organization and business formats, from wholly owned businesses to franchises, to joint ventures and firms specializing in management contracts. The best example of a franchisor is USA-based Cendant, the largest hotel chain in the world in 1999, with 515,267 rooms worldwide. Yet within Cendant there are many autonomous groups with well-known names, with accommodation targeted at different markets, such as Ramada, Howard Johnson Motels, and Days Inns. Likewise Accor, the French hospitality leader, had seventeen brand names at the last count (www.accorhotels.com), including Novotel, Sofitel, Ibis and Formule 1. Some companies specialize in managing hotel properties through management contracts but do not own them. Hyatt is an example of this approach. Other companies extensively franchise their hotels for others to operate. To compete with these large chains individually owned properties join together in marketing consortia giving the appearance of being international groups such as Best Western or Logis of Great Britain. Table 2.2 shows the size and international scale of the accommodation business. The hospitality experience has indeed come a long way from 'bed and breakfast'.

Another recent factor is the greater participation of hotel companies and investors from the Far East and Third World nations as their governments recognize the enormous value and potential of international tourism and business travel. Accommodation as part of the wider hospitality experience is a clear function of economic growth. The range of goods used by the hotel industry is vast and covers most of the manufacturing base of an economy, from building materials to the full range of furniture and fittings. Moreover, hotels also use the full range of professional services from advertising agents to merchant banks.

Yet the hospitality accommodation experience is about much more than economics, global representation and sophisticated products and services. Above all it is about the human element of service, and the fulfilment of the specific needs of the customer. Indeed, as hotels in a particular market segment become more physically similar, as their facilities become standardized and predictable, so the aspects of service and quality become the competitive edge between hotels and companies. Businesses now recognize and give full strategic attention to the components of such service and quality. They are properly concerned with human resource management, with providing their employees with better training and work conditions, with understanding their customers' needs more carefully and responding effectively to them. President of the American chain Four Seasons

Table 2.2 *Top 15 hotel chains 1993 and 1998*

1993 Rank	Hotel chain	Rooms	1998 Rank	Hotel chain	Rooms
1.	Hospitality Franchise Systems	384,442	1.	Cendant (was HFS)	515,267
			2.	Bass (includes Holiday Inn)	452,820
2.	Holiday Inn World Wide	340,881			
3.	Best Western International	272,743	3.	Best Western	304,512
			4.	Choice	292,009
4.	Accor	250,319	5.	Marriott International	286,377
5.	Choice Hotels International	229,784	6.	Accor	280,161
			7.	Starwood (inc. Sheraton)	210,569
6.	Marriott International	173,048	8.	Promus	188,686
7.	ITT Sheraton Corp.	129,714	9.	Patriot American	105,201
8.	Hilton Hotels Corp.	94,924	10.	Hilton Corporation	102,555
9.	Forte	78,691	11.	Carlson	102,380
10.	Promus Cos.	78,309	12.	Hyatt	93,729
11.	Hyatt Hotels/Hyatt International	76,057	13.	Sol Melia	65,083
			14.	Granada (includes Forte)	56,112
12.	Carlson/Radisson/Colony	75,986	15.	Hilton International	53,651
13.	Club Mediterranee SA	65,128			
14.	New World/Renaissance Hotels	55,591			
15.	Hilton International	52,930			

Hotels, Isadore Sharp (1992), summarizes it as follows: 'Until the late 1980's, most hospitality companies saw service as peripheral. Now, competition is driving service to the top of the corporate agenda'.

It is also important to place the accommodation industry as a prime element of the overall tourism industry. For this purpose a tourist may be considered to be a traveller for pleasure, or on business, or visiting friends and relatives. The scale and contribution of the tourism industry cannot be stressed enough in the economies of the world today. As an invisible export, acquiring large sums of foreign currency from overseas visitors, it outstrips the major UK exports of petroleum, financial institutions, civil aviation, sea transport and consultancy firms. In 1998 there were 23.4 million overseas visitors to the UK spending £12.6 billion, more than double the arrivals in 1980 (BHA, 2000).

The actual number of hotel businesses in the UK is difficult to assess. It is dependent on the definition of utilized. Residential accommodation may cover hotels, motels, holiday camps and holiday centres, guest houses, inns and boarding houses and hostels. The BHA estimates that there are over 60,000 hotels and guest houses in the UK (BHA, 2000). The British Tourist Authority and the Tourist Boards have 22,807 registrations offering over 900,000 bed spaces. Most of these will be larger properties (more than 10 bedrooms). With the number of bed spaces (i.e. a double bed equals two spaces), certainly in excess of 1 million in the UK, the scale of the hospitality industry's accommodation provision is enormous.

Table 2.3 *Analysis of UK hotels by turnover (£)*

Turnover (£000)	Number (1996)	Number (1999)	% Share ('96)	% Share ('99)
1–49	1095	525	9.6	5.0
50–99	2660	2105	23.2	20.2
100–249	3565	3300	31.1	31.7
250–499	2310	2045	18.6	19.6
500–999	1125	1285	9.8	12.3
1000–4999	735	980	6.4	9.4
5000+	145	185	1.3	1.8
TOTAL	11,615	10,425	100.0	100.0

Source: Keynote Ltd (2000a)

The number of businesses remained steady in the 1990s, although VAT-registered hotels' turnover leapt from £6.9 billion in 1994 to an estimated £11.5 billion for 2002. As mentioned earlier, this UK national industry, as with many other European countries, is still primarily based on smaller businesses. This is illustrated in Table 2.3. The majority of VAT-registered hotels, therefore the relatively larger ones, had turnovers in 1991 below £500,000. Indeed the single most occupied band was a turnover between £100,000 and £249,000. Such revenue is derived from four operating departments within the hotel. This was estimated in 1992/93 (Kleinwort Benson, 1991) to be 54 per cent from room sales, 37 per cent from food and beverage, 4 per cent from telephone, and 5 per cent from laundry/leisure. This rooms revenue resulted from an average occupancy of 62 per cent. By 1998 average occupancies were up to around 75 per cent (BHA, 2000), with revenue broken down into rooms (68 per cent), food and beverage (24 per cent), telephone (2 per cent) and other (6 per cent). The change in this sales mix reflects two trends. The first is to build budget hotels without any food and beverage facilities so that food and beverage revenues are now a much smaller proportion of hotel revenues in total. The second is the growth in the use of mobile telephones, which has adversely affected hotel sales and profits.

However, in order to understand a hotel's operation it is necessary to understand not only its level of turnover, but also its operating costs. Table 2.4 reproduces figures from a report in the *Caterer & Hotelkeeper* (Tarpey and Walsh, 1993), prepared in conjunction with Pannell Kerr Forster Associates, along with more recent data for 1999. It gives a detailed breakdown of the UK hotel revenues and expenditure by reproducing a profit and loss account for the UK hotels' sector as if it were a single company. Comparison between 1992 and 1993 clearly shows how the industry responded to an economic downturn by cutting costs dramatically so as to achieve a higher level of operating profit on a lower sales figure. The data for 1999 clearly shows how this was maintained in the longer term. Also the change in sales mix referred to above has led to considerable increase in profitability. In addition, the introduction of yield management systems in hotel reservations has greatly helped manage occupancy rates, rooms revenues and profits.

Whilst the recession of the early 1990s took its toll on employment within the hotel and catering sector, longer-term trends still highlight a gradual increase, with forecasts for considerable skill shortages if and when the economic upturn arrives. The trend has been one of recession redundancies followed by a slow improvement. Department of Employment statistics show that in 1980 there were 241,700 people employed in the hotel sector alone, and that this rose by 17.2 per cent to 283,200 in 1990. In 1991, when the economic downturn really pinched, this figure dropped to 260,000. This figure has remained largely unchanged throughout the 1990s. It is significant that approximately 60 per cent of the workforce is made up of women, of whom 32 per cent are part-timers. Indeed around 44 per cent of all hotel workers are part-timers. Wages assume tremendous importance in such a labour-intensive industry and payroll is on average 27 per cent of turnover in UK hotels.

Table 2.4 *Breakdown of hotel operating costs*

	1992 %	1993 %	1999 %
Turnover	100	100	100
Wage costs	34	32	27.3
F & B costs	22	21	10.5
Other purchases	23	22	22.8
Operating profits	21	25	39.4

Note: F & B = Food and beverage
Source: Tarpey and Walsh (1993) and TRI Hospitality Consulting (2000)

ACCOMMODATION OPERATING SYSTEMS

In Chapter 1, it was identified that a hotel was an operation made up of a set of 'core' operating systems, augmented by a number of 'ancillary' operating systems relating to the size and grade of provision. The core operating systems of any accommodation provision relate to reservations, reception, housekeeping, and billing. Each of these systems or departments of the operation will be briefly introduced. A detailed analysis of these systems may be found in the companion volume to this text – *Hospitality Operating Systems* (Ball *et al.*, 2002).

Reservations

Most accommodation operations have a reservations system of some kind. This is largely because the operation has fixed capacity, that is to say there is a fixed number of bed spaces. In order to ensure the most efficient use of these spaces, and the most profitable use in the commercial sector, advance bookings enable occupancy to be maximized. Reservations can either be computerized or charted manually on well-established formats, often referred to as density charts. The overall aim of the department is to maximize occupancy at the best possible average room rate, so-called REVPAR (revenue per available room). Reservations may also be the centre for guest history information and guest correspondence.

Reception

Although accommodation operators prefer to take advance reservations, customers can also arrive on the day without an advance booking. Whether they have a reservation or not, all customers need to be 'received', a function performed by the reception staff, and known as the check-in procedure. Reception is a key method of giving information to guests throughout the stay, a customer care role sometimes augmented by the concierge department in larger hotels. Concierge is a point of information and also of many guest services in the larger city-centre hotels, providing the guest with theatre booking facilities and other travel and entertainment arrangements.

Housekeeping

The main back-of-house department linked to accommodation, housekeeping has an overall responsibility for maintaining standards of cleanliness and the presentation of the principal accommodation product, the guest's bedroom. Staff and departmental systems are concerned with the servicing of bedrooms, bathrooms and corridors, including the replenishment of linen, arranging guests' laundry needs, and the checking of rooms for faults, maintenance requirements and safety. The liaison and communication between housekeeping and reception is clearly crucial in ensuring maximization of guest satisfaction during the stay, and room occupancy, ensuring there is complete agreement on the readiness of rooms to be sold and occupied by incoming guests.

Billing

At the end of a stay, all guests have to check out of their rooms and settle their accounts with the hotel. For individual clients, this will normally entail asking reception or cashiers (in larger properties) for their final account or bill. Payment is then made by a method normally previously agreed, and most often by cheque, credit card or charge card. In commercial properties, many firms have special accounts with the hotel and the guest merely has to check the particulars of the bill and sign the document. Payment is then handled directly between the firm's and hotel's accounts department. The summation of the daily totals of bills paid and accounts settled becomes the hotel's daily banking summary, the sales turnover attributable to a particular day's business.

CURRENT ISSUES AND FUTURE TRENDS

Each sector of the accommodation sector has some specific issues dealt with in each of the following chapters. But of relevance to all sectors are three key issues that have emerged in the late 1990s. These are security and assets, technology and disintermediation, and design.

Security and assets

The American President, George Bush, stated after the terrorist attacks of 11 September 2001 that the 'world had changed forever'. Certainly the immediate effects of this event were a major and serious downturn in demand for hotel accommodation. In Europe, it was 4 star city hotels that had the greatest reduction in demand. Average occupancy was down 18.7 per cent, but 26.5 per cent for 4 star properties, due largely to a decline in both business and leisure travellers from the USA. This event was so extreme that at least one crisis seminar was held by industry leaders to discuss the situation. However some accommodation providers, notably budget hotels and holiday villages experienced little or no downturn, as they are heavily reliant on domestic customers. Different events impacted on these businesses, such as foot and mouth, train crashes and floods.

Clearly there is little the industry can do about such external occurrences except have contingency plans in place for responding to a decline in demand. However, customers do expect that hotels are safe places to stay and hotel companies need to ensure that they have appropriate security measures, not only to safeguard their guests but also their employees and the property. In fact, security and assets have been recognized as two of the five major challenges within the industry in this new millennium by the International Hotel & Restaurant Association (IH&RA, 2000).

Technology and disintermediation

The internet, and information and communication technologies (ICT) in general, were identified in Chapter 1 as of major significance to the industry. Technology too is one of the IH&RA's major challenges. In the accommodation sector a key issue is the way in which ICT is changing the channels of distribution for hoteliers and other providers. A channel of distribution refers to the way in which a hotel company communicates with its customers and how they communicate with it. Such channels include advertising through a variety of media such as television, press and direct mail, and selling through travel agencies, central reservations offices and directly through each individual property. The rapid growth of the internet and the marketing of rooms directly through hotel company websites, as well as other portals such as lastminute.com, has transformed how these firms do business. By 2002 it is estimated that up to 25 per cent of all hotel reservations will be from the internet. This mode of booking allows customers to deal directly with the hotel and thereby no longer use intermediaries, such as travel agents (hence the term 'disintermediation'). There are a number of implications of this. Customers may pay less by booking directly, hotels do not have to pay commission, distribution costs are considerably reduced, and so on. Delegates at the 3rd Annual European Hotel CFO Forum in 2001 identified this as a key issue which required some innovative thinking to address the uncertainty that this created (www.ehotelier.com).

It has also been argued that the internet creates a level playing field so that small independent hotels can more easily compete with the larger chains. A search engine directed to find a hotel in a specified location will not differentiate between big and small companies. However, chain portals do have some advantages over the smaller businesses, so independent hotels continue to recognize the need to join consortia to assist them with their sales effort. For instance, SRS-WORLD-

HOTELS has 400 member hotels, located in 250 destinations in 65 countries. In 2000 this global marketing consortia generated 1.2 million room nights for its members, 8 per cent of which were through their website.

The other major effort that hotel companies are engaged in is to enable the wide variety of computer systems now utilized in properties to be fully integrated. There are as many as 18 different IT systems, of which the principal ones are reservations, property management, inventory, and stock control. Historically the hotel industry has tended not to purchase off-the-shelf software, but proprietary systems specifically designed for one aspect of the hotel business. Such systems do not 'talk' to each other and hence information is not transferred easily from one system to another. The American Hotel and Motel Association currently have a major working party looking at this issue in an effort to resolve it (www.ahma.com).

Design

Each year, Pannel Kerr Foster organize an industry event based around a debate, where four industry experts put the case for or against a motion. In 2001 the motion was that 'design, design, design has replaced location, location, location as the three most important aspects of hotel management'. The suggestion was that hotel success was now based less on where the hotel was placed, but more on how it was designed. The reason for this proposition was due to the success of a particular type of hotel, so-called 'boutique' hotels.

Boutique hotels began in the early 1980s. Two such hotels were designed and opened in 1981. The Blakes Hotel in South Kensington, London was designed by celebrity stylist Anouska Hempel. In San Francisco, the Bedford in Union Square, was launched and is now one of 34 boutique hotels currently operated under the flag of one of the most well known operators of such properties, the Kimpton Group. In 1984, the Morgans Hotel in New York, designed by French stylist Andree Putnam, was opened by Ian Schrager, another pre-eminent operator of the boutique concept.

Definitions of boutique hotels vary, but operators, designers, and owners would agree on their major characteristics. The first is obviously design. These types of hotel are very individual in terms of their 'look'. They may be in old or newly built buildings, but their exteriors and interior design are always distinctive. The aim is to create an environment which creates a sense of style, distinction, warmth, and intimacy. In many boutique hotels each guestroom is individually designed, making every single stay unique, even for their repeat guests. For example, the Library Hotel in New York City offers a different theme (from romance to music) in every guestroom. Technology also enhances the design and ambience. It is used to promote emotional contact between the guests and the hard attributes of the building through effective lighting and music. It is also provided for the convenience of hotel guests, including features such as in-room DVD players, flat-screen television sets, cordless phones, and computers with high-speed internet access and the latest monitor genres. Of key importance is the extent to which such technology is both leading edge and fashionable. The second feature of the boutique concept is the nature of the guest experience. Most operators insist that this type of property should not exceed 150 rooms, so that every guest can be recognized by employees, acknowledged by name and given individualized service. In larger properties, particularly those operated by Schrager such as the Paramount

Hotel (594 rooms) and the Henry Hudson Hotel (821 rooms), it is a less personalized service but with more emphasis on entertaining guests by creating a theatrical atmosphere through design, colour, lighting, art, and music. Entertainment is an important dynamic in creating a lively, chic and trendy mind-set and is not limited to events such as live music and performances. The boutique concept itself *is* entertainment because it has a hip restaurant, trendy lounge, and 'in' bar. The third feature is the target market, which could be defined as the 'image conscious'. Such people tend to be early 20s to mid-50s, with mid- to upper-incomes, often working in the media and fashion.

Figure 2.4 *Boutique hotel*
Source: Twenty Nevern Square

There are clearly two types of boutique property, depending on their location. The first type is city based, where location is of major importance. However a 'good' location for this type of hotel is based not on proximity or convenience, but on the trendiness of the neighbourhood. Most city boutique hotels are located in trendy and exciting cities such as New York, London, San Francisco, and Miami. As the concept develops, more and more companies are targeting less cosmopolitan cities than these, looking for locations with vibrant economies and high-end socio-economic groups, with hotel stock built by the chains. The second type of boutique hotels are in resort destinations. These tend be different from city hotels being more exotic, smaller, and highly intimate. Location is also important for resort boutique properties which are typically found in well-hidden, tucked away, deserted corners of the islands or the mountains. The more difficult it is to reach the destination by means of common transportation, the more fashionable the location is considered. Here the guest experience is not based on technology, which tends to be deliberately excluded so that guests can 'get away from it all'. These hotels have features such as traditional spas, rose petal baths, private individual plunge pools, honeymoon packages, and art and painting sessions.

Boutique hotels bring certain benefits in terms of operations and profitability. Besides strong customer demand, the economics are favourable for operators. For example, in the context of disintermediation they can easily reach their target markets at low cost. Once established, boutique hotels also tend to have a higher percentage of repeat business compared to the industry in general, which may reflect a smaller degree of volatility when going through difficult economic times. Nevertheless, smart boutique hotels must continue to adapt to the incessantly changing needs, tastes, preferences, and fashions in order to remain competitive in this market.

Given the importance of location, even to boutique properties, it is not surprising that the industry audience at the PKF debate overwhelmingly voted against the motion. 'Location, location, location' remain the three essential features of any successful hotel.

CONCLUSION

From this introductory review of the sources of accommodation demand, it can readily be understood that awareness of the markets available is essential to the manager of a successful accommodation business. More than that, it is necessary to recognize the users and their differing needs, and their changing needs, as trends and socio-economic factors alter and influence. Demand patterns change, market characteristics change, the needs and tastes of consumers change and competition increases. The hospitality manager must keep fully up-to-date with this turbulent and ever-changing market place, and be familiar with the principles of market segmentation.

Awareness must lead to action, and the successful businesses respond quickly and effectively, not waiting for the competition to take an unassailable lead. Already European and American companies are reacting to the demographic trends, developing new accommodation products with features particularly relevant to the older guest and the disabled. Accor have for some years been planning a new brand of Mediterranean coastal properties with full medical facilities and qualified staff, and even in provincial France one can come across small hotels describing themselves as suitable for the 'troisième age' (retired person). Companies are also reacting to topical issues and concerns within their markets. In the USA a number of major hotels have started recycling and energy conservation programmes, partly to save money and partly to promote a better image, to attract the sections of the market that are increasingly environmentally conscious. Hilton International has introduced a customer care programme directed at its increasing Japanese market segment, providing its guests with '*Wa No Kutsurogi*' service – meaning, 'comfort and service the Japanese way'. Part of this programme is a guarantee of Japanese-speaking staff and hotel literature translated into Japanese.

In recent years the drive to know your market segments better and respond to their wants has led many hotel chains towards branding their hotel products, such as Accor in France and Cendant in the USA. Through proper product branding, firms aim to win brand loyalty from consumers who desire consistency in the quality and provision of goods and services.

This differentiation of a group's hotel products began in the USA with organizations like Quality Inns, developing alternative products at different standards and different prices to suit different markets. This form of branding must be complemented by a sophisticated central reservations system, with the consequential ability to refer clients from one outlet to another, making immediate bookings, whether direct or through a travel agent. The loyalty factor can then be consolidated by repeat business recognition schemes, loyalty clubs that offer the customer ever-increasing benefits and privileges. Hilton introduced its 'Honours' programme in 1987 and in one year the membership was up to 1 million. It has even begun a 'Gold Passport Club' for frequent users and, for the most special deals and privileges, there is a special club for its 1000 top customers. Clearly, Hilton believes in looking after and keeping hold of its top income-generating clients. Small, individually owned businesses and global hotel chains alike know that they must identify their markets, and provide the type of residential facilities at the level of price and quality desired. This approach will give their operators the upper hand in the increasingly competitive industry of hospitality accommodation.

SUMMARY

This chapter has identified that the UK accommodation industry has an annual turnover of approximately £11 billion and it includes nearly 60,000 businesses. People stay away from home for a number of reasons, principally on business, enjoying leisure or for 'institutional' reasons. They expect their accommodation provider to have a wide range of products and services available to them, depending on the type of unit they are staying in. The mix of different types of property, ranging from luxury 5 star hotels down to backpacker hostels, typically reflects the nature of economic development in a country. Two key factors are the relative importance of service industries as opposed to manufacturing, and within services the level of tourism demand.

The industry is increasingly international and dominated by the large chains. These chains are becoming larger due to mergers and acquisitions. Although the principal source of revenue (TRI, 2000) is room sales (52 per cent), companies also make money from selling food (29 per cent) and beverage (11 per cent) and other services (7 per cent). The key element of cost is labour (27 per cent of sales). Food and beverage is less profitable due to its materials costs. Many chains have deliberately designed hotels without such facilities. The core business of accommodation provision is therefore made up of four systems – reservations, reception, housekeeping, and billing.

The sector faces three major challenges. There are concerns about security and assets, the need to effectively exploit new information and communication technologies, and how to gain competitive advantage from architecture and design. There are now some hotels, called boutique hotels, that have created a niche market based on their image and design.

FURTHER STUDY

Ball, S., Jones, P., Kirk, D. and Lockwood, A. (2002) Hospitality Operating Systems, Continuum: London.

www.ehotelier.com

www.ih-ra.com

QUESTIONS

Develop a profile of accommodation provision for the town or borough of a city in which you live or study. Where are the properties located? When were they built? What is their capacity? What markets do they serve? Who owns and operates them?

CHAPTER 3

Business and conference hotels

INTRODUCTION

The last century has clearly witnessed the most unprecedented development of trade and industry, from national to international boundaries, from the Western economies to the Far East. Driven by technological advances and a consumer-based society, economies have become more complex and volatile, and have moved from a purely manufacturing base to more mixed economies, often service industry dominated. As a result the business community has assumed a vital role in society, and service industries such as the hotel sector have become crucial elements in the provision of necessary services to enable businesses to operate effectively.

The first period of rapidly increased business-oriented travel came in the 1920s and 1930s between the World Wars. Companies began to grow, often from their original location; they began to distribute goods and to travel to inform consumers about their products; and they began to be conscious of selling and promoting. The advent of better forms of transport facilitated this new approach. This period has been described by Medlik (1981) as one of 'rapid development of transport, by car, motor coach, and by air, bringing new custom to hotels, which had to adapt themselves to the increasing restlessness of holiday makers, and to the increased volume of business travel'. Since the Second World War, the importance of business travel to the hotel industry has very often superseded the significance of recreation travellers. Hotel companies, developing into ever larger chains and groups, have primarily targeted business locations for new sites and properties. These locations have varied from commercial and market towns, to the major cities and conurbations, from business parks and industrial estates, to roadside and airport sites. The hotel group Swallow, based in the north-east of England, reported in the mid 1990s that 85 per cent of all bookings to its 35 hotels were from guests travelling on business or attending meetings and conferences. Indeed in 2000, there were an estimated 1.3 million conferences in the UK generating sales revenues of £6 billion. Most of the total were non-residential with 51 per cent in hotels. This market is valuable to hotels not only because of the income it creates, but also because demand is at a different time to peak leisure demand – lowest in the summer and highest in September, October and November.

This level of hotel revenue from the business community is all the more significant when one considers that such trade is often at a high average room rate, high food and beverage spend, and at a much greater margin of profit than that obtainable from the leisure and holiday market. Across all industrial sectors, firms have become much larger organizations in the last 30 years, conglomerates covering the globe, with the subsequent need for national and international travel, for high quality accommodation and services, and for impressive venues for important meetings and conferences. These needs provide the hotel industry with an outstanding opportunity, and the multi-national hotel chains are in a hugely competitive battle to win the custom of business travellers. Indeed as we shall explore in this chapter, the entire travel industry is forming alliances and joint ventures in order to exploit more effectively the relentless growth in worldwide business activity. When one considers that the computer giant IBM has an annual travel and accommodation budget for its UK division alone of £15 million (Craymer, 1994), one can understand the strategic significance of business customers to airlines, to travel firms, and to hotel companies alike.

HOTEL DEVELOPMENT AND LOCATION

The location of business and conference hotels has been determined by the level of economic activity, the characteristics and the needs of the demand from business. Centres of commerce like London provided an early impetus for hotel development, but so did the growth of manufacturing industry and the railways. Stations became prime sites for business hotels, some with direct walkways from platform to hotel reception. Indeed one of the most prestigious companies earlier this century was British Transport Hotels, actually owned by British Rail. Industrial towns throughout Britain were also key locations, as business people began to meet clients, hold sales meetings and negotiate with suppliers. The 'commercial traveller' entered the vocabulary and hotels began to advertise themselves with this new market in mind. Hotel groups still target business towns. In 1993 the marketing manager of Mount Charlotte's Thistle brand stated that, 'we plan to have a Thistle hotel in every industrial city in England by the end of 1995' (D'Ambrosio, 1993). Likewise, many of the new Novotel properties, such as the Glasgow hotel opened in 2001, are based in city centres. Indeed Accor have begun to add the word 'city' or 'centrum' to the names of such properties to indicate the nature of the hotel's location, for instance Novotel Glasgow Centre or Novotel Praha Centrum. London, as the UK's commercial centre, continues to have new hotels developed such as the Hilton Trafalgar Square, opened in 2001, and the Marriott at Canary Wharf.

More recently the motorcar has become the principal means of travel for business executives, as sales of company car fleets blossomed and motorways and dual carriageways afforded fast and convenient routes. The 1960s saw the advent of hotels located primarily for the road user, such as the original Post Houses of the then Trust Houses Ltd, and the introduction from America of the concept of the motel, the motor hotel. To this day, hotel and catering companies seek sites near to the major roads and motorways, attracting the business traveller with their time-saving location, ample car parking, accommodation, food and drink under one roof. This is particularly true of budget hotels (discussed in Chapter 5).

Locations have also changed with the changing pattern and structure of industry. The shift towards service companies and technological firms, and the decline of heavy industry and manufacturing, has meant that new criteria have entered the location decision process. Many of the new firms in electronics and consumer services relocated to new towns and business parks, away from the high rentals of city centres and away from traffic congestion and parking difficulties. Such firms also sought the new pools of labour in the developing urban areas. The development of corridors of electronics-based industry, as in the Thames Valley, also developed new centres of commerce in towns like Reading and Bracknell in Berkshire. Naturally, hotel chains followed the demand. The French company Campanile in 1992 developed 12 new hotels near to business centres as diverse and geographically spread as Dartford in Kent, Wrexham in North Wales and Washington in Tyneside. The company positions its hotels on main roads to capture business travellers and tourists, as do Forte Travelodge and Whitbread's Travel Inn.

We have already noted how the hotel accommodation industry has followed the major forms of transport of the day, from railways to roads, and more recently the sudden development of air travel has influenced location of hotel businesses. The aeroplane has changed the pattern of international trade and travel out of all recognition. Since the 1950s, in particular, travelling by aircraft for both holidays and business has become an integral part of the modern industrialized society. As a result airports have become prime centres for hotel development, and a drive around Heathrow or Gatwick Airport is a drive past a cordon of hotels representing almost every international hotel chain. Airports attract business people for travel, for meetings and conferences, and as the road systems to airports have improved, so they become points of convergence and convenience, whether or not the airport itself is to be used. As a result, airport hotels have become a hybrid of business and conference centres, with the additional market of airline crews and airline passengers also on their doorstep. In the early 1990s, the American-based group Choice Hotels opened its European flagship property at the Charles de Gaulle airport in Paris, including extensive conference facilities and fast shuttle services to and from the airport. According to the Keynote Report (2000a), one fifth of all the major hotels built in the 1990s were airport hotels, such as the Sofitel at the new Athens airport.

This latter example of international development highlights a key trend in the location decisions of major hospitality companies; to seek out the centres of commerce throughout the world and be represented. One reason for such worldwide development is the fact that many hotel chains feel that they have saturated the business market in their home countries. 'The history of the UK hotel industry in the eighties was the history of expanding hotel chains which grew to capture more than one third of all hotel rooms in the country. Now expansion is on a global basis', was how consultant Paul Slattery introduced the International Hotel Groups Directory of 1991. Already the recently liberated countries of Eastern Europe have attracted interest, with Accor opening two Sofitel in Poland in 2001 and Novotel properties in Russia, Hungary and Poland in 2002. The rapidly developing markets of the the Middle East, Latin America and the Far East are also high on the agenda for expansion (www.novotel.com).

Before leaving the subject of location, a recent trend regarding the venues for meetings and conferences must be established. As businesses have reviewed their style and manner of conducting in-company meetings, training courses and seminars, so many have chosen to return to the peace and tranquillity of the countryside. Country house hotels have found some new and lucrative business as a result, and have found the need to create or upgrade their facilities for smaller gatherings of senior executives. Such hotels can provide a calm and relaxing ambience in which business people can focus their minds on decisions affecting the future of their company. Such locations may also provide the leisure element which many conference organizers now feel is a significant aspect. Hotels with golf courses are an example of this trend, where leisure centres are as important as the conference room technology. Scottish hunting lodges, historic castles and stately homes such as Lucknam Park are some of the venues now utilized by the business community (Butler, 1992). In East Sussex for example, the three red-star Netherfield Place Hotel may often sell all its 14 bedrooms to a single company mid-week, providing the perfect environment for a relaxed meeting. This mid-week business is clearly greatly complementary to the weekend country house trade, especially out of the holiday season. Netherfield Place has had to upgrade its business-oriented technology, as so many business people now need support systems for their laptop computers. It can also provide business executives with recreational pursuits, including archery, clay pigeon shooting, and nearby golf. A leisure centre and swimming pool is on the agenda for the future. There are also some purpose-built residential conference centres, although many are developed by converting large houses and stately homes. Such centres have 16 per cent of the UK conference market.

SIZE AND SCALE OF THE SECTOR

The significance of business travellers to hotels is clearly illustrated by the UK Tourism statistics of 2000. These figures show that 66 per cent of business travellers use hotels, compared with only 18 per cent of recreational travellers. This importance is further endorsed by the analysis of overseas visitors to the UK in the same year. The average stay of business travellers was shorter, 3.4 days on average, whereas the holiday tourist averaged 5.8 days, but the business traveller spent £103.50 per day and £351.90 per visit, whilst the holiday traveller spent only £46.70 per day and £270.90 per visit. The British Hospitality Association suggest that the business market counts for 39.5 million nights in the UK, with an expenditure of over £2,000 million (BHA, 2000).

The larger international chains have thus become more and more dependant on this enormous market. Keynote (2000a) identify that about 'two-thirds of most leading hotels' occupancy rates is accounted for by the business and conference market', and that Hilton Hotels, owned by the British company Ladbroke plc, has reported that 70 per cent of its revenue comes from business travellers. This international revenue from business is still concentrated on the USA and European trading areas, though Japan and the fast developing economies of the Far East, such as Singapore, Malaysia and Korea, are beginning to be greatly influential. However, it is important to note the recent comments of the British Hospitality Association 'Europe dominates world tourism, absorbing half of the world's receipts and two thirds of arrivals – America comes a distant second with 27 per cent' (BHA, 2000).

For hotels to maximize their revenues and profits, they need to be in a mutually beneficial arrangement with the key players in this large business and conference sector. In particular, there needs to be a nurturing of key accounts, the multi-national corporations such as IBM mentioned earlier. Such firms have professional travel managers or buyers who contract specific travel agents to obtain the best possible deal on the travel and hotel elements of their executives' business trips. For example, IBM (UK) Ltd, contracted the Thomas Cook agency to work with specific hotel chains in getting the best rate available for its 2000 employees who, at the time, regularly travelled on business, some 35,000 bed nights, at an average room rate of £54.13 (Craymer, 1994). These figures dramatically illustrate the size and scale of the business, conference and airport-based sector of the hotel accommodation business. It is now a truly global industry with a complex scenario of hotel chains, travel agents, travel suppliers, travel buyers and conference organizers, increasingly linked by the modern technology of central reservation systems.

These central reservation systems (CRS) have done much to augment the scale of the international business market. Originally developed by the world's major airlines, they have become the focus of all computerization of the travel industry. Hotel chains and international consortia of hotels are aware that they must be a part of such systems, that their own bookings networks must be linked to one of the major CRS, such as Sabre or Galileo. Only then can they be involved in a system, which attracts business travel buyers, because they can book the airflight, the hotel accommodation, the car hire and any other travel-related service required in one transaction. Swallow Hotels reported that in the year following linkage with the Sabre and Galileo CRS, it secured £500,000 of extra business revenue.

MARKETS SERVED

When reviewing the sources of demand for hotel accommodation in Chapter 2, it was established that across the worldwide hotel industry, business travellers account for 37.1 per cent of demand, conference delegates 13.4 per cent and government officials 5.5 per cent, a business-oriented market of at least 56 per cent of total accommodation demand. The profile of this market and the needs of the market are subject to rapid change. World trade is increasingly international and competitive, and today's business people need the services and products that a modern technological environment demands. However the market can be segmented into a number of different levels and during a recession in Europe, company travel budgets are often cut drastically and business trip expenses reduced. As a result a good deal of price and product differentiation has taken place, and the large chains like Accor and Thistle have branded their hotel divisions to be attractive to a range of users and budgets. In the UK, Granada Group plc introduced a clear branding and pricing strategy, with a one price per room approach. At the budget end of the market, a business traveller could stay in a Travelodge at £39.95 per room, or a Post House at £49.95, or a Heritage at £59.95 and so on through to its Grand and Exclusive collections of hotels, with service and facilities appropriate to each price level.

The business market

The business traveller market is recognized as having particular needs, and bedrooms are being upgraded to provide better work areas, and dataports, that is,

Figure 3.1 *Hotel conference facilities*
Source: Swallow Hotels

facilities for lap-top computers to be hooked up. There is also an executive lounge with an area for meetings, a business secretarial service and complimentary refreshments. A basic but important feature for an hotel near a motorway is ample parking, which is free, and being near Heathrow, there is a courtesy coach service to and from each airport terminal, also free of charge. Fast check-in and check-out is another crucial service. Business hotels offer a variety of room rates. In most business hotels there are special corporate rates for company bookings, including a travel agent corporate rate for reservations through firms such as Thomas Cook and American Express Business Travel. Such bookings are subject to a travel agents' commission of 6–8 per cent. There is also a local privileged rate for those companies in the area, which use the hotel regularly.

The conference market

The conference market is divided into those on a day-delegate rate, including room hire, lunch and refreshments, and a 24-hour rate, to additionally include breakfast, dinner and accommodation. The latter is excellent business for the hotel, and ensures good take-up of the food and beverage outlets. Training courses have proved a particularly useful source of demand in an area where firms need to constantly update their employees on changing technology, service and production systems, and on management techniques and practices. There are two distinct types of training course delegate, from the course that is held totally within the hotel, to

Figure 3.2 *Hotel meeting room facilities*
Source: Sheraton

the use of the hotel for residential purposes only, as many firms now have their own well-equipped training centres.

Conference organizers, like the previously mentioned company travel buyers, are the important people for hotels to satisfy in this sector of the market. All arrangements must be checked in great detail, and the hotel must deliver the promise and ensure that the conference goes smoothly. Particular issues are transport arrangements, including car parking and transfers, timing of the catering to be in line with the programme of the conference, and excellent communication between all the hotel departments concerned, from reception to the conference and banqueting office to the food and beverage team. Message handling is often a problem for all business people when away from their offices, and hotels must ensure this issue is dealt with efficiently. Leisure clubs and indoor swimming pools are an important attraction to conference delegates and business travellers alike, as they take time to unwind and keep fit at the end of a long day.

A new development is the provision of stand-alone conference facilities adjacent to budget hotels. Whitbread have opened three Touchbase units in 2001 located on Travel Inn sites. These provide nine private, fully equipped and affordable meeting rooms with bright natural light, climate control and ergonomically designed seating, whiteboards, flipcharts, overhead projectors, stationery, telephone and marker pens, plus LCD projectors available when required. There are also 18 'hotdesks' at which people can work, equipped with digital phones, high speed internet access and laptop recharge points. Customers have access to unlimited hot beverages whilst using the facility and can purchase snack items when needed (for a virtual tour go to www.letstouchbase.co.uk/tour).

The airport market

Airport hotels also cater for a number of different sections of the airport and airline users market. Accommodating the air crews from various airlines is a regular and lucrative market. Pilots and cabin crew staff need regular stop-overs in a nearby hotel between flights. Airlines agree a room rate with the hotel, and often allocate their staff a daily amount of money to be spent on hotel services, known as a *per diem*. Air crew business has some special needs, with the emphasis on basics like efficient laundry service for uniforms, ironing facilities, leisure and health and beauty salons, as well as good transport to and from the terminal buildings, and in some cases their own lounges and recreation areas. They may even require black-out curtains in their bedrooms so that they may sleep during daylight hours between flights. Also, the hotel must be geared to check-in and check-out at all times of the day or night, dependent on flight times. Another airport connected business which calls for fast flexibility is that of delayed flights. Bad weather, technical difficulties or terrorism scares can all lead to airlines needing to accommodate large numbers of people at short notice. Airport hotels normally build up cooperative relationships with certain airlines, with an agreed rate for food and accommodation. There needs to be a pool of nearby and willing staff to suddenly organize meals and rooms for what may be hundreds of customers.

The final airport related market is that of in-bound and out-bound passengers. Passengers arriving at airports often require immediate hotel accommodation, particularly after long-haul flights, or such a stay may be part of the original package. Many hotel companies form agreements with airlines and offer special inclusive rates for these independent travellers. Here is another reason for being interfaced with the airlines' CRS bookings networks. Airport hotels also try to tap the out-bound market, where passengers need to be in the area of the airport the day before the flight. Indeed, many airport hotels have developed 'Take-off/Touch-down' packages to include free car parking at the hotel for the duration of the trip, and of course there is the courtesy coach to take clients to and from the airport terminal.

With a market profile so business-oriented as the above indicates, there remain particular challenges for maximizing occupancy at business, conference and airport hotels. There are predictable troughs in the trading pattern which need to be tackled. Holiday times, particularly when schools are also out of term-time, mean that a lot of business people are away on holiday as well, not travelling on business or attending conferences. As a result there can be some worrying weeks at Christmas, Easter and in August, when alternative strategies need to be adopted in order to fill the hotel bedrooms. Furthermore the age profile of many of the travelling business people mean that they are precisely the age-group that have young families to take on holiday. Weekends can also be a problem, as most business clients check out on Friday morning to return home. This is when the leisure facilities may be utilized by weekend break customers, whilst the function rooms could be promoted as the venues for local wedding receptions.

THE PRODUCT OFFERING

The business traveller now needs more in their hotel bedroom than a comfortable bed and a well-lit desk area at which to work. Today's business market needs business systems and technology at hand in their hotel, such as the fast communication systems of today, like fax machines and electronic mail. The refurbished Athenaeum Hotel & Apartments in London highlights in its brochure the features that many executives now look for in a hotel bedroom:

- CD and video in every room with free video and CD library service

- Two-line telephone

- Voice mail

- Fax and modem facilities

- 110/240 volt converters

- Full air-conditioning

- Power showers

- Personal room safes

- Full valet service

- 24-hour room service

- Bedside controls for lighting and air-conditioning.

Whilst location, price and levels of service and quality remain essential factors, it is the features like those above that are now being demanded by the top end of the market. In 2001, Holiday Inn in the UK announced new features specifically designed to attract business travellers. These included a choice of three types of pillow (firm, soft synthetic, or feather), redesigned décor (downlighters, soft wood furniture, and fabrics in bold colours), separate data and telephone lines, and breakfast check-out service (the hotel bill is taken to the guest's table in the morning).

The products offered by this sector of the hotel industry are becoming more and more sophisticated, as hotels try to keep pace with technology changes in the office and in the area of communications. However, such businesses must not forget the basics of service and quality, and with this in mind, many of the business hotel chains are embarking on product branding to ensure consistency. This form of branding includes setting standard specifications, consistent quality and consistent marketing. Many large organizations are implementing Total Quality Management (TQM) programmes in order to be absolutely clear on the specifications of service and product standards. The conference market has been particularly targeted by hotel chains as an area where consistency must be achieved. Marriott has drawn up a seven-point 'no-risk meeting plan' feature, to ensure success. This includes cost quotations, meetings with management, a guarantee of meal breaks and refreshment breaks being served on time, even a complimentary pager for conference organizers. Hotel groups are agreeing standards for conference table settings, from notepaper to pens and name cards, all with the group's logo and consistent print-style. There will also be a standard range of conference equipment available, from flip charts to video-monitors and for international venues, simultaneous translation facilities.

ORGANIZATION

The successful operation of any hotel requires the effective coordination of a number of individuals and departments. Business and conference hotels need that coordination to be both effective and efficient: fast yet smooth. The business person is often under pressure and needs to work quickly, and though courtesy is always necessary, so is speed of response. The management of an organization needs to be clear as to the needs of their clients, and have systems and procedures which ensure their satisfaction.

In an Economist Intelligence Unit survey (1991) of business and conference hotel users, communication between management and the key departments came out as the most crucial factor. A successful conference, for example, is the culmination of many different people's commitment to the task. Though many are involved, the end result must appear as an effortless realization of the demands of the conference organizer. 'Without a shadow of a doubt the most critical factor for any hotel/conference venue is to get their act together in terms of communication between management, marketing and front of house,' said one organizer.

Increasingly business and conference hotel operators are effective forms of service organization. Heskett (1990) defines such successful service firms as those that 'have a targeted market; well-defined service concept; a focused operating strategy; and a well designed service delivery system'. We have already seen how hotel companies are going about achieving three out these four factors. At the service delivery system level, i.e. operations, hotels are being radically transformed. Integration and communication are the aims of such an approach, and all must be wrapped in an appropriate management style and structure. Organizations are becoming less hierarchical with reduced layers of supervisors and managers. The empowerment of hotel employees which results will only be successful if those empowered are given the training and the motivation to enable them to grasp new responsibility and authority for the betterment of the guest experience. The most expensive reservations system in the world will be an asset in obtaining customers for a business hotel, but it is the service and the staff that will keep those customers, not only for the unit but for the whole group. The extent to which hotel organization is being transformed is illustrated in Figure 3.3, which shows the typical organization structure of a business and conference hotel in the late 1980s, compared with Figure 3.4 showing the 1990s.

CURRENT ISSUES AND FUTURE TRENDS

The development of CRS, global booking networks, is undoubtedly still going to be a key issue for the future of business and conference hotels. It means that only the largest hotel chains and consortia can possibly consider the capital outlay involved.

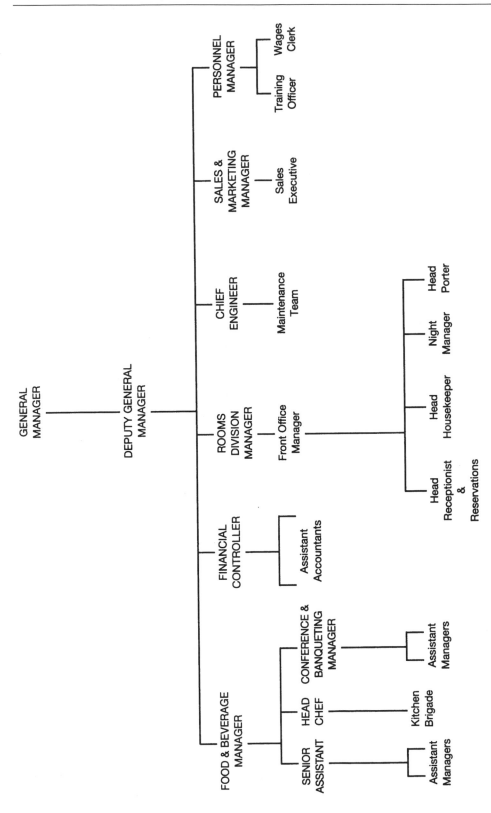

Figure 3.3 *Organization chart of a hotel in the 1980s*

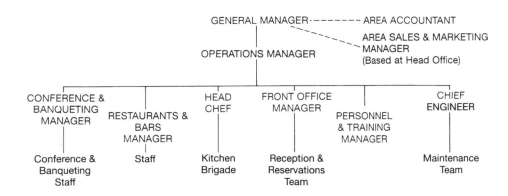

Figure 3.4 *Organization chart of a hotel in the 1990s*

It is going to be increasingly difficult for the independent hotel to compete with the financial power of these multi-national organizations. Such organizations are spending even more money on advertising themselves direct to the travel trade as well as direct to the customers. Alliances are being formed all the time, such as Radisson's move into Europe via marketing and reservations links with Edwardian Hotels of London and SAS Hotels of Scandinavia. Hotel companies are joining forces with the travel firms themselves, as in 1992 when Forte Hotels signed a 5-year international marketing deal with American Express. This joint programme included the promotion of Forte Hotels in American Express magazines, and the encouragement by hotel staff for guests to pay by the American Express charge card.

Paradoxically, technology could also be a threat to some conference hotels as video-conferencing becomes a reality. There is the possibility that business people will need to travel less and attend less meetings and conventions if more communication can take place via satellite television from one continent to another. Certainly modern dedicated conference centres will provide tremendous competition to hotel facilities in the major commercial centres. A recent example from Germany is of a conference centre in Karlsruhe with the capability of accommodating up to 16,000 delegates in all, in rooms suitable for gatherings of between 10 and 5000 people, with simultaneous translations into nine languages, plus television cable connections and a video-conferencing studio. In May 2000, Swissotel Ltd, a division of Swissair, signed a 20-year agreement with Marylebone Warwick Balfour, which will invest £6 million in the hotel, mainly to extend its conference space.

Traditional hotels may also find the competition hotting up from all-suite hotels, principally developed in the USA, but now often featuring meeting rooms and conference facilities. The Boston-based Guest Quarters Chain has properties with up to 250 suites plus meetings facilities for around 75 delegates. These suites include 1 or 2 bedrooms, separate lounge, full kitchen and bar, and a grocery delivery service if guests do not wish to use the in-house restaurant.

Trends and issues to be addressed on rather more mundane, but nevertheless important, revenue sources concern food and beverage sales and telephone revenue. Many hotels are reporting lower bar spends and generally healthier lifestyles associated with lighter lunches and breakfasts. The trend to involve celebrity chefs in hotel food service continues (see Chapter 12). Furthermore, the advent of mobile phones and car phones, plus charge cards, has greatly reduced the telephone revenue. Sales have reduced from £4 per guest per night in the early 1990s down to less than £2, a significant sum over the whole year. It has recently been estimated that telephone revenue counts for about only 2 per cent of total turnover across the UK hotel sector, down from a high of nearly 8 per cent. This is evidently a trend of serious implications for the industry. However the range of better facilities has allowed hotels to raise the room rates, while conference and meeting rooms provide increased opportunities to gain sales from non-residents. The other big trend is the incorporation of leisure facilities into business hotels. This is discussed in the next chapter.

CONCLUSION

The importance of the business traveller and the conference delegate has been established. The major international hotel groups will continue to target this market sector, and expect hotel management to respond effectively to the needs of these particular customers. The environment of fast-moving change requires management to keep in the closest touch with the market. This approach demands that operations managers are aware of the business world at large, in their local, national and international community. Above all, it requires managers to monitor the changing needs of their customers, the companies and the travel buyers, the conference organizers and the travel agents, the airlines and the airport managers.

However, hotel management must never lose sight of the day-to-day operation within their business. The business market demands high levels of quality, and in a highly competitive situation, there is choice available in abundance. Service must be guaranteed, and requirements fulfilled. The business traveller of today needs flexibility of options, not rigidity of routines in the way hotels are run. The implications for the quality and training of personnel are clear. Major companies like the Marriott Corporation are aggressively advertising the caring, flexible approach adopted by and instilled into its front-line employees. A recent campaign highlighted instances of exceptional customer service by specific members of its staff in some of its international business hotels, proclaiming how the company empowers its employees to use initiative in ensuring customer satisfaction. The business traveller may well require the information and communication technology of the moment, but he or she also needs to experience the real meaning of hospitality.

SUMMARY

This chapter has identified that a major market for hotel accommodation is the business traveller. A significant segment of this market is conference business, whilst airport hotels also have some specific characteristics. This market is estimated to contribute 39.5 million nights in the UK. Hotels serving this market tend to be located in city centres and transport hubs such as airports, railway stations, and motorway interchanges. The products and services vary from meeting the basic needs of business people at the budget end up to sophisticated communications technologies and meeting facilities in 4 and 5 star properties. Hotels typically have at least one member of the management team responsible for marketing to and dealing with business clients.

FURTHER STUDY

www.accor.com

www.hiltongroup.com

www.jarvis.co.uk

www.sixcontinents.com

QUESTIONS

Select two hotel chain websites. Compare and contrast these chains' locations, prices, and product/service offer to the business traveller.

Type in 'hotel' into key word search of an archive held by a trade publication (such as www.businesstraveller.com or www.ehotelier.com). What trends are evident in the UK business hotel market?

CHAPTER 4

Resort hotels

INTRODUCTION

At first sight the terms in this chapter may appear confusing and perhaps overlap with the section on small hotels and guest houses. This is because traditionally resort hotels have been known in the British market as those hotels located in seaside 'resorts' such as Blackpool, Brighton and Scarborough. Such towns have been dominated by small, independently owned and operated hotels. But this chapter focuses on a different set of accommodation types. Since the Second World War the term 'resort' in this country has taken on a new, American meaning. To be a resort, a property must be in its own spacious grounds and offer a central basic theme activity, such as a championship golf course, with a wide range of supporting activities (anything from water sports to hunting), and be exclusive. As distinct from conventional hotels, resort hotels are positioned as destinations in their own right. In other words, there is no need for guests to go anywhere outside of the resort itself, it is completely self-contained.

Internationally, although owned and/or operated by hotel companies, resorts comprise not just hotel accommodation but also apartments, condominiums, villas and houses that may be owned, leased or time shared by individuals. Such resorts, for instance South Seas Plantation in Florida, include not only places to stay but also restaurants, shops, a marina, private beach, 18-hole golf courses, tennis courts and other recreational facilities. They are in effect little villages, providing everything that both holiday and long stay guests may require.

In the UK the situation is slightly different. There are two main types of resort hotel categories. First, there are country resort hotels that are hotels located outside main towns or in the country with extensive leisure facilities. Although also enjoying peaceful, rural settings, country resort hotels with their extensive leisure and recreational facilities and profit motivation have a different emphasis compared to traditional country house hotels. They are operated on a large scale, often 100 hotel rooms or more, and are either converted existing hotels/mansions or purpose-built properties. They are commercially driven, which has meant that they have had to appeal to a wide client base – business, conference and local markets – as well as the leisure market, served by more traditional country house hotels. They have responded positively to increased leisure time by adding extensive leisure and recreational activities to their properties.

Second, there are those holiday villages and holiday centres where the operators, such as Center Parcs and Holiday Club Pontin's, have ploughed heavy investment into the development and up-grading of facilities and accommodation. If using an international definition of 'resort' hotels, these resorts would still not be 'exclusive' enough despite this investment. However, in terms of the UK marketplace their impact is still significant and as they share the other characteristics of resort hotels they are included here. The policy of these resort hotel operators is to provide a range of accommodation – apartments, villas, chalets and so on – as well as full-service hotel rooms, and in this respect they appear very similar to some resort properties abroad.

This chapter therefore seeks to focus on resort hotels in the UK defined as country resort hotels, and modern-style holiday villages and holiday centres.

SIZE AND NATURE OF THE SECTOR

It is increasingly the case that these types of accommodation provide customers with a place to stay on their second holiday or short break. Low cost air fares mean that the majority of British leisure travellers take their main holiday overseas, in destinations that have a better climate and lower prices. UK operators recognize the need to combat the British climate and therefore have invested in large-scale all-weather facilities, such as Center Parc's 'sub-tropical swimming paradise'. Likewise at the centre of each Butlin's Resort is the Skyline Pavilion. This is a distinctive canopy covering a variety of bars and restaurants, shops, sideshows and arcades. The Pavilion has a central stage area that hosts live entertainment during the day and in the early evening – so that as their website states 'no matter what the great British weather is doing outside, there's always plenty to do and loads of weatherproof fun to be had!'.

Country resort hotels

It is difficult to gauge accurately the entire market size of this type of resort property. However the number of corporate hotels is more easy to estimate, as the majority are operated by hotel companies in the UK. There are 11 Marriott Country Club Hotels across the UK each has its own swimming pool, gym, sauna, and a health and beauty salon. There are also 18-hole championship golf courses at country club hotels Forest of Arden in Central England, Dalmahoy in Scotland and St Pierre in Wales. De Vere Hotels operates 11 country resort hotels with a golf and leisure orientation, including the world famous Belfry Hotel. In three locations – Belton Woods, Slaley Hall and Cameron House – it is possible to buy a time share of a lodge in the grounds of these country estates. The Moat House chain has 30 of its 43 hotels providing Club Moativation, which includes a swimming pool, fully-equipped gymnasium, saunas, steam rooms and spa. The Jarvis chain, which also includes the Ramada brand in the UK, has 18 hotels with Seb Coe Health Clubs and another 14 with Poolside Leisure Clubs. Hilton's concept is called LivingWell in which they have invested £70 million. There are 80 such health clubs, some of which are in business rather than resort properties.

Holiday villages and centres

The holiday village and centre market was estimated to be worth £539 million in 2000. In the 1990s two major companies dominated this market – Scottish &

Figure 4.1 *Typical resort property*
Source: Turnberry

Newcastle (S & N) owned Pontin's and Center Parcs, whilst Rank operated Haven, Warner and Butlin's holiday villages. In 2000 and 2001, S & N disposed of their two brands in both cases to private investors, whilst Rank sold its brands to Bourne Leisure. Subsequently Bourne sold the Oasis holiday village to Center Parcs. There are, at time of writing, 3 Butlin's, 8 Pontin's and 19 British Holiday parks (rebranded Warners and Haven locations) in the UK. In addition to these chain-operated brands, there are also an unknown number of independently owned and operated holiday villages, such as Barend in Scotland, Gurnard Pines on the Isle of Wight, and Croyde Bay in Devon. The latter is interesting since it is owned and operated by UNISON, a British trade union for public sector workers.

Both sectors of the resort hotel market sector in the UK are dominated by hotel and leisure companies. This matches trends worldwide. The results of a 1994 survey of 16 worldwide resort areas showed that large hotel chains such as Hilton, Sheraton and Marriott commanded aggregate market shares of 70 per cent of total available rooms (Angelo and Vladimir, 1994). At that time none of these chains had UK-based resorts. By 2001 Marriott was well established and Four Seasons was planning to open a new resort property in Fleet, Hampshire in 2002. Club

Table 4.1 *Major operators of holiday village and centre resorts in Britain*

	Number of resorts
Butlins	3
Center Parcs	4
Haven	56
Holiday Club Pontins	8
Warner	13
Total	84

Source: Individual holiday village websites (2000)

Mediterranee remains the largest European resort operator, with resort hotels in over 100 destinations worldwide. The most publicized resort development in Europe has been Disneyland Paris which operates 5,211 rooms in 6 hotels.

THE RESORT HOTEL MARKET AND CUSTOMERS

Both types of resort hotel are more dependent on leisure customers than conventional hotels. In addition, although the core market for revamped holiday centres used to be the C2D socio-economic groups, this is changing in line with new competitors (such as Center Parcs) and with country resort hotels both of which are marketed as relatively up-market resorts to the middle and upper classes. Therefore, resort hotels now tend to be positioned as 'country clubs' offering peace and relaxation as opposed to excitement and entertainment (which traditional holiday centres used to provide) and target more up-market families with their high standards of service and accommodation.

Increased leisure time, the growth of the short-break market and annual weekend breaks, the increased demand for mid-week breaks from the 60-plus market, and a greater interest in sport, health and fitness activities have all contributed to the new popularity of holiday centres in the UK and have moved them away from the traditional base of providing holidays for price-conscious families. Operators like Butlin's and Pontin's have been expanding their seasons and coming up with new brands in a bid to encourage a more diverse and up-market clientele. For example, Holiday Club Pontin's divided its holiday centres into four categories:

- Family favourites – centres targeted at the value-for-money family holiday market.

- Chalet hotels – premium accommodation in three and four star chalets.

- Reserved for adults – centres aimed at customers over 50 years old.

- Coast 'n countryside – centres that provide a base for touring holidays.

In terms of market segmentation, Center Parcs regards the overall holiday experience as the company's main attraction and therefore targets young families; young retired people and peer groups (such as squash or golf clubs), all in the

ABC1 social groups. Its typical customer therefore remains leisure seekers who holiday mainly as a family unit. Interestingly, up to 50 per cent of this core market are repeat customers (a very high level compared to conventional hotels). This company achieves very high levels of occupancy throughout the year (plus 90 per cent). A factor that helps them do this is that they only sell three- (Friday to Sunday) or four-day stays (Monday to Thursday) or combinations thereof. In the summer months longer holidays are sold, whilst during the rest of the year the short breaks are more popular. High occupancy is also helped by the fact that the company has no plans to open any more UK villages, thereby limiting supply. Nonetheless business is so strong that two of their four locations are having additional luxury villas built to accommodate up-market demand.

Center Parcs has always provided some meeting rooms and associated facilities in order to target businesses for conferences and training seminars. However, in reality the company has found it very difficult to mix markets in its villages. For instance, business users and all-male sports groups are not easily integrated into a predominantly family, holiday environment. Likewise business customers may wish to stay for periods outside their normal three- and four-day stay periods. Recently they have developed a new marketing strategy and appointed a Sales Manager with specific B2B responsibility. They have also installed a new feature comprising high ropes, abseiling and climbing, designed for team building and management development exercises.

In comparison, country resort hotels target more diverse customer groups. Their extensive facilities allow them to avoid seasonal trading troughs by matching the availability of accommodation to specific, different market needs and also enable them to target local markets (a market actively avoided by holiday centre operators). They are geared more to the weekend, short break and overnight business markets than the long holiday market, their average stay being usually no longer than two nights. Although their guests appear to be similar in terms of demographics to hotel guests generally (usually between 35 and 54 years of age) they show a stronger bias than other hotels towards more affluent groups. They are also often popular with overseas tourists, in particular those from Japan and the USA. An example is Dalmahoy Hotel Country Club Resort, near Edinburgh. Its target markets are the Edinburgh area for membership and golf; the UK for conferences and short breaks; and Scandinavia, Germany and Japan for recreation holidays or breaks during business trips in the UK. Sports tourism may therefore be as important to these resort hotels as business tourism. It is also a growing and lucrative market, for example, spending on golf tourism (holidays where golf forms the main part of the experience) by Europeans is estimated to be £1270 million per year with an average spend of £224 per golfer (Hegarty, 1993). There are currently 64 hotels, specifically for golf tourism in the UK, 28 in England, 27 in Scotland and 9 in Wales.

Whilst business tourism, in the form of conferences and overnight stays, contributes approximately half of country resort hotels custom, an important additional form of revenue to these hotels is from their sports and leisure facilities. For example, annual membership of their golf and leisure clubs often contributes an additional 20 per cent of revenue. This can optimize hotel occupancy by adding up to 20 per cent to room occupancy levels. In addition, local membership means that they are able to replicate demand to other centres for overnight stays. According to Mintel, the health and fitness industry in the UK is worth £1.25

billion and 14 per cent of the population use a health club. De Vere's health clubs have a membership of 20,000 of which 70 per cent are people living near to the property at which they are a member. Location is a key factor in health club usage. Resort hotels in country locations may have relatively small memberships, so that the majority of users are hotel guests; whereas hotels near or in urban locations with health clubs may have members outnumber guests by more than four to one.

Another market for hotels of this type is the incentive travel market. Country resort hotels such as Gleneagles in Scotland and Hanbury Manor in England have more recently become popular as incentive travel destinations. Incentive travel is used by all kinds of employers to reward their managers/employees for high levels of performance in the workplace. Incentive planners are attracted by the ambience, exclusivity, up-market image and the flexibility offered by the extensive grounds and facilities in these country resort hotels.

LOCATION

It will be obvious by now that one of the most important factors affecting the location of resort hotels is the requirement for extensive land. For instance, a golf course, which is an integral part of a country resort hotel, is estimated to take between 120–75 acres of land (and of course several resort hotels comprise more than just one course). The Wentworth Golf and Country Club in Surrey is located in over 700 acres of land. Due to the high cost of land in the UK and the planning problems associated with such large developments as resort hotels, the growth of this sector has certainly been restricted. Many schemes have also fallen foul of conservation worries, a problem characteristic to resorts worldwide due to their requirements for beautiful, natural settings as well as the need to artificially landscape facilities such as golf courses and accommodation units (in the case of holiday centres). This also explains why holiday villages continue to be operated in locations that were fashionable or easy to get to in the 1950s, such as Weston-super-Mare and Bognor Regis.

However, resort villages are not always unwelcome additions to rural areas. They require not only a large population (anything between 5–8 million people) within a certain catchment area, often no further than a two hour drive away, in terms of customers but also a local labour pool. The Sherwood Forest Holiday Village (a Center Parc) employs hundreds of people on site, the majority of which come from the surrounding area, and it employs far more people indirectly through the use of local suppliers and firms. For all resort hotels, accessibility is very important. Country resort hotels, due to their reliance on both business and leisure tourism, require locations that are near to commercial centres. Also, if they are targeting overseas markets they will need to be close to an airport or a railway station. The ideal location characteristics for a resort property are as follows:

- a total site of at least 130 acres, to include one golf course as a minimum (sometimes an existing course and clubhouse, with fine impressive, extensive grounds, may be deemed suitable);

- a large town/city within 20 miles (a good commercial centre), with a population of at least 200,000;

- a nearby airport or railway;

- close to a community that has some attraction to overseas markets;

- close to local markets for golf, entertainment and conferences;

- fast and easy access.

In England, the such hotels are within close proximity to major cities such as London, Southampton, Birmingham and Derby.

An important location decision criterion for Center Parcs, throughout Europe, has been its targeting of countries with a very changeable climate, its 14 Centers are therefore located in the Netherlands, Belgium, France and the UK However with nearly 3000 beds to fill 102 times a year they look for locations within two hours drive of at least 2 million people. This is why these newer villages have quite different location characteristics to the traditional centres, which are typically located at the seaside.

PRODUCT OFFERING

Many business hotels have added leisure and health clubs, which blurs the difference between them and resort properties. However, the true resort hotel is designed entirely around its extensive recreation and leisure facilities. They are year-round centres/clubs/villages where innovative and extensive indoor and outdoor facilities form an integral part of the resort. A country resort hotel such as Hanbury Manor, in Hertfordshire, offers the following products and services:

- 200 acres of parkland;

- 18-hole golf course designed by Jack Nicklaus II;

- tennis courts;

- putting greens;

- croquet lawn;

- jogging trail;

- walled garden;

- 36 acres of pinetum;

- clay shooting;

- archery;

- hot-air ballooning;

- horse riding;

- fishing;

- three restaurants;

- 96 five-star bedrooms;

- cocktail bar;

- swimming pool/spa;

- health and beauty facilities (such as aromatherapy, massage, steam rooms, sun bed, sauna, facials, body treatments, hairdressing, etc.);

- fitness studio;

- dance studio;

- gymnasium;

- crèche;

- squash courts;

- conference facilities for between 10 and 100 people.

Besides offering the use of these facilities, Hanbury Manor also provides services such as professional coaching, lifestyle evaluations and tailor-made fitness plans. This example demonstrates that resort hotels provide a 'complete experience', not just the use of facilities. It is these facilities, which have helped develop the reputation of this hotel, and many other resort hotels in the UK, as up-market golf and leisure-oriented hotels. Added to these facilities, the fact that such hotels often have a higher number of rooms than conventional hotels, means that they can attract conferences and corporate entertainment events at premium rates. The sports and leisure orientation of resort hotels (see Figure 4.2) is therefore a key differentiating feature over conventional hotels, so much so that companies such as De Vere and Whitbread have become the largest operators of golf courses in the UK.

To keep pace with rising consumer expectations, all holiday centres are investing in better quality accommodation, restaurant facilities and general comfort. Butlin's for example, underwent a £43 million accommodation upgrade which included the introduction of new three-star standard County bedrooms in hotels or Suites at Holiday World. Centres now also provide a choice of self-catering or full board catering, a trend that reflects transatlantic resort influences. Guests can choose from a range of cafés, bars, and restaurants offering everything from a quick snack to a full meal. The provision of self-catering facilities has been the reason why holiday centre operators have often not been included in the 'hotel company' category. However, an operator such as Center Parcs provides extremely high-quality self-catering accommodation and the option to hire fully serviced villas, or even hotel rooms at the Elvedon Forest Holiday Centre in Suffolk. Each villa is relatively secluded from neighbouring villas and is supplied with an open fireplace, central heating and colour TV connected to a video-film network. Villa rental prices are however not fully inclusive of all facilities, they only include access to the swimming facilities.

The Center Parc concept has more selling features than just high standards of accommodation. Perhaps its main 'unique' selling point is the central complex, this provides a sub-tropical atmosphere (it is covered by a transparent sliding all-weather dome) with shops, restaurants, terraces, sports facilities (Jardin des Sports) and the pool complex. The pool area comprises a sub-tropical dome (kept at a constant 30 degrees centigrade) with artificial wave pool and waterslide, bubble

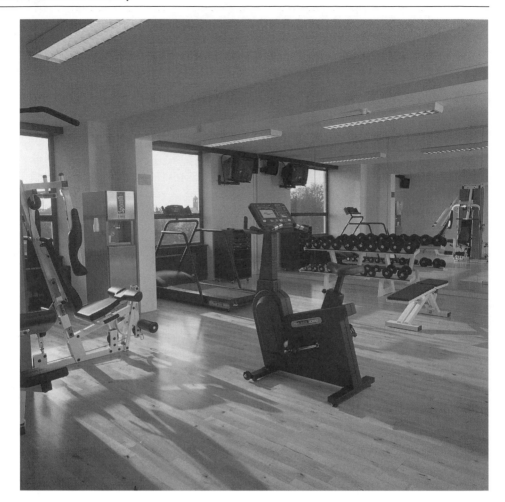

Figure 4.2 *Hotel fitness centre*
Source: Holiday Inn

bath, hot whirlpools, children's pools, solaria, saunas and outside heated pool. There are over 10 different types of restaurants and bars on site, ranging from Le Sapiniere, where average spend per head is £35, to the value-for-money Country Pancakes and Huckleberrys.

ORGANIZATION AND STAFFING

The prominence of sports, leisure and recreational facilities in all types of resort hotels means that their organizational structures and corresponding staffing requirements are quite different from traditional hotels and holiday centres. Studying the contribution of different operating departments reiterates this point. Non-room turnover at De Vere's golf hotels was estimated to be 62.5 per cent of total hotel turnover, compared with 50 per cent in conventional hotels in the UK. This incorporated not only restaurant and bar revenue but a high level of revenue from green fees and pro shops. Meanwhile, Center Parcs earn up to 60 per cent from villa rental, 25 per cent from catering, 15 per cent from shops and nearly 10 per cent from other recreational activities. As a result of product development, the company is likely to increase its average spend per customer whilst on site, so that in the future the contribution from non-villa rental sources will be higher. These statistics have obvious effects on the organization and management of resort hotels, and also mean that break-even points are harder to figure out due to the complexity of the operations.

A hotel executive may know little about the different operational demands of the sports and leisure areas, therefore, an experienced leisure/recreation manager has an important role to play in resort hotels, as illustrated in Figure 4.3. Golf, in particular, because it has its own etiquette and set of specific rules, needs professionals/experts managing the facility. They will have a better appreciation of customer needs and the confidence to know that what is being offered meets with expectations. Safety of course is another important operational aspect which must be managed correctly, and is made more complex by the addition of guests involved in recreational and sporting activities.

Successful resorts also tend to achieve higher occupancy and higher sales per room than other categories of hotels. Whereas average occupancy achieved by English hotels in 1999 was just over 50 per cent, De Vere's golf hotels achieved 67 per cent, whilst their room yields were some 11 per cent higher than other UK hotels. However, corporate country resort hotels are probably the most expensive hotels to operate. They average a higher number of employees per room (due to their high service levels), and thus their payrolls are much higher than for other kinds of hotels.

Holiday centres, in terms of the number of staff employed, are large establishments. Center Parcs, for example employs over 800 people in total, over a quarter of whom work in its catering outlets alone. In addition, occupancy rates of plus 90 per cent all year-round mean that productivity is paramount. Butlin's, Pontin's and Warner's also report high occupancy rates, in the 70s, as a result of their far more flexible and relaxed style and their more sophisticated packages. Over Christmas Butlin's Holiday Worlds sometimes cater for over 62,000 guests. Just like other service sectors, customer care is an important aspect of staff training. Warner's operated a 'Quality Through People' customer care training programme and Center Parcs has, as one of its goals, an approach to guest service that is second to none.

STANDARD OPERATING PROCEDURES

Once again, extensive leisure amenities, the scale of operations and the holiday 'experience' (offered particularly by holiday centres and villages) make some of the operating procedures for these hotels distinct. The economics of leisure and sports facilities are similar to those of a hotel. The purpose is to maximize yield through full utilization of capacity. For accommodation this means that all rooms/villas are occupied to their optimum capacity, while for sports like golf, all courses are fully booked by complete foursomes spaced at proper ten-minute intervals with the maximum number of playable hours.

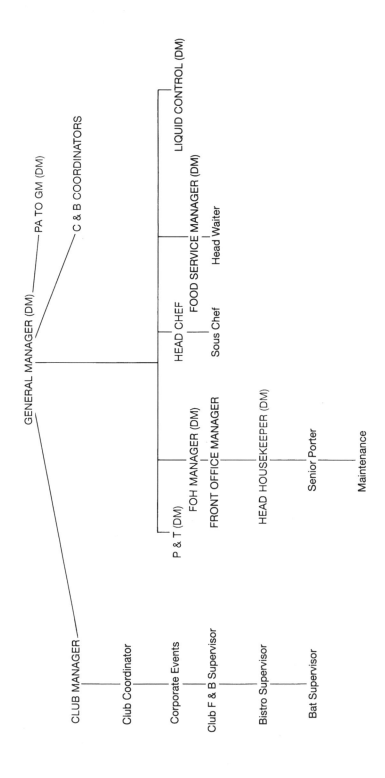

Figure 4.3 *Organization chart of a resort hotel*

Excepting changes in the weather for outside activities and the different popularity of certain sports, systems can be installed in order to maximize facility use and manage the capacity of these amenities. Corporate country resort hotels, for example, operate different 'use' categories such as 'peak' and 'off-peak' membership and computerized booking systems for sports facilities are used by all types of resort hotels.

An important operational task in the large capacity holiday centres is the management of large peaks in demand, due to their less varied demand and specified arrival and departure dates. For example, at certain meal times when all restaurants and snack bars are busy (on arrival days demand is exceptionally high), procedures that assist in managing these trading peaks include the use of queuing systems or in some instances bookable facilities. Services such as laundry are also often best contracted out in order to help with the huge demand for linen on change-over days. The pre-payment of short breaks or long holidays also reduces the front-of-house operation (and relieves the need for a major cashiering function) on arrival and departure days. Center Parcs, for instance, request that for bookings taken more than eight weeks in advance a deposit is paid within 10 days of receiving booking confirmation and that the total cost is received in the period before the start of the holiday. For bookings within eight weeks of the holiday the whole cost is payable immediately. The reservations function of this company is therefore very important and it is also likely that, compared to conventional hotels in this country, substantial interest may be earned on these pre-stay payments, particularly as the Parcs can be up to 60 per cent booked two months prior to arrival.

Many non-accommodation facilities in resort hotels, such as retail outlets, bars and restaurants, utilize computerized point-of-sale equipment in order to monitor these facilities and as a feedback system for recognizing demand trends. These information systems are particularly significant given the importance of these additional sources of revenue.

Country resort hotels tend to use the conventional mix of hotel distribution channels. However, business and conference houses, incentive planners and sales representatives overseas are particularly important sources of business given their characteristics of demand. Meanwhile, many holiday centres are keen to work with the travel trade, they all operate efficient booking systems and commission structures. Their long and short holiday breaks are easy packages to sell through this route and there is the possibility for agents to earn extra commission by selling add-on items such as rail travel to and from the holiday centre. However, in reality most holiday villages operate through direct selling only, in other words, its holidays are not available through travel agents. The internet is an increasing source of such reservations.

CURRENT ISSUES AND FUTURE TRENDS

So far resort hotels have been responding to meet changing customer expectations and aspirations and the tastes of an increasingly affluent, more widely travelled leisure consumer. In the future, it is likely that UK leisure trends will follow the pattern in the USA. The market will then be driven by affluent and active middle-aged and early retired consumers. Resort hotels, particularly corporate country hotels because of their quality of accommodation provision and high service levels, will be the best placed to benefit from this expected growth in active leisure demand, as conventional hotels do not have enough of the facilities necessary to meet this emerging demand.

The sector will however continue to be constrained in terms of new supply, due to the sizable land requirements and inclement weather in this country. In addition, all resort operators will have to take more note of the environmental impact of their operations. Center Parcs has led the field so far environmentally; in 1990 it won the English Tourist Board's inaugural award for Green Tourism and has won many such awards since then.

The key market for the future will be the short break market, rather than the long holiday market. Holiday centres in particular should continue to target ABC1 families with children under 14 years of age, a group of consumers that are set to increase (in a four-year gap it was estimated that there was a growth of 100,000 more under five-year olds in the population).

Following overseas trends again, there is the potential for UK resort hotels to become more mixed developments. In other words, a hotel, villas, condominiums, and homes for time-share could all be developed on the same site. The real estate opportunity could therefore really be exploited for those resort operators who own their own properties, extending their expertise into different accommodation forms. An example of an existing type of mixed resort in Europe is the Hyatt La Manga Club Resort in Spain. This was upgraded in order to attract business year-round and to put it on a competitive footing with top ranked destination resorts worldwide. The resort is set in 1400 acres and comprises a 192 room five-star hotel, 72 apartments (ranging from studios to extensive villas in their own grounds), three 18-hole championship golf courses, 18-court tennis centre with gymnasium and spa, a beach club for water sports, a soccer field, crown bowling and equestrian centre, and a range of different types of restaurants. This could, assuming investment was available, be the future type of resort development in the UK, given the success of present operators and the ever increasing demand for relaxation and leisure.

SUMMARY

This chapter has identified that leisure is a major market for accommodation providers. A significant segment of this market is holiday villages specializing in providing short break family holidays, whilst resort hotels also have some specific characteristics. In the UK, hotels serving this market (and Center Parcs) tend to be located in the country, whilst holiday villages are traditionally located at the seaside. The products and services vary widely from self-catering to serviced accommodation, all styles of restaurant, and a range of sports, leisure and health facilities. Hotels typically have at least one member of the management team responsible for leisure facilities.

FURTHER STUDY

www.centerparcs.co.uk

www.devereonline.co.uk

www.british-holidays.co.uk

QUESTIONS

Select two holiday village websites (include Center Parcs as one of these). Compare and contrast these villages locations, prices, and product/service offer.

Type 'resort hotel' into the key word search of an archive held by a trade publication (such as www.caterer.com). What trends are evident in the UK resort hotel market?

CHAPTER 5

Budget hotels

INTRODUCTION

In contrast to most traditional forms of accommodation provision, budget hotels are a relatively new phenomenon within the UK. Up until they emerged, in the mid-to-late 1980s, budget accommodation in Britain was dominated by guest houses, inns, farmhouses and other forms of bed and breakfast provision. Consequently, budget hotels had to compete with a vast, and diverse, range of pre-existing, low cost accommodation in order to establish themselves and penetrate the market-place. Where such competition was largely absent, as in the USA, for example, budget hotels were able to capture the market more easily and, therefore, develop earlier and consolidate more rapidly. For this reason the motel has been a significant feature of the USA accommodation industry for a much greater period than its British counterpart.

Given this historical background, it could be argued that the budget hotel is not a particularly innovative concept. Within the British context it could be seen as simply a repackaging of low cost accommodation in such a way as to be defined as a hotel. Consequently, a new product is created by systematically stripping out many of the features of conventional, full service hotels in order to create a lower service offering. This can then be provided at an appropriate tariff to the existing market for low cost accommodation.

On the other hand, the rapid growth of budget hotels and the high occupancy levels that they typically achieve has been interpreted by some as evidence that a new market has been created. It is argued that a significant slice of budget hotel customers have never previously patronized other forms of low cost accommodation. Viewed in this way, budget hotels can claim to be highly innovative, since both a new product and a new market have been established. The extent to which budget hotels constitute an innovative feature within UK accommodation provision will be explored in the remainder of this chapter.

DEFINITION

In order to understand the nature and operational characteristics of budget hotels it is necessary to define the product/service combination at the outset. Unfortunately, there is a lack of definitional consensus among both academics and industrialists alike. This leads to confusion as to which hotels are budget hotels and what are the requirements to become one. Through common usage the term has come to imply that rooms are offered at lower tariffs than industry norms and with facilities and services that do not match the usual provision found in traditional hotels. However, the lower tariff rates and service provision are not the only factors which differentiate budget hotels. Indeed, as these hotels have developed they have diversified and this adds to the definitional confusion. As Roper and Carmouche (1989) point out, budget hotels should not be regarded as a homogeneous sector of the hotel industry as there is substantial segmentation within this type of provision.

Projection 2000, offers a basic but useful starting point. 'Budget hotels offer 2/3 star accommodation at 1/2 star tariffs. Mainly located on major roads, they are designed with "no-frills" convenience as a priority ... The budget hotel has two principal differences when compared with a standard hotel or guest house: price and location.' The key features identified here are those of lower tariff, reduced facilities and locational characteristics.

The reductionist approach to facilities and services used by budget hotels has called into question the appropriateness of the term 'hotel' when describing that which is left. Conventional hotel guide/classification schemes had difficulty in embracing budget hotels given their level of product/service offering. However, both the AA and RAC have acknowledged the importance of budget hotels and have altered their classification schemes in ways so as to capture them.

As the AA (2000) states:

> In 1987, the AA introduced a new category of hotel called 'Lodge'. This was necessary to meet the rapid expansion of this style of property throughout Britain. Lodges generally provide a high standard of accommodation with a wide range of facilities required by the business and leisure user, but often provide none of the traditional hotel 'services' expected, and the catering operation is usually housed in an adjacent block. Lodge accommodation usually means two star standard but for the above reasons, does not qualify for a star rating. It would seem that any attempt to define budget hotels using only the tangible features of tariff, facility levels and location will be limiting. So much so that the word hotel has to be eliminated and replaced by the term 'lodge'.

The English Tourist Board (ETB) sought to widen the definition by seeing budget hotels not only in terms of their facilities but also in terms of what these facilities might mean for customers. They stated that such hotels provide a highly standardized and branded product, with simple front- and back-of-house operations, offering a standard national room charge (excluding breakfast) with minimal public/common facilities and offering no discounts. The RAC provides a similar insight: 'Lodges are designed to provide inexpensive overnight accommodation for the traveller. They are usually located on major road networks or on the outskirts of urban areas. Food service is usually provided by adjacent motor way or roadside restaurants.' Despite using the term 'lodge', the interesting features highlighted here are the use of the reference to the market as 'the traveller' and its general concurrence with the definitional characteristics offered by the ETB.

The English Tourist Board has followed the lead of the AA by recognizing budget hotels in their classification schemes by again using a lodge classification. This has been introduced to ... 'acknowledge the purpose-built bedroom accommodation that is springing up along our major roads and motor ways'.

In summary, the main features that these three major classification schemes have identified as being pertinent to the budget hotel concept are as follows:

- lower tariffs than industry norm;

- two/three star standard of accommodation;

- limited facilities and services;

- aimed at the transient market;

- located on major road networks or in secondary urban locations (retail parks);

- catering is usually provided by an adjacent food operation;

- purpose-built in terms of location and design;

- standardized operational procedures and charges nationwide;

- branded network of hotels.

It is a compound of these features that will be utilized as a definition of budget hotels for the remainder of this chapter. They are generally good quality, value-for-money bedrooms designed and marketed in such a way as to appeal to the travelling public.

GROWTH OF THE SECTOR

Forte Hotels initially fuelled the penetration of the budget hotel in the UK with the introduction of their first Travelodge in 1985. As with other sectors of the UK hotel industry, the prosperous years of the late 1980s facilitated rapid growth in provision. However, whilst three-, four-, and five- star hotels suffered at the hands of economic recession and the Gulf War at the turn of the decade, the budget sector flourished with demand increasing and outpacing the supply. Conditions of economic stringency seemed to have less impact on the budget sector. Indeed, the economic necessity of 'trading down' from high tariff hotels could have actually benefitted budget hotels. However, this point should not be over-emphasized since the building of new budget bedroom blocks was slow during the difficult 1990–3 trading period. By 2000, Keynote (2000a) reported that there were an estimated 35,000 budget-priced hotel rooms in the UK, representing approximately 5 per cent of all hotel rooms. In addition the price range has broadened in the sector between £19.95 to £65.00 per room per night. The size of the sector and its importance, the major brands and their number of units is illustrated in Table 5.1.

Whitbread and Compass have emerged as market leaders with the Travel Inn and Travelodge (originally developed by Forte) brands respectively. Both of these groups have successfully completed a degree of synergy between these new brands and their previous line of business. Whitbread, like a number of other brewery-related companies such as Scottish & Newcastle, already had a portfolio of appropriately located, low cost accommodation in the form of their public house estate. Purpose built bedroom blocks, adjacent to the public house and/or roadside restaurant were used to improve accommodation facilities and provide the standardization required of a brand. A total of 227 Travel Inns, situated predominantly in the UK's largest cities and airports, have made Whitbread plc the largest budget hotel chain. Compass, too, has integrated this hotel concept into

Table 5.1 *Major operators of budget hotels in the UK*

Brand	Hotel group	Number of budget hotels	Number of budget hotel rooms	Tariff (£)
Express by Holiday Inn	Six Continents	+60	n/a	42.95
Travel Inn	Whitbread	227	14,500	41.95
Travelodge	Compass	213	10,695	42.95
Premier Lodge	Scottish & Newcastle	116	n/a	42.95
Ibis	Accor	34	3705	64.95

Source: Company websites

its existing chain of motorway service areas, under the Moto brand, and the Little Chef chain of roadside restaurants (see Chapter 14). In March 2000, there were 195 hotels in the Travelodge chain, including the newly opened Edinburgh Travelodge and the Heathrow Travelodge.

The remainder of the UK budget hotel sector is made up of North American and French motel concepts which have been 'imported' into the UK. These imported brands do not have the advantage of synergy with existing units. They are sometimes handicapped, for expansion, by the lack of suitable development sites. This problem is not as acute for a domestic operator with an existing chain of underdeveloped roadside sites/units. However, the greater maturity of both the French and USA motel markets gives these overseas brands more exposure to the operational learning/experience curve than their UK-based counterparts.

The majority of the budget hotel brands mentioned above are operated in an owner–operator capacity by the hotel group who owns the brand. However, due to the highly standardized nature of the product and the strength of the brands involved, franchising is likely to become a dominant feature of the budget hotel sector. In the USA, franchising of budget hotel concepts is big business with franchisees continuously being sought by franchisers. It is likely, that with the involvement of foreign hotel groups (Accor, Choice, etc.) that franchise agreements will become as common in the UK as they are in their home countries. For example, the majority of Travel Inns operate under franchise to other Whitbread businesses such as Beefeater, Brewers Fayre and TGI Friday's. Compass are just about to start franchising out the Travelodge concept to Jarvis hotels, who are opening a hotel in Edinburgh.

THE BUDGET HOTEL CUSTOMER

It could be argued that the economic recession of the early 1990s could not have come at a better time for the budget hotel operators. With the standard of accommodation on offer at the lower tariff rates, the budget hotels were in a perfect position to capitalize on trends in business and consumer travel expenditure cutbacks. It has been accepted that the budget hotel has two main target markets through which to maximize its profit potential. The first and core market is the business traveller. It has been estimated that this target market represents around 60 per cent of all bedroom sales in the budget sector, and dominates the Monday to Thursday market. These transient business travellers are thought to be junior managers in large corporations on £50 per night expense accounts who would rather utilize the high standards of the budget hotel than use a local independent hotel or guest house with whom they have no guarantee of standards. This business user was joined by a large number of middle managers who have been forced to 'trade down' from traditional full-service hotels due to cuts in what is seen as unnecessary expenditure. In 2002, the Premier Lodge budget chain has an advertising campaign that specifically identifies its tariff of around £50 in comparison with that of Holiday Inn three-star hotel rate of around £90.

The second target market is the leisure user. The average consumer now travels more frequently, further away from home and more independently than ever before. This trend, in conjunction with the increasing number of families who take short break holidays within the UK has led to more demand for affordable, quality accommodation in convenient locations. Room pricing is attractive to the family market with rates charged per room, not per person. This is also ideal for visitors who do not intend to physically stay in their hotel for the total duration of their visit. These are consumers who are not looking at the hotel as a venue at which to spend their time, but as a functional place in which to rest, eat and drink. This new provision therefore has encouraged a demand from customers hitherto not users of traditional hotels. These could be guests who decide to stop at a budget hotel to break a journey overnight instead of travelling straight through, or those who utilize the simple and straightforward convenience of the accommodation instead of stopping with friends or relatives when visiting. The budget hotel and its different culture and atmosphere from traditional hotels has, to some extent, diminished the class structure of the hotel system due to its informal, impersonal and simple mode of operation. The budget hotel is not a home or exclusive club of any one set of users, it is simply a place of rest which holds no barriers against usage. Due to its lack of public areas it holds no informal dress codes and can therefore be considered to have 'classless' appeal. This enables a wide variety of potential users to be targeted.

Budget hotel users appear to be attracted by the fact that they can pay for the combination of facilities that they want to use. Paying full price for full service makes little sense if you have neither the time, nor the inclination, to use the services provided. Slight alterations to the product/service offering can therefore appeal to a particular group of users and segment them for particular targeting. Segmentation of budget hotels has occurred in order to target certain user groups more specifically.

It is expected that foreign visitors will take an increasingly important role in income generation for the budget sector in the future. The French, for example, are more accustomed to the philosophy and culture of the budget concept and are a prime market in the south of England following the Channel Tunnel opening.

In summary, a number of different types of budget hotel customer have been identified. These include:

- business users down-trading from hotels with higher service levels;

- business users trading up from bed and breakfast style accommodation to standardized accommodation facilities;

- transient UK leisure users who are attracted by low tariffs – particularly for family occupancy;

- overseas leisure users already familiar with the budget hotel concept within their home market;

- first time/new users attracted by 'value for money', i.e. the ability to pay only for those facilities which they actually use.

The future for the budget hotel market appears to be continued growth. The supply has segmented and niched remarkably early in its UK life-cycle, possibly due to the experience of operators in other countries (France and the USA). It is likely that the customer markets will continue to segment in response to their needs for particular combinations of product/service offerings.

LOCATIONAL CHARACTERISTICS AND SITE CHOICE CRITERIA

As stated above, site location is of similar importance to price in the marketing mix for budget hotels. The correct location is the key to the success of a budget hotel. It must be situated in a place with easy access. Adequate car parking space is important. Land and planning permission must be available at the right price. These criteria therefore limit the choice of sites available to potential developers and operators. Budget accommodation cannot be provided, economically, on premium-priced land. For example, city centre locations have been off-limits due to the price of land, therefore budget hotels were forced into out-of-town 'secondary' urban locations on main trunk roads. This fits in well with recent building developments in the form of retail and leisure parks in out-of-town locations, and many new retail and leisure developments include planning for a budget hotel. Motorway service areas also made attractive sites. Budget hotels are now being built in cities, but often their room tariff is adjusted upwards to reflect this location. For instance, the Travel Inn in central London had a rate of £74.95 in early 2002.

Campanile in 1992 insisted 'further growth in this sector will depend on finding the right sites in the right locations'. The importance of national coverage and the creation of a nationally recognized brand has already been indicated, and is necessary if a critical mass is to be reached. Problems have arisen to some extent in achieving such a national coverage due to high land prices and poor availability of suitable sites in some regions. The south east has been particularly difficult for the budget hotel developers who cannot afford the land prices demanded due to the necessity to maintain low room tariffs. So despite having considerable market potential, with the operation of the Channel Tunnel, future growth in the south east cannot be guaranteed. It is those budget hotel developers that already possessed suitable sites that have been able to develop at the greatest rate. Forte's roadside presence through their catering operations allowed them instant access to ideal locations for accommodation expansion.

Compass, who merged with Granada who had taken over Forte, believe that they still possess some prime sites for development, but it is logical to assume that

Figure 5.1 *Budget hotel built adjacent to existing property*
Source: Premier House

the first sites to be developed would be those with the most potential and that it is only the less favoured sites which are left to be developed. Consequently, the rate of expansion will be restricted by financial expediency. It can be argued, however, that it would be advisable to develop as many sites as necessary to create a full national network of budget accommodation, even if some of the sites may not be as profitable as some of the others. A full national network of budget accommodation controlled by a central reservation system would allow for total loyalty from travellers wherever they go.

There are basically two types of site – existing roadside properties with scope for expansion and redevelopment, or greenfield sites. Existing properties by the roadside are often public houses owned by breweries. The property is developed by the addition of an adjacent bedroom block, often with restaurant facilities being provided in the original 'shell'. Budget hotel concepts on this kind of site are reinforced by the roadside presence of strong branding in the form of signage, as each of the buildings is unique. Roadside diners, such as Little Chef, may also be adapted in this way. Alternatively, budget hotels can be developed on greenfield sites as 'new builds'. In this case, the property itself is tailored and built to create a differentiated product. If there is no pre-existing restaurant provision, a branded outlet such as Chef and Brewer is co-located with the unit. This kind of budget hotel development is illustrated in Figure 5.2.

Figure 5.2 *Budget hotel on greenfield site.*
Source: Premier House

The financial situation with regard to site purchase and development through to payback is shown in Table 5.2. The stated cost per room varies from brand to brand from £20,000 to £45,000. Consequently, the potential profitability of the budget hotel concept is clear and explains why there are so many hotel groups seeking new locations currently in the UK. With one budget hotel operator quoting operating costs of around £5.00 per room per night including laundry and staffing it appears that net profit opportunities are potentially great in both the short and long term. Not only do these sites represent a good return on capital employed, but it is also highly probable that the investment value of a completed unit would far outweigh the costs required to construct it. For example, the above hypothetical budget hotel would result in an overall value of around £2,000,000.

PRODUCT/SERVICE OFFERING

The main features that distinguish the budget hotel have already been identified. This section will outline in detail what it is that makes up the operation of a budget hotel and what the tangible components of the accommodation provision are. The AA identifies that lodges must meet the minimum standards for two stars with the following exceptions:

Table 5.2 *Site purchase and development costs*

Costs		
(i)	Cost of land purchase	
	Land acquisition, 1 acre	£400,000
	Plus legal fees @ 4%	£16,000
	Agents fees @ 1%	£4,000
	Total land purchase costs	£420,000
(ii)	Costs of construction	
	40 rooms @ £25,000 per room	£1,000,000
	plus associated fees:	
	Structural engineer @ 3%	£36,000
	Quantity surveyor @ 3%	£36,000
	Total costs	£1,492,000
Asset valuation of the completed unit		
	40 rooms @ £45 per night	£1,800
		365×
	Total income p.a.	£657,000
	Target rate of occupancy @ 75%	
	Target income p.a.	£492,750

- porterage need not be available;

- foyer or reception area seating to be available, although its existence may be limited;

- writing facilities are optional;

- a bar is not required;

- light refreshment and breakfast facilities in neighbouring restaurant (where available) will be acceptable;

- room service is not required;

- telephone need not be provided in-room;

- 100 per cent en suite facilities are required.

This demonstrates that the budget concept places less emphasis on traditional hotel services and offers customers a different atmosphere and product. Roper and Carmouche (1989) argued that the budget concept is a utilitarian purchase owing to the limited product offering and that the customers' motivation to purchase is related to convenience and occasion. This leads to a parallel being drawn to the fast-food industry where the emphasis is on the tangible product and less on the service (in its traditional restaurant sense). The product is 'trustworthy' reliable and standardized, to allow for customer expectations to be met irrespective of which unit they visit.

It is the design of the accommodation provision that holds the key to the success of the operation. A strict set of standard operating procedures is made possible by regulating the design of the bedrooms and reducing the consumer/staff interaction. Campanile stated that since their bedroom blocks are pre-fabricated and since every room is built to the same specification, then any two Campaniles are identical. This is seen as a strength, 'If people like the product they will keep coming back, knowing what they are going to get and how much it will cost' (Day, 1992).

It is this concentration on the product design and operation at all budget levels that makes the budget brands suitable for franchise. The budget hotel is designed to maximize revenue-earning potential, whilst maintaining low build and maintenance costs. The design then, is crucial to the profitability of the budget concept. Revenue is small in comparison to traditional hotels; therefore costs have to be more keenly controlled. The maximization of revenue earning space is demonstrated by the role ergonomics plays in the design of budget hotels with few if any public areas, standard room layout allowing for easy maintenance and economics of scale to be gained from suppliers. Even though the market is far from saturated, competitive rivalry is already showing in the sense the niche sub-segments of the sector are already emerging. These niche brands are competing in this value-for-money market by offering more value-added features or by 'stripping down' further to an even more utilitarian product in order to offer an even lower tariff. This sub-segmentation and niching was seen in Table 5.1 that demonstrates where some of the major brands fall in terms of price and product offering.

Formule 1, a French brand, has gone for the basic product with automated payment, room allocation and entry to the hotel. No staff/consumer interaction is necessary at all. Four rooms share a bathroom and toilet (which are self-cleaning) and only a pre-packed continental breakfast is available as refreshment. The rooms are very modern in design with metal and plastic finishes being preferred to wood and traditional bedroom designs. The Formule 1 brand has been remarkably successful in France, but is yet to achieve anything spectacular in the UK. The first unit opened in Doncaster in 1991. The Travelodge and Travel Inn brands appear in the middle of the market. They dominate, with over 60 per cent of the budget bed stock between them. This domination at mid-level budget is probably what has encouraged other operators to look for other methods of creating a differential advantage for themselves. Compass and Whitbread enjoy the benefits of being market leaders with a national network of accommodation provision and centralized reservation services. This enables the advantages of critical mass to be accrued and results in average occupancy rates in excess of 80 per cent. All of these brands at this level provide an en suite bathroom and toilet, with remote control colour TV. Most have double beds and a bed settee.

Whitbread, like Scottish & Newcastle and other brewers, have realized that there are market opportunities within the budget sector by re-establishing the 'coaching inn' concept. Their philosophy in the building of budget bedroom blocks adjacent to public houses or restaurants is that the majority of travellers would prefer to eat and drink in a 'pub' or restaurant than in a cafeteria (as with Travelodges being adjacent to Little Chefs). 'Business travellers do not want to be cooped up in their rooms all evening, after a quick steak and chips. Beefeater are comfortable pubs, where they can chat over a couple of pints, just as they might in their local' (Baker, 1994).

Scottish & Newcastle Premier Lodges have gone one stage further in the budget stakes by providing satellite TV in each room with a direct dial telephone. The trend in this 'one-upmanship' may prematurely kill off the budget sector. If all the competitors follow suit in this bid to add value to their products the resulting 'facilities drift' could end up providing just another three-star product. For example, Holiday Inn developed a Garden Court at the opposite end of the spectrum to Formule 1, which offered all the facilities of a three-star hotel including conference and meeting facilities but without the traditional services. However, they have subsequently decided this concept was too elaborate for the budget market place. Instead they have developed their Express at Holiday Inn as their brand for this segment.

MANAGEMENT AND STAFFING

Where the accommodation has been built adjacent to an existing catering operation, it is likely that the same management (frequently a couple) will run both the food and accommodation operations. However managing a budget hotel differs somewhat from a traditional small hotel. The reception area (if there is one) may not be staffed constantly. Little direct supervision is required except for cleaning and maintenance. The cleaning may be contracted out to another company and therefore the staff involved in running the accommodation side of the operation are minimal. The standard procedures for each brand allow for little of the management's individuality to influence the accommodation provided, this is controlled by head office and the manager's main role is that of cost and quality standards control.

Marketing is controlled most often by head office with high proportions of bookings coming via central reservations services. Skill requirements are therefore reduced from the traditional hotel provision, with emphasis on retailing and property management rather than interpersonal skills.

CURRENT ISSUES AND FUTURE TRENDS

Budget hotels were the fastest-growing sector of the UK market in the 1990s. This continues to be the case in 2001. All the main players are announcing plans for expansion and new players are entering or are expecting to enter the UK market in the near future. Despite this growth, and a tariff increase, average occupancy remains steady in the low 80 per cent range. Scottish & Newcastle have announced plans to spend over £100 million on building nearly 50 Premier Lodge hotels in the UK with intentions to have 148 hotels opened by the end of 2002. Climat De France had an unfortunately short trading period in the UK. Its only British unit opened near to Manchester on a retail park, but quickly went into liquidation, possibly indicating the importance of a critical mass to enable expensive advertising and central reservations systems to be put into practice. The competition at the lower level of the budget sector could depend upon the success of franchising policies by the brand owners and the uptake by franchisees in the UK. It is unlikely that within the next five years the UK will reach the saturation point that the USA has reached. Budget hotels are here to stay and prosper for at least the next ten years in their current format. Technological advancements may enable further improvements to be made to increase convenience. Future locations are likely to include further development of city centres and airport locations. There is also the possibility of budget hotels being built close to hospitals as 'patient hotels'. Budget hotels have carved themselves a suitable niche within the accommodation provision currently available elsewhere in the market.

It has been interesting to see that budget hotels have been least affected by adverse trading conditions following the outbreak of foot and mouth in the UK and the downturn in international travel following the World Trade Center attack in New York. Operators in both the UK and USA account for this by identifying that the decline in air travel has actually increased car travel, which accounts for nearly 100 per cent of all budget hotel arrivals. Also the diverse nature of the market segments served means that they are less susceptible to a downturn than brands identified with one particular market.

SUMMARY

In the late 1980s branded budget hotels were an innovation. By 2001, they are the most common form of chain property and continuing to expand rapidly. They have specific characteristics related to their location near main highways, low tariff structure, and limited facilities. They are often purpose-built adjacent to restaurant facilities of various kinds. The two largest UK chains are British owned Travelodge and Travel Inn, although a range of non-British chains have entered the market, sometimes on a franchise basis. This type of hotel is easy to construct and operate, and achieves high levels of profitability based on high rates of occupancy. New technology is making them even more profitable through internet reservations and credit card access to the property and rooms.

FURTHER STUDY

www.hiexpress.co.uk

www.travelinn.co.uk

www.travelodge.co.uk

QUESTIONS

Select two budget hotel chain websites. Compare and contrast these chains' locations, prices, and product/service offer.

Type in 'budget hotel' into the key word search of an archive held by a trade publication (such as www.caterer.com). What trends are evident in the UK budget hotel market?

CHAPTER 6

Guest houses and small hotels

This sector of the industry can be said to present the 'human face of hospitality'. As far as the accommodation sector is concerned, the majority of operating units, around 70 per cent have less than 25 bedrooms, and many of these are operated by the owner or the owners of the property. It is therefore a classic entrepreneurial business that relies heavily on the enthusiasm and expertise of many thousands of people.

In this chapter, an understanding of the nature and characteristics of the guest house and small hotel sector within the UK is developed and the commercial pressures and priorities facing operators within this sector are identified, the markets in which guest houses and small hotels operate are described; and organizational structure and functional activity of operations in this sector are explored. Finally current issues and future trends are highlighted.

DEFINITION OF THE TYPE OF OPERATION

The small, independently owned guest house and hotel continues to dominate the accommodation sector in the UK, Europe and internationally. Definition of their activities is included in SIC 66 *Hotels and Other Residential Establishments* (see Table 1.1), along with motels, holiday camps, boarding houses, hostels and other similar establishments, providing furnished accommodation with food and service, for a monetary fee. In general, the classification is governed by the Fire Precautions (Hotels & Boarding Houses) Order (1972) which covers premises sleeping more than six persons (three bedrooms), including both guests and staff. Further, attempts to define what represents a 'hotel' have been numerous. In some cases, these are legal definitions as in the Development of Tourism Act 1969. In others they are academic definitions, as for instance those by Burkart and Medlik (1981) and Medlik (1994). Such definitions tend to be very broad due to the diversity of physical facilities, geographic location, markets served, and manner of business operation. However, they agree that a hotel broadcasts the fact that it is in business to provide accommodation, food, drink and other facilities in return for monetary charge.

There is however a legal difference between a guest house and a hotel. The Hotel Proprietor Act (1956) states '... [a hotel is] an establishment held out by the proprietor as offering food, drink and, if so required sleeping accommodation, without special contract, to any traveller presenting himself who appears willing and ready to pay a reasonable sum for the service provided and who is in a fit state to be received'. Unlike a hotel, a guest house has no legal obligation to receive all persons who arrive at the door, and has the right to be selective.

Guest houses also differ in that they tend to have the character of an extended family, welcoming guests into the household in a very person-to-person manner. Finally, the English Tourist Board defined a guest house as '... an establishment, licensed or unlicensed, which provides accommodation, meals and sometimes other services for residents only'. Thus, in the UK, a guest house is variously described as a private hotel, a guest house, bed and breakfast, or a boarding house. Indeed, owners often use the terms interchangeably to suit the specific guide book, or market segment, in which they wish to be represented. They tend to be smaller than hotels (4 to 9 rooms), with more limited facilities for residents. In 1999 the English Tourism Council, the Royal Automobile Club (RAC) and Automobile Association (AA) combined to create a new overall rating scheme for this type of serviced accommodation. Customer care and guest service are emphasized in these diamond ratings, rather than the range of facilities, as follows:

- one diamond – clean and comfortable accommodation, providing breakfast and a helpful service;

- two diamonds – an increased level of quality and comfort, with greater emphasis on guest care;

- three diamonds – well maintained, with practical décor, a good choice of breakfast dishes and a higher degree of customer care. At least 40 per cent of the bedrooms have private or en suite bathrooms;

- four diamonds – an even higher level of customer care, comfort and quality;

- five diamonds – excellent level of customer care.

For the purposes of this chapter, guest houses and small hotels are therefore defined as follows. In terms of physical facilities, service capacity, number of employees and market share they represent small scale accommodation providers, in comparison to the largest units of operation in the UK. The businesses are financed by one individual or small group, directly managed by its owner, or part owner, in a personalized manner and not through the medium of a formalized management structure.

It can then be seen that compared to a budget hotel, guest hotels and small hotels welcome a much smaller number of customers. The owner manages and operates the property him or herself, on a daily basis, and does not employ managers to do the job for him. The business is not part of a chain of similar establishments, it is privately owned and operates as an independent business. As such, the owner is totally responsible for making all business decisions.

SIZE AND NATURE OF THE SECTOR

There are limited and often inconsistent sources of statistical information relating to the guest house and small hotel sector in the UK. This is due, in part to:

- the absence of universally accepted organizational definitions;

- many operate below the VAT registration threshold level;

- not registered with officialdom as offer fewer than three rooms for let;

- no government policy for compulsory registration;

- seasonal and intermittent patterns of operations;

- active avoidance by operators aiming to avoid bureaucratic, legal and fiscal scrutiny;

- general inconsistencies in the manner in which they are counted.

As a result, accurate information regarding supply is difficult to obtain and, of what does exist, it is the smaller properties which are often missing. For instance, in presenting the number of hotels per UK geographic region the HCTC excluded establishments owned and managed by self-employed people. That is to say the very types of businesses which are the focus of this chapter. Furthermore, in calculating UK hotel stock Harrison and Johnson (1993) took the HCTC base of 52,200 units, discarded units which were guest houses, other non-hotel establishments and those having less than the required number of bedrooms, to arrive at an estimate of approximately 19,000 hotels. This left 33,200 accommodation units in the UK in limbo, many of which may fall into the guest house and small hotel sectors.

Drawing on available information from the national tourist boards, which readily admit that the statistics are anything but comprehensive, Table 6.1 gives an indication of the numbers of hotels and guest houses in Britain. However, it still does not identify the number which could be classified as 'small'.

Table 6.1 *Number of hotels and guest houses by region (2000)*

	NITB	STB	ETB	WTB	TOTAL
Hotels	133	2,508	20,987	717	24,345
Guest houses	140	1,420	8,246	1,100	10,906
Total	273	3,928	29,233	1,817	35,251

Source: National tourist boards

Despite these problems, a vast amount of information about these accommodation providers can be found in the printed media. The national tourist boards (NTBs) produce official *Where to Stay* guides to hotels and guest houses, which are revised annually. In addition, there are a wide range of other directories organized and published by, for example:

i.   motoring associations e.g. AA, RAC;

ii. good food guides e.g. Egon Ronay, Taste of Scotland/Wales;

iii. consumer associations e.g. Which Hotel?, Good Hotel;

iv. professional associations e.g. BHA Hotels & Restaurants of Britain;

v. other e.g. Signpost, Best Loved Hotels, Ashley Courtenay.

Until 1999, each of these different organizations used their own grading and classification schemes to assess and monitor overall quality, and some still do.

The high proportion of small businesses in the accommodation sector has been traditionally explained by a number of factors.

Relative ease of entry

The capital investment required is lower than in many other industries, specialist knowledge and qualifications are desirable, but not a prerequisite, and there is no compulsion to join trade or professional associations or similar organizations which have codes of practice such as consumer protection schemes.

Market demand highly diverse

Market demand is highly segmented, many of which do not lend themselves to satisfaction by standardized corporate properties. As a result, this diversity of demand is often best satisfied by a wide range of small establishments offering a wide variety of locations, quality ranges, physical facilities, and special interests/activities to niche markets.

Consumer satisfaction

The nature of accommodation provision is such that the small establishments may be better suited to respond quickly to customer needs and expectations, in a highly personalized, flexible environment. As such they are well positioned to provide specialist services which have the potential to add quality, variety and authenticity to the products offered to the tourists.

Economic viability

The small, often family, business can be economically viable in a limited, specialized or local marketplace, where there is often not enough profit for large businesses with their high overhead costs. As such, Kleinwort Benson described this sector of the hotel industry as the equivalent of the 'corner shop' (Kleinwort Benson Securities, 1991). It occupies a niche, is convenient for the local market, is usually run by local people, offering a limited product range, but nevertheless enjoys strong customer loyalty.

However, these mainly positive factors have to be located within the realities of the 1990s. The following points highlight the continuing domination of the smaller business and its significant role as an employer. Regrettably, this is tempered by the fact that their viability is threatened by operating only a small number of rooms, mainly at low market levels, resulting in relatively low turnover and profit earning potential. As such, for many guest house and small hotel operations it represents a high risk business.

Ownership

Kleinwort Benson estimated hotel room stock, which is not owned by the large groups accounts for around 66 per cent. This represents a 15 per cent decrease from 1987, and 25 per cent since 1936. In 1999, the HtF estimated that 60 per cent of all firms in the hotel and catering industry were operated as sole proprietor or partnership, and were frequently family run (HtF, 1999).

Employment

There are 127,000 persons self-employed in the hotel and catering industry, which represents approximately 11 per cent of total employment in the sector. Small businesses having ten or fewer employees accounted for 70 per cent of hotels in 1999.

Size

Using one hotel establishment as a unit of measurement, estimates of the percentage of hotel stock which falls into the 'small' category (50 rooms or less) vary between 65 per cent and 75 per cent, while the average room size of a small independently owned hotel is 15, compared with 89 in group owned properties in the UK. In Wales, for example, 60 per cent of hotels have less than ten rooms, and guest houses have approximately three letting rooms.

Market level

Seventy-five per cent of all UK hotels operate at the two-star/unclassified market level, compared to around 18 per cent of corporate owned hotels, and achieve an average annual room occupancy of 45 per cent to 55 per cent. This grouping accounts for around 78 per cent of the small accommodation providers.

Turnover and profit earning

The industry has the highest number of low turnover companies of any industry in the economy. More than 90 per cent have a financial turnover of less than £250,000. Moreover, the independent hotel delivers a trading profit per room seven times less than the corporate hotel, reflecting a general lack of the economies of scale enjoyed by the larger groups.

Risk factor

During the 1990–3 recession many small businesses were trading at levels which were below their critical break-even point, bringing about a dangerous situation of banks and creditors deciding to foreclose on business. At the time, the National Westminster Bank commented that 'it was an unfortunate fact of life'. For the remainder of the 1990s business remained relatively stable, with wide variations in performance depending on location. Small hotels and guest houses in seaside resorts that had invested in their tourism and conference infrastructure, such as

Blackpool, Bournemouth and Eastbourne, have survived. Other towns have been less successful in providing their hotel operators with a high standard of income.

MARKETS SERVED

The main demand occurs during April to September inclusive, concentrated on July to September, which continues to account for 60 per cent of overseas visitors and 40 per cent of UK trips. However, while the pattern of trade remains highly seasonal, the spread is not as severe as in previous decades, in part due to the fact that these sectors are now seen as ideal vehicles for the robust short break and shoulder season market. Furthermore, the nature of the product encourages a high level of core repeat business (50 per cent) while passing trade from touring customers with no forward reservations accounts for about 50 per cent of bookings.

The profile of typical customers is made of two main markets, the domestic and the overseas. The domestic market is dominated by the leisure, secondary or short break holiday guest using guest houses and small hotels for short stays of 4 to 7 nights mainly during April to September. The majority travel by private car, average party size is four, drawn mainly from ABC1 socio-economic groups, and are aged 35 plus. Approximately 80 to 90 per cent of accommodation arrangements are made independent of travel agents or tour operators, with guests booking directly with the individual operators. While 5 to 10 per cent of customers purchase inclusive packages, with the remainder booking through Tourist Information Centres and travel agents. A surprising number of small hotels now have a website and take internet reservations. Generally, of all persons taking domestic breaks of at least 4 nights duration, 10 per cent use guest houses, while 20 per cent use small hotels.

The overseas market is also dominated by the leisure guest with over 40 per cent of overseas visitors on their main holiday, 25 per cent on an additional holiday, and 11 per cent visiting friends and relatives. The average length of stay in the small hotels and guest houses tends to be 2 to 3 nights. Around 80 per cent of guests belong to AB socio-economic groups, tend not to be accompanied by children, and are aged between 25 and 54, with the 25–34 age group alone accounting for 33 per cent of all visitors. Approximately 77 per cent make independent accommodation arrangements, with only 23 per cent booking through travel agents. Generally, of all overseas tourists 32 per cent use small hotels, and 31 per cent use guest house accommodation, providing that quality expectations are satisfied.

Market segmentation is becoming an increasingly vital issue in the hotel trade, and no more so than to the guest house and small hotel sectors. Standard market segmentation approaches based on socio-economic, lifestyle, interests, and geographic factors are as applicable and as implementable to the guest house and small hotel sector, as to the large corporate groups. The range of variables which can be used include age-group, lifestyle, interests/activities, mode of travel, vacation type, season of travel, length of stay, average spend, method of reservation, newspaper readership and purpose of visit.

From these variables, guest house and small hotel operators can develop the profile of the specific market segment they wish to target. In particular, the locations are well positioned to exploit the growing demand for environmentally sound, outdoor pursuits, special interest courses, and itinerary planning for car tours. This can best be achieved through linking with other accommodation providers, activity/interest specialists, and transport companies. In this way clearly defined and priced, attractive packages can be developed and communicated to core and specialist markets.

As the majority of guest house and small hotel reservations come direct from the guest, by-passing travel agents, which account for around only 15 to 17 per cent of reservations, exposure in guides and directories represents a key method to target specific segments. Furthermore, it has been found that the more individual the property, the more likely a directory will be used as an information source on which to base purchase decisions, as such astute entries are vital to small hotels and guest houses. Other than those produced by the national tourist boards, a selection of the guides and directories most favoured by the UK guest houses and hotels are listed in Table 6.2.

Table 6.2 *Reservation sources of information*

Automobile Association (AA)	Royal Automobile Club (RAC)
Ackerman	Good Food Guide
Johansens	Michelin
Les Routiers	Ashley Courtenay
Egon Ronay	Good Hotel Guide
Signpost	Which Hotel?

There are six priority segments for the guest house and small hotel sectors.

i.   UK short break, promoted directly to the customer, by-passing the travel trade.

ii. USA/Canada independent travellers reached through direct mail, press coverage, consumer advertising, carefully selected wholesalers, retailers and BTA/NTB press departments.

iii. Special interest and activity, e.g. golfing, craft course, walking, bird watching.

iv. European holidaymakers, travelling independently and to a lesser extent travel operators. This segment is best targeted through retail travel agents which tailor make itineraries to the customer's specifications, e.g. 'Go As You Please' car touring types of programmes;

v.   Families are a durable segment which need is nurtured by devoting more effort to providing children's menus, meal times, baby-sitting services, entertainment and activities, and appropriate pricing policies.

vi. Visiting friends and relatives will be recommended to use a local guest house or small hotel of sound, established reputation and reasonable price as a substitute to staying with friends and relatives.

However, it should be emphasized that guest houses and small hotels are continuously struggling to attract these priority segments, as they lose market share to the hotel groups. This is due to corporate groups having the capacity to advertise nationally being capable of offering overall greater quality, consistency and value for money, ease of purchase through central reservation services, as well as a full range of locations and invariably a wider range of facilities than the small operators. Thus, the days of the totally independent small business are history if they want to stay in business. In the 2000s the way forward is through linking into marketing consortia which can cost-effectively reach these segments through combining resources, offering a full range of locations, and often a central reservation service. This strategy is more fully discussed in looking at future trends in this sector.

LOCATION

The majority of existing guest houses and small hotels can be found in secondary and tertiary locations, reflecting historic travel patterns of both domestic and overseas consumers, e.g. seaside resorts, country coaching inns. As a result they are generally a smaller, lower market level, serving mature or declining markets, suffer from a high degree of seasonality and general demand fluctuations, and produce lower trading profits. For this grouping of accommodation providers, Conrad Hilton's much quoted three success factors for hotels of 'Location, Location, and Location' has a different interpretation. There are very few guest houses and small hotels that are sited in prime locations. Most are well hidden, up long driveways, in the back of towns and remote scenic areas. However, perhaps their location is in fact a major strength, as the charming names adopted by the guest houses in particular reflect their attractive location, e.g. Hill Top, Beach Dunes, Riverside, Wood End. This combination of name and location characteristic, which is typical of many of the small accommodation properties, can be illustrated with a quote from one small hotel's brochure: 'Poised above Tobermory Bay, in the Sound of Mull, the Western Isles Hotel combines friendly hospitality with breathtaking views over an ever-changing vista of mountain and sea.'

When selecting a location for a guest house or small hotel, decisions are influenced by a mix of personal and business factors. Personal factors would include the likes of: get on well with the locals; can pursue hobby/sport; enjoyed the area during previous holidays; and pleasant environment for the children to grow up in. While business factors focus on: demand actual/potential; tourist attractions in the area; proximity of competition; capital investment requirements; length of season; profit earning capacity; potential for future growth or diversification; eligibility for public sector financial grants; and projected return on investment. However, frequently the personal factors override the business, which may not bode well for a sound commercial future.

PRODUCT OFFERING

Guest houses and small hotels are found in all grades of properties from de luxe, to unclassified. In tourist areas, like seaside resorts, such properties are often clustered together, with whole streets turned over to visitor accommodation. This is illustrated in Figure 6.1. In rural areas, the former use of the building is often obvious by its name that will include words such as mill, farm, manor, castle, parsonage, old school, almshouse and vicarage. For instance, Contin House is a former Church of Scotland manse built in 1774. It is now a traditional Highland Lodge. It has been tastefully refurbished to achieve a very high standard of accommodation whilst retaining the homeliness of a private house. The house is situated in its own garden, surrounded by pasture land, on a peaceful island in the River Blackwater.

Figure 6.1 *Typical small hotels in a British seaside resort*
Source: A. Carpenter

The majority of owners are genuinely interested in their guests and pride themselves on the warmth of welcome and quality of service. Furthermore, hosts are usually local people with a good knowledge of the area so they can advise on all tourist information requirements. The viability of the sector has strengthened as domestic and overseas visitors have become bored of the bland, standardized sameness of many of the corporate group-owned hotels. As a result they are seeking out a more personalized, individualistic environment offering a specialized product – often a style of living to which the guest would like to become accustomed!

Hopefully this trend will continue, provided the small operators can deliver increasing high standards in the physical product and service elements to match customer expectations. However, this may be a problem as many operators are in a situation where they cannot afford to put off refurbishment programmes, but cannot afford to finance them on present levels of revenue. The realities are simple, profit margins are low and cash flow cannot support additional borrowings required, when such improvements are unlikely to yield substantial revenue growth. In certain circumstances, funds from public sources, and government assistance, are generally available to alleviate the burden of refurbishment. For instance, the Wales Tourist Board is encouraging guest house improvements in resorts through allocation of Section 4 funds to assist in upgrading. However, there seems to be an inbred reluctance among small operators to get involved with such public sector schemes, perhaps, because it is feared that it may result in red tape or threaten individuality.

The ideal components of the core product of a small hotel consist of:

- a warm welcome;

- comfortable facilities;

- attractive location;

- satisfaction of perceptions of value for money;

- pride in preparing and serving good quality local produce;

- 'caring', represented by the owner taking a personal interest in their guest;

- efficient, friendly staff mirroring the attitude of 'mine host', tailoring customer service to each individual guest's needs;

- availability of special interest and activities programme;

- easy to purchase, attractive packages of all the components needed for a tourism experience.

Perhaps the most critical of these components to the success of the operation is the human, caring element – mine host and the staff. Take that out and the unique selling proposition disappears, the heart of the operation has been extracted. With all the components in place, the owner has a clearly focused, differentiated market proposition, a specialist product with which to strengthen their market appeal in niche markets and prosper.

ORGANIZATION AND STAFFING

There is a timeless quality to the organization of guest houses and small hotels, with traditional hospitality values and personal objectives mixing with commercial imperatives. As a result business organization frequently reflects the historic way of doing business, rather than any revolutionary, modern management system. In order to better understand factors which influence business organizations, two issues need to be discussed: degree of income dependency, and 'amateur' status.

First, three main levels of income dependency on the business can be identified, each of which will result in differing attitudes and motivations towards organization and staffing. The hotelier or guest house owner may run the unit as their primary source of income. They are therefore likely to be heavily reliant on overdraft facilities and loan capital. Second, the business may be a secondary source of income, whilst the owner carries on their 'real' profession. Finally the owner may be in the 'comfort zone'. The property has been purchased outright, and the owners seek only to achieve a 'comfort level' in terms of level of income generation to sustain a desired life-style.

A second issue is the 'amateur' status of guest house and small hotel operators, which has historically been a characteristic of these sectors. Operations are often started by an individual with enthusiasm for the social aspect of the business, but with only very basic knowledge of business practice and operations. Many have been 'in business' before as opposed to 'running their own accommodation business' and have no idea of the reality. Indeed, Boer (1992) commented that the supply of unskilled entrepreneurs to the hotel industry continues seemingly unabated.

As a result of these two factors, owners bring different levels of commitment and abilities to the business organization. Frequently, motivations are highly life-style driven, rather than commercial, which often results in operating below optimum. In addition, outdated management mentalities and general management weaknesses are common. Such business flaws were masked during the more buoyant 1980s, but the 90s were less tolerant of the inexperienced amateur. This prediction is as relevant as it was post-war, when Moncrieff (1947) advised that 'For too many people, the idea of running a small hotel has a curious fascination. Hotelkeeping is a serious business in which there is little room for optimistic, inexperienced amateurs. Only by being shrewd and careful can a modest income be earned.'

No matter the size of the accommodation unit, marketing, housekeeping, maintenance, food and beverage, and human resources all need to be professionally planned, managed and controlled, profits maximized and accurate records maintained. What is different in the small operations, is that it is the owner alone who has to cope with these tasks, without a team of subordinates to delegate to. It is the ability to successfully juggle these roles, a strong engaging personality, combined with excellent service, which will influence the success of the operation. The following quotation sums up the complexity of small operations and is very apt relative to the specific nature of the accommodation sector: '... it takes a lot to become an entrepreneur. It demands the dedication to work long hours, and to persuade others to work long hours, at a kaleidoscope of tasks, ranging from immediate response to operational emergency, through to cool appraisal of planning and development for the future' (Milne and Thompson, 1988).

In order to effectively cope with this 'kaleidoscope of tasks', the operator surrounds himself with a team of experts to give the benefit of their specialist knowledge and advice. Managing a small business can be a lonely affair, unlike the large corporate groups there are no superiors, or a head office, to ask for specialist advice. Thus, this team of professionals is a substitute for the more formal support network of a large firm, with the organizational structure being one of 'hub and spoke'. This is illustrated in Figure 6.2.

Within the operation the organizational structure is simple, reflecting more the image of an extended family, rather than any hierarchical configuration. Family members are looked to first as a source of convenient and economic labour. From that core of 'staff', employees will be kept to the minimal required to cope with the differing seasonal demands. Remote, out of town, locations may find it difficult to attract and retain good quality staff and such hotels generally need to provide staff accommodation.

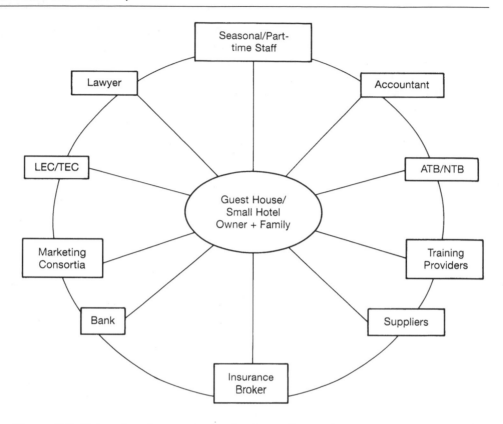

Figure 6.2 *Hub and spoke organization for the small operation*

Training is generally done 'on the job'. However operators are currently being encouraged to increase the training provision for their employees through, for example, the Welcome Host programme. This was designed to improve the standards of service and hospitality provided to tourists and launched in the UK by the Wales Tourist Board in 1992 and Scottish Tourist Board in 1993. In most areas TEC/LECs provided a subsidy to reduce the price payable by participants to encourage the use of Welcome Host training providers.

STANDARD OPERATING PROCEDURES

It would be easy to theorize about the range of standard operating procedures such small operations should have in place, in terms of induction packs, customer care procedures, purchasing specifications, etc. But the reality is that, in the main, no such formalized procedures exist. The owner/manager is so directly involved in the day-to-day operation that he knows intuitively what needs to be done in the best interests of the business. There is no need to document every step, it is implicit, rather than explicit, and for the owner and staff the procedures are just all part of the daily routine to be followed. Thus, while a 600 page standard operating procedure manual is appropriate to the massive McDonalds corporation, it is not as relevant to the smaller operation. However, standard forms are frequently in use for the likes of booking charts, forward booking forms, guest registrations, staff records and general accounting functions. For those establishments which employ a significant number of persons, a standard induction pack may have been developed to cover standard house procedures of customer care, phone answering, taking of reservations, personal presentation, and general conduct.

CURRENT ISSUES AND FUTURE TRENDS

In 1989 it was predicted that the small accommodation operator had a future. In 1994 there was less certainty about this. However, in the early 2000s the increasing need for wide geographic coverage, the relative ease of entry into the sector, coupled with customers who increasingly search out more differentiated products, have ensured their continuity. So long as the small business operator continues to offer a professional, unique, highly personalized, quality product.

For those tough guest houses and small hotels which survived the effects of foot and mouth, now is the time to plan, to stand back from today's pressures and take a strategic view of the future. However, one of the problems that is faced within this sector is the uphill struggle to persuade the owners into the need and value of thinking strategically. This has never been more important as the dominant competition, the corporate groups, have access to all the tactics available to the independent owner, but in addition they have many more opportunities and resources denied the small operator. As such, the smaller operators have little hope of changing the rules of the competitive game.

For the future two strategies have emerged through the chapter, appropriate to the small accommodation sector. At first glance they may seem to be in conflict: product differentiation and cooperative networks. The first urges the operator to be unique, specialized, a loner while the second recommends that he becomes a team player. However, together these two strands of strategy can present a winning combination.

Product differentiation

In current hotel product marketing there is seldom reference to a 'common' hotel product, but more to a specific type of hotel, e.g. fishing, golfing, country house, non-smoking. Thus, for the early 2000s, the guest house or small hotel needs to consider the possibility of transforming an 'all-purpose' operation into a more differentiated product, capitalising on its unique selling points of the personalized environment, cherishing the customer, and customizing the product offering to their individual needs. In doing this the operators are developing niches in which corporate groups have no particular interest or advantage. Thus, the small operator is offering a specialized product, with a distinctive image, serving the needs of a targeted market niche.

Cooperative networks

The trend in the tourist industry as a whole is towards greater integration through cooperative networks which bring together all components of the tourism product, i.e. airlines, car hire, accommodation, credit card companies, special activity programmes. Such cooperative networks enable the packaging and effective distribution of a compound tourism product, of which the guest houses and small hotels are part. As a result, in the early 2000s astute small accommodation management is becoming more that of a 'team sport'. Operators are developing cooperative networks to assist them with: professional advice and support, centralized marketing, access to central reservations systems (CRS) and global markets, financial services, access to public sector funding and information. This can be seen mainly in the form of marketing consortia such as Consort, Best Western, and Pride of Britain. Indeed with respect to CRS involvement Go & Welch (1991) state that: 'From the standpoint of the smaller operator it is hard to see how overall independence of action can be maintained, without becoming less visible to the public and sales agents, consequently losing market share.'

CONCLUSION

It is obvious that guest house and small hotel ownership and operation brings with it tremendous, stimulating 'highs' and just as extreme, depressing 'lows'. It is agreed that it is exciting, challenging, and very hard work with the future not secure and filled with many uncertainties. Survival will depend upon well balanced management expertise, marketing muscle, traditional values of hospitality, value for money, high quality, investment in staff training, and importantly a revival of the 'entrepreneurial spirit'. At a more basic level, successful operation is dependent on steely determination and a toughness which is intolerant of amateurism. Guest houses and small hotels may not be perfect, in every aspect of their operation, however they represent the human fact of hospitality within the UK accommodation sector as a whole. Without them the hospitality industry would be bereaved and much less vibrant.

SUMMARY

This chapter has defined the small hotel and guest house sector of the accommodation industry. Businesses in this sector are very small and operate throughout the UK. They serve a number of different markets, but find it difficult to compete with chain operations in the budget sector. Successful small hotels focus on delivering good service. The newly introduced diamond rating scheme by the English Tourism Council emphasises this characteristic. Their size means that they tend to have a distinctive 'hub and spoke' organization structure, centred around the owner. There is no doubt that the sector faces very great challenges.

FURTHER STUDY

www.britishresorts.co.uk

www.englishtourism.org.uk

www.farm-holidays.co.uk

QUESTIONS

Select two tourist boards in the UK. Compare and contrast the locations, prices, and product/service offer of small hotels and guest houses you are directed to by the Board websites.

CHAPTER 7

Hospital hotel services and residential care

INTRODUCTION

Hospitals and residential care homes provide accommodation for two major groups – the sick and infirm, or people who are unable to look after themselves for a wide range of reasons. One major segment of the population falls into this category, namely the elderly. Those aged over 65 make up 14 per cent of the population but they account for nearly half of health and social services expenditure. Those aged over 75 and especially over 85 use care services even more intensively. Nearly two-thirds of social services gross expenditure on the care of older people is spent on residential and nursing care. Quite simply more people are living longer. In the UK the number of people aged over 85 has nearly doubled since 1981 and will double again by the middle of this century. At the same time, arrangements for their residential care have changed. There has been a 38 per cent fall in the number of NHS beds designated for older people since 1983, whilst the number of nursing and residential beds in the independent sector has risen by 242 per cent (Audit Commission, 2000). In 1994, 18 per cent of older people were hospital in-patients at some time, compared with 13 per cent in 1982. On the other hand the average length of stay in geriatric wards fell by 45 per cent between 1990 and 1995, due to the pressure to release beds and increase throughput in the NHS. Such reduction in the length of stay in hospital allows less scope for recovery and rehabilitation, and places increasing demands on social services. It is quite clear that these services face a major crisis and that providers need to engage in new ways of doing things.

In the UK, most hospitals are managed within the National Health Service, whereas residential care homes are predominantly owned and operated by the private sector, but are heavily regulated by social services. According to the Audit Commission (2000), this growth in the elderly and shift from hospital to residential homes has put pressure on both health and social services. This shift was not well planned and has created major challenges. The NHS has found itself less able to discharge people from acute hospitals and be confident that appropriate community care will follow. Local authority social services departments have found themselves squeezed between demands from the NHS on the one hand and from the independent sector on the other. So health and social services are locked in a vicious circle. They need to agree their respective responsibilities and to set deadlines and improve the arrangements for long-term care assessments.

NATURE AND SCALE OF HOSPITAL AND CARE HOME PROVISION

There are around 500 National Health Service (NHS) Trusts in the UK at present. Most of these control the 1200 NHS hospitals that there are in the UK. The size and nature of hospitals varies from units of around 20 beds up to more than 500 beds. The size and complexity of the hotel services department varies accordingly, smaller hospitals may employ two or three hotel staff, with larger units employing over 100 staff in the Hotel Services department. Very small hospitals are often managed by a nearby larger unit.

Since the early 1980s all hospitals have been obliged to participate in Compulsory Competitive Tendering, which has included putting their 'hotel' services (largely cleaning and maintenance) out to tender. This has encouraged hospital hotel services management to carefully review the work carried out to ensure that it is done as effectively as possible, as well as giving value for money. All hospitals must ask outside companies to submit tenders for the catering, hotel and other services every 3–5 years. Most of the in-house services submit tenders and in a lot of cases the contracts are given to these (called Direct Service or Direct Labour Organizations), but many are also given to contract companies.

In addition to NHS provision, there is also the commercial health sector. People who prefer private medical care pay for the facilities and service similar to those in a three- or four-star hotel. Medical insurance often covers the cost of this. There are an estimated 230 independent (private) hospitals, often run by specialist health care companies. Most NHS hospitals also have a small number of private rooms run along similar lines.

As well as hospitals, there are also a large number of residential and nursing care homes throughout the UK. There are a total of 18,600 homes, owned by 12,000 independent owners offering over 500,000 beds, up from 140,000 in 1992. Such homes concentrate on providing long-term accommodation, with a range of additional services such as meals and minimum nursing support through to 24-hour medical supervision. One study in Yorkshire (Herne, 1994) identified that on average there were typically 14 to 41 residents, of whom 88 per cent were women. Their ages ranged from 65 to 101, with an average age of 86. The average length of stay was 3.5 years.

DEMAND FOR HOSPITAL AND CARE HOME SERVICES

The 'users' of a hospital include the patients, salaried or volunteer staff, and visitors, who may be either visiting patients or visiting staff as part of their jobs, such as delivery people or sales representatives. A typical large general hospital may have 20 wards with around 25 in-patients in each ward, 100+ out-patient visits per day, around 200 medical and paramedical staff, 200 support staff, and 500+ visitors per day.

Most people, at some time in their lives, attend a hospital either as out-patients, day patients or staying in hospital for one or more nights. They may be confined to bed or may be physically fit enough to be up and around. For every patient in hospital there is usually at least one visitor each day. Some of these visitors are able to stay overnight (usually the parents of young patients) and so accommodation is also provided for them. In most hospitals the patients are outnumbered by the medical, paramedical and other staff. Staff within hospitals, often work on a shift basis to give 24-hour cover. Volunteers may provide services such as hospital radio, libraries, etc., as well as reception services. These have to be catered for according to the hospital's customs. The great variety of staff in hospitals and their varying requirements for living and working accommodation means that hotel services must be flexible. Living accommodation is often provided for at least some of the medical and paramedical staff, particularly junior doctors and nurses in nurses' homes and doctors' residences.

Accommodation provision in the care home sector, especially with regards to elderly residents, provides particularly complex challenges. Elderly people may originally enter a home because of one main reason. Either they have social problems resulting from bereavement, loneliness, or lack of family support; or they are mentally or physically frail. As they grow older, additional problems may arise simply as a result of ageing or the degenerative nature of their condition. The most common combination of conditions might be dementia, arthritis, and failing eyesight or hearing or both. As a result of this care home managers face five major challenges in caring for their very vulnerable clients (Herne, 1994). First, the 'elderly' are not one single group but many disparate groups from different generations, ethnic backgrounds, and social origins. Second, there is evidence that elderly people in care homes are afraid to complain for fear of retribution. Third, there is evidence to show that elderly people are resistant to change and like set routines. Fourth, many require special diets as part of the treatment for their medical conditions, such as diabetes, or just for general health reasons, such as overweight. Finally, residents may require help with normal functions such as eating or going to the toilet.

PRODUCTS AND SERVICES

Hotel services within hospitals are the same kind of services that a hotel provides for its guests. These services consist of food and beverage provision, cleaning services, portering, laundry and transport. This chapter will concentrate on accommodation provision, as food and beverage service is discussed in Chapter 16. It will demonstrate the importance of hotel services to the patients, residents and staff of these facilities.

Hotel services are one of the most important services provided in a hospital. The service has three main objectives, the most important being to control the spread of infection through the effective cleaning of all areas within a hospital. Second, the hospital building and its contents must be kept in the optimum condition, and this is accomplished through the careful scheduling of regular cleaning and maintenance using the correct equipment and materials. The third objective of the department is to provide a bright and cheerful atmosphere for staff and patients. This cheerful environment comes not just from the physical surroundings of the hospital, which of necessity are often fairly utilitarian, but also from the attitude and manner of the staff. Hotel staff, like all hospital employees have a role in the care of patients and it is from this role that many staff acquire high levels of job satisfaction. The hotel services staff often feel the same sense of pride as the medical staff when patients go home after successful treatment.

Accommodation for patients in hospitals is usually in wards of between 2 and 30 beds, although in some hospitals single rooms are provided as well as the wards. Day rooms are often provided and in some hospitals a separate dining area is located on the wards. Single rooms are provided with private bathrooms for private patients, usually with a higher standard of furniture and furnishings. Also provided in hospitals are out-patients and day-care facilities, operating theatres, laboratories and consulting rooms; and a variety of areas for physiotherapy and other specialisms. A greater emphasis is being placed on day visits to hospital and shorter stays than in the past, meaning that out-patients areas are expanding and patient bed numbers are reducing. Some hospitals have specialist facilities such as burns units or labour wards, depending on the type of hospital.

The aim of hotel services within a hospital is to provide a specialized cleaning service of the appropriate standard for all these areas within the constraints of the budget. As a general rule an allowance of around 3 hours per bed per week is allocated to cleaning in hospitals. Unlike many other establishments within the hospitality industry, the aesthetic appearance of these areas within a hospital is not of prime importance, although in private rooms or in private hospitals a standard of appearance similar to that in a three- or four-star hotel is normally found. In public sector hospitals, the surfaces, furniture and fittings are purchased with a very strict budget in mind, both for the initial purchase and for their cleaning and maintenance. Surfaces and furniture are expected to be durable, as wear and tear is heavy and replacement may only be possible on a very infrequent basis, hence, for example, metal framed beds and heavy duty vinyl floors are selected for many areas.

Because of the high hygiene requirements of many areas within a hospital, surfaces which are easy to keep to these high standards are usually present. Surfaces are chosen according to the areas for which they will be used, for example smooth floorings may be selected for ward areas, theatres and treatment rooms because they provide limited scope for microbial growth. In contrast in day rooms and offices the comfort of the user may be considered to be more important and floors may be carpeted and walls papered. However, many hospitals, as in the private health care sector, now want to make their patients' stay as pleasant as possible, and more consideration is being given to the choice of surfaces and furniture which create a pleasant environment. Carpet and furniture manufacturers are providing items which are practical from the hospital point of view. These specially designed items are usually stain resistant and easy to keep clean, but also warm, comfortable and attractive. Fire resistance is an important consideration in hospitals so inherently fire resistant wall and floor coverings are normally in place. Textile items such as curtains are purchased with fire resistant finishes which have to last for up to around 60 washes.

HOSPITAL ACCOMMODATION PROVISION

The Audit Commission suggest that a number of key questions have to be resolved in order to get the balance between health and social service care. These questions are:

- Where should the boundaries of responsibility lie between the NHS, social services, housing and other agencies?

- What is the role of the NHS in long-term care?

- Should national standards be set for care and, if so, how should these be implemented, funded and measured?

- What is the correct balance between acute, preventative, and rehabilitative services?

- Should direct payments be extended to older people to strengthen the user's influence? If so, what does this mean for the role of social services?

- Are new arrangements required to develop care management skills further?

Given these challenges and the increasing demands on the health service, the UK government announced a new NHS Plan in 2000, covering all aspects of health provision including hotel services (H M Government, 2000). The NHS Plan has set targets for the introduction of ward housekeepers by 2004, who will be accountable to the nurse in charge of the ward. Ward housekeepers will enhance patient care by helping clinical staff to deliver basic aspects of care. Most importantly, the ward housekeeper will be responsible for supervising the delivery of food and a clean patient environment. There were 72 Acute Trusts in 2002 who were identified as having Ward Housekeepers, or the basis of a Ward House-keeping Service already in place.

The government has also provided £62 million over two years to fund the Clean Hospitals project (NHS Estates, 2001). This project is designed to ensure that all patient areas, visitor toilets, out-patients and accident and emergency units are thoroughly cleaned and kept clean. Chairs, linen, pillows, furniture, floor coverings and blinds which are dirty will be cleaned or replaced. Ward sisters and charge nurses will have the authority to ensure that the wards they lead are properly cleaned. In some cases, NHS trusts will have to adjust contracts with external cleaning companies to ensure nurses can take the lead in ensuring wards are properly cleaned. Every NHS trust has to nominate a Board member to take personal responsibility for monitoring hospital cleanliness, and report to the Board following regular check-ups. The Patients' Forum in each trust will monitor standards and use unannounced inspections to do this. National standards for cleanliness will form part of the NHS Performance Assessment Framework. Every hospital's performance will be measured against these standards by the end of 2000. The independent NHS watchdog, the Commission for Health Improvement, will inspect and report on this aspect of NHS care.

RESIDENTIAL CARE

Because many older people need ongoing care following a spell in hospital, the NHS and social services work together to assess their needs and organize necessary care. However, according to the Audit Commission (2000) some local authorities do not specify when things should be done. In those that do, standards vary, with the time allowed from assessment to putting a care package in place, ranging from 5 days to 26 weeks. Authorities should agree times and these should be as short as possible. The quality of the assessment process also varies. This matters because assessment often determines whether older people are able to go home or require care in a residential setting.

Social services departments are introducing care managers to assess the needs of older people and to arrange packages of care with providers of services within a framework set by the authority centre. Such managers should be supported by reducing restrictions on choice, introducing service level agreements with providers and delegating budgets (backed by financial support and advice). Furthermore service reviews should be a priority to ensure value for money. Social services departments need to develop more sophisticated funding and contracting mechanisms to promote improvements in quality and innovation, and eliminate unhelpful bureaucracy. Finally, they need to improve and extend their monitoring capabilities to reduce the risk to vulnerable older people.

CARE IN THE COMMUNITY

There is an alternative to residential care, often preferred by elderly people. The policy of caring for vulnerable people in the community – as far as possible in their own homes – rather than in large, depersonalized institutions, has developed gradually over the last 30 years. Although social services departments and health authorities are the lead agencies, housing is a key building block in making the policy work. Currently over 1.3 million people in need – those with mental health problems or physical disabilities, frail older people and those with learning disabilities – receive help with their housing, at an annual cost of more than £2 billion. Housing provides a stable base for independent living, together with access to support services and informal care networks. Housing agencies help vulnerable tenants with practical issues such as claiming housing benefit, or resolving disputes with neighbours. Over 25,000 homes each year are adapted to assist those with impaired mobility.

However significant strains are emerging. The stock of social housing has shrunk by over 1 million dwellings since 1981, and many of the high quality homes have been sold, while an increasing number of elderly people seek support to continue living at home. There are 110,000 fewer psychiatric beds than there were 40 years ago; alternative provision is made in specialized housing projects or by supporting people with mental health problems in mainstream accommodation. As health services have refocused on acute care, and social services have targeted their resources on higher-level needs, there is an increasing concentration of people with lesser degrees of vulnerability and dependency in the stock that remains.

The growing pressures on housing authorities, and weaknesses in the way that some are responding, mean that the needs of many vulnerable people are not being met. Some councils lack basic data on individuals' needs, and what is available to meet these needs. For example, there is no register of adapted properties in some areas. Local authorities are constrained by the stock of social housing they have available, and many properties for letting (such as unadapted inner-city tower blocks) are unsuitable for vulnerable people. Frail older people and people with physical disabilities are waiting up to two years for routine adaptations. Not only is the delay distressing to users, but additional costs are incurred through more demands on homecare and the increased risk of institutional solutions.

The difficulty of blending housing and community care objectives is illustrated vividly by the experiences of frail older people and those with mental health problems. There are 530,000 units of specialized housing for community care clients, much of it sheltered housing for the elderly. But many authorities have continued to provide sheltered housing on a traditional basis, without rethinking its role in a changing world. A serious consequence of this inflexibility is the domination of crisis response – hospitalization, homelessness services, high intensity support in specialized schemes – at the expense of effective prevention. If vulnerable people living in mainstream accommodation do not receive basic support – with budgeting, shopping and other everyday skills that most take for granted – they may fall into difficulty and ultimately abandon the tenancy. Failure to invest in early intervention, often because there is no obvious means of funding it, is a false economy. For example, a tenancy crisis followed by hospitalization, followed by resettlement into social housing, costs over £5,000 for people with mental health problems. In effect, many become trapped in a 'revolving door' syndrome.

ORGANIZATION AND STAFFING

Staffing accounts for around 90 per cent of the total cost of the hotel service in hospitals. The staff are employed either by a contract cleaning company such as Mediclean or by an in-house service department. Both of these operate on a contract basis to provide the cleaning service. The organization and reporting system of hotel services varies slightly depending whether the service is contracted out or not. This is illustrated in Figures 7.1 and 7.2.

The Cleaning Services Manager (or Assistant Hotel Services Manager) is responsible to the Hotel Services Manager for the management of all aspects of the service. Usually they will have a number of years experience, often having previously held a post as Assistant Hotel Services Manager and will usually hold a management qualification in the field of Hospitality Management. In private hospitals this post is usually called Housekeeper, although as they are normally fairly small units the job is often combined with that of the supervisor. The Cleaning Services Manager in hospitals is responsible for controlling the budget given to the department and must allocate money to cover the costs of all the staff, equipment and materials used to clean the hospital. The Cleaning Services Manager is also responsible for the recruitment of all the staff within the department; this may be delegated to the Assistant Services Manager. The Manager

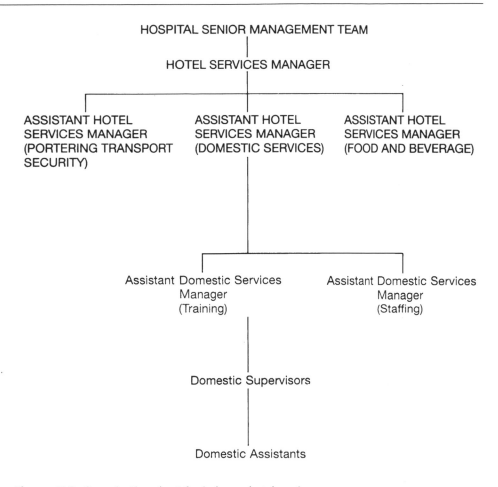

Figure 7.1 *Organization chart for in-house hotel services*

is responsible for the organization of training of staff. The operative staff (ward maids, hotels, etc.) are usually trained by the supervisors, however induction and issues such as health and safety or fire prevention are often organized and carried out by the Manager or Assistant. The Manager is responsible for maintaining the quality of the cleaning service and has to ensure that the standards agreed for each are adhered to. This involves installing quality control mechanisms and in-depth liaison with the Infection Control Committee and the senior hospital management. In hospitals where a contract cleaning company is used, the Manager is responsible for liaison with the cleaning company and for ensuring that standards are maintained by them.

In larger hospitals, usually one or more Assistant Services Managers are employed. They are often people with a hospitality management qualification and one or two years management experience. The Assistant carries out the more routine tasks delegated by the Cleaning Services Manager, such as recruitment, induction and training of operative staff, the distribution of cleaning supplies and ensuring quality control procedures are carried out effectively. Often Assistant Domestic Services Managers are given a specialized function within the department such as training or quality control.

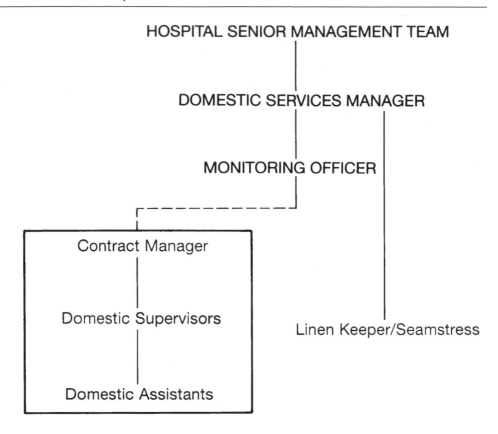

Figure 7.2 *Organization chart for contracted hotel services*

Where a contract cleaning company is employed, their work is monitored by Monitoring Officers who are responsible for ensuring the standards of cleaning are maintained throughout the hospital. This is done by spot checking a number of areas each day and reporting back if standards fall below a pre-agreed acceptable level.

Supervisors are responsible for ensuring that the required standards of cleaning are met, through the day-to-day management of staff in their specific area of the hospital. Usually the supervisor is responsible for a team of cleaners or for a specific area within the hospital, whether it be either a ward or a department. Supervisors are responsible for the cleaning of the area, and, in wards, often for the service of meals and drinks. They are generally responsible for ensuring that the staff work the correct hours according to their contracts and are punctual and efficient. They are responsible too for their appearance, attitude and hygiene. Training of new staff and re-training of existing staff is an important aspect of their jobs. They are responsible for ensuring that the correct cleaning and food supplies are available in their work area, as well as liaising with the nursing staff to ensure that the cleaning is carried out with the least disruption of other services. The supervisor is also concerned with the control, distribution and cleanliness of equipment and materials used in the area. Supervisors in some hospitals will be responsible for the distribution of the correct quantity of linen to the wards. Most supervisors undertake some cleaning duties along with the hotels. They may also undertake some tasks which are traditionally nursing duties, such as make beds and provide hot drinks. The department for which the supervisor carries out these duties has to transfer money to pay for these services to the Hotel Services Budget. The supervisors are responsible for reporting complaints, criticisms and compliments to the Hotel Services Manager so that appropriate action may be taken.

Cleaners are mostly part-time, and carry out cleaning duties according to the needs of the department. Cleaning methods are tightly prescribed in hospitals and the hotels will receive at least two or three days training when they commence employment. Most work is carried out during the day, particularly in the morning. In areas which are used only during the day, e.g. out-patients wards, operating theatres, etc., cleaning is carried out at night when they are empty. Normally two or more hotels work together in quiet areas especially at night. As many areas in a hospital are busy 24 hours a day the hotels must work around the other users of the area. In particular they must try not interrupt the work of doctors and other medical staff and try to fit in with the routine of the other hospital staff in the area. The hotel is sometimes the only link a patient has with normal daily life and patients may confide their fears and sometimes their symptoms to that person rather than to the nurses or doctors. It is up to the hotel to pass on the information if it appears to be important. In many hospitals the hotel staff are responsible for the service of food and drinks to the patients, although in some hospitals this task has been assumed by the nursing staff so that they have more social contact with the patients. The hotel staff are often also responsible for washing up after each patient's meal. Many hospitals have a linen room and employ linen assistants and sometimes seamstresses. They are responsible for receipt, checking, repair, marking, storing and distribution of clean linen. Seamstresses will make items such as curtains, although in many hospitals all items are bought in ready made. They are also responsible for the provision of certain of the staff uniforms as well as any mending.

Supervisors, and hotel and linen room staff may be employed by a contract company rather than by the hospital. A contract manager is usually employed by the contract company to ensure that the work is being carried out effectively and to the correct standard.

HOTEL SERVICES OPERATION

Because there are very tight financial and quality controls in place in hospitals, the organization and planning of the cleaning service is carried out with a great deal of attention to detail. In order that this planning can be carried out satisfactorily, the Hotel Services Manager will draw up a very detailed description of all the areas which have to be cleaned along with a detailed list of their contents. This is normally done by walking around the building in a logical way, listing each area and its contents on a pro-forma, which is often a plan of the building. The information collected in this way is up-dated regularly. Times for the cleaning of each item in each area are usually available and these are allocated to each of the areas. When the times are totalled, a cleaning time for each area is available. This is illustrated in Figure 7.3

In order to decide what the staffing requirement is for the areas, extra time is

Patient Care Duties
Ward Standard Hours Summary

Date – 15.05.94

Hospital No 1	Hospital Name: St Mary's	
Ward No 6	Ward Name: Top Floor	Number of Occupied Beds – 14
Task Type: Weekly		

Code	Task Description	Unit of Measure	No of units	Weekly Freq.	Secs/ Occ.	Total Secs	Total Hrs
100	Dust bed	bed	22	1	66.48	66.48	1.11
106	Dust bed curtain rail	bed	22	1	3.97	3.97	0.07
108	Change locker bag	bed	14	14	3.00	41.99	0.70
109	Move ward bed	bed	14	1	10.17	10.17	0.17

Figure 7.3 *Extract from ward cleaning hours summary*

then added to this to allow time for staff to have breaks or to rest. From this the number of staff needed to clean an area can be calculated, depending on the hours they are expected to work. Most of the hotel staff in hospitals are part-time workers, working varying lengths of shifts, depending on the areas in which they work and the hours of cover needed. Staffing can be worked out on a day-to-day basis depending on the work that has to be done, related to factors such as the number of patients in a ward and any changes in occupancy. Longer term staffing decisions can also be made based on the figures achieved in this way, such as Christmas and Easter holiday cover.

When the number of staff has been calculated, the number of supervisors can be assessed depending on the areas to be covered, the number of staff and the hours of coverage needed. Usually one ward or number of areas close together will need one supervisor who works full-time, but this will relate to the shape and size of the buildings. Staff rotas (telling staff the hours they are expected to work) and timetables (telling staff what they have to do during the hours they are at work) can be worked out from this information. These procedures can ensure that a cleaning service is provided at the minimum cost to the hospital.

In many hospitals the linen is dealt with by the nursing staff and in others by the hotel staff. Various systems are used for the collection and distribution at ward level. Linen is divided into three categories before being sent to the laundry. Soiled linen is not infectious and is bagged and sent to the laundry according to hospital practice. Linen which has been in contact with blood, faeces, vomit or urine is called fouled linen. It is bagged separately, usually into a plastic bag, and the top tied securely. Special category linen has been in contact with any of a number of serious infectious diseases such as hepatitis or typhoid. This is bagged and the top tied with water soluble alginate thread. The bags are placed directly into the washing machine to reduce human contact with the infected linen. Hotel staff are often responsible for stocking the ward linen cupboard regularly.

As hospitals have to work to certain guidelines and standards in order to prevent the spread of infection, any decisions about cleaning must relate to the standards of hygiene required for the area. Three standards are commonly adhered to in hospitals. A reasonable, non-clinical standard of appearance and cleanliness is provided in areas such as waiting rooms, day care facilities and offices. In areas such as wards, treatment rooms, etc., a clinical standard must be maintained meaning that all surfaces must be kept clean and free from infection. High risk areas such as operating theatres and isolation units are areas which must be kept to a very high standard of cleanliness in order to prevent the risk of infection. Staff are usually required to wear special protective clothing including hair and shoe coverings in these areas.

Hygiene standards are monitored in most hospitals by the Infection Control Committee, who take samples from surfaces in different areas on a regular basis to check that microbial growth is within safe limits for the area. The results of these tests are reported to the hotel services team and they are obliged to act on them. The Environmental Health Officer visits once every 6 months to ensure that hygiene policies are adhered to.

In order to maintain the very strict standards of hygiene, hospitals have very tight quality control measures. The supervisor, Assistant Hotel Services Manager or the Monitoring Officer check the work of the hotel staff regularly. Checking is done with the help of checklists, or in many hospitals with a computerized monitoring system similar to the hand-held computerized stock control equipment used in supermarkets. All areas are checked frequently, but no routine of checking is established. Each area is divided in a number of sections, each section is checked and failures to achieve the required standard are noted. A failure rate of more than 5 per cent is considered unsatisfactory and action is taken either with the hotel staff and supervisors or with the contract company.

In order to implement the high standards of work required, all staff in the department are given fairly extensive training. Cleaners are usually given around three days training by their supervisors in the day-to-day work required of them, whereas training in such issues as health and safety, and fire procedures is carried out by the Hotel Services Manager or the assistant. Training of the supervisors and managers is usually a combination of on- and off-the-job training carried out over the first few weeks or months of employment.

Because of the rigid quality control mechanisms in place in hospitals, the types of cleaning equipment and materials to be used have to be carefully selected, although similar selection procedures to hotels are usually followed. The variety of items is minimized so that staff are less likely to be confused about what equipment and materials to use in a specific area. However, in order to control the spread of infection, colour-coded cloths and other items are used. For example all items used in ward areas may be green, whereas items to be used in toilet areas may be red. Generally, in most areas neutral synthetic detergents are used. In baths, showers and toilets, sanitizers are used. Traditionally in hospitals, disinfectant and bleach were used a great deal, however today their use is minimal except in areas where there is a serious risk of infection. Vacuum cleaners used in hospitals are usually purchased with very high levels of filtration, usually around 99 per cent to minimize the possibility of microbial spread. Usually floor maintenance machines (polishers) have vacuum skirts to avoid the spread of dust when they are used for polishing or buffing.

Many hospitals now have procedures for dealing with complaints and compliments made by the hospital patients. This means that staff are encouraged to maintain high standards of work as well as customer care skills.

113

CURRENT ISSUES AND FUTURE TRENDS

This is an area which is undergoing a great deal of change and will continue to do so. The use of contract cleaning companies will become more common as it means that the responsibility for cleaning can be lifted from the hospital management to experts in the field with minimal oversight by the hospital staff.

Hotel staff are taking over more of the non nursing duties, such as bed making and service of meals from nursing staff on the wards to allow them more time to use their nursing skills. The hotel services department charges the other departments for the use of their staff. Allied to this, awareness that cleaning is a skilled job – very different from household cleaning in the home – is growing, consequently the standards of training and supervision are becoming higher and more respect is given to jobs within the Hotel Services Department. In order to give more credence to the training given to hospital hotel staff, awards such as Investors in People are being sought by many hospitals. Also many staff in this area are being encouraged to achieve National Vocational Qualifications.

There is at present a policy within the health care sector to provide a more acceptable and positive experience for people attending hospitals. Complaints mechanisms have been set up in many hospitals and they are gradually adopting more of the service skills used in the hotel industry, so more customer care training will be needed by hotel staff. Standards of facilities are improving and are gradually becoming similar to those provided in hotels. Also more attention will be paid to the selection of surfaces, furniture and fittings so that they are easily and cheaply cleaned, as well as looking good. This will affect the methods and frequencies of cleaning used by the hotel staff. Improved quality standards are being reflected in the fact that some Hospital Hotel Services are acquiring BS 5750, the British Standard for Quality Systems.

Hotel Services Departments within hospitals will be expected to be more financially accountable than ever before, as budgets allocated will be tighter and any other department in the hospital will be expected to pay for the hotel services used.

Hospitals have been aware for many years of the psychological effects on patients of their stay in hospital, particularly if it is a long stay. Patients often feel worthless and that they are missing their normal daily life. The Hotel Services Department has to have a greater part to play in making the patients feel welcome and valued. Patients who are physically not too unwell in some hospitals help out with some of the cleaning duties for the staff, which gives them an occupation instead of long hours of sitting in bed.

SUMMARY

In some respects this sector of the accommodation industry has experienced the greatest change during the 1990s. The shift in provision from hospitals to residential care and nursing homes has been significant. The high profile that both health and social services have, both in terms of the media, the government and general public, often suggests a permanent state of crisis. Certainly this is a very large sector of the UK industry with very specific services that are needed by its users. New initiatives in the public sector are likely to continue the great rate of change managers have experienced in the last decade.

FURTHER STUDY

www.nhsestates.gov.uk

www.hospitalcaterers.org

QUESTIONS

In what way is the provision of long-term residential services different to the provision of accommodation to short stay hotel guests?

CHAPTER 8

Hostels and halls of residence

INTRODUCTION

Hostels are houses or halls of residence for groups who have specific needs, typically students, young workers, tourists and organized parties. The majority of hostels came into existence in response to a demand for safe, affordable, long-term accommodation. Education establishments, universities, public schools and private colleges, have had a long history of associated accommodation provision and many children of the middle and upper classes were 'sent away' to be educated. Then in the late 1800s, large numbers of young people moved away from their homes for the first time to find work. They too required secure and respectable accommodation that ideally gave them access to social and leisure activities with people of their own age and interests. Hence the development of YMCAs and YWCAs (Young Men's/Women's Christian Associations).

One exception to the traditional demand for long stay hostel accommodation is the Youth Hostel movement. It became a fashion, between the First and Second World Wars, that young workers and student groups left the towns to walk and cycle around the countryside. There was in fact very little alternative, apart from the traditional British seaside resort holiday, as this period pre-dated the charter flights to Spain and other popular destinations. Before 1950 foreign travel was considered unusual and not for the masses. Youth Hostels were common in Germany in the early 1900s and provided inexpensive overnight lodging for one or two nights. The idea spread rapidly throughout the rest of Europe and in 1932 the International Federation of Youth Hostels was formed. In 1980 the International Federation of Youth hotels had 50 national members.

To some, the term hostel has become synonymous with poor quality, short-term accommodation. It is thought of as provided by charities, such as the Salvation Army, for the very poor or homeless in society. In this context it is used as a derogatory term signifying the occupants' failure to take care of themselves and implying a residence giving the very minimum of comfort and security for little or no monetary return. For these reasons this type of hostel is not considered part of the commercial letting industry. Although this type of accommodation plays an important role in society, it is still just one very small element of the total hostel provision. As we shall see in this chapter, much hostel accommodation is of a very high standard indeed.

DEMAND FOR HOSTEL ACCOMMODATION

The management of accommodation and the experience of the hostel product certainly differs according to the needs of the user groups. The majority of commercially let hostel accommodation is provided for the younger members of society. College halls of residence, youth hostels, the YMCA, YWCA, school study centres and the like all exist predominantly to serve the needs of youth. Security, affordability, a functional living environment and easy access to leisure activities are equally important to each user group.

Young workers

CACI Acorn profile projections show that there are many more young workers in society than ever before, and that the young working society in general is much more mobile and willing to move away from home to take up a job. Young people between the ages of 15 and 29 years are estimated to make up 25 per cent of the total population of the UK and most seek work in their late teens or early twenties. With such a mobile population, it is reasonable to assume that not all young workers will be able to find permanent suitable accommodation immediately, and not everybody likes the privacy or isolation given by privately rented housing. Therefore for young workers in their first or second jobs, hostels can provide a residential place, either as a long-term home base, until the occupant moves on, or as a short-term solution, until more suitable alternatives can be found.

Students

It is in the interest of Universities and Colleges to provide hostels or residences, as it keeps the students close to the lecture rooms and libraries and involves them in college activities. This is especially true of institutions built on 'greenfield sites' away from existing population centres, such as Keele and Warwick. Some universities can only guarantee a student place in a hostel, for the first year of study. Student populations engaged in the higher education sector have been seen to increase consistently over the last 20 years and most universities and colleges have been unable to keep pace with the demand for rooms.

When choosing a place at university, students express a preference for those educational establishments that can offer a place in halls of residence. Usually it is the student's first time away from home and a room in college implies that they do not have to worry about maintaining their accommodation, or preparing their own food, or remembering to pay the household bills.

Tourists

In Europe as a whole, 2 per cent of all holidays taken by young adults are spent in youth hostel accommodation. The tradition of youth hostelling is not quite so established in the UK but there are 230 YHA hostels in England and Wales and 300,000 active members. The YHA is a registered charity and membership is essential for anyone wishing to stay in one of its hostels. The YHA is by far the biggest provider of this type of accommodation and the only obvious competition is the small guest house sector of the industry. However many of the hostels are located away from centres of population and form the backbone of walking and trekking holidays in remote locations.

Figure 8.1 *Typical youth hostel*
Source: A. Carpenter

Conferencing and activity breaks

Higher education institutions in the UK are largely state funded through the Funding Councils. However, universities, as autonomous self-governing bodies, will seek to increase their total income as this will enable them to provide improved facilities. Since halls of residencies or student hostels are used for an average academic year of 36 weeks duration in each year, the time they are left empty represents an under utilized asset that can be used for conferences and a variety of other letting purposes and therefore commercial activities.

Venue Masters (formerly the British Universities' Conference & Exhibition Venues Organization) represents more than 90 universities and colleges, all of whom offer a wide range of accommodation to conference organizers, part-time students, holiday makers on activity breaks and individuals looking for budget accommodation. There is no doubt that this type of venue has advantages for a wide range of potential user groups. Facilities usually include a considerable amount of purpose-built accommodation in an academic environment. The average number of standard bedrooms in a university is 1000 and just over 500 en suite bedrooms. However this varies quite widely. The University of Bradford has 100 standard and 60 en suite rooms, whilst Cardiff has 1800 standard and 3000 en suite (www.venuemasters.com). In 2002, day delegate rates ranged from £15 to £30, whilst 24-hour delegate rates were from £35 to £85. The range of associated facilities is impressive and can include lecture rooms, language laboratories, computer workshops, television and film studios, exhibition areas, sports and recreation facilities and libraries.

Occupancy patterns tend to be short term, the letting periods are limited by the needs of the full-time student body who come and reclaim their rooms as each new term begins. However, in most cases, conference and activity break organizers need only a few days or at most a couple of weeks to complete their programme of events. The unpretentious nature of the study bedrooms and the functional nature of the catering facilities is offset by the vast scale and capacity of the venues. University bursars and caterers are used to dealing with large numbers of young adults throughout the year, and residential events of a thousand delegates in the middle of the summer vacation does not confront them with problems they have not met before.

Organized school activity workshops

Organizers of schools' parties use hostels to provide budget accommodation in support of school activities. Residential visits to youth hostels, activity centres, nature study centres support the work of pupils studying elements of the national curriculum. Complete hostels can be booked to ensure school parties do not disturb other residents and centres will plan the itinerary of the visit to ensure maximum benefit is gained.

THE HOSTEL PRODUCT

Hostels are clearly not hotels. They do not provide the same level or range of service and they do not consider the people who use them as guests. Nor is hostel accommodation a by-product of another overriding activity. Hostels therefore cannot be compared or considered in the same way as accommodation provided by the hospital service or the prison service. The motivation to use hostel accommodation is created by the user for either short-term or longer-term living space and to give the user access to leisure or work. The level of intervention by hostel management, in the living activities of the residents, is much less than most serviced accommodation, as hostels become the home of the user, if only for a very short time. The management of hostels is, therefore, less intrusive and less sophisticated than in a hotel or guest house, in some cases the relationship becomes more related to that of landlord and tenant than of hotelier and guest. It is therefore not unreasonable to expect people who use hostels to provide much more in the way of goods needed for day-to-day living.

The range of facilities provided by hostels and the associated intensity of service is reflected in the prices charged, but the significant advantage of hostel accommodation over the commercial alternatives is that they all provide the resident with an increased level of security and to some extent safety through supervision.

A typical study bedroom in a university hall of residence has to fulfil two basic needs of the student, first to act as a home bedroom where the student lives, and second as a place where they can work at their studies. It is equipped with a single bed, wardrobe, wash handbasin, bookcase, coffee table, desk and desk chair and an easy chair; soft furnishings are kept to a minimum in order to reduce maintenance. Bathrooms, shower rooms, and toilets are usually shared, but some of the newer halls have ensuite facilities. If a hall of residence does not include its own dining facilities, it is likely that self-catering kitchens will be provided between several rooms and most rooms have access to small food preparation areas to make hot drinks and re-heat pre-prepared food items.

Figure 8.2 *Typical hostel bedroom*
Source: University of St Andrews

YHA hostels, on the other hand, are constantly upgrading their facilities, but most bedrooms are still dormitory style, sleeping from 4 to 12 people. It is, however, increasingly common to find hostels that have twin rooms on offer and smaller dormitories that can be used as family rooms. In keeping with the youth hostelling culture, bedding is restricted to a laundered linen sleeping bag although pillows and duvets are provided. Youth Hostels provide evening meals and breakfast in communal dining rooms and the food is usually pre-plated for convenience of service, hostel residents are asked to help clean up afterwards, again in keeping with the hostelling culture. The time of access to hostels is somewhat restricted, visitors are not allowed into YHA hostels after 10.30p.m. at night and lights are turned off in the dormitories at 11.30p.m. Residents are not encouraged to get up too early in the mornings either, most hostels are 'closed', until 7.00a.m.

It used to be that entry to a YHA could only be gained by the young traveller if they had made their journey under their own efforts, walking, cycling or by canoe. These days many hostels have car parks and do not mind if residents have used the bus to get there.

The YMCA movement came into being in 1844. It was the inspiration of George Williams, a devout Christian who felt that there was a need for secure hostels for young working men. From its earliest beginnings, religious belief has not been a barrier to entry into a YMCA hostel and hostel managers admit both young men and young women. Single rooms are available on either a bed and breakfast basis or as self-catering bed sitting rooms. Most residents stay for extended periods of up to two years or more, most residential hostels have extensive leisure and sporting facilities and some have limited restaurant facilities.

Founded in 1855, the Prayer Union and the General Female Training Institute, came together as the YWCA to develop residential accommodation and a forum for common interest and debate. It operates 60 hostels in England and Wales, many of which have long waiting lists. It has no connection with the YMCA movement and is centrally managed from its head office in Oxford. It offers hostel accommodation aimed at young people between the ages of sixteen and twenty-five. The YWCA does not insist that residents are Christian or female although the organization still has a strong religious foundation.

MARKETING

The demand for hostel accommodation is dependent upon the extent of the booking period, the pricing strategies and the membership practices adopted by the hostel management. Little external marketing is carried out by hostel operators where residents stay for long periods of time and particularly where prices are consistent with, or marginally below, the value of commercial letting policy.

Long-term residential lets

Halls of residence in the university sector and young workers' hostel places are always in demand and waiting lists are not uncommon. In these environments, internal marketing is carried out to maintain an atmosphere of understanding between residents and the hostel management. It would be easy to assume that because the hostel residents regard the rooms as their temporary homes that they, as a client group, become a captive audience. Common marketing strategies include direct mail to residents' rooms, keeping residents informed of changes in routine, improvements to the administration of their accommodation, and activities in which they can join. Notice boards and posters involve residents in the activities of the hostels and at the very least keep them informed of what's going on. By far the most effective marketing is carried out by personal contact and word-of-mouth, in common with most closed communities, students' opinions are formed by the people they talk to and hall wardens are a major source of information.

121

Short-term residential hostels

Where hostels rely exclusively on short-stay residents, such as in a youth hostel, it makes sense to encourage users to join the hostel's membership. This identifies people who have used the hostels in the past and hopefully will use them again in the future. The membership fee fulfils two roles for an organization. First it helps to maintain cash flows throughout the year regardless of the occupancy levels of the hostels. Second it provides the organization with a database of names and addresses to which it can directly market itself, knowing that these are the people who know and like the organization and can be encouraged to re-buy. Membership magazines, accommodation guides, newsletters, promotional offers all are typically used as ways of affecting buyer behaviour and encouraging repeat business.

OPERATION OF HOSTEL ACCOMMODATION

Just as the marketing of a hostel varies according to whether it has long-stay lets, as in the case of a student hall of residence, or short-stay lets, as in a youth hostel, so also does the operation of these facilities.

Halls of residence

A typical university may have between five and twenty halls of residence accommodating between 200 to 2000 students. If the university is one of the newer 'red-brick' universities, built during the 1960s and 1970s, the halls of residence are likely to be located on campus, whereas older universities may have halls spread through the local area. They typically consist of mainly single study bedrooms and usually are big enough to justify their own catering facilities. Perhaps 20 per cent of all such accommodation will be self catering. In addition, some halls of residence may have twin bedded accommodation. This style of room is only let in term time on a single sex occupancy basis and they are not popular with the majority of students who value periods of privacy and quiet study time.

The Accommodation Services Department would coordinate various student contracts in the halls, as well room renting and leasing schemes in the private sector, which supplement the total stock of rooms available to students. Rooms are allocated to incoming students at the beginning of each year. New students are asked to complete letting contracts, which specify the payment of fees and the rules of the college in terms of both their behaviour and their understanding of their responsibilities as residents. Students entering college for the first time, students from outside the immediate locality of the college, and overseas students are usually given priority. Allocation is based, where possible, on the students' personal needs. For instance, smaller halls may be set aside for occupancy by mature students, or even students with young children, so that additional facilities such as a crèche and a self-service laundry may also be provided.

The Head of Accommodation Services would typically report directly to the college principal for all issues that may arise from the management of the halls. Each of the halls is likely to have a Warden who is given some responsibility for general student conduct, and to act as the first point of contact in a crisis or emergency. They are usually drawn from among the university's staff or student body and live in an apartment or room in the hall for which they are responsible. If the Warden is a student, they are usually either final-year students, or post-graduates. They are given some compensation in rent as payment for their services.

Within the Accommodation Services team, support will be provided to the wardens both in terms of dealing with the residents and dealing with the hall of residence. Should a warden have a problem with a resident, a 'Student Services Manager' is usually available to provide advice. Ultimately, if problems continue, the conditions outlined in the student contract will be enforced and students be asked to leave the halls if their behaviour warrants it. Likewise, if an emergency occurs at any time of the day, the Estates Manager is likely to have a service engineer available to deal with the problem. In addition there will be available emergency contractors from the gas, electricity and water utilities.

As well as Student Services, Estates Managers, and Wardens, the accommodation service is also likely to include Cleaning Services Managers with responsibility for day-to-day cleaning and maintenance of the halls. Supervisors may work throughout the day and can help the cleaning services manager with planned maintenance, the planning of redecoration and replacement of furnishings such as carpets and curtains. They also ensure that the halls have adequate supplies of cleaning materials and that cleaning equipment is regularly serviced and in good working order. Typically, cleaning staff work for a limited period of the day, with most cleaners being employed for three hours each morning. Students are expected to make their own beds and provide their own bed linen and towels, they are asked to keep their rooms generally tidy. Cleaners will only ensure the cleaning of floors, flat surfaces, sinks and bathroom equipment. Student rooms are cleaned once every two weeks, although most rooms are inspected every two days for student safety. Daily cleaning is provided for all shared areas such as bathrooms, toilets, kitchens and corridors. Jobs are assigned to cleaners who individually will be responsible for a block of rooms and its service areas, supervisors inspect the work to ensure that the tasks have been carried out correctly. Cleaning Service Managers may, on occasions, organize a group of staff to carry out jobs that require a team effort such as carpet shampooing, window cleaning or intensive cleaning of the lobby or public area.

The Accommodation Services Manager is likely to coordinate the department through regular contact with staff. These meetings serve a particular purpose at the end of each academic term as it allows for the halls to be organized for the residential conferences booked by the conference office, or equivalent. This office has the responsibility of maximizing the use of the vacated halls of residence and academic facilities. Costs associated with the University's physical assets, its campus and buildings, still continue to be accumulated regardless of occupancy levels in the halls. Any income and profit that can be earned during the holiday periods helps to offset these costs and provide money for further investment.

Universities promote themselves as an exhibition and conference venue in various ways, such as tourist information literature, direct mail to prospective clients, and through advertising material produced by a consortium of universities. Typically bookings are taken centrally by the conference office staff and this is communicated to the Accommodation Services Manager in the form of a request for accommodation. Similar requests are sent to the college caterers and campus managers who control access to the lecture rooms and sports facilities. In essence, the facilities of the college, including all the hostel accommodation, become available for the use of the conference office.

The role of the Cleaning Services Department changes with the type of room occupant. When rooms in the halls are let to conference delegates, they have to be fully serviced daily, beds are changed daily, with linen provided by the Cleaning Services Department, along with towels, soap and other accessories. This increased level of service inevitably means a change in staff working patterns and longer working hours, the housekeeping role becomes much closer to that expected by a hotel guest, as the intensity of the service is increased. Nonetheless, colleges and universities, with thousands of student rooms, still have remarkably few staff in relation to the numbers of room occupants.

Hostels

The informal culture of the hostel movement is reflected in the informality of its organization. The YHA, YMCA and other similar types of hostel operator rely on small teams of people who maintain the standards of the organization according to their rules and operating methods. Organization charts appear very flat in this style of hostel, with one or two people being responsible for the practical operation and management, and a mixture of full-time, part-time, casual, or, in some cases, volunteer staff providing the labour force. In a bigger hostel the scale of the operation demands a more formalized structure as the management task increases.

CURRENT ISSUES AND FUTURE TRENDS

Hostel accommodation provision forms only a small part of the accommodation industry. Its origins are rooted in responses to very precise needs. It is worth noting that organizations with clearly targeted user groups, or market segments, are successful in attracting high occupancy levels. The demand for hostel accommodation is not diminishing and most organizations are opening new hostels or refurbishing old ones as funds allow. However, recently the YHA has faced severe financial crisis due to the foot and mouth disease. To the end of October 2001 the 228 hostels in England and the UK lost £5 million of its annual £30 million. However, it is believed that the demand will increase again. Hostels are frequently very busy and have found a new market segment in school groups, who occupy hostel accommodation outside the traditional holiday periods. YHA hostels are moving closer towards the standards of facilities and service expected by holiday makers who traditionally would have used guest houses or small hotels.

With regard to universities and colleges, it is difficult to envisage a time when all students will be guaranteed a place in halls of residence. Whether or not student attendance at university declines, student accommodation is a key factor in attracting students to any one particular institution. The student hostel is part of the total package offered by educational establishments and can directly contribute to the students' ability to study. The competitive nature of this sector will encourage re-development and new-build projects which will provide flexible accommodation for alternative uses outside the traditional term times.

SUMMARY

This chapter has identified that the provision of hostel accommodation is on a very large scale indeed, serving a diverse range of different markets such as tourists, students, school parties and conference delegates. Much of the accommodation is found to be operated by universities, who use their halls of residence, not only for long-term lets to their students, but also exploit them for conferences, activity breaks, and other short-term lets. Whereas in the past youth hostels provided very basic self-catering accommodation, often shared with others, the modern hall of residence is typically a single en suite room.

FURTHER STUDY

www.venuemasters.co.uk

www.yha.org.uk

www.ymca-wales.org

QUESTIONS

Select a hostel from the YHA website and a university website. Compare and contrast the product/service offer of these two providers of hostel accommodation.

PART 2

THE FOOD SERVICE INDUSTRY

CHAPTER 9

The foodservice sector

INTRODUCTION

The author and broadcaster Derek Cooper wrote in 1964:

> I have the utmost sympathy for caterers who are trying hard to do a self-respecting job in the face of almost universal indifference ... There is, alas, no reason for optimism on the eating front. For the minority prepared to pay for the privilege, there will always be a small number of good restaurants. The majority of us will continue to put up uncomplainingly, perhaps even with a sort of masochistic pleasure, with this kind of bad food and bad service.

Thus Cooper put the blame, if blame there need be, for poor standards of catering in Britain fairly and squarely on the consumer. He argued that if the consumer refused to accept food and service that was inadequate, then the caterer would have to improve those standards or go out of business. But he wrote that in the 1960s. Do the British public still have such low expectations? How has the industry responded to consumer needs?

This chapter examines the nature of foodservice provision from a consumer perspective. It discusses the foodservice consumer and the reasons they may have for eating out. It describes and analyses what has been called the 'meal experience'. It then goes on to give an overview of the size and scale of this sector in the UK, before looking in more detail at the operating systems used in the industry. All the major systems and technologies are explained, including both back-of-house systems such as call order and cook–chill and front-of-house service systems, such as table service and self-service. It concludes that the industry in the 2000s is very different from that of the 1960s, not least because the British customer has at last stopped being indifferent to poor food and lousy service.

WHO EATS OUT AND WHY?

Obviously there are many different types of customer – male and female, young and old, single people and families, rich and poor. It is essential that foodservice operators are aware which of these customers their operation will attract. It may attract all of them, although this is unlikely. Most people have preconceived ideas about the suitability of certain foodservice establishments for certain types of customers. For the purpose of economic analysis and research, the population in Britain has been broken down into 'socio-economic groups'. Basically this is the subdivision of the population into groups with broadly similar incomes, occupations, education levels and resources. This has been used as one way of identifying distinct market segments. More recently, this kind of demographic segmentation has been replaced by a more sophisticated analysis based around so-called 'life-style groups' based on psychographics.

The implications of such segments are many since research has shown that 'expectations, values, usage and attitudes are likely to vary between groups. Members of different groups are likely to give different priorities to certain needs, and the upper socio-economic groupings are likely to be able to satisfy certain needs more easily than others' (Cannon, 1980). Thus to answer the question, 'What factors contribute to the customer's enjoyment of a meal?' is by no means easy. For each type of customer, with each type of need to be satisfied, there is an operation that will be satisfactory. All we can do is look at those factors that contribute to the meal experience in some way or another and draw some general conclusions about how they affect the customer.

Probably everybody in the UK has 'eaten out' at some time in their life. As we have seen in Chapter 1, there are many different sectors of that industry, each catering for very different consumer needs. Essentially, however, there are some sectors of the industry that cater for people who have no choice but to eat there – hospitals, institutions, prisons, and so on – that have a captive market; and those restaurants, cafés and cafeterias where the consumer chooses to eat. In some cases, this choice is very restricted, on a train for instance, or in a staff dining-room, but in most cases, the choice is vast. If people decide to eat out, then it follows that they have decided on this course of action in preference to some other. In this respect, the foodservice operator is competing with alternative experiences that might attract consumers' hard-earned disposable income, and these may be far removed from any gastronomic delights. The consumer may choose to go to the theatre, to play squash, to visit the races, and so on. So let us look a little more closely at why a person chooses to eat out instead of some other pleasurable activity.

Graham Campbell-Smith (1967) lists a total of 43 different reasons why people may choose to eat out. It is really no surprise then that there is such a rich diversity of eating-out establishments available to the public. However, six basic reasons have been identified (Jones, 1988) as to why people eat away from home:

- *Convenience* This factor includes all those people who are away from home for some reason – shoppers, commercial travellers, commuters – who are physically unable to return home at normal meal times. It would also include people who do not have the time to eat at home and eat out in conjunction with some other leisure activity.

- *Variety* Just as people do not go to see the same film every week, people are stimulated by trying new foods or drinks in different restaurants. Also, people who live in circumstances where meal experiences are limited, such as in hostels at universities or colleges, or in poorly equipped bed-sits, may choose to eat out for this reason.

- *Labour* The desire to have someone else prepare, cook, serve and wash up a meal most certainly influences some people's decision to eat out. Or for medical and other reasons domestic help may be required, which may not be available. The popularity of fish and chip shops is a long-standing example of this, as is the recent growth in takeaways and fast-food operations. By 2020 50 per cent of all UK meals will be prepared outside the home.

- *Status* Both for personal and business reasons people may choose to impress their guests by taking them out to a fashionable and/or expensive restaurant. In many parts of the world, the business lunch is an accepted way of sealing successful business transactions, while in the USA the executive even has a working breakfast. On the personal level, eating out may be partly attributable to conforming with the social pattern of the neighbourhood.

- *Culture/tradition* Eating can be described as 'a part of our cultural heritage, and a manifestation of kinship'. In Britain, celebrations of special events such as anniversaries and birthdays are often associated with eating out, although not to the same extent as the Belgians and the French under such circumstances.

- *Impulse* This is rather like saying that sometimes people have no particular reason for eating out, they do so on the spur of the moment, so that it is a catch-all for any circumstances that have not been included previously. But there is no doubt that in certain businesses, notably retailing, impulse-buying is very significant and that it contributes to sales in the catering industry too, especially with regards to vending and takeaways.

A study by the American National Restaurant Association (Goldman, 1993), identified five main reasons for eating out in the USA, summarized as:

- *Doing the easy thing* This is a simple replacement of eating at home with eating out to save time and effort.

- *Having a fun time* This sees outing as a reward or a treat, usually in celebration.

- *Having a nice meal* This decision is based on eating out for the pleasure of doing so.

- *Making sure everyone has something to eat* This relates to providing a convenient way of feeding family members, each of whom are operating on a different schedule.

- *Satisfying a craving* This is the most impulsive reason for eating out. It is especially important in the takeaway and home delivery markets.

Whether there are five or six reasons for eating out, the important point that is being made is that many people do not eat out just for the food. It is all too easy for the catering student and professional caterer to believe that because the food is the most visible product of a restaurant, and that is what the customer most obviously pays for, the food is the be-all and end-all of successful catering. As we have seen, however, customers may be eating not to satisfy hunger at all (although in most cases they will be) but to satisfy other needs like social contact, status and curiosity.

These different reasons and circumstances surrounding eating out are reflected on how much people spend of their income on meals eaten outside the home. In 1999, according to Family Spending National Statistics, the average weekly household expenditure on restaurant and café meals was £9.40, takeaway meals £3.10, meals bought and eaten at the workplace £1.50, and state school meals just 40 pence (Keynote, 2000b). Since this is an average, the spending behaviour of different groups varies greatly, but overall this is a growth of 28.8 per cent on restaurant meals and 19 per cent on takeaways in the four years from 1996. Expenditure on workplace meals and school meals has seen no growth during this period.

FACTORS IN THE MEAL EXPERIENCE

Food

Although people do eat for reasons other than simply to satisfy their hunger, food is what is still the heart of the experience. But because most people in the Western world eats every day, everybody is an expert about the subject. People know what they like and expect to be served it. For many years in the UK, the most popular meal was prawn cocktail, steak, chips and peas followed by ice cream. However the recent growth in healthy eating, has seen a decline in the popularity of red meat and an increase in fish and chicken consumption. From the operator's point of view, it is extremely unlikely that we can change the consumers' preconceived ideas about food. The customer has partly chosen the restaurant on the basis of what type of food is served and will select from the menu those dishes that are most appealing. The palate is a delicate instrument that should be cared for and educated. Indeed in France school children are taught to appreciate food as part of the national curriculum. All the various sensory impressions or sensations such as odour, taste, texture and variety complete the gastronomic experience throughout life. The successful caterer is the one who ensures that the appearance, aroma, taste, texture and temperature are all just as the customer expects them to be.

- *Appearance* The expression 'looks good enough to eat' has not become a cliché, by chance. Food has to look good on the plate – a factor that all the major catering firms are aware of. They spend a great deal of time and effort in ensuring that their units sell a product that looks good. A key feature of restaurant food in the 1990s was the development of plate service so that the food is served exactly as the chef designed it.

- *Aroma* The second thing that will affect customers' reaction to the food, even before they eat it, is the smell. Dining out in an Indian restaurant or buying fish and chips would not be the same without their own particular aroma. Some operators even exploit this factor by ensuring that the ventilation leads out onto the street in order to attract customers. Although this may be very effective for fresh bread shops and doughnut houses, not all cooking smells are desirable. While eating food, much of the sensation is derived from the olfactory centre of the nasal cavity, without which most of what we eat and drink would lack its subtlety. In drinking a vintage wine or a good brandy, much of the enjoyment is derived from its 'nose' and the same can be said of other gastronomic experiences.

- *Taste* The taste buds of the tongue are only able to detect four basic flavours – sweet, sour, salt and bitter. It is the many variations of these four that combine to create the unique flavour of a particular food. For the consumer, the combination of flavours is quite important and can be used to good effect in various dishes: sweet and sour pork, lamb with mint sauce, and so on. It is also relevant to the sequence of dishes since generally sweet items are left until the end of a meal lest they upset the palate.

- *Texture* There are many textures of food – rough or smooth, hard or soft, fluid or solid, dry or moist, and tough or tender. The consistency and shape properties of food are experienced by pressure and movement receptors in the mouth. It is these that signal our dislike of food that is rubbery, slimy or tough and a customer's choice of a rare, medium or well-done steak is partly derived from the influence of texture upon the palate.

- *Temperature* Customers enjoy the variety that temperature can add to a meal – a piping-hot stew followed by ice cream for instance. Wealthy Victorians ate a sorbet in the middle of their long banquets in order to refresh their jaded palates as the citrus-based ice was refreshing. But temperature not only provides variety, it affects flavour too. The sweetness of a dish is accentuated when served hot, while the saltiness of a soup is reduced at a high temperature.

Service

Customers are not familiar with, nor care for, the problems of providing service. They are only concerned that the service is of the standard that they expect. If they are in a hurry then they will go to fast-food outlets that will provide a speedy meal; if they are out to impress, they will go to a sophisticated restaurant providing gueridon service. There are many differing styles of service, each tailored to meet the particular needs of a certain type of client expectation.

Social groups AB do spend more than any other group (40 per cent of their expenditure on eating out) in restaurants, hotels and steak bars where 'service' is provided, whereas groups DE spend 30 per cent of their expenditure in cafeterias, pubs and cafés. This of course reflects the cost and value for money as much as an attitude towards service, but there is no doubt that consumers who are not used to full silver service or gueridon work feel uncomfortable in those situations where it is provided. Campbell-Smith (1967) argued, 'At the lowest level of socio-economic grouping, there is probably no need to have more than four or five types of eating establishment, from a general café to a fish and chip shop, hamburger bar, bacon-and-egg speciality restaurant and possibly a simple snack and sandwich bar.' Whilst the way this is expressed is somewhat condescending, in practice this mix of restaurant types is precisely what we find today at motorway service areas! The expectations of the British public are much higher, with regards to the range of restaurants now available, the variety of product range, and the improved standards reflected in fast-food and roadside catering, compared with the popular catering outlets and transport cafés that Campbell-Smith was familiar with.

There does appear to be a trend for customers to complain more than in the past. This is not necessarily because they have more to complain about, but they are becoming less reluctant to do so. This is particularly true among male customers, in the AB category and over-45 age group. And it is slow and poor service that is most frequently complained about. According to the latest survey by the *Square Meal Eating-out Guide* (1999), the time taken to serve customers topped the list of complaints, with 17.8 per cent complaining about this problem, compared with only 15.5 per cent in the previous year. Overall, however, complaints about service fell to 26.1 per cent (from 30 per cent) of the guide's readers, with dramatic declines in reported cases of rude or snooty staff and of rushed or inattentive service.

Cleanliness and hygiene

In the USA, the preoccupation with hygiene was developed sooner than in Britain. But with the influx of US-style operations, some of their ideas about cleanliness have been introduced. As we shall see, disposables, which are probably the most hygienic means of serving food, have become more acceptable, and we shall probably see other ideas, such as cellophane-wrapped cutlery, crockery and so forth, assuring us of their pristine state, on tables in restaurants in Britain quite soon. The power of advertising and the media to influence people is also making consumers more and more aware of personal hygiene and hygiene in the home, which is bound to affect attitudes to eating out. Already there is a growing movement towards the banning of cigarette smoking in public places and many places, including cinemas, canteens and public transport have segregated areas for smokers and non-smokers.

Whether justified or not, Britain does not have a very good reputation for cleanliness. Tourists from abroad find our streets, parks, buses and public buildings dirty and litter-strewn in comparison with their own countries, and this attitude is extended towards our hotels and restaurants. The caterer is aware that cleanliness and hygiene are selling points and that the regulations laid down are only a minimum standard to be met. In the *Square Meal Eating-out Guide* (1999), poor hygiene was low on the list of the complaints.

Essentially there are three areas of concern for the foodservice operator: staff, equipment and environment.

- *Staff* Customers will not expect staff to wear a uniform, although most foodservice operations do encourage staff to wear a uniform as part of their overall image, fast-food outlets are a good example of this. However staff will be expected to be smart and clean. People tend to ascribe cleanliness to particular aspects of appearance – clothes, which they expect to be well-pressed and stain free; hair, which should be clean and looked after well; nails, which should be clean and manicured; and body odour, which should be neutral, i.e. neither sweaty nor overly perfumed.

- *Equipment* Customers will notice if equipment is not clean since it is literally put under their very noses. All table appointments, cutlery, crockery, and so forth, must be clean and polished and not defective in any way, for instance, cups chipped, plates cracked or forks bent. Furniture too must be well maintained.

- *The environment or room itself* As most restaurants and food service outlets have direct access onto the street and have a great deal of human traffic in and out of them, they collect a lot of dirt and dust. The operator must ensure that floor and wall surfaces are cleaned regularly and fittings such as pictures and prints and lights are dusted properly.

At this point one might reasonably presume that the next factor that influences the customer's enjoyment of a meal will be that indefinable factor – atmosphere.

Ask anyone why they go to a particular restaurant and they will probably say one of the three things – they like the food; it is good value for money; or they like the 'atmosphere'. But, if you ask someone to explain what 'atmosphere' is, they are not usually able to define what they mean. They may say that they like the surroundings, the music played there, the other customers or some other aspect of the operation, but usually they will not be very clear about it. This is because so many of the factors that contribute towards creating an atmosphere are received by the customer on a subconscious level. So rather than talk about atmosphere in vague terms, we will look at these factors in some detail.

Décor

'In the year since redesigning its Notting Hill outlet, Wimpy International has trebled its turnover there. And at the THF Cavendish Hotel, a redesign has improved bar turnover by 50 per cent.' (Hempel, 1979). So good interior design is obviously important to an establishment's success. As we saw in Chapter 3, boutique hotels have based much of their success on design. But to analyse what is good and what is not so good is very difficult. Newell (1965) wrote: 'Atmosphere is ethereal, evasive and indeterminate. The response of an individual to atmosphere is personal and . . . the individual's reaction to any combination of the factors [which influence atmosphere] can only be determined or controlled by rudimentary principles.' The problem lies in the essential paradox that customers need to feel 'at home' in their surroundings, without feeling that they are at home. Thus the décor of a restaurant must be different without undermining the sense of security of customers; it should provoke feelings of pleasure and relaxation rather than tension and anxiety. Complaints about décor have decreased over the past year. The décor must also play an integral part in the whole surroundings, whereas if customers are paying a lot for a meal, then they will expect plush surroundings, whereas if customers want a quick, cheap meal, then they will expect functional rather than decorative décor. Recently, interior design has been seen as an important feature of a restaurant concept, with debates in the food columns of newspapers about whether it was more important than the food. Creativity and innovation have become watchwords for the industry as design becomes a more integral part in hospitality and leisure developments.

Lighting

The lighting in a foodservice operation is determined in conjunction with the décor. In the same way that colours can affect moods, brightness or dimness can too. Generally, bright light will promote a sense of warmth and sociability, whereas dim lighting will have the reverse effect. Thus restaurants that aim to attract couples will have dim lighting that will make the partner appear to be more attractive and increase the sense of relaxation, whereas restaurants catering for groups of people will be bright to aid sociability. Lighting can also have the effect of distorting true colours, for instance, butchers have used a particular light bulb to enhance the redness of raw meat, while the effect of ultra-violet light on white is well known. The caterer must ensure that the lighting does not have an adverse effect upon the appearance of the food, décor and customers. Lighting should also reflect the time of day, so that at lunchtime it is more acceptable to eat in a bright environment than at dinner. Finally, lighting in conjunction with turnover can help to establish a fast turnover of customer by creating a brisk atmosphere.

Air conditioning

In the USA, with their far greater extremes of heat and cold, air conditioning is found everywhere. This is not the case in Britain and generally the problems of heating and ventilation are dealt with separately. Restaurants are busy places, or should be, with customers coming in and going out, with waiting staff to-ing and fro-ing, so that it is very difficult to maintain a constant temperature. Similarly, the proximity of the kitchen must give rise to cooking smells that may stimulate the appetite but can just as easily be off-putting. There are two aspects to heating the establishment – actual and psychological. Both the illumination and the colour scheme can affect the customer's sensation of warmth and other factors have a similar effect. For instance, a convected air curtain over the entrance gives an immediate sensation of warmth for people coming in off the street in winter, or of coolness in summer. Similarly, an obvious radiant source of heat like a coal fire also creates a feeling of warmth, even if its contribution to the actual room temperature is minimal. It can also have the undesired effect of making people feel too hot – customers have even been known to ask to be moved to another table because they are too hot from fake gas-fired 'coal' fires that give off no heat. As far as the actual temperature is concerned, the most pleasurable temperature for people sitting down is around 18°C. This will be affected by the number of people in the room since sitting ten customers in a room will produce about as much heat as a one kilowatt fire. In this respect, heating that is controlled by a thermostat is desirable: if not, a small thermometer placed in the room will give the caterer an indication of the room temperature. Customers will also strongly object to sitting in a draught. The source of most draughts is doorways or windows. Screens near the service doors and entrance should help to eliminate draughts and likewise, windows should be checked and possibly double glazed, particularly those with an easterly or northerly aspect. At the same time, it is desirable that the air in the room be circulating and moving to remove unwanted smells and to help maintain the ambient temperature. This must be done in a controlled way, using fans or extractors. In the kitchen, too, extractor fans must be properly sited and maintained correctly to minimize cooking smells in the restaurant itself. Finally, there is growing concern about smoking in public places. More and more outlets are providing no-smoking areas in parts of their operation.

Furnishing

The functional design of restaurant furniture reflects greatly upon customers' enjoyment of meals and the length of time they will spend in the establishment. It will also affect the number of covers that can be accommodated in the food service area and thereby influence customers' sense of security and intimacy. This same factor will also affect the profitability of the enterprise, so that a great deal of research has gone into the design of tables and chairs, to the extent that the Council for Industrial Design set up an Advisory Committee on Hotels and Restaurants that has made recommendations concerning restaurant furniture.

Consumers, of course, are not concerned with this detailed analysis; their only concern is comfort and well-being. Thus, if customers are in parties of four or six, they will prefer to sit at a round table, which enhances personal contact and conversation, rather than at a rectangular table, which, from the caterer's point of view, will increase the seating capacity. Likewise, it was found in popular catering units that fitted booth seating, where there were places for four people, couples preferred to sit next to each other since it was difficult to talk to each other when facing each other across the table without addressing the people on either side. This meant that the seats had to be made sufficiently long and wide to allow people to turn inwards without discomfort. Customers, too, are fussy about where they sit in a restaurant. Many people, for instance, will insist on sitting so that they are facing into the room, partly so that they have something other than a wall to look at and partly because they feel more secure with a wall behind them. Finally, according to research by the Council for Industrial Design, women seem to have different sitting habits to men. Men prefer to slump back or lean on their elbows in a relaxed position, whereas women can sit upright for longer periods without suffering the same amount of fatigue as men. Obviously it is impractical to have two sorts of chairs, but if a restaurant wishes to encourage people to linger over their meal, it must provide chairs with arms.

Acoustics

Restaurants are noisy places, or they would be if care was not taken to reduce the level of noise. In fact, reducing the level of noise of movement and bustle used to be the first step taken by restaurateurs who want to upgrade their premises. Modern design which tends to have hard surfaces for walls, few fabrics, wooden or tiled floors, and metal furniture and fixtures seems to run counter this argument however. The most important point to note with regard to levels of acceptable noise is that age group rather than social class is the determining factor, young people being able and willing to accept much higher levels.

There are three contributory factors to noise in a restaurant (apart from outside or extraneous noise that presumably could be avoided if necessary).

- *Voices* Customers need to communicate with each other and with the staff. Therefore the general level of noise should not exceed that which makes ordinary conversation impossible. Obviously, the more people in the room, the more noise there is, but as one can hardly request customers to talk more quietly, the caterer must reduce the general level of noise by reducing the input from the two other factors.

- *Operational* Eating and serving food can be a fairly noisy business. Apart from the noise derived from serving food, there is also noise caused by movement. Some floor surfaces are much noisier than others, for instance, tiling as opposed to carpeting. But in addition, the décor can contribute. Carpeting and curtains can reduce noise, while a textile wall fabric made in France called *mur de silence* was credited with reducing noise from an adjacent room by up to 90 per cent. The same report states that if 'premises are carpeted, the electricity heating bill can be reduced by 12 per cent, according to research conducted in Japan'. The main factor contributing to this saving is pile height, irrespective of whether the carpet is wool, nylon, polyester or acrylic.

- *Music* Most experts agree that music has a direct and strong effect on the customer's mood. It is used in many different environments – on Waterloo Station or in supermarkets to speed up the flow of people, in factories and workshops as 'music while you work', and extensively as background music in hotels and restaurants. It can achieve many things for caterers so long as they are aware of one essential point – that background music is forced upon the customer whether they like it or not, and if they do not like it then the restaurant loses customers. Otherwise, music may be used to create an environment of bustle until the restaurant fills up and then be turned down to allow for conversation. It can reinforce the particular image of the restaurant by playing appropriate music: rock music in the Hard Rock Café, and chamber music in the Ritz. It has even been suggested that music can be used to overcome customers' prevailing moods of depression on a wet, rainy day by playing bright and cheerful tunes.

Newell (1965) proposes the following points to consider:

- No vocals because people listen to vocals.

- No 'top ten' because they are fashions and become dated too quickly.

- A balance of light pop, film themes, musicals and any music that will have lasting popularity.

- Not mass-produced but carefully considered for the particular style of restaurant.

Size and shape of the room

This factor will certainly affect the atmosphere of the eating environment by creating feelings of intimacy or spaciousness. As we have seen, the operation can affect people's reactions to the room by careful use of colour, patterns and lighting. Unless the restaurant is purpose built, operators may have to resort to employing the skills of the interior designer to modify establishments where the ceiling is too high or too low, the room is too narrow, too small or whatever. Many high-street sites, for instance, are designed with shops in mind and therefore tend to be long and narrow (the wider the frontage onto the street, the greater the expense of buying or renting the site) which is why so many catering units in such sites have mirrors along one wall, in order to create an illusion of width.

Clientele

This factor is one over which the caterer only has limited control. Most certainly, however, customers' enjoyment of the meal will be affected by the other customers in the room. In general terms they will feel at home and reassured if the other customers are of a similar age, wearing similar clothes and behaving in a similar way. Whereas they will be upset if others are behaving too loudly (or too quietly), or if they are casually dressed when they are formal and vice versa. In most instances, however, the restaurant will reflect the socio-economic and age group that will be attracted to it, as outlined above. A person who dines at the Savoy will expect to eat in formal, reserved surroundings with others of middle age and thick wallets, and someone eating in a Harvester will expect to see children.

The only control that caterers have over clientele is that of refusing to serve customers, which so long as the restaurant is not an inn as defined under the Hotel Proprietors Act 1956, they are perfectly entitled to do. It was the practice in years gone by to refuse customers on the basis of their dress, and some places still insist that male customers must wear a tie, although this practice appears to be dying out.

THE FOODSERVICE SECTOR DEFINED

In order to discuss the foodservice industry in some depth, it is first necessary to define the industry. However, to the best of my knowledge nobody has yet attempted to do so in the UK, primarily because foodservice is seen as a part of the hotel and catering industry as a whole. This assumption was perfectly reasonable forty years ago or so, when, with a few exceptions, the main establishments serving meals were hotels and inns. However, since 1945, the entire complexion of hotelkeeping and catering has changed with the development of institutional and industrial catering, the growth of the 'popular' catering sector and in recent years, the boom in fast food. Thus there is now a very real need to separate the provision of accommodation from the provision of food and drink in order to appraise and evaluate the foodservice industry in its own right.

In effect, this textbook has already defined foodservice by the way it is organized. The second half of this text has ten chapters, each of which is devoted to a specific sector. In some cases these sectors match sectors as defined by the Standard Industrial Classification, in other cases they discuss and analyse foodservice provision outside of the SIC, as illustrated in Figure 9.1. The underlying principle for classifying the industry into these sectors is the focus this text has on operations. If this text were only concerned with the size and scale of the industry, then the SIC would be the best way to organize the text. However, this text focuses on customers needs and how the industry responds operationally to these needs. Varying customer needs result in a different set of priorities of factors in the meal experience. These alternative sets of priorities have led to the development of specific kinds of operation to serve each of these markets. For instance, fast food grew up to satisfy the need for a high value, quick service meal item. The sectoral classification is also consistent with the original text in *Foodservice Operations* (Jones, 1988), where the issue was discussed. 'This division (sic) is not arbitrary but an attempt to examine particular aspects of food service, and in many respects it is a classification that many caterers would accept as being identifiable in the industry ... The diversity of the industry means that there are some operations which cannot be easily classified, [such as] takeaways and vending. Each chapter has a subtitle [which] attempts to put into a single sentence the features or problems of that sector which differentiates it from any other' (Jones, 1988). These differentiating factors are identified in Table 9.1.

Since the first edition of this textbook, written twenty years ago, the foodservice industry in the UK has changed significantly. In Chapter 1 a particular trend referred to as 'blur' was identified. Such lack of distinction used to arise due to the firms that operated in this industry. 'The distinction between one sector and

Table 9.1 *Sectors of the foodservice industry*

Sector	SIC classification	Differentiating factor
Restaurants	part of 6611	'the quintessential foodservice outlet'
Hotel foodservice	6650	'for people staying away from home'
Motorway and roadside	part of 6611	'foodservice for the motorist'
Licensed trade	6620 and 6630	'food for people out for a drink'
Fast food and takeaways	6612 and part of 6611	'meal package for people in a hurry'
Employee feeding	6640	'for people at their place of work'
Welfare catering	9310, 9320 and 9330	'for people unable to feed themselves'
Travel catering	none	'for people on the move'
Outside and social catering	none	'service where it was never intended'

another is blurred when the same firm operates in more than one sector ... [the] industry's classification is meant to illustrate the essential feature of providing food and drink under particular circumstances' (Jones, 1988). Today, particular brands are not so easy to classify in the way proposed. The distinction between a restaurant and a pub is based on the idea that food sales exceeds drink sales in the former, and vice versa in a pub. However brands like J D Wetherspoons and All Bar One may find food sales greater than 'wet' sales in one trading period, but not in another. Likewise, some brands that were developed for the high street as restaurants or fast food outlets, may now also be found on the roadside or in employee feeding. Despite this blurring, there remains some value in separating out operations in the way adopted in order to identify the key features of these types of business.

In Chapter 1, key statistics relating to the hospitality industry as a whole were identified. In this part of the book, each chapter on a sector of the foodservice industry will also identify key operating statistics in terms of the size and scale of each sector. It is therefore unnecessary to duplicate this information here. Nonetheless there are some key facts, based on this author's estimates derived from a composite of a number of sources, that need to be emphasized. In 1998, the hospitality industry employed approximately 1.88 million people (HtF, 1999), with around 1.6 million workers engaged in the provision of foodservice. Of these around 70 per cent were female employees. Over 0.6 million of these employees work in the not-for-profit sector of the industry, such as healthcare and education. These employees work in around 175,000 commercial outlets and 90,000 non-commercial operations (education, health, public sector, etc.). (Foodservice Intelligence, 2000). Commercial types of business providing foodservice are 53,000 pubs, 48,000 hotels, 28,000 quick service outlets, 25,000 restaurants, and 18,000 leisure venues. In the not-for-profit segment, there are 35,000 outlets in education, 30,000 in healthcare, and 21,000 in the employee feeding sector. Between them all they served 8.5 billion meals in 1999. The financial turnover of the industry in 1999 was estimated to be £22 billion (Foodservice Intelligence, 2000). Arguably the largest single catering operation in the UK is the National Health Service, which spends over £450 million each year.

FOODSERVICE OPERATING SYSTEMS

In Chapter 1, different types of foodservice operation were identified as having different combinations of eight core systems (Figure 1.3). Each of these will briefly be discussed here. A full and detailed exploration of these is provided in the companion text to this, *Hospitality Operating Systems*.

Stores systems

The foodservice industry handles a wide range of materials, many of which are perishable and susceptible to contamination by bacteria. Foodstuffs therefore need to be stored under conditions that are both safe and secure. Most operations would have ambient, chiller and freezer storage areas. Two main storage systems operate, either shelved or bulk storage. In shelved storage, items are broken down from the cases or packages in which they are delivered and individually stored on shelves. Bulk storage involves storing items in bulk and only breaking these down when needed in the preparation or production area. It is only large-scale operations, such as central production units or flight catering kitchens, that adopt this system.

Preparation systems

The extent to which preparation of food materials is conducted on the premises depends on the extent to which the menu is based on fresh or pre-prepared foodstuffs. Many restaurant and quick service concepts are based on dishes which are purchased chilled or frozen and only require simple defrosting and preparation prior to service. More up-scale, traditional restaurants however undertake a great deal of preparation of foodstuffs with separate sections of the kitchen devoted to meat, fish, vegetables, and bakery preparation.

Production systems

Production systems vary according to the scale and variety of output, as well as the policy with regards to on-site preparation. Menu items may be prepared individually, usually in response to a customer order. This is the traditional *à la carte* or call order system. Alternatively they may be prepared, usually in bulk, prior to specific customer orders. This is the traditional *table d'hôte* system. In operations that are based on pre-prepared dishes, the system is simplified so that it is, what has been termed, 'assembly-serve' (Jones, 1988).

Holding systems

In traditional foodservice operations, the production area is adjacent to the dining area, so food is served hot directly from the kitchen to the customer. With the *table d'hôte* system, this food is usually kept hot during the service period. However, as identified in Chapter 1, some operations are 'decoupled'. Food is produced in a different place and at a different time to when it is served. In these cases either the cook–chill, cook–freeze, or sous-vide system may be used to hold the food at a safe temperature.

Transportation systems

In decoupled systems, dishes and meals need to be transported in their chilled or frozen state from the kitchen to the dining area. A variety of systems exist for doing this in hospitals, flight catering and other sectors adopting this approach.

Service systems

Lillicrap (1971) identified nine styles or types of service including gueridon, full silver, plate/silver, plate, family, counter (or cafeteria), snack bar, French, and Russian. Of these, the last two – French and Russian styles – are hardly used at all in the industry today; likewise, cafeteria service developed during the 1970s with several variations designed to increase throughput such as free-flow, scramble and carousel systems. In addition, there is also buffet service, tray systems, trolley service, and automatic vending. Subsequently further systems analysis has been carried out (Cousins and Lillicrap, 1999) and five main types of front-of-house service style have been identified.

- *Table service* This is service to customers sitting at a laid cover. It includes silver service, family service and plate service.

- *Assisted service* This is any combination of table service and self service. For instance, many restaurants have incorporated self-help salad bars into their operation.

- *Self-service* Customers select from either a single counter or several counters of food and drink items, often using a tray, and pay at a till point. Alternative configurations of counters are known as 'free-flow', 'scramble', echelon and carousel.

- *Single point service* Customers are served at a single point, and food may be consumed on the premises or taken away. This includes take-aways, kiosks, vending, food courts and bars.

- *Specialized or in situ* This refers largely to the service of food and drink to customers in places not primarily designed for foodservice consumption. It includes tray serve systems, such as in hospitals or on airlines, trolley service, home delivery, drive-ins, and hotel floor service.

Clearing systems

Whilst the service system explains how meals are served to customers, each of these also includes a way of clearing away equipment used by the diner.

Dishwash systems

There are two main dishwash systems designed to reflect the scale of the operation (assuming that washing up by hand is no longer employed in the industry!). Large-scale operations employ so-called flight wash-up systems, developed originally for the flight catering industry, whereas small-scale operations employ single line systems.

Whatever back-of-house and front-of-house systems are adopted, the operational activity will centre on the effective and efficient delivery of the meal experience. The range and scope of such activities can be exemplified by considering the typical operations manual of a foodservice outlet. The manual for a fast-food restaurant is illustrated in Figure 9.1.

1. Introduction
   - Background to the company
   - Organization chart
2. Finance
   - Cash and turnover summary
   - Weekly stock and usage sheet
   - VAT
   - Weekly finance reports
   - Payroll
3. Products
   - Delivery
   - Storage
   - Ordering
   - Recipes
   - Food preparation
   - Method
   - Presentation, holding and serving of each menu
   - Packaging
   - Portion control
   - Stock control
   - Menu storage, relating to different times of the day
4. Equipment
   - Specifications
   - Operation
   - Cleaning
   - Maintenance
5. Marketing
   - Advertising
   - Public relations
   - Point-of-sale/display material
6. Job descriptions
   - Managers
   - Supervisors
   - Crew members
7. Training
8. Staff
   - Recruitment
   - Selection
   - Engagement

   National Insurance Contributions
   PAYE
   Absence from work
   Holidays
   Discipline, warnings and dismissal procedures
   Food hygiene and safety policy
9. Standard forms
   Standard letters
   Job application form
   Medical Questionnaire
   Staff engagement form
   Contracts of employment
   Disciplinary procedure

Figure 9.1 *Franchised fast-food operations manual contents*
Source: Acheson and Wicking (1992)

ISSUES AND TRENDS

The foodservice industry has probably experienced a greater level of innovation than the accommodation industry. These have largely centred around the production of meals rather than their service. Such advances, whether they are process redesign or new technologies, have enabled meals to be produced more quickly and in larger quantities at lower unit cost. This, in combination with trends in consumer expectations, has led to significant improvements in the quality of provision throughout the industry. Whereas in the 1970s, consumer experts such as Egon Ronay, could rightly criticize whole sectors of the industry, such as motorway service areas, schools and hospitals, today all sectors of the industry now perform to high standards of provision. Although as we shall see, as customer expectations continue to rise, a number of initiatives have been implemented to improve standards, such as raising standards at motorway service areas (see Chapter 12), the better hospital food campaign (see Chapter 16) and investment in rail catering (see Chapter 17).

As in the hotel sector, the UK foodservice industry has also seen a large number of mergers and acquisitions. In 1999 Allied Domecq exited licensed retailing by selling Punch taverns, McDonalds Restaurants acquired the Aroma coffee-bar chain, and Scottish & Newcastle purchased Greenalls. In 2000 Bass focused on retailing and disposed of its brewing interests, Granada hospitality and Compass merged, and Rank disposed of its Tom Cobleigh chain of pubs. Many major chains are now both hotel operators, foodservice companies and licensed retailers, notably Whitbread, Six Continents, and Compass.

Catering is one of the few big industries in the UK that is still growing (JHIC, 2000). It is a £51 billion market forecast to grow at an annual compound growth rate of 7.2 per cent between 1999 and 2004. Almost as much money is spent on buying food away from home as is spent on grocery food. A major factor in this is the growth in disposable or discretionary income. Another major factor is the shift away from a goods economy to an experience economy. Whilst the price of food declined in real terms by 1.4 per cent between 1994 and 1998, the price of catering increased by 3.5 per cent (JHIC, 2000). Customers are willing to pay more for services and the right experience because they *value* such interactions. In another survey of 1012 adults (Keynote, 2000b), 78 per cent of all adults identified going to a restaurant as a good night's entertainment. This was true across all age groups. Going to the pub was also thought of as entertaining by adults under 35, but as people got older it became less attractive. Increasingly, the key factor that influences eating out behaviour is life-style rather than demographics. Twenty per cent of couples with children, whatever their age, are likely to eat out at least once a month, whereas 35 per cent of young people who live on their own do so.

This shift to experiences being valued by customers means that firms need to think in terms of 'modal segmentation' for their marketing planning. This means that they have to identify the moods of their customers rather than their demographics (age, sex, ethnicity). Research by the Henley Centre (JHIC, 2000) identified four factors that drive the choice of venue for a night out. These were: who is in the group, how much energy the group has, where the venue or chain of venues are located, and whether or not they are offering a special deal or special event. Such research suggests that hospitality businesses should think in terms of targeting and 'hosting' specific types of relationship, such as couples, families, work colleagues, and so on. It is much more likely now that special occasions such as birthdays or anniversaries will be celebrated with a meal out than ever before (Keynote, 2000b). They should also recognize that often they might be part of a chain of experiences. In the Henley study only 13 per cent of people who had eaten out went out just for that activity, the vast majority went somewhere else such as a pub, club, coffee bar or friend's house.

Finally, healthy eating has emerged as an issue, reflected by the foodservice industry in its provision of vegetarian options, healthy alternatives and menu selections. However, in reality, the average British consumer's behaviour is contradictory (JHIC, 2000). They say that they want to eat more healthy food, but consumption of unhealthy foods has changed very little over time. The reasons for this are that people do not always know what is healthy or not, their concerns are really about food safety (BSE, GM foods, e-coli) rather than a good diet, and they see stress as more damaging than fat or cholesterol. Hence people will drink alcohol and eat fatty foods to indulge themselves and relieve stress, which they see as the greater evil.

SUMMARY

This chapter has examined the nature of demand for foodservice and the reasons why people eat out. It explored the concept of the meal experience, and the various factors that influence customers' enjoyment of a meal. Nine different sectors of the industry were identified, along with their specific characteristics. Finally the different systems used to deliver foodservice were identified.

FURTHER STUDY

Ball, S., Jones, P., Kirk, D. and Lockwood, A. (2002) *Hospitality Operating Systems*, Continuum: London.

www.caterer.com

www.chainleader.com

www.indicater.com

QUESTIONS

Go to the www.chainleader.com website and type 'design' into their search engine. This will take you to over 50 'virtual tours' of foodservice outlets throughout the USA. Select three restaurants and consider how each of them goes about delivering a meal experience to its customers.

CHAPTER 10

Restaurants

INTRODUCTION

In many respects the difficulty in analysing this sector lies in the origin of restaurants. As Derek Taylor (1977) points out, before the Second World War 'the most common route for restaurateurs was to acquire a following when acting as a head waiter elsewhere and then to set up their own shingle'. The famous Quaglino's restaurant was established in just this way. Thus restaurants tend to be owned and operated by individuals and individualists. There is no neat formula for opening and operating a successful establishment. However, some firms have deliberately set out to create a chain of units which depend for their success on mass appeal, so that two broad groups of restaurant can be identified, namely popular catering units and 'speciality' restaurants. The restaurant sector has also been significantly influenced by ideas developed in the USA.

This does not refer only to the introduction of US 'cuisine' (hamburgers, fried chicken or exotic ice creams) but to the significant influence over the last twenty years of US ideas and techniques on the British foodservice operations. These ideas and techniques are not only applicable to US foodstuffs – for example, fast-food techniques have revolutionized the traditional British fish and chip shop. The extent of US influence is great. For instance, the development of the popular catering sector of the industry was significantly influenced by three British operations based on US ideas – Kentucky Pancake Houses, Wimpy Bars and Golden Egg restaurants; the nationwide chains of roadside restaurants (notably Little Chef and Happy Eater) were developed from a US prototype; the largest growing sector of the industry, fast food, is based firmly on US practices; and coffee shops and grill rooms in hotels originated in the USA.

The impact of American ideas has continued on into the 1990s. Home delivery is a development from the takeaway, but instead of customers having to visit the shop in person, all they need to do is telephone their order and the meal will be delivered to their home. Drive-ins have been slow to develop in the UK, partly due to its different climate and car size, despite the fact that Rank opened the first roadside 'drive-up' fast-food facility on the A1 near Darlington in 1981. Convenience stores provide self-serve food and drink facilities in retail outlets, while food courts operate several catering concepts in one location, sharing the seating capacity. They are found at rail and air terminals, such as Euston and Gatwick, and in shopping malls, such as the Newcastle Metro Centre.

RESTAURANTS DEFINED

There is no easy way to identify this sector. A restaurant has been defined as an 'establishment where refreshments or meals may be obtained' (Oxford English Dictionary). Many different types of establishment may be included in this definition: snack bars, cafés, speciality restaurants, popular catering units, and so on. In the last chapter, this sector was identified as 'the quintessential foodservice operation'. The key point is that this is the sector where customers of choice go to have a complete meal experience. There are various ways in which a classification of restaurants may be made.

The spectrum

This analysis, carried out in the USA, assumes that there are three most important variables – menu, service style and price. It originated in order to define restaurant categories in hybrid markets, so that in theory there should be room for at least one of each type of restaurant, since they each appeal to a different market segment. Eleven types of restaurant are defined:

takeaway;

snack stand;

limited menu, low price, self-service;

limited menu, low/moderate price, self-service;

limited menu, moderate price, service;

full menu, low/moderate price, service;

full menu, low/moderate price, self-service;

full menu, moderate price, service;

full menu, moderate/high price, service;

luxury menu, high price, continental (gueridon) service;

social caterer.

The major problem with this classification is that although it could be applied to the UK, as yet no data have been compiled on this basis. In an early study in the USA the Spectrum study yielded some interesting information. Over 55 per cent of sales were in operations with a full menu, so that speciality restaurants (like McDonalds) were tending in the USA to extend their menus to provide greater appeal. Second, over 60 per cent of sales were made in operations that provide service as opposed to self-service. This contradicted slightly the third point, that nearly 70 per cent of the market was through low- or moderately low-priced outlets.

A restaurant typology

This approach (Powers, 1985) to restaurant classifiction, attempts to analyse restaurant types using completely different criteria, namely the sophistication of the system and the system's innovativeness. The classification is shown in Figure 10.1.

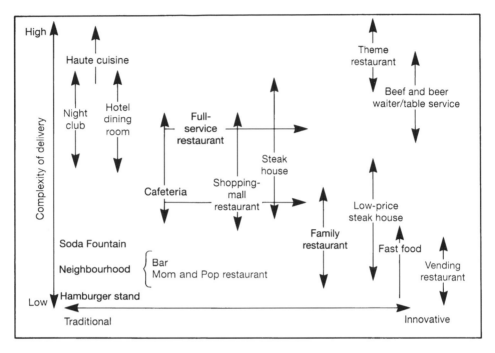

Figure 10.1 *The restaurant typology*
Source: Powers (1985)

Expanded restaurant typology

This classification (Muller and Woods, 1994) was also developed in the USA. It explicitly recognizes that the growth and significance of multi-unit restaurant chains has altered for ever the structure and make-up of this sector. It proposes five types of restaurant, each of which has distinctive menu characteristics and operational features. These are: quick service, offering low price, speed, and consistency; mid-scale restaurants, based around menu choice, value, and comfort; moderate up-scale, delivering ambience, flexibility and a 'fashion statement'; upscale outlets which deliver an experience, style and ambience; and business dining, based on location, price and value. Each of these five types of chain has distinctive menu characteristics, strategic focus, and operational imperatives. Of these five, three can be identified as matching UK styles of restaurant quite closely, (quick service we consider in Chapter 14).

Restaurant chains, such as Garfunkels, Beefeater, Pizza Hut, and Harvester, share many of the characteristics of the mid-scale restaurant. There is a fairly broad menu appeal, with large portions, and commodity items; the focus is on standard operating procedures, building traffic volumes and pricing points; and operational success is based around the size of the facility, cost controls and the execution of process standards. The moderate up-scale concept is exemplified in the UK by

TGIFridays, restaurants operated by My Kinda Town, and some pizza/pasta chains. Here the menu is trendy and fashionable, based on a limited inventory with some cross-utilization; the focus is on energy and service, with some innovation; and keys to success are 'theatrics', good staff, and strong concept/décor. Finally, the up-scale restaurant in the UK is typified by Conran's chain of restaurants which includes private dining, a wide range of cooking styles from modern British to Traditional Asian and a they offer a wide selection of trendy bars and restaurants to choose from. More typically UK up-scale restaurants are not chains but are represented by the high-profile restaurateurs operating just one or two restaurants, such as Prue Leith, Gary Rhodes and Antony Worrall Thompson. This style of restaurant has a menu which is complex, highly presented and customized; the strategic focus is on price to screen out 'unwanted' custom, high product differentiation and a quality image; the key to success is largely based on the individual skill and expertise of the restaurateur or chef.

Concept categories

The American National Restaurant Association has developed, in conjunction with CREST, the idea of 'concept groups' (Goldman, 1993). This further develops three of the five types of restaurant mentioned in the extended typology. The quick service segment is subdivided mainly on the basis of core product, into 'concept groups' of chicken, donut, Mexican, pizza, and so on. Mid-scale restaurants are made up from seven concept groups – cafeteria, casual dining, family style, hotel, steakhouse, speciality (seafood, ethnic), and varied menu. Finally, the up-scale segment has concepts described as casual dining, high check (high priced), moderate check (moderately priced), hotel, speciality, and varied menu.

On the basis of the above classifications, this chapter is concerned with those restaurants which operate as stand-alone outlets, offering mainly full menus, in the mid-scale and up-scale segments. Thus takeaways, fast food (or quick service outlets), hotel restaurants, and roadside/motoway diners are specifically excluded, and each of these is dealt with in subsequent chapters.

DEVELOPMENT OF THE RESTAURANT SECTOR

The restaurant industry in the UK has developed over the last seventy years in five distinct stages.

1930 to 1955 – depression and war

Prior to the 1930s, restaurants in the UK were limited to either local taverns or 'coaching houses', or large hotels where customers were expected to wear evening dress and the atmosphere was very formal. The situation was much the same in the USA, where for the average family in small cities and towns dining out was an occasion. The working man's restaurant and boarding house were strictly 'meat and potatoes'. During the 1930s however, the Aerated Bread Co. (ABC) and J. Lyons opened tea shops in urban centres throughout the UK. These quickly developed the service of more substantial meals and became the first national chains of restaurants. In 1931, Frank and Aldo Berni also opened their first restaurant which was, after the Second World War, to turn into the first chain of steakhouse restaurants.

The Second World War was to have a major impact on the development of the UK restaurant industry. Whereas in the USA the industry continued to innovate and develop, in the UK business almost ceased altogether. First the bombing of major cities literally knocked down restaurant premises, as well as, not surprisingly, deterring customers from eating out! By May 1945, nearly 24,000 hotels and pubs had been destroyed or damaged by bombs and fires (Tarpey, 1993a). Second, there were major food shortages during the War that lead to food rationing that continued for some years after the end of the conflict. Indeed the Meals in Establishments Order of 1942 imposed restrictions on the number of courses to be served, introduced a maximum price for a meal, and prohibited consumption of meals in public after midnight in London, and 11.00pm elsewhere. This decline in the restaurant industry was matched by tremendous growth in the industrial foodservice sector. Factories were encouraged to provide meals for the workers and schools were enabled to provide a two-course hot meal at a reasonable price. So although the number of establishments increased by 30 per cent between 1941 and 1946, and the number of meals served almost doubled during the same period, this growth was due to industrial, institutional and military catering.

1956 to 1970 – 'Never had it so good'

From 1950 onwards the restaurant industry began to make up lost ground, but only very slowly. Consumers were not free to eat as much as they could afford until the end of rationing in 1954. And the emphasis was on dining at home. So between 1954 and 1967, during which time Macmillan, the British Prime Minister, coined the phrase 'you've never had it so good', there was only modest growth in demand for restaurant meals (O'Connor 1993). Thus the average rate of growth in expenditure on food by caterers and restaurateurs was only 2 per cent per annum during the 1960s. At the same time, spending on food by households was almost static, indicating that people were eating out slightly more. One of the first major studies on eating out habits in the UK was undertaken in 1965, sponsored by Smethurt Foods. This National Catering Inquiry showed that 40 per cent of people surveyed ate away from home daily at their workplace or nearby, whereas only 25 per cent of people had a meal for social reasons at least once a week. The main reason for not eating out socially was given as the cost. But the same study also reported that 'some married couples admitted to being stumped for conversation when alone at table' and that a large number of people avoided up-market restaurants due to 'snooty waiters and flamboyant, incomprehensible menus' (Tarpey, 1993b).

During this period the only major mid-market restaurant chain to develop was Berni Inns, largely through converting public houses into steakhouse restaurants. In the mass market, the Wimpy, Golden Egg and Kardomah restaurant chains developed, but unlike in the USA where this style of restaurant had developed as fast food, these chains offered table service. The British also remained very conservative in their eating habits. The traditional meal of roast meat with potatoes and two vegetables, followed by a sponge pudding was very much the norm. The 'carvery' style restaurant was developed on this tradition by Lyons who opened their first 'carvery' in the 1960s.

The relatively slow development of the restaurant industry up to 1970 was probably due to a number of factors. First, the foodservice industry as a whole was dominated by the licensed trade. There were over 70,000 public houses in the UK, a high proportion of which were owned by the big six brewers – Bass Charington, Allied, Whitbread, Watney Mann, Scottish & Newcastle, and Courage. In the 1950s and 1960s, these companies regarded pubs as retail outlets for selling their product – beer. There was also a unique form of franchising public houses in the UK, known as the tied-house system. In effect, the brewers leased their property to the pub 'landlord' at a peppercorn rent. In return the brewer had exclusive rights of supply to those licensed premises. Landlords of tied-houses received little or no training in catering and were not encouraged to develop the food side of their business. A second factor that held back restaurant development was related to the dominance of public houses. Licensing law in the UK prohibited young people from using pubs. Under 14s were not allowed in at all, and under 18s were not allowed to purchase or consume alcohol. As the 'local' was often the centre of social life outside the home, there was no tradition of eating out as a family in the UK. Finally, commercial television – ITV – only began in 1958 so that national advertising of restaurants was not possible until the 1960s. Even then the BBC continued to capture a high proportion of viewers and ITV advertising was dominated by fast-moving consumer goods.

However, the range of opportunities for eating out was extended during the 1960s in two ways. The first roadside diner was opened by Trust Houses as a Little Chef in 1963. Originally based on a US concept, the diner was quickly developed to reflect British expectations. The menu was very similar to that found in restaurant chains located in high streets and the service style was table service. The second development was related to ethnic cuisine, both Indian and Chinese. Restaurants offering both these menu styles grew up from the historic association of the UK with Hong Kong, Singapore, India and Pakistan. Many people of these former colonies had rights of citizenship and immigrated into the UK during the 1950s and 1960s. Such immigration was often associated with political and social upheaval in their home countries. For instance, many Asian immigrants arrived from Uganda during and after the dictatorship of Idi Amin. Their culture encouraged entrepreneurship and their experience led to them opening restaurants, usually in high street locations. By 1970 there 'were about 4,000 Chinese restaurants' in the UK and a growing number of Indian restaurants. Over half the people surveyed in the National Catering Inquiry of 1965 had experienced this style of cuisine.

The 1970s – signs of competition and innovation

The restaurant industry grew significantly during the 1970s largely due to the overall growth in consumer expenditure. In 1974 the Trends in Catering survey was commissioned by the Hotels and Catering Economic Development Committee. In 1975, this showed 460 million meals a year were consumed away from home, with an expenditure of £2000 million (excluding alcohol). This was the equivalent of two meals a week for the average Briton, and represented 4 per cent of total consumer spending.

The 1970s was a period during which new chains emerged to compete in a number of market segments. The Happy Eater chain was founded to compete head-to-head with Little Chef in the roadside dining sector. New steakhouse chains, such as Beefeater, Angus Steak House and Chef & Brewer developed to compete with Berni Inns. Steak house restaurants originated in the licensed trade sector of the catering industry. Their origins and continued success are built on a menu based around steak, which requires a limited amount of kitchen equipment, i.e. grill and deep-fat fryer, and hence capital investment; little technical expertise for the preparation, cooking and service; popularity of the meal item; pre-portioning of the product from the supplier; relative ease of storage and reasonable shelf-life; and little or no wastage. This type of restaurant served plated meals with a table d'hôte menu, comprising three starters, usually soup, prawn cocktail and one other; rump, sirloin or fillet steak grilled to order; ice cream or cheese board; followed by coffee or a selection from a range of speciality coffees. The price of the meal is based on the cost of the main item and since, to attract custom, pricing is competitive, strict portion sizes are shown on the menu and are supported with illustrations of how each dish should be presented on the plate.

In 1974 the first McDonalds restaurant was opened in Greenwich, a south London suburb. In 1976 Peter Morton opened the London Hard Rock Café, Bob Payton opened the Chicago Pizza Pie factory, and Roger Myers and Karen Jones opened Peppermint Park and Coconut Grove in 1979. These were signs that the restaurant industry was about change dramatically during the 1980s.

The 1980s – a rapidly maturing industry

In a 1980 survey of 680 establishments of all types, the commercial operation of speciality restaurants was investigated. Restaurants identified as selling French or Italian cuisine were the smallest of all restaurant types surveyed – 43 per cent served less than 50 covers per day and only 7 per cent recorded over 200 covers on average per day. This was a reflection on the average amount spent per head of £7.50 exclusive of VAT and service, which is considerably higher than the average for other sectors. 'Ethnic' restaurants (which include Indian and Chinese cuisine) had an average spend of around £3 per head, but a correspondingly higher turnover with 70 per cent of them having a turnover of 50 covers or more per day. There was also a significant difference in policy with regard to takeaway food sales. Only 15 per cent of French and Italian restaurants had some takeaway trade, and this only accounted for approximately 10 per cent of their sales. For 'ethnic' restaurants, however, takeaway sales were important – 'over a quarter of Chinese and Indian restaurants got between 20 and 50 per cent of their business from takeaway meal purchases'. It seems that many operators recognize that a change in service style, towards more self-service and takeaway operations, is one of the most significant developments in the industry.

Although nearly 90 per cent of restaurants were independently owned and managed, the performance of these single units and the approach of their owners was very different from that of chain restaurants. In the mid-1980s the average turnover of an independent restaurant was £115,000 compared with £270,000 in a chain unit. This reflects the size of the units: independent units averaging less than 60 seats, chain units around 80. The independent restaurateur also tends to open longer hours to achieve this level of turnover. In comparison, in 1986 a typical managed public house had an annual turnover of £210,000, of which 20 per cent derived from food sales.

This was reflected in the way in which the large brewers operating such chains organize and manage these outlets. Nearly all of them developed separate divisions for such restaurants with an operations director whose background is in catering rather than the licensed trade. In 1986, Bass operated Toby Restaurants, Grand Metropolitan Berni Inns, and Allied-Lyons had the Vittle Inns chain and New England Restaurant Group. Such divisionalization, the increasing sophistication of the customer, and the much greater levels of competition have led the chains into broadening the product range on offer and diversifying out of the steak-based concept.

Until the opening of the first McDonalds in Britain in 1975, most UK restaurant chains operated table or plate service, or, in small snack-bar units, counter service. These high-street restaurants found it increasingly difficult to continue this style of service for several reasons. A very large increase in high-street rents and rates necessitated maximizing the seating capacity of restaurants. Table service does not necessarily have higher staffing costs than a comparable fast-food operation but the staffing cost per unit sale is lower due to the higher turnover of fast-food restaurants. Customers' tastes have changed and effective marketing by the new operators has forced the traditional popular catering units to rethink their policies.

There was also a significant shift in taste away from red meat towards more healthy eating. This had a major impact on the steakhouse chains. Berni diversified out of steak into a number of branded concepts, but eventually Grand Metropolitan sold 150 of their 208 outlets to Whitbread who absorbed them into their Beefeater chain. The 1980s also saw the emergence of family style restaurants such as Harvesters and TGIFridays. The first UK-based TGIFridays was opened by Whitbread in March 1986. There was also significant growth of restaurants based around pasta and/or pizza. Between 1984 and 1986, the number of UK pizza restaurants increased from 110 to 450. For instance, Whitbread expanded its Pizza Hut chain from 20 to 75 units, claiming that sales had responded outstandingly to television advertising.

1990s onwards – growing sophistication and competition

The development of theme restaurants towards the end of the 1980s was of major significance within the UK. It marked a major and permanent change in how the British think about eating out. Right up until the mid-1980s, most restaurants were seen as a substitute for eating at home. Such substitution was either necessary, convenient or in order to celebrate a special occasion. But eating out was still not perceived as a 'leisure experience'. Unlike the French who are said to 'live to eat', the British continued to 'eat to live'.

With the growth of theme restaurants the British have decided that eating out is fun, that it is a leisure activity, and that it is more than just the consumption of food. As Thomas (1994) says in defining a theme restaurant, it is 'largely a destination ... [with] an intangible, overall ambience and theatre which takes you somewhere other than where you are'. Eating out is now a part of the lives of most consumers, with 62 per cent of consumers stating that they eat out during the evenings and 51 per cent of consumers claiming that they dine out in restaurants during the day. Between 1995 and 1999 food sales increased significantly in the

Figure 10.2 *Typical mid-scale restaurant (The Crab and Dragon)*
Source: The Pelican Group plc

pub sector, taking a higher share in the overall restaurant sector. Household expenditure on eating out has also increased by 17 per cent between 1994 and 1998. A key influence on this substantial increase was the economy, particularly the level of disposable income. Between 1995 and 1999 disposable income increased by over 5 per cent, resulting in a higher level of income to spend on eating and drinking outside of the home. The 1990s saw a change in people's life styles. Lives became more hectic and the increase in the number of working women resulted in less time for home cooking, thus encouraging eating out. Moreover, there have been a number of specific brand restaurants that have targeted particular customers, e.g. city-centred outlets targeted at office workers, fast food and cafés aimed at the pre-family category.

Figure 10.3 *Typical moderate up-scale restaurant*
Source: TGIFridays plc

SIZE AND SCALE OF THE RESTAURANT SECTOR

In 2000, there were 45,875 restaurants registered for VAT (Keynote, 2000c). This number of outlets has grown slightly from 1996, before which economic recession had seen a downturn in restaurant businesses. Of these restaurants, only 2 per cent generate sales of over £1 million per year. The majority, around 78 per cent, have an annual turnover of £50,000 to £249,000. The total sales of the restaurant sector (excluding fast food) in 1999 were estimated at £5.4 billion. The fast food sector increased at around 4.5 per cent per annum between 1995 and 2000, the restaurant sector experienced a steady annual sales growth of 5.5 per cent at current prices in

1999. The sector employed an estimated 361,700 workers in 1999, of which 54 per cent were part-time.

The UK restaurant sector remains fragmented, with a large number of independent businesses operating locally but a growing number of national chains. Of the largest restaurant chains, three are based around families (Harvester, Toby Restaurants, Brewers Fayre), two around pizza (Pizza Hut and Pizza Express), one based on steak (Beefeater) and one (Little Chef) is a roadside chain. The main restaurant chains are illustrated in Table 10.1 (fast-food chains are shown in Table 14.3). The top brands dominate their sectors: Pizza Hut has one third of the pizza restaurant market, Beefeater one-third of the steakhouse sales, and Little Chef has no direct competitor.

Table 10.1 *Major operators of chain restaurants 1993 and 2000*

Trading Name	Owner/Franchiser 1993	No. Outlets 1993	Owner/Franchiser 2000	No. Outlets 2000
Little Chef	Forte	350	Compass	435
Pizza Hut	Whitbread/Pepsico	293	Whitbread/Tricon	439
Beefeater	Whitbread	280	Whitbread	257
Wimpy	Wimpy International	230		
Perfect Pizza	Scott's Hospitality	241		
Toby Restaurants	Bass	200	Six Continents	127
Big Steak Pubs	Allied-Lyons	170		
Pizza Express			Pizza Express	256
Brewers Fayre			Whitbread	380
Harvester			Six Continents	129

Source: Keynote (1994)/Company Reports/Trade Press/Keynote (2000c)

In addition to these main brands, there are also a number of smaller chains based around 'theme' concepts. City Centre restaurants is the UK's largest independent restaurant company with 210 restaurants. Its brands include Garfunkels, Deep Pan Pizza, Café Uno, Frankie & Benny's (whose menu may be seen in Figure 10.4), Est Est Est and Wok Wok. Compass operates the Harry Ramsden chain of fish restaurants, and a new independent chain Fish! has recently come into the market. Scottish & Newcastle operate the Old Orleans theme restaurant chain, whilst Whitbread have the TGIFridays franchise (32 outlets). Other Whitbread restaurant brands include Café Rouge (103 outlets), Bella Pasta (73 outlets) and Mamma Amalfi. Chains with around 20 to 30 outlets inlcude Angus Steak House, Ask (pizza concept), Brannigans, Conran Restaurants, Chez Gerard, Mongolian Barbeque, Nandos (up-market chicken concept), and Yo! Sushi. A clear trend in the branding of restaurant chains is the use of the exclamation mark!

UNDERSTANDING THE RESTAURANT CUSTOMER

If the restaurant sector is made up of a number of different types of restaurant, it

Minestrone soup
Prepared to Mamma's own recipe, topped with fresh parmesan.
£2.65

Garlic Pizza Bread
Our best pizza dough freshly baked.
£2.15

Baked Flat Mushrooms
Filled with Cousin Luigi's herb and garlic stuffing, served with a spicy tomato dip.
£3.15

Potato Skins
Filled with either bacon and cheese or cheese and chives, served with a sour cream dip.
£3.65

Mamma's Cheese Bake
A blend of our finest cheeses, baked on Mamma's Neopolitan sauce and served with warm ciabatta bread for dipping
£3.95

BBQ Chicken Wings
Our classic BBQ wings served with celery, honey and mustard sauce and sour cream. Enough for two to share
£5.95

Frankie's Fried Calamari
Crisp fried in our garlic and parmesan flavoured coating, served with a warm Neapolitan sauce.
£3.95

Avocado and Prawns
Fanned avocado and prawns served with a generous helping of spicy 1000 island dressing.
£3.95

Meatballs on Spaghetti
Classic New York home-style meatballs. Prepared to our own recipe mounded on spaghetti tossed with Cousin Mario's beef ragu.
£6.65

Penne Pasta, Pesto and Chicken
The house favourite. A great combination of sliced chicken breast, pasta pasta, pesto sauce, (pine nuts, basil, parmesan cheese and olive oil) and diced tomato. Served with lots of freshly ground black pepper.
£6.95

Frankie's Steak Ciabatta Sandwich
A chargrilled 4oz* sirloin steak on toasted ciabatta bread, dressed with a pesto mayonnaise, topped with crisp lettuce and red onion.Served with tomato, mozzarella, pesto oil and house fries.
£6.75

Chicken Parmigana Sandwich
Frankie's famous chicken parmigana served as a classic New York style sandwich. Served in ciabatta bread with house fries.
£7.25

Warm Chicken Salad
Sautéed pieces of chicken breast, red onion and mushrooms glazed in our balsamic dressing over mixed salad leaves with cucumber, peppers and tomato. Served with a portion of ciabatta bread.
£7.75

Avocado and Bacon Salad
Diced avocado and crispy bacon served with honey and mustard dressed salad leaves, mozzarella and croutons.
£7.75

Figure 10.4 *Restaurant menu*
Source: Frankie and Benny's

follows that each of these is directed towards market segments. For instance, Muller and Woods propose that each of their types of restaurant has distinctive 'customer decision attributes'. The mid-scale restaurant offers value, comfort, table and counter service, with a appropriate menu mix and choice. In using a moderate upscale restaurant the customer is making a 'fashion statement' and seeking ambience. The up-scale restaurant customer is very much into the full meal experience, with a great deal of style, ambience and service. While the business dining customer wants an easy purchase decision, value, and an accessible location. The differences between these styles of restaurant are illustrated in Figures 10.2, 10.3 and 10.5.

Dining out in the UK has steadily increased over the past decade. In 1999 50.8 per cent of those surveyed ate out at lunchtime and 62 per cent in the evening. Between 1994 and 1998, household expenditure on eating out increased by 17.2 per cent. By 1998, £6.73 was spent per week on eating out, in comparison to 1992 when the average amount spent per week on eating out was only £1.72. A key influence to this increase is the greater amount of disposable income, which has grown by 5.4 per cent in the past four years alone. With the number of choices and outlets emerging, the five types of restaurant most frequently visited are 'English', Chinese, Indian, Italian and pizza style outlets, which between them have nearly 70 per cent of the market.

Figure 10.5 *Typical up-scale restaurant*
Source: Conran restaurants

LOCATION OF RESTAURANTS

The diverse types of operation and wide range of market segments served make it difficult to be precise about the criteria for selecting a restaurant site. In addition, UK legislation and planning restrictions on the development and use of business premises for catering purposes often mean that foodservice operators have a limited choice as to where to locate their outlets, especially in towns and cities. There are therefore two ways in which an operator can go about selecting a site for a restaurant. The first way is to identify a location and develop the right kind of restaurant for that site; the second way, is to define the restaurant concept and then seek a location with the appropriate market demographics. The first approach is usually adopted by independent restaurateurs operating single units; whereas the latter is the approach adopted by chains.

Goldman (1993) compares and contrasts these two approaches, as follows.

The preselected location approach

The first step is to carry out an analysis of the secondary data available with respect to the chosen location. This is followed by a primary market study which reviews the competition and establishes the needs and wants of people in the area. Both this primary and secondary data enables the specification of life-cycle categories and trends, from which it is possible to draw up a specification of market segments. These segments are usually defined by age, income, and family structure. From this specification, a customer profile is drawn up, which then enables a restaurant concept to be defined.

The preselected concept approach

In many respects this is the reverse process. The operator starts with a well-defined concept, identifies the customer profile, defines the segmentation, collects secondary data on several potential areas, carries out primary research on likely suitable locations, and then selects the most appropriate market area.

Whichever of these two approaches is adopted the operator needs data on a number of key characteristics in order to determine the suitability of the location in general, and the specific site for the restaurant. Location selection criteria include factors such as population density, population mix, economic characteristics, geographic features, employment characteristics, and levels of competition. Site selection criteria include traffic flow, visibility, access, utilities, and traffic patterns. In the USA Melaniphy (1992) suggests that there are as many as twelve different types of site on which restaurants may be developed. The structure of the US industry, economic profile, geographic features, and other factors may mean that not all these apply to the UK. Types of restaurant site that are typical of the UK include city or town centres (so-called 'high-street' locations), retail or shopping centres, adjacent to or within leisure or tourist attractions, commercial areas, residential areas, or out-of-town sites.

OPERATIONAL FEATURES

In 1981, Jones wrote 'In view of the wide diversity [in the restaurant industry], no clear service style can clearly be identified.' Since then, Cousins and Lillicrap (1999) have redefined styles of foodservice, so that it is now possible to say that predominant style of service in restaurants is 'service at a laid cover'. Within this category food is served in a number of ways.

Plate service

This style of service has the food item plated then individually served to each customer. In the 1980s, this was typical of the 'pub grub' segment of the market. With the growth of bistros, family restaurants and in particular nouvelle cuisine and other styles of gastronomic cooking, this style of service has also been adopted in up-market operations. Plate service is particularly suitable for this as it enables the chef to present the food artistically.

Family service

This style is ideal for use in restaurants serving Far Eastern cuisine. Eastern eating habits differ from the European concept of eating a sequence of courses, including a principal dish or main course. In India, for instance, food is traditionally served on a large tray, containing different dishes and accompaniments, and people help themselves to small amounts from one dish at a time, although there is no hard-and-fast rule for the order in which the food should be eaten. Likewise, in China, every bowl, from a wide selection is available to all diners and they serve themselves from each dish with chopsticks. Thus, in opening restaurants in Britain, Indian and Chinese restaurateurs have adapted their service style to meet Western demands, in a similar way to their adaptation of the cuisine to Western tastes. Family service is the practice of serving food in dishes, from which customers are expected to help themselves as they are placed on the table. Apart from maintaining links with tradition, this style of service requires fewer staff than silver or gueridon service requires, and also less training in service skills in necessary. The key element to the success of such operations is ensuring that the temperature of the food is maintained. This means that the kitchen must serve very hot food into heated dishes, customers must be supplied with hot plates, and that the dishes are kept hot by lamps or hotplates placed on the table. The restaurateur may also find that disposable table linen is preferable, as, in serving themselves, the customers may not be as efficient as a waiter and spillages often occur.

Silver service

This used to be the 'standard' style of service found in restaurants and hotels. Food is presented on 'flats' (serving trays) or in dishes to the customer and then served by the waiting staff onto the plate. Silver service originated because food is traditionally served on silver flats to enhance the appearance and maintain the temperature of the food and it provides the customer with a degree of 'service'. It is becoming out-dated because the economic necessity of using stainless steel instead of silver has removed one of the main attractions of 'silver service'. If food can be presented attractively on the plate from the kitchen then the need for service equipment, dishes and flats is reduced, along with capital investment and operating costs. Also, silver-service waiting staff require a level of skill and consequent training that simpler food service methods eliminate.

Gueridon

This style of service was developed during the Edwardian era and is symptomatic of the Edwardian's gastronomic indulgence. A gueridon is a table or trolley placed beside the customer's table at which the waiter prepares, fillets, carves and sometimes cooks the dishes to be served. This style of service is flamboyant and emphasizes the personal attention and service that a customer receives. It is also associated with menu dishes that are of the highest quality, and are very expensive, being based on classical French cuisine. For this reason, gueridon service is restricted to restaurants catering for a market that is prepared to pay the high prices that must be charged to cover operating costs. High costs are due to several factors – the service is labour intensive requiring a chef de rang and commis de rang

161

to serve an average 10 to 12 customers; staff must be trained extensively and paid a salary commensurate with their high level of technical skill; fewer customers can be seated in a restaurant operating gueridon service than other styles of service due to the need for space to move trolleys around the room; and this style of service requires relatively greater capital expenditure in equipment than other styles of service which, due to the expectation of clientele, is usually in silver plate.

FUTURE TRENDS

Many types of business, including restaurants, may be franchised, but the foodservice market is particularly suited to this form of operation. A franchise has been defined as a form of licensing under which an individual or company joins in partnership with an experienced organization for their mutual benefit. Such an agreement can be seen to extend advantages both to the franchiser (the organization granting the franchise) and the franchisee (the person buying the franchise). The number of franchise operations in Britain is changing all the time, particularly with the development of fast food, but restaurants that are franchise operations include TGIFridays, Pizza Hut and Pizza Express. A major trend in the latter half of the 1990s was the extension of new franchised brands into the UK, such as Taco Bell, Wendys, KFC, ChiChis, and so on. More recently a number of UK-based firms have successfully developed their own concepts such as Sunnyside Up.

Many of the chains are continually trialling new concepts and developing new brands in an effort to attract a new market segment or increase market share. These new restaurants are often located on sites where the chain has an existing restaurant with declining demand. Recognizing the 'daisy chain' of consumer behaviour, whereby customers meet in one place, may go on somewhere else, eat in a third location and go on to a club, the British city and high street often finds these outlets clustered together, with competing brands literally opposite or next to each other.

Finally, in addition to the well established ethnic restaurants, new-style cuisines have and will continue to become more widespread. This includes Thai, Indonesian, Japanese, Vietnamese, Lebanese, Caribbean and Cypriot styles of cooking. This is because the British holiday maker has now travelled further than the Mediterranean resorts to more exotic locations and because there has been an increase in the number of British citizens originating from these locations. New chains such as Yo! Sushi demonstrate this trend. But increasingly we are seeing the development of multi-ethnic menus, with dishes from a range of different origins, and so-called fusion cuisine, which creates dishes using cooking methods and ingredients from across different ethnic sources. Health and diet continue to influence menu planning, but more in response to consumers' perceptions of the need to eat healthily rather than their tendency to do so. The move from red meat to chicken and fish continues but is not rapid. The vegetarian restaurant chain Cranks ceased trading in the early 1990s and there seems no prospect that a new entrant will come into the marketplace offering only vegetarian food.

CONCLUSION

Restaurants in some form or another have a very long history, and there is no doubt that they will continue to serve food and drink for many more years. Despite the growth of fast-food outlets and takeaway restaurants, people enjoy dining out, and restaurants satisfy this demand, whether they are unique or part of large chains. Furthermore, it appears to be the latent ambition of many people in the catering industry to run their own restaurant business. This sector, perhaps more than any other, offers the opportunity to individuals to fulfil this ambition. A restaurant requires less investment than a hotel, it is smaller in scale than many other types of operation and has greater status attached to it than public houses or outside catering. In many respects, it fulfils the criteria of a business suitable for any budding entrepreneur. However, at the same time, it must be recognized that a restaurant is a risky business venture. Although there are examples of staggeringly successful restaurateurs, there are equally many unsuccessful restaurateurs. The main reason for this is that apart from being proficient and expert caterers, restaurateurs must also understand the market in which they operate. The restaurateur is selling a non-essential product – it is a luxury item – and must compete with other products for the customers' hard-earned disposable income.

The sector is made up of a number of different restaurant 'products' each of which is at a different stage of their life-cycle. Ethnic restaurants, especially Indian and Chinese outlets, are at the mature stage. The number of outlets has remained largely unchanged since the 1970s and the menu and concept is equally predictable. Steak-house restaurants are also at the mature stage, if not in decline, due to more health-conscious consumers. Family restaurants have grown rapidly in the 1980s and are now reaching maturity, with consequent 'thinning out' of major brands. Theme restaurants continue to develop and are still at the growth stage of their life cycle. But the most significant fact about the UK restaurant industry is the attitude the British customer now has towards eating out. Until the emergence and growth of theme restaurants in the late 1980s, people dined out to eat, often because it was convenient, sometimes in order to celebrate. Nowadays however, more and more people are treating the eating out experience as a leisure activity in its own right. Restaurant dining is not a substitute for eating at home, it is one of a range of leisure pursuits to be enjoyed. This more than anything will continue to transform the restaurant sector in years to come.

SUMMARY

This chapter has looked at the restaurant sector of the hospitality industry. It identified that there were a number of different ways in which restaurants could be classified, such as the restaurant typology and concept categories. The UK restaurant sector grew up in five distinct stages over the last seventy years, and is continuing to grow at a rapid rate in the new millennium. Many of the largest restaurant chains were developed in the 1980s and continue to be successful brands today. Despite the high profile of chains, the industry also includes a very large number of independently owned and operated businesses. Chain operators will tend to adopt a preselected concept approach to the location of their outlets, whereas most independents have a preselected location around which they fit their concept. Part of the concept will be the service style that is used. The chapter identified four main styles, typically found in restaurants, namely plate service, family service, silver service and gueridon service. The chapter concluded with a review of current issues and future trends, which were identified as franchising, branding, and so-called fusion cuisine.

FURTHER STUDY

www.ccruk.com

www.whitbread.co.uk/enjoy/restaurants

QUESTIONS

Go to City Centre Restaurants website (www.ccruk.com). and select three of their brands. Determine what type of restaurant they are, using the Spectrum analysis, their expanded restaurant typology; and their NRA concept categories.

CHAPTER 11

Foodservice operations in hotels

INTRODUCTION

Good cooking was brought to Britain by the great chefs and hoteliers who came from the Continent to work in the grand hotels of Britain in the 1880s and 1890s. For a long time the only place where one could eat in style was in a hotel, and during their heyday these hotel restaurants were very successful, although not necessarily very profitable. Hotel restaurants were usually the loss leader designed to entice the clients to book bedrooms. Restaurants acted as positive attractions and in assessing profit and loss many genuine costs were ignored or forgotten in hotels. But with the increase in the growth of restaurants, the narrowing of the gap between the rich and the poor and the increase in travel for business rather than for pleasure, hotels have increasingly become a facility for accommodation rather than for dining in. By the 1960s, the image of many hotel restaurants was old-fashioned and uninspiring, and the early 1970s saw a conscious effort by hoteliers to improve this image, typified by Trusthouse Forte's development of La Fontaine and La Piazza restaurants in the Grosvenor House Hotel in London. Hoteliers attempting to expand their market and attract new custom, have to create a new image. As Bruce Whitehall wrote in 1981 (cited in Jones, 1981) about many hotels' attempts to promote weekend food sales: 'an establishment which is full of expense account businessmen throughout the week may have difficulty in projecting the informality and liveliness increasingly appropriate to the British Sunday'.

Things remained little changed during the 1980s, until the recession hit in the early 1990s. As a result of this, there has been a quiet revolution in terms of how foodservice is carried out in hotels. It is a 'quiet revolution' because many hotels are not able to transform their provision due to constraints such as their star rating. Hence some provision, notably lounge service, room service, bars and banqueting has changed very little. The major change has been in terms of restaurant provision and breakfast service. In the mid-1990s two alternative strategies were pursued. Either hotels, in keeping with the strong brand image of the hotel, branded their restaurant provision; or they created unique restaurants to compete with independent theme restaurants.

THE HOTEL FOODSERVICE SECTOR

It is extremely difficult to establish the number of foodservice outlets that exist within UK hotels. In Chapter 2, we identified that it is even difficult to establish the number of hotels in the UK, let alone how many restaurants and bars they may have. In 1999, it was estimated that there were 11,450 hotels in the UK most of which would at least serve breakfast to their customers, this number has decreased over the years, a result from acquisitions and mergers. Approximately 29.6 per cent of the sales turnover of these businesses derives from the sale of meals, and a further 11 per cent from the sale of beverages. In 2000, this was estimated to be sales of £1.5 billion in food sales and £1 billion in beverage sales. If other lodging accommodation is included, such as bed and breakfast, youth hostels and holiday camps, the number of outlets increases to 49,000 (Foodservice Intelligence, 2000), with total food sales of £4.7 billion.

The main market served by hotel foodservice operations is of course the hotel guest. Hence the market segments using these outlets reflect the nature of markets attracted to the hotel property, as discussed in the chapters in Part 1 of this text. However, hotels also serve non-residents, competing directly with the restaurant sector. They also provide banqueting facilities for both residents and non-residents. Provision can therefore be divided into four main areas: restaurants (which typically account for 68 per cent hotel catering sales), banqueting (20 per cent), room service (8 per cent), and bar/lounge service (4 per cent). However, this breakdown of a hotel's catering sales mix needs to be treated with some caution. First, there can be wide variation between different types of hotel. Obviously budget hotels have hardly any foodservice provision, whereas business and resort properties may have extensive conference and banqueting facilities. Second, even within the same segment, hotel provision varies, often due to the original design of the property. For instance, the Churchill and the Cumberland are four-star London hotels within 100 metres of each other. The former has a restaurant, carvery, coffee shop and Japanese-style restaurant, while the latter has one restaurant. Third, the sales mix can vary from year to year. During the period 1990 to 1993 there was a marked decline in demand for banqueting due to the recession, which gradually began to pick up again in 1994. Figure 11.1 illustrates the nature of hotel foodservice.

FOODSERVICE OPERATIONS IN HOTELS

In order to adapt to the changes in demand for foodservice, increases in the tourist market and the need to improve profitability, hotel operators have had to examine critically all aspects of their operations. The foodservice manager in a hotel must therefore have a very clear idea of what each aspect of the operation is attempting to achieve and which customers' needs the unit is serving. This will ensure that the essential operational features of the coffee shop or floor service, for example, are recognized and maintained. After all, a hotel does not need to have three or four different types of restaurant, if all its clients' needs are the same.

Restaurants

Hotel restaurants vary widely in terms of the size and service style. A unique feature of hotel foodservice provision is breakfast meal service. Unlike the USA, where chain restaurants and fast-food operators have developed the breakfast

Monday Morning

This is typically the quietest morning. People are checking out of the hotel after their leisure break or having travelled down the night before preparing for an important early-Monday morning meeting. During the rest of the week we get plenty of our business residents using the Traders restaurant for breakfast.

Monday Lunchtime

We are getting into the heart of the week's business. We have business customers – anything from middle managers to managing directors. We also get some leisure customers who are here for a few days' break. But the bulk of our customers are business people. They are effectively adopting the hotel as their home while they are with us. We need to remember this and treat them well. It can be stressful for business people, especially if they spend a lot of time on the road. The hotel and Traders become a kind of haven.

During the day

During the day the business customer is looking for efficiency from us. They may be meeting colleagues or customers. We need to be friendly to them but to remember that they are conducting their business and want to appear professional. This means we need to be professional to them (they can take advantage of our meeting rooms and facilities if they need to). However, it is important not to be afraid to approach business people and offer them more to eat or drink. The knack is in getting the timing and style right.

The kind of business conducted in the lounge is varied. You get people doing business reviews. You get reps calling in to see people. You get recruitment agencies holding informal screening interviews in the lobby. The meetings are usually one-to-one. These meetings continue all day.

In Traders near leisure and tourist destinations you get people using the Traders lounge for afternoon tea and cakes before doing more sight-seeing. These people stay during the week and are usually retired professional people – very much the traditional Posthouse customer.

At lunchtime we also get day conference guests. We get conferences taking place drawing people from a 50-mile radius. They usually have food laid on as part of the conference but some do use the Traders restaurant. We also get older guests coming in for a meal.

Early evening during the week

Early evening we get some families with young children coming in for a meal. These are local people from different backgrounds. We also get some people popping in on their way back from work in local offices for a quick meal and a drink. Between 7.30 and 8.00 we get business people who have checked in, showered and want something to eat and a couple of drinks. We also get people having a few drinks with us after their conference. Later in the evening we get younger couples coming in to eat and some families with older children in their teens.

Friday afternoon

This marks a real change. The business people generally check out and people coming for weekends away check in. The demands on and of Traders change dramatically.

The Weekend

At the weekend we get families staying with us for a break. We also get people staying overnight because they have a family function to go to, like a wedding. Over the weekend you see a lot more children in Traders. It is very important to make families and their children feel welcome. In the past children in licensed premises have been treated as second class citizens. We need to reverse this and help the parents to relax. We don't want the parents to feel embarrassed and hide away in their rooms and not spend money with us.

We get all kinds of families who are attracted by the excellent value we offer. We also get couples for romantic weekends away and older couples too.

On Saturday afternoon we get people popping in to watch a cricket or football match on our sports TV channel. They usually have a few drinks with us while the match is on.

The service needs to be flexible enough to reflect these different markets.

Figure 11.1 *A week in the life of a Trader's Restaurant*
Source: PostHouse Hotels

market, in the UK breakfast is almost only eaten away from the home when staying in hotels. Until the 1990s, there were basically three types of restaurant found in hotels – the coffee shop, the carvery and the silver-service restaurant.

Plate-service restaurants

Typically, plate service is found in the 'coffee shop' – an American concept introduced into hotels during the 1960s. The operation is usually open from early morning until late at night, serving breakfast, morning coffee, lunch, afternoon tea and supper. In some cases there are different menus from each of these meal periods but more often than not one menu is in use throughout the day. The service style is table service or plate service, with all dishes portioned and plated in the kitchen. This American concept developed for a number of reasons. First it reduced the operating costs of conventional silver-service restaurants by introducing plate service, which increases the number of customers served per member of staff by up to 60 per cent, eliminating the capital investment in service equipment and reducing the floor space per customer by up to one-third. Second it provides a meal and beverage facility that serves throughout the working day to guests travelling from abroad, who may arrive from different time zones and require full meals at unusual times. Third it modernized the image of hotel restaurants by introducing a more contemporary and relaxed atmosphere, and meeting the growing demand for snack meals rather than traditional three- or four-course meals. Finally it met the growing demands of the American tourist market and the youth market. Today coffee shops are found on the high street (see page 204).

Carvery

A carvery-style operation is not a new idea – restaurants were operated in this way in the early part of this century. The basic concept is that roast meat joints form the basis of the menu. These are carved in the room and customers serve themselves from the carvery counter, selecting whichever meat and vegetables or salad they choose. The name 'Carvery' was in fact the registered brand-name of restaurants operated in this way by the J. Lyons organization and other firms have had to find other names to describe their operations, such as 'The Chef's Table'. The typical carvery menu comprises a three-course table d'hôte menu, with a selection of five or six starters, three of four roast meats and possibly one or two alternative main courses and a selection of sweets. Waiting staff take the customer's order and may be responsible for serving the first and third course, and coffee if required, while the customer is served at the carvery counter by a 'trancheur' or 'carver', who is usually dressed in chef's whites. The counter may be a straight line or bow-shaped and consists of boards for carving, hot cupboards or overhead heat lamps and bains-marie for vegetables. Sauces and accompaniments may either be served at the table by waiting staff or customers may help themselves at the carvery counter. The advantages of this style of operation are: the presentation and carving of meats and food items in the restaurant is a promotional tool and enhances sales; customers are allowed to select as much as they wish for an all-inclusive price, that promotes a sense of value for money; the menu requires a smaller kitchen area and fewer kitchen staff to prepare the dishes, as little or no cooking to order is done during the service period; and since there is an element of self-service, fewer waiting staff are required for a carvery than in a traditionally-organized restaurant. For the carvery supervisor or manager, there are specific potential problem areas. The policy of allowing the customers to help themselves to as much as they wish makes control and pricing very difficult. Many such operations have abandoned this policy by either stating on the menu the portion size or using portable carving trolleys with the trancheur serving customers at the table, rather like gueridon service. Since joints are pre-cooked, close control of the appearance and palatability must be exercized, and unused meats may be reused in rechauffe dishes or in cold meat salads to reduce waste.

Silver-service restaurants

This style of service is based around the service of food with a spoon and fork (or other appropriate service gear) from dishes or flats by waiting staff at the customer's table. This style of service was very common in the archetypal hotel restaurant of the 1960s and 1970s. Such a restaurant would typically offer an à la carte menu of individually priced dishes, based on classical French cuisine, along with a set price table d'hôte menu. Tables would be laid with linen cloths, silver cutlery, and crystal glassware. In many respects, especially in four- and five-star hotels, these operations had remained unchanged for a hundred years. Unlike carveries and coffee shops, these restaurants would be open only for lunch and dinner, and often they were staffed by men.

There are hotels that continue to operate one or more of these three types of restaurant. This is largely because hotel general managers and head chefs, with a Swiss hotel school training, are extremely reluctant to overturn the tradition of the 'hotel restaurant' based around classical cuisine, especially in London, and there has been a very low return on capital investment from hotel foodservice. However, a new style of hotel restaurant provision emerged in the 1990s not based around the restaurant/carvery/coffee shop profile. In essence the aim is to look at restaurant provision as a profit centre for the hotel and market it as a restaurant in its own right. This means that hotels are copying trends in the restaurant sector of the industry. Hotels can follow two strategies to achieve this and implement this strategy in two different ways. One strategy is to create a standard brand, just as the hotel is branded; the alternative is to create a unique restaurant modelled on current fashions and trends in that sector. To implement either of these alternatives, the hotel company can do so itself; or it can go into some kind of joint venture with another partner to do it for them.

The alternative strategy is to incorporate an existing restaurant brand into the hotel. For instance, the Hilton group has two Chinese restaurants franchised by the Zen chain and two Japanese outlets franchised by Hirolo in four of its hotels (Edwards, 1993). Likewise, the tropical brasserie theme of Trader Vic's, a Polynesian style restaurant/bar operation, has been incorporated into 21 hotels worldwide. The UK restaurant chain My Kinda Town is expanding overseas by adopting this strategy. The SAS hotel in Brussels has a Henry J. Bean franchise within it, with a franchise fee of around 7 per cent of turnover. Sometimes the restaurant chain is part of the same group as the hotel in which it is incorporated. For instance, Forte's Excelsior Hotel at Heathrow has a Wheeler's restaurant.

The alternative to branding is to create a unique restaurant aimed at attracting anyone seeking to eat out. For instance, Hilton opened an American-themed diner called Ike's at their hotel in Croydon. Operated by the hotel, it has its own budget

Figure 11.2 *Hotel restaurant menu*
Source: PostHouse Hotels

and sales targets. The same is true of the Pavilion restaurant at the Grosvenor House Hotel. This 130-seater restaurant has a 'bright, informal, non-hotel image'. It serves around 2500 customers with an average spend of £21. The Churchill Hotel also developed its own restaurant concept with a distinctive décor, ambience and menu.

The alternative to creating your own unique restaurant in the hotel is to get a restaurateur to do it for you. An example of this was Nico at Ninety, the joint venture between Nico Ladenis, the established chef-patron, and Forte's Grosvenor House Hotel on London's Park Lane. This restaurant was more up-market than the Pavilion and Ladenis had complete freeedom to operate the restaurant as he wished. He negotiated a five-year lease for the space within the hotel, although Forte funded the refurbishment costs of £250,000.

Lounge service

This type of service is now only provided in four- and five-star hotels or in those hotels where there is no coffee shop. The main food and beverage items served in the lounge are morning coffee and afternoon tea (see Figure 11.3). These are served in the lounge, partly for guests' comfort and partly because the traditional hotel restaurant needs to be cleaned and prepared between each meal service. Lounge service also provides for the service of alcoholic drinks to residents at times when the hotel's bar must close to comply with the licensing law. Nonetheless, lounge service is labour-intensive and demand is erratic, which accounts for its decline. It is common for a member of the restaurant staff to be rostered on lounge duties.

Room service

Room service must be provided in those hotels who wish to attain a four- or five-star rating, but like lounge service, room service is expensive to operate and demand is uncertain. In a study of hotel room service (Buick, 1994), 83 per cent of the hotels that were surveyed saw room service as important from the operation's point of view and 94.4 per cent felt it was an important service for their guest. Some hotels have replaced a few room-service facilities with vending machines, such as in-room cocktail bars or soft-drinks vending machines and shoe-cleaning facilities in corridors. To comply with the licensing law that only residents and their bona fide guests may purchase alcoholic drinks throughout the 24 hours of a day, they must be sited in the guest's room or designed only to operate for residents, i.e. using a special key. For those hotels that continue to provide traditional room service, breakfast accounts for 56 per cent of the total meals served by room service, followed by 35 per cent of dinner meals, and then lunch and snacks at 6 per cent and 3 per cent respectively. To simplify the service, hotels have encouraged the trend towards continental breakfasts, either by making continental breakfasts inclusive in the room tariff and charging extra for a full English breakfast or by making the latter only available in the hotel's restaurant or coffee shop.

There are three basic systems for providing service in a guest's room.

Figure 11.3 *Hotel afternoon tea service*
Source: Consort Hotels

Floor-pantry system

Floor service staff are based on each floor or every second or third floor and operate from a service pantry. The pantry is stocked with the goods and the equipment necessary to provide beverages and snack-type meals for those rooms that the pantry has to service. Any dishes or drinks unavailable in the pantry are collected from the main kitchens or dispense bar as required. The main advantages of this system are two-fold. Staff should be able to respond quickly to a request since they are located close to the rooms. Second, a customer who uses room service a great deal can achieve some rapport with the server responsible and feel a greater sense of well-being from the personal attention.

There are, however, several disadvantages with the system. Demand is erratic, peaking at breakfast time and in the early and late evening, so that extra staff must be employed at peak periods. Second a hotel with ten floors may employ five room-service staff, one for every two floors. If several guests on the same floor require service, one server is rushed and provides poor service, while others are doing nothing. Third, a server stationed in a floor pantry at times of slack demand feels isolated and lacks job satisfaction. Fourth, control of materials, foodstuffs and beverages is made more difficult by having several points and stock-taking also takes longer. Finally, ordering by guests is made difficult. Either they telephone the floor pantry directly, in which case they may be unable to place an order if the waiter is busy, or they telephone the switchboard or reception to order, from where it is relayed to the floor waiter, which is time-consuming and places extra strain on telephonists and receptionists. Because of these drawbacks this approach to floor service is rarely found, except if a hotel has a so-called executive or concierge floor.

Centralized floor service

To overcome most of those problems identified above, many hotels operate a central floor service, from which all floor service staff operate. As each order is telephoned into room service, the staff serve the orders in turn, irrespective of the floor the orders come from. This type of service is possible using high-speed lifts. The advantages of a centralized system are that fewer staff are required to provide a comprehensive service, especially during off-peak periods; control is made easier since the central point is usually located close to the main kitchen; equipment stock levels are lower, since it is not necessary to equip individual floor pantries with beverage-making facilities, etc.; valuable and expensive floor space is saved on each floor that may be better used for revenue making; the room-service telephone is staffed 24 hours a day by a member of the team; job satisfaction is enhanced by working as a member of a team and by sharing out the work load equitably between the servers.

Through reception

The most popular system for providing room service, according to Buick's (1994) survey, 60 per cent of hotels channelled guest enquiries for room service through reception, with only the restaurant having direct contact with the room service department.

One of the criteria for achieving four- and five-star status is that the hotel must provide 24-hour room service. Up to the 1970s, it was common for a guest to be able order anything from the hotel's extensive à la carte menu to be served in the room. During the 1980s most hotels reduced the scope of this provision as only a small proportion of certain dishes were ever ordered. Floor-service menus were devised to include the most popular items from the à la carte menu, plus some snack items from the hotel's coffee shop. In the 1990s, this provision has been further modified so that there is often a breakfast menu, a lunch/dinner menu available from late morning up till about midnight, and an all night menu with considerably fewer menu items. Typical dishes on room service menus are 'standards', such as grilled steak, American-style hamburger, club sandwich and Caesar salad. As we move into the 21st century, some hotels are leaving the 24-hour service and adopting a more practical alternative of only offering room service between the hours of 7.00am and 11.00am.

Demand for room service can vary quite widely according to the market profile of the hotel. For instance, the Churchill Hotel accommodates a large number of guests from the Middle East who make extensive use of room service, especially during the night. Changes to foodservice provision in other parts of the hotel have also affected room service. It was the case that guests were encouraged to take breakfast in their rooms, because silver-served breakfast meant that restaurants were crowded and slow. With the switch to buffet-style self-service breakfast, hotels now discourage room service. It is estimated that room service generates 4.2 per cent of a hotel's total food and beverage sales and although room service is slow, 70 per cent of respondents agreed that they would prefer to continue with room service.

Banqueting

Banquets, conferences, wedding receptions and dinner dances are an important source of revenue for most hotels. But it would be a mistake to believe that the hotel sector exclusively carries out function catering – outside caterers, banqueting houses, institutional and industrial caterers are other types of foodservice business involved in the 'banquet' trade. Functions vary in size from small private parties for 10 or 12 people up to large affairs for 1000 or 1200 people; they may be family celebrations, social events or business functions; the meal may be lunch, dinner or wedding breakfast; and the dishes may range from only canapés, as at a cocktail party, up to those to be found in a six- or seven-course menu. This diversity means that each function is different and must be approached individually, taking particular note of the function organizer's particular requirements. To enable the foodservice manager to do this, details of each function are usually entered on a function form or banqueting memorandum. Function forms have a number of advantages.

A well-planned form ensures that the caterer discusses all the essential points with the function organizer. It may be used as a contract between caterer and organizer. It can be circulated to all relevant departments of the hotel or establishment so that all staff are informed about the function.

The staffing of the banqueting department of a hotel will depend on many factors: the size of the banqueting rooms, time of year, popularity of the hotel, availability of staff, management philosophy, and so on. Broadly speaking a distinction can be made between hotels that have a banqueting manager and full-time staff and hotels that do not. Obviously the larger and more popular the banqueting facilities, the greater the likelihood that full-time personnel will be employed.

In organizing the banqueting operation in a hotel, pre-planned menus are often devised. These have both advantages and disadvantages. Pre-designed menus should ensure that the principles of good menu planning are adhered to. Function organizers with little catering experience may select dishes that they themselves like, without considering the impact that these dishes may have upon the meal as a whole. Second, menus that are planned in advance enable the banqueting manager to quote a price to the customer immediately, since they are pre-costed. The cost of a menu determined by the customer has to be calculated from scratch. Menus can be designed that accommodate the availability of both kitchen equipment and service equipment, without placing unnecessary strain upon the stocks of plates, cutlery, pans, etc. The quality of food served is likely to be higher if the kitchen staff are preparing dishes that they are familiar with and have prepared often.

The dangers of pre-planned menus are that they may not be flexible enough to cater for the wide range of customer demand. They may be too stereotyped and lacking in originality. They may be unresponsive to changes in the conditions of supply of goods and commodities, especially fresh meat, fish and vegetables. They may reduce job satisfaction due to staff having to prepare and serve the same dishes repetitively. It is therefore wise for banquet menus to be changed every two or three

Figure 11.4 *Hotel banqueting suite*
Source: Hilton Hotels

months and both banquet and kitchen personnel should be involved in their compilation.

The second element of planning is applied to seating and table plans for functions. In most cases all the possible seating arrangements of a particular function room will be well-established from constant use. The two main table arrangements for functions are formal (top table with sprigs) and informal (rows of round tables).

The third element of planning is ensuring that the proper number of staff are available and fully briefed before the start of the function, especially if they are casual staff. The briefing should include details such as the location of guest and staff toilets, the table or station each waiter is to serve, the menu and details of each dish, the order of service, who to see if a guest requests something unexpected, and so on.

Different service styles are adopted because of the diversity of functions. Broadly speaking these service styles are silver service; family service; plate service; and buffet service. Each of these service styles is discussed elsewhere and they are listed here in decreasing order of staffing requirements. The choice of which particular style of service to use will depend upon how much the customer is prepared to pay; the availability and expertise of the service staff; the size of the function room in relation to the number of guests to be served; the nature of the menu items selected; and the time of year, since cold dishes rather than hot tend to be served from buffets and are therefore more appropriate for the summer months.

Plated service is particularly the style of choice in London hotels, increasingly linked to cook–chill production. Hotels are attracted to this as the cook–chill entrée (and other courses) can be purchased from specialist suppliers economically, banquet production does not disrupt operations and staffing of other food and beverage outlets in the property, waiting staff need less training, and they are able to serve fifteen guests each instead of the ten with silver service.

Buffet style service

A buffet can be defined as a refreshment bar and the original style of buffet for a hotel or restaurant was a counter stocked with cold drinks, beers, wine, hot beverages, tobacco, pastries, cakes, sandwiches and ice cream. Today, of course, such a buffet is more likely to be found at a railway station than in a hotel or restaurant. Buffet service in the modern restaurant refers to the presentation of a wide selection of dishes on a buffet table or counter from which customers help themselves. It is a style of service particularly suitable for banquet catering or catering for guests staying on demi-pension or full-board terms, since the all-inclusive price can be calculated to allow the guests the freedom to select their own meals. The type of dishes served tend to be salad items, although there is no reason why hot dishes cannot be served. If they are, however, equipment such as plate warmers and hot-plates must be made available to keep the food hot and more service staff will be needed to help the guest with the service.

The main advantage to the operator of adopting this style of foodservice is that it greatly reduces the number of staff required for the meal service, while a neatly laid-out buffet presents the food in an attractive and spectacular way. It is not a service style that is appropriate for formal occasions. Important points to consider in operating a buffet are as follows. In order to accommodate the food for a large number, the buffet table may need to be quite long, in which case it may be advisable either to have two separate service points or to split the buffet in two identical sections so that guests may start at either end of the table. Dishes and flats must be replenished as soon as they are empty and where necessary redressed to maintain an attractive presentation. Staff must be available behind the buffet to advise the guests and help with their selection. Thought must be given to presenting the dishes on the buffet in a colourful and appetizing manner. There must be an adequate supply of plates and service equipment, and finally the buffet table should not be placed near to a radiator or in direct sunlight.

There are, however, problems with buffet service that must be recognized and dealt with. Wastage may occur if the quantities of each dish are not estimated accurately in advance. This is made difficult by the variety of dishes presented, so that predicting accurately which dishes will prove most popular is made more difficult. The type of food suitable for buffet service is perishable, and the method of presentation at normal room temperatures will tend to hasten the rate of spoilage. Suitable buffet dishes tend to be highly priced: cold joints of meat, dressings relying on oil, and so on. In addition, to present the food as attractively as possible, the decoration of the dishes will increase both food and labout cost. The preparation of a good buffet is a skilled job, making difficult demands upon the expertise of the kitchen staff; and futhermore, by placing a buffet in a room the seating capacity is reduced, and thus revenue also is potentially lost.

FOODSERVICE ORGANIZATION IN HOTELS

The internal organization of food service in a hotel will depend upon the size, style and turnover of the unit, which as we have seen can vary quite widely from one hotel to another. It will also be greatly influenced by the management policy of the hotel company's directors. In a small hotel, the director may well also be the manager and the management structure may be relatively simple. In effect, control and direction is in the hands of one person, with supervising staff reporting directly to that person. In much larger hotels the management structure is very much more complex and various grades of managers and supervisors can be identified. Within such a hierarchy, the role of food and beverage managers varies widely, and in many hotels, he or she will have two distinct functions.

In some hotels, the manager will be responsible for carrying out, rather than instigating, policies with regard to the provision of food and drink. This will cover all aspects of food service – monitoring suppliers and foodstuffs received, monitoring standards of cuisine and service, staffing the restaurants and bars, promoting food and drink sales, liaising with the customers themselves, appraising costs and turnover and most importantly, ensuring that a satifactory gross profit margin is maintained. In this respect, a food and beverage manager is no different from managers in other sectors of the catering industry.

As a member of the management team, the food and beverage manager will be placed on call, usually during a day or evening shift, to be responsible for all the activities of the hotel's operations. In addition to routine duty management tasks such as checking security, supervising staff and so on, the duty manager is expected to deal with any ordinary events such as staff absences, guest complaints, and so on. Thus, a food and beverage manager in a hotel needs knowledge and skills of hotelkeeping in addition to those of catering. At the same time, within the larger hotels, he or she is supported by specialist staff such as personnel and training managers, controllers and sales personnel whom other sectors of the industry do not employ, at least within the unit. The food and beverage manager in a hotel is very much a part of the management team within the hotel; in popular, industrial and institutional catering, the manager is usually in sole charge of the unit.

CURRENT ISSUES AND FUTURE TRENDS

Major trends in hotel foodservice in the USA (Weinstock, 1994) were more conceptualized and casualized dining rooms; standardizing menus and three-meal coffee shops; cutting wine prices; competitive prepackaged, all-inclusive banquet meals; and more healthy menu items. All of these can also be applied to the UK hotel foodservice scene.

The top two challenges were to 'help restaurant managers develop an entrepreneurial style that customers have come to expect at independent restaurants'; and 'create marketing and promotional programs to drive sales'. As we have seen, hotel operators have adopted four different approaches to this entrepeneurial challenge based around branding and/or joint ventures. With regards to marketing and promotion, three UK trends emerge. First, hotels no longer just think of their guests as their market. They are segmenting their foodservice offering into different markets with promotions aimed at each. So a hotel located in a business area may target office workers and business people at lunchtimes through local advertising and promotions. Many hotels have successfully developed Sunday lunchtime trade by promoting family lunches or 'brunch' aimed at local householders. Second, there is an increase in 'loyalty dining cards'. These are 'smart' cards that entitle the holder to a discount related to how frequently the customer uses the outlet. Hilton, Hyatt and Intercontinental hotel chains have all introduced this concept for their guests. Finally, hotel foodservice managers are working closely with suppliers, especially wine and spirits suppliers, to carry out in-house promotions.

There continues to be the trend of inviting high profile, so-called celebrity, chefs to take over the running of the hotel restaurant. Such arrangements vary, but increasingly they are joint ventures or leases. In 2001 Gordon Ramsay took over the restaurant at Claridges Hotel in London. In 2002, it was announced that Gary Rhodes would operate a restaurant in the refurbished Cumberland Hotel on London's Hyde Park Corner.

CONCLUSION

The foodservice manager in a hotel has a wide range of service styles and operations to deal with. Each of them has its special problem and the manager must be familiar with all the different needs and requirements. Each of the main areas will have a different clientele. In the restaurants, the customers will either be residents or non-residents. For many years, the residential diner was regarded as the cornerstone of hotel restaurants. Today, however, the hotel cannot rely upon residents to provide them with the turnover required to operate a successful restaurant. Thus the hotel's restaurant must compete, in its own right, with other foodservice operations found locally. Thus, the larger hotels have a selection of restaurants to compete with the variety of restaurants found in any main street – an up-market, speciality restaurant, a coffee shop or fast-food operation, a grill-room or steak house-style restaurant, and so on. Futhermore, to enhance this competitive stance, these restaurants have a strong base and are marketed with the aim of attracting customers who are non-residential.

The room-service customer has a different need. Any guests who require refreshment do so for reasons of thirst or hunger that need to be satisfied quickly and/or discreetly and their expectations are that the service will be prompt and as good as they might get in the hotel's bar or restaurant. Finally, the guest at a function or banquet is there because it is a special occasion, be it a social event or business meeting. Therefore, the essential qualities of a good banquet are a smooth running, efficient, service, care to keep to the arranged schedule and food that is as good as that a customer in the hotel's restaurant might receive.

SUMMARY

Generally foodservice in hotels is not discussed separately from its accommodation provision. It is therefore difficult to obtain precise figures as to how much foodservice is carried in this sector. There are four main types of activity in hotels. The first is restaurants, which are often similar in concept and service style to those brands found in the high street. Hotels also provide lounge service and room service, although only in four- or five-star properties. Finally, a major market is banqueting, which in some properties can generate more revenue than the three other types of business put together. The management structure in hotel foodservice is more complex than in other sectors. Typically there is a Food and Beverage Manager to whom reports a manager of each of the types of foodservice (restaurant, lounge/floor service, banqueting) and an executive chef. Trends in the sector include a growing use of cook–chill meals, especially for banqueting, and growing synergy between hotels and established restaurant brands.

FURTHER STUDY

www.fourseasons.com

www.savoy-group.com

QUESTIONS

Go the Savoy Group or Four Seasons website. Select two of their hotels and compare the scale and nature of foodservice in these two properties.

CHAPTER 12

Motorway and roadside dining

INTRODUCTION

Roadside dining is not a new idea. The original coaching inns were established in order to serve customers travelling the length and breadth of Britain by road. Just as the railway was significant in the development of hotels, the motorcar has played a major role in the development of the catering industry. In the 1950s, the number of cars increased by over 200 per cent, and by nearly 140 per cent in the 1960s. By 1992 there were 20 million vehicles on the road, nearly 16 times more car traffic than fifty years earlier. Between 1989 and 1999 motorway traffic increased by a further 42 per cent, yet motorways account for less than 1 per cent of total road length in the UK. The impact of this growth on the foodservice industry was first felt in the 1960s. Prior to the emergence of restaurant chains, roadside catering was either provided by pubs and hotels, or the archetypal transport café. But in 1959 Forte opened the first Little Chef. This was based on American style roadside diners orginally and was little more than a hamburger and hot dog stand. Quite quickly these units were developed into table service restaurants.

One year later in 1960 the first motorway service area (MSA) was built on the M1 at Newport Pagnell. At this time it had 20,000 vehicles per day passing by; in 1998 it was over one million vehicles a week, averaging 88,000 a day. The first MSAs were fairly rudimentary, consisting of little more than a petrol filling station, toilets, and a cafeteria. Since the original legislation that enabled these MSAs requires operators to pay annual rents that increased with turnover, there was little incentive to invest. An editorial in the Daily Mirror in the late 1970s stated that 'British Rail catering, on the way up, passed motorway cafes, on the way down, some time ago' and certainly during that time motorway catering faced a great deal of criticism. In fact in 1978, the situation was so serious that the government set up the Prior Commission to look into the whole question of motorway service areas. The report said that the service areas provide many things including petrol, breakdown/repair facilities, toilets, retail shopping, catering in a wide variety of units and even overnight accommodation. But the legislation that had originally set them up was too detailed and complex. Therefore revised conditions were established and operators were granted 50-year leases. Thereafter provision had to guarantee 24-hour parking, petrol, toilets and some form of catering.

In the 2000s two main sectors remain distinct – motorway service catering and roadside restaurants. Each of these will be looked at separately, even though Compass has a significant role in both sectors. Current trends and future developments in motorway and roadside catering will be considered at the end of the chapter.

180

MOTORWAY SERVICES

It is possible to clearly specify motorway service areas as all sites in England are currently owned and controlled by the Department of Transport. However, in the first major change since 1978, the UK government announced in August 1992 changes in policy towards deregulation. These changes included reduction in the minimum interval between MSAs and hence an increase in the number of possible sites, MSAs have to be 15 miles apart; privatization of site ownership, largely by enabling the existing leaseholders to purchase their sites; relaxation of control over site development, by enabling private sector developers to apply directly to local authorities; and some modifications to the restrictions placed on operators with regard to minimum levels of service. These restrictions required a minimum number of parking spaces in relation to the existing and projected traffic flows past the site, disabled access, 24 hour petrol, and a minimum level of catering. During the consultation between the DoT, MSA operators, motoring organizations, local authorities and other interested parties, it had been proposed to allow the sale of alcohol at MSAs and the development of large retail stores and leisure complexes. These proposals were rejected. MSAs exist solely for the convenience and use of the travelling public – motorists, coach passengers, and commercial drivers. There is also the growth of accommodation provision at MSAs. Such budget hotels have already been discussed in Chapter 5.

Size of the sector

Only 1 per cent of all public roads in Great Britain are motorways. There are just over 3000 kilometres of such highways. However, motorways carry per kilometre very much more traffic than other roads. During the 1980s this type of road had 20 per cent growth, compared with only 2 per cent on principal and trunk roads. By 1999 there were 84 MSAs in Great Britain, 30 more than a decade ago. Roadside restaurants had sales turnover of £570 million in 1999 (Keynote, 2000b), a growth of 26.7 per cent since 1995. In 1998 it was estimated that over 250 million people used MSAs, yet independent research showed that two-thirds of these people used the free facilities but bought nothing. The sector employs around 8000 staff, of which the majority are catering staff.

In 1996 Granada made a take-over bid for Forte. As it already operated Granada motorway service, it sold Forte's 21 strong Welcome Breaks in 1997 to Investcorp of Bahrain for £476 million. Welcome Break served 20 million meals a year and its turnover in 2001 was estimated to be £520 million. In 2001 Compass Group and Granada demerged from one another, eventually leading to Compass announcing that they planned to drop Granada's name all together. The Granada units were rebranded Moto. In 1998 investment firm Nikko acquired Roadchef. It is estimated to have an annual sales turnover of £280 million. The market is dominated by three main operators – Moto (42 MSAs), Welcome Break (21 MSAs), Roadchef (19 MSAs) – who operate 95 per cent of all MSAs. These operators also operate MSA-style units on principal and trunk roads. For instance, Welcome Break have two service stations on the A50, both of which have a Burger King and a Little Chef restaurant.

Markets served

One third of British adults have visited a MSA for a meal (Keynote, 2000b). Slightly more men than women use them, and younger people rather than older – which probably reflects the frequency of travel on motorways by these groups.

It is quite clear that MSAs serve the motorist when sales are analysed. Out of more than an estimated £1610 million total sales turnover, two thirds is derived from petrol sales. Catering represents just over half of the remainder, with retail shops a third. In 1992 the average customer spent £1.14 in the MSA restaurant (Mintel, 1992). The early 1990s have seen a great deal of market research by the major operators in order to understand more closely customers' needs. Granada's research (Tarpey, 1994) showed that its typical customer (75 per cent of the sample) was male, aged 25 to 44. In view of the fairly basic needs that MSAs satisfy, this largely reflects the pattern of motorway usage. So MSAs are used by ABC1 socio-economic groups predominantly, which reflects their levels of car ownership, mobility and affluence. But MSA usage varies quite widely throughout the year. For instance, on Saturdays throughout the soccer season, large numbers of fans use the motorway network to get to and from matches. Likewise, bank holidays and seasonal holiday periods may cause significant increases in usage, as in the case of MSAs in the north of England at the beginning of Glasgow's traditional holiday fortnight in July.

Location

It was the Department of Transport (DoT) that decided on the location of MSAs. Until 1992 it had a policy to provide sites about every 40 kilometres. Sites were acquired by compulsory order and then leased at peppercorn rents to operators prepared to develop the site. Deregulation in 1992 revised this to enable more frequent services, within 25 kilometres of each other. In view of the current size of the MSA network, this in effect means that new MSAs are likely to be built around the M25 or on new sections of motorway. Such development costs vary between £10–£30 million depending on the size of the site and extent of the facilities. These high costs have tended to prevent new entrants investing in this market. Adjacent sites are usually leased to different operators in order to increase competition. However due to the change in ownership of many sites – Granada took over Forte for instance, and then sold some of its sites to Compass – this is now not always the case.

Style of operation

A fairly typical MSA, serving one side of the carriageway, would have parking for 200 cars, 20 coaches and 50 HGVs; a petrol filling station and associated retail shop; a restaurant for up to 300 customers; a general shop; toilets and showers for men, women and disabled persons; and probably a fast-food outlet as well (as illustrated in Figure 12.1). Other facilities may include telephones, amusement arcades, baby changing rooms, bank ATMs, picnic areas, specialist retail outlets such as bookshops and gift shops, children's outdoor play areas, business centres, with internet access, tourist information centres and an area where drivers can join the AA or RAC. From the foodservice perspective the most distinctive feature of provision is the large-scale cafeteria provision which is almost unique to this sector. However, a significant, recent trend has been the building of fast food and other branded foodservice outlets on MSA sites. This is particularly the case with the provision of fast food takeaway provision. Thus Moto have a franchise agreement with Burger King. Welcome Break have McDonalds or Burger King, and KFC on some MSAs. And Roadchef opened their first Wimpy counter service operation on the A1M in 1994.

Figure 12.1 *Typical motorway service area*
Source: Hunting Aerofilms Ltd

But the heart of the operation remains the self-service cafeteria. These too are branded – Welcome Break have the Granary (in 2001 being converted into Food Connections), along with Red Hen, Caffe Primo and Brioche Doree. Roadchef have On Route cafeterias, Wimpy and Costa Coffee brands whilst Moto's brands include Upper Crust, Ritazza, Harry Ramsdens and Stopgap.

ROADSIDE DINING

The development of roadside dining, and especially the branded chains, is a story of new entrants growing rapidly, only to be taken over by the major players in the market. From its conception in 1959, Little Chef has dominated the marketplace. In 1973, a second chain, Happy Eater was set up and grew to rival this dominance. Then in 1986, Little Chef (with 270 units) and Happy Eater (with 85) merged when Forte bought Imperial Hotels, although they continue to be marketed as separate brands. At this time new companies entered the market with the intention of developing a chain of roadside restaurants. Kelly's Kitchens were created, owned by Bass, and then sold to Forte when 17 outlets had been built to be converted into Little Chefs. AJs Family Restaurants was set up by the former director of Happy Eater. This too grew to around 40 units before being sold to Little Chef. At the time of Granada taking over Little Chef there were 335 outlets. Now owned and operated by Compass, this number has continued to grow to 435 by 2000.

Definition and size of the sector

This sector of the UK foodservice industry is defined by its dominant brand. When we talk about roadside dining in the UK, what we are refering to is Little Chef. Other chains such as Happy Eater and AJs Restaurants have been taken over by this brand leader. In many respects it is a remarkable story. The hospitality industry during this century has seen a number of new concepts develop in the UK – fast food, budget hotels, food courts, family restaurants, and so on. But none of these concepts have come to completely dominate their segment or entirely replace the provision that was there beforehand. So although hamburger chains have impacted on fish and chip shops, there are still a large number of independently owned and operated fish and chip shops in the UK. But by the roadside, the traditional, independently owned 'transport café' has become almost extinct. There is now one unit for every 100 kilometres of the UK's principal and trunk roads. This success is one of the first examples in the UK of effective branding in the foodservice industry. The consistent standard of provision by roadside diners was so superior that market share was quickly established and maintained.

There were over 500 roadside restaurants in the UK in 1992, of which over 80 per cent were in England. The sector had an estimated sales turnover of £449 million, which represents about 45 per cent of the total roadside market (Mintel, 1992b).

Markets served

Just as on motorways, the average customer reflects the profile of the motoring public. Ironically, the very feature that led to the concept's success branding, has apparently failed to establish any major differences between the brands in the minds of most customers. One market survey in 1991 indicates that less than 30 per cent of respondents had any brand loyalty and this has probably been true for many years. A survey conducted by Happy Eater in the 1970s, before its takeover by Forte, showed that the principal reason people stopped at these outlets was to use the toilet facilties, not to have a beverage, snack or meal. Customers therefore tend to stop when they need to, rather than drive on to the next outlet out of brand preference. It is also the case that although the brands try to differentiate themselves, there are major similarities in the nature of provision. So although Happy Eater aimed at the leisure traveller with the family, and Little Chef more towards the business traveller, location rather than segmentation was the key factor in attracting custom.

Figure 12.2 *Typical roadside diner*
Source: AJ's Restaurant

Location

The cost of developing a site ranges from £250,000 up to £500,000. This kind of investment therefore requires the application of careful site selection criteria. Until the late 1980s, most developments were on greenfield sites. In the last ten years, such sites have become more difficult to find and the emphasis has switched to locating diners at petrol filling stations. In effect, small scale MSAs are being developed. The involvement of petrol companies and motor traders in roadside catering development reflects a trend: more and more new sites will tend to be located on petrol station sites. There are three main reasons for this. First, food and drink is not the only reason that motorists have to stop. Research has shown that in order of importance they stop to use toilet facilities, because of tiredness, to eat or drink, to buy petrol and to let the traffic clear. Second, petrol stations have both spare land for development and existing access off and on to roads, which makes planning applications easier. Finally, motor traders are facing stiff competition for tyre and exhaust sales due to the growth of specialist retailers/fitters, so they are seeking new ways to generate income and utilize space.

The single most important criterion for selecting a site is obviously the number of people likely to stop at the facility. However, simply counting the traffic flow is inadequate. Whilst traffic flow gives an indication of the total potential market, it does not indicate what proportion of these may use the facility. The potential usage is determined by other factors such as the location of other roadside facilities, ease of access to the site, and length of journey being undertaken. For instance, one operator opened two sites almost simultaneously. The site in Humberside had an extremely high traffic count, whilst the other in Norfolk a low count. But because many of the passers-by in Humberside were travelling probably less than two miles, from their home to work or shopping, whilst those in Norfolk were travelling at least 20 miles from one town to another, the latter operation was more successful.

Style of operation

The typical roadside diner comprises a table-service restaurant with seating for between 90 and 120 customers, a call order kitchen, toilet facilities, a small retail space often by the cash desk, and car parking for up to 50 vehicles. A distinctive feature is the restaurant's exterior and signage aimed at attracting the attention of passing motorists. AJs further developed the Little Chef/Happy Eater concept by adding a self-serve salad bar in the restaurant and a take-out counter. Subsequently, co-branding and micro-footprinting has seen many Burger King units installed within or alongside Little Chef operations.

The menu offers a wide range of items, drawing on a range of culinary traditions in order to appeal to all market segments. An example of a roadside menu is shown in Figure 12.3. Menus typically incorporate photographic illustrations of dishes which are designed to increase their appeal, influence consumer choice, and thereby increase average spend.

CURRENT ISSUES AND FUTURE TRENDS

The development of non-motorway 'service areas', the location of roadside restaurant brands on MSAs, and the development of budget hotels mean that the issues that face both motorway and non-motorway provision are increasingly the same and future trends will reflect this. Changing consumer tastes, that are affecting all sectors of the foodservice industry, are also impacting on this sector. The switch to healthy food choice and towards snacking or 'grazing' rather than main meals, has resulted in menu redesign and a gradual decline in average spend. The major trend up to the 1990s had been to extend the product range to provide a 'one stop shop' for all the needs the motorist may have. Sales have therefore grown from the purchase of additional items. Having reached the limit of what can be made available, the future trend will be to focus on increasing the frequency of purchase. Thus in redesigning nine of Granada's MSAs, an effort has been made to 'get the salesman, who's using [the car park and toilets] ... into the service area to use the facilities' (Webster, 1994) and once inside attention has been paid to design,

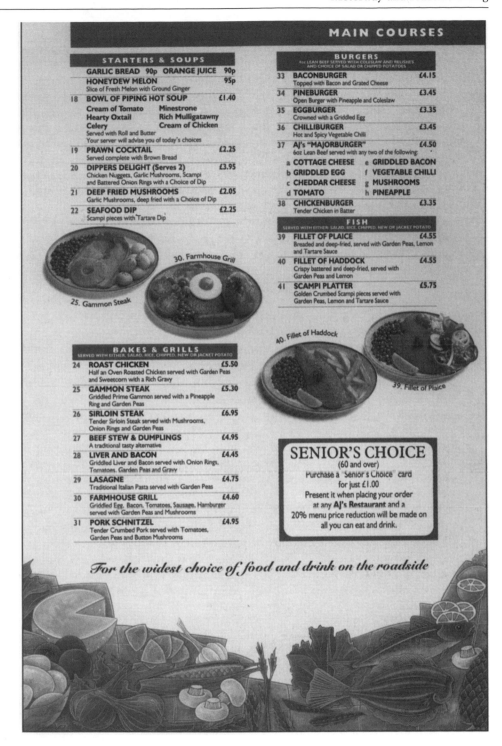

MAIN COURSES

STARTERS & SOUPS

GARLIC BREAD 90p ORANGE JUICE 90p

HONEYDEW MELON 95p
Slice of Fresh Melon with Ground Ginger

18 BOWL OF PIPING HOT SOUP £1.40

Cream of Tomato   Minestrone
Hearty Oxtail   Rich Mulligatawny
Celery   Cream of Chicken
Served with Roll and Butter
Your server will advise you of today's choices

19 PRAWN COCKTAIL £2.25
Served complete with Brown Bread

20 DIPPERS DELIGHT (Serves 2) £3.95
Chicken Nuggets, Garlic Mushrooms, Scampi
and Battered Onion Rings with a Choice of Dip

21 DEEP FRIED MUSHROOMS £2.05
Garlic Mushrooms, deep fried with a Choice of Dip

22 SEAFOOD DIP £2.25
Scampi pieces with Tartare Dip

25. Gammon Steak

30. Farmhouse Grill

BAKES & GRILLS
SERVED WITH EITHER: SALAD, RICE, CHIPPED, NEW OR JACKET POTATO

24 ROAST CHICKEN £5.50
Half an Oven Roasted Chicken served with Garden Peas
and Sweetcorn with a Rich Gravy

25 GAMMON STEAK £5.30
Griddled Prime Gammon served with a Pineapple
Ring and Garden Peas

26 SIRLOIN STEAK £6.95
Tender Sirloin Steak served with Mushrooms,
Onion Rings and Garden Peas

27 BEEF STEW & DUMPLINGS £4.95
A traditional tasty alternative

28 LIVER AND BACON £4.45
Griddled Liver and Bacon served with Onion Rings,
Tomatoes, Garden Peas and Gravy

29 LASAGNE £4.75
Traditional Italian Pasta served with Garden Peas

30 FARMHOUSE GRILL £4.60
Griddled Egg, Bacon, Tomatoes, Sausage, Hamburger
served with Garden Peas and Mushrooms

31 PORK SCHNITZEL £4.95
Tender Crumbed Pork served with Tomatoes,
Garden Peas and Button Mushrooms

BURGERS
4oz LEAN BEEF SERVED WITH COLESLAW AND RELISHES
AND CHOICE OF SALAD OR CHIPPED POTATOES

33 BACONBURGER £4.15
Topped with Bacon and Grated Cheese

34 PINEBURGER £3.45
Open Burger with Pineapple and Coleslaw

35 EGGBURGER £3.35
Crowned with a Griddled Egg

36 CHILLIBURGER £3.45
Hot and Spicy Vegetable Chilli

37 AJ's "MAJORBURGER" £4.50
6oz Lean Beef served with any two of the following:

a COTTAGE CHEESE   e GRIDDLED BACON
b GRIDDLED EGG   f VEGETABLE CHILLI
c CHEDDAR CHEESE   g MUSHROOMS
d TOMATO   h PINEAPPLE

38 CHICKENBURGER £3.35
Tender Chicken in Batter

FISH
SERVED WITH EITHER: SALAD, RICE, CHIPPED, NEW OR JACKET POTATO

39 FILLET OF PLAICE £4.55
Breaded and deep-fried, served with Garden Peas, Lemon
and Tartare Sauce

40 FILLET OF HADDOCK £4.55
Crispy battered and deep-fried, served with
Garden Peas and Lemon

41 SCAMPI PLATTER £5.75
Golden Crumbed Scampi pieces served with
Garden Peas, Lemon and Tartare Sauce

40. Fillet of Haddock

39. Fillet of Plaice

SENIOR'S CHOICE
(60 and over)
Purchase a "Senior's Choice" card
for just £1.00
Present it when placing your order
at any AJ's Restaurant and a
20% menu price reduction will be made on
all you can eat and drink.

For the widest choice of food and drink on the roadside

Figure 12.3 *Roadside diner menu*
Source: AJ Restaurants

in order to encourage impulse purchases. But there is still scope to grow. The research quoted earlier showed that only one in ten people of the sample had eaten in this kind of operation in the previous month. The use of faster and more efficient cars on new and more roadworthy motorways, results in shorter, more comfortable journeys. MSAs are therefore increasing their advertising and improving their catering facilities to persuade motorists to stop and to guarantee them good service. A future idea that some operators are considering is the opening of a shopping mall in an attempt to lure motorists off the motorway to shop. There remains huge market potential in this sector.

The acquisition of Little Chef, first by Granada and then by Compass, has a seen a rationalization in the chain. In 2001, 35 smaller units were closed and only 12 new ones opened. Co-branding has also been further developed. In 2001 seven units were trialled co-branded with Harry Ramsdens, Upper Crust bagettes and Ritazza coffee. Sales increased by 30 per cent, so Compass plans to convert 150 Little Chefs to this format over the next four years. The cost of this is approximately £250,000 per outlet. The menu has also been adapted to include steak and salmon in order to encourage more dinner business, especially from adjacent budget hotels.

The strong branding of outlets does assure higher standards, but standards still appear to be low. In 2000 a consumer report by *Which?* Magazine reported poor quality in 39 different MSAs around the country, operated by all three of the major operators. Only one meal out of 39 was rated as excellent. In response to this, Welcome Break are explicitly competing on the basis of quality. Following a critical report by Egon Ronay of standards in UK MSAs, Welcome Break have employed the Ronay organization to survey all their outlets, approximately 100 restaurants and cafés over 21 sites, once a month. To underpin quality improvements the organization has reviewed its menus, standard recipes and ingredients in order to improve food quality. A further £500,000 was invested in replacement equipment, especially coffee-making equipment to improve beverage quality. And a £250,000 training centre was opened at the Membury MSA. Likewise in 2001, Roadchef announced a £30 million investment programme designed to redevelop three MSAs and upgrade the infrastructure on many others. This strategy and investment may be important given the entry into the market of a French roadside caterer – Eliance. Standards on French MSAs are thought to be higher, although Eliance is currently undercutting their competitors by 10 per cent. They currently have three brand new MSAs and plan to open 17 more in the next few years.

In 2000, the Office of Fair Trading (OFT) decided to investigate possible anti-competitive behaviour by MSA operators. This followed complaints from the general public that prices were too high when compared with similar brands on the high street. In response the operators argued that their prices reflected the fact that they were legally obliged to remain open for 24 hours and provide significant infrastructure that was non revenue generating such as access roads, parking, and toilets. Clearly competition in this sector is increasing.

SUMMARY

In some respects, roadside dining is not significantly different to the restaurant sector as whole. Many of the restaurant and fast-food brands found in high streets, shopping centres and suburban locations are also found at the roadside. The differentiating factors of this sector are the market served, ie the motorist, and the specific location of these outlets. The operation of motorway service areas (MSAs) also has some specific characteristics due to the way in which these are built and licensed. Most of the outlets are owned and operated by major chains. A major trend is the linkage of these outlets with budget hotels.

FURTHER STUDY

www.roadchef.com

www.welcomebreak.co.uk

QUESTIONS

How does the food on offer and meal experience differ in this sector compared with the average high street?

CHAPTER 13

Licensed trade foodservice

INTRODUCTION

Hospitality can be defined as the 'friendly and generous reception and entertainment of guests and strangers' (Thompson, 1993). This definition is consistent with hospitality's origins in the inns and taverns of Britain and the warm welcome for which they are still famous. This sector of the wider hospitality industry is still of economic and social importance, but it is experiencing major change. Ian Sproat MP, the Undersecretary of State for Tourism in 1994, suggested that 'the British pub provides a unique attraction for visitors to this country'. Research commissioned by the Brewers' Society in 1992 indicated that British pubs were popular with tourists. One American visitor remarked, (Brewers' Society, 1999a) 'I like them. I don't understand them – but I like them.'

This confusion is perhaps not surprising as the British system of bar ownership and operation has evolved over time to become like no other in the world. This chapter will explain how this historical development affects the present structure of the trade and how licensed operations are managed. It will also outline the current size and scale of the sector and key features of operations. Finally, the future will be considered – how licensed foodservice might be affected by current trends and the way in which pubs may evolve to meet those changes.

DEFINITION

Historically, licensed premises were called alehouses, taverns, or inns. Alehouses tended to sell only beer; taverns have become what is now commonly called a 'public house' or pub; and inns provided accommodation as well as food and beverages. Today public houses and bars are licensed for the 'sale of drinks for consumption generally on the premises' as defined by the Standard Industrial Classification (2000), but the sale of food accounts for a substantial portion of the receipts of these establishments. The licensed trade includes public houses, clubs, wine bars, and any bar where alcoholic drink and often food is offered for sale. Each requires a different type of license in order to be able to sell alcoholic beverages, which can stipulate the range of drinks that may be sold and the opening hours of the operation. Such premises and the food and drink sold, represent an important part of British social life as well as contributing considerable sums to the national economy through the tax which is paid on alcohol.

DEVELOPMENT OF THE LICENSED TRADE

The British public house has its origins in the Saxon inns and taverns which brewed beer and served food for villagers and travellers. As settlements grew in size and number, the pubs became communal meeting places for social interaction. The Industrial Revolution increased urban prosperity so that consumption of beer, particularly by thirsty factory workers, grew steadily. The Ale-house Act of 1828 repealed and codified the many statutes then in existence and formed the basis of subsequent liquor licensing. In 1830, licenses were issued to beerhouses in an attempt to reduce the consumption of spirits, but, in fact, more drunkenness ensued because beer became more readily available. By the following year more than 30,000 new beer shops were opened and this process brought the total in existence to 50,000 by the middle of the century (Medlik, 1978). By 1869 these 'beerhouses' had proliferated to such an extent that the British Government felt the need to monitor their operation because of the crime and disorder associated with heavy drinking.

Since then, both public house premises and their managers need to be licensed by local magistrates who have discretionary powers to restrict or revoke licenses in the public interest. These licensing laws had their origin during the First World War, when it was felt necessary to reduce the opening hours of licensed premises so as to concentrate the efforts of workers, especially in munitions factories, upon essential war work. Licensing regulations remained unchanged until 1988, when pubs were allowed to extend permitted opening hours in line with those of mainland Europe.

Ownership patterns have also evolved in a uniquely British way. Until the 19th century, all public houses were independently owned. The brewers, numbering far more than they do today, sought to increase loans made to publicans in return for the exclusive right to sell the brewer's beers in the pubs. By the end of the 19th century, with the stagnation of beer sales and tightening of licensing controls, the competitive forces increased. These informal loan arrangements were turned into outright acquisitions to prevent outlets falling into the hands of competitors. This process is called vertical integration and it meant that brewers could either run their pubs themselves by employing managers or selecting tenants who were 'tied' to sell their beers in exchange for a rental fee.

From the 1950s many mergers and acquisitions gave rise to a concentration of large numbers of tied outlets within a small number of large brewing companies, and, in economic terms, this is called an oligopoly. Since the 1960s many felt that this oligopolistic arrangement was acting against the public interest in reducing consumer choice and artificially raising prices. The Monopolies and Mergers Commission (MMC) report of 1989 was the twenty-third investigation into the licensed trade since 1966 which reported that a complex monopoly existed in brewing. The result of this report was the Beer Orders of 1990 by which licensees were permitted to purchase draught cask-conditioned beer from a 'guest' brewer. From 1992 onwards brewers' control of tied outlets was limited to 2000 per company.

SIZE AND SCALE OF THE SECTOR

In Great Britain 51,500 bars generated sales in 2000 of £13.75 billion, 1 per cent increase on the previous year's sales (Foodservice Intelligence, 2000). The sector employed over 830,000 people including 80,000 self-employed persons in 2000. There are over twice as many females as males employed in the public house trade, reflecting the part-time nature of much bar work.

The number of pubs in the UK declined by more than 7000 between 1995 and 2000, according to research company Foodservice Intelligence. Operators are aware that the public house is in danger of losing its time-honoured status as the centre of community social activity and may become yet another leisure activity, alongside watching videos or playing on a computer. To counteract this, the number of meals served and the value of food sales have increased. While alcohol is still the mainstay of the public house's income, it is representing an increasingly small proportion. Food income, however, has almost doubled in the decade from 1982 to 1992 and, by 1996, is forecast to represent more than one third of public house turnover. This is illustrated in Table 13.1.

Table 13.1 *Product mix of public houses % 1993–7*

	1993	1995	1997
Alcoholic drink	63	63	59
Catering	16	17	18
Soft drinks	8	8	8
Gaming, telephones, etc.	13	13	15

Sources: Mintel (1998) and author's estimate

The average sales mix shown in Table 13.1 hides wide variation. At one end of the sector there are pub restaurants which predominantly sell food. This segment was estimated to have sales of £1.29 billion in 1999 (Keynote, 2000b). At the other end the sector there is the basic pub, predominantly selling alcohol, of which beer is the largest seller. But even in the pub sector, food now represents on average nearly 16 per cent of turnover, with sales of £940 million in 1999.

Despite, or perhaps because of, these changes, the public house remains the most visited leisure venue, with around 70 per cent of the population paying at least one visit during the year (BMRB International, 1992). The typical public house drinker is likely to be male aged 25 to 49 years old and in the C1 social class (Keynote, 2000b). Women however, figure prominently in the once a week drinking category, and evening drinkers tend to be from the younger age groups. A Keynote (2000c) survey revealed that the public house is by far the most popular place to eat out at lunchtime, with food sales exceeding £3 million. The frequency of evening visits to the pub for a meal are less than in the daytime with over 17 per cent of adults visiting a public house for a meal once a week. Women are more likely to eat in a pub than men and the largest percentage of diners were in the age group of 25- to 34-year-olds. The consumer perception was that public houses food offered good value for money and was the best source of traditional British food, but that drinks were sometimes seen as expensive compared to the price paid at supermarkets. This is due, in part, to the control over wholesale prices which is exerted by major breweries, with liquor prices to the 'tied' trade far exceeding 'free' trade levels. With the advent of the Single Market in 1993, restrictive personal allowances for the import of duty-paid alcohol were abolished. This meant that travellers returning from the Continent could bring back unlimited amounts of alcohol for personal use, and current estimates suggest that this traffic represents around 12 per cent of the take-home trade.

Food being available is the second most popular reason for choosing a pub, after it being the 'local' within walking distance. The availability of food is of particular importance to women, people over 45 years of age, and those in the AB socio-economic group, i.e. the most affluent and the E grouping, comprising a large number of retired people. There are no significant variations in the pattern of pub visiting throughout the UK.

CURRENT STRUCTURE OF THE LICENSED TRADE

Since the Beer Orders of 1989, big brewers were required to dispose of around 14,000 pubs. The licensed trade sector has therefore become divided into three clear sectors: independent, pub companies and brewery owned pubs.

Independent sector

The free houses (free of brewery tie and often run by sole proprietors) accounted for around 30 per cent of the 50,000 total pub outlets in 2000. This phenomenon has occurred partly because national breweries have had to dispose of pubs above the statutory limit, and also because entrepreneurial operators have been quick to seize unique opportunities to break into the market. Within the independent sector, nearly all pubs are owned and managed by the operator.

Pub companies

Independent chains of pubs, i.e. not owned by a brewery, have over one-third of the market in terms of pubs owned. The majority of these, around 14,500, are leased or tenanted pubs. The major operator is Nomura with trading names or subsidiaries such as Inntrepreneur, Phoenix Inns, Unique Pub Company and so on. It operates 7000 pubs. Punch is the second largest operator with 5200 properties, followed by Enterprise Inns and Pubmaster. Punch operates not only regular pubs but also 'concept' pubs that are branded, such as Qs (sports bar), Great Local (neighbourhood bar), and Bar Room Bar (sells pizza from a wood-burning oven). One independent multiple operator with an innovative approach is JD Wetherspoon of London. Tim Martin established this company in 1979 and drew upon his legal training to convert prime high street sites into profitable managed free houses that numbered 438 in 2000. Wetherspoon's offer branded catering in one standard menu in all their managed outlets.

Brewers

Following the Beer Orders, some national brewers responded by re-focusing upon a single primary activity. National brewers recognized that beer-reliant pubs may not survive, and they re-furbished their managed estate in order to increase branded catering. The total number of national sector tenancies reduced by 50 per cent since 1989 because of the need to conform to the Beer Orders, and remaining tenancies were replaced with longer commercial leases. In 2000 only three national companies both brewed beer and owned pubs. These were Whitbread (4000 outlets), Scottish & Newcastle (3000 pubs) and Bass (2750). This was then reduced further to two when Bass sold its brewing business in the spring of 2000 to focus purely on retailing.

Pub chains now tend to 'brand' their outlets. For instance Scottish & Newcastle have four major styles of pub, as follows.

- **James H Porter** – community pubs with a great range of beers, wholesome value for money food and great entertainment in a safe, comfortable environment.

- **Cooper's Kitchen** – based in attractive rural locations specializing in home cooked food, well kept cask ales and great atmosphere with the highest standards of hospitality.

- **Baroque** – is a contemporary bar/café targeted at the more discerning customer. The design uses fresh contemporary ideas, natural wood and stone to achieve a truly atmospheric ambience.

- **Football Crazy** – a traditional broad-based community pub in the colours of the local football team as its point of difference. The requirement is for a franchisee with a genuine passion for football and a customer base who are 'united' by a desire for a football atmosphere at their local.

CURRENT OPERATION OF LICENSED PREMISES

It is difficult to describe an 'average' licensed unit. They range from old to new, in a variety of architectural style and interior decorations. Despite changes in the total number of outlets, their ownership and the development of pub brands, customers are still most likely to use the pub nearest to their home most often. (Lang, 1994). Like many hospitality operations, licensed trade units are focused upon operational matters such as preparing the premises and product for the arrival of the customer. For licensed premises, opening hours are those prescribed by law, and so the operation of supplying food and drink must revolve around those hours. In all licensed operations, whether independently or brewery owned, the manager holds the justices' licence and is responsible for everything which happens on the premises, although a licence may be held jointly by two persons. The nature of the trading hours of public houses often demands that the manager and staff live on the premises. Traditionally, public houses have been run by married couples, with one partner being responsible for liquor ordering and service, while the spouse deals with the cooking and cleaning. In many operations, this is still the case, particularly in small country properties, but in larger operations, the licensee, male or female, takes on a more executive than operational role. In the past, working behind a bar has been regarded as a temporary, low-skill and low-paid job, but recent calls for increased professionalism by organizations such as the British Institute of Innkeepers have encouraged greater staff training with the aim of improving product quality and reducing staff turnover.

Faced with rapid changes that have challenged its traditional stability coupled with the most prolonged recession in 50 years, its future is unsure. In the face of this hostile environment, public house operators have switched focus from drink to food, which has shown growth of 16.2 per cent between 1995 and 1999 (Keynote, 2000b). Free houses (without brewery ties) and managed houses have been particularly proactive in developing catering with tenants and leaseholders concentrating more on 'wet' sales. A survey by Mintel showed that approximately 20 per cent of pubs serve food all day, 50 per cent do so at lunchtime and in the evening, and 20 per cent serve at lunchtime only. The type of meals served is related to the style of the operation. It was estimated in 1991 that 8 per cent of sales were cold food only, 63 per cent were both hot and cold food served over a food counter, and 29 per cent of sales were 'restaurant sales'.

This has developed following 'two broad patterns' (Jones, 1988): snack meals and restaurant meals. Snack meals are consumed while having a drink in the bar area. They range from sandwiches up to hot, plated meals. Typically food is displayed in glass-fronted cabinets and plated by counter staff, according to customer's requirements. Customers may serve themselves from this counter, or if an order has to be placed, be given a ticket to be served when the meal item has been prepared. In this style of operation, the tables are 'pub style' and not laid up for meals. Often the customers collect their own cutlery and accompaniments from a service point. This may mean that the furniture is not ideal for eating a meal, as tables are smaller and lower than those found in restaurants. This is illustrated in Figure 13.1.

Restaurant meals in licensed premises are provided in an area exclusively set aside for the service of meals. Of the 29 per cent of food sales served in pub restaurants, just under half is served in restaurants 'within' the pub, and just over half in restaurants attached to but separate from the pub itself. Tables are laid up in advance, customers order from a menu and items are prepared and served to order. Therefore the distinction between what is a pub and a restaurant becomes indistinct. Perhaps the relative floor area of dining area to bar may be used as a guide, so that where the restaurant is less than 50 per cent of the total floor area the operation may be considered to be a pub. Alternatively, or as well, if 'wet' sales, i.e. sales from drinks, are greater than sales from food.

Thompson (1994) believes that larger public house operators have recognized the value of branded restaurants that offer a recognizable concept and standardized product offering. They have developed from 'steakhouses' into popular restaurants serving a wide range of food. The menu of one of these pub restaurants is illustrated in Figure 13.2.

Figure 13.1 *Typical pub foodservice*
Source: A. Carpenter

LICENSED HOUSE MANAGEMENT

As in many hospitality operations, the public house product includes such intangibles as atmosphere and warmth of welcome, and the professional licensee is fully aware of their importance. Traditionally, the acquisition of a licence was regarded as attractive to candidates with a service pension seeking a comfortable semi-retirement in congenial surroundings. Today, individual tenants or lease-holders too, have become more business-oriented and professional. This section will consider how licensed premises are managed and what skills are required of its managers. These skills are becoming more important because the licensed trade is currently in a stage of transformation to cope with a hostile environment. So the professional licensee needs social, technical, business and marketing skills

Social skills

The public house licensee comes into contact with many different types of people and so an ability to 'handle' people is important. These include customers, staff, suppliers (local, regional and national) and agents of regulatory organizations (police, customs and excise, income tax, weights and measures, public protection, etc.). Operationally, the licensee must be a good judge of character as his legal responsibilities include the duty to run an orderly house. This means that the

❏ **STARTERS**

GARLIC BREAD	£1.25
CHEESY TOPPED	£1.75
PRAWN COCKTAIL with Granary Bread	£2.95
HOMEMADE SOUP with French Bread	£1.95
KING PRAWNS in Filo Pastry with Dip and Salad Garnish	£2.95
HOMEMADE PATÉ and Toast	£2.50
GARLIC MUSHROOMS & French Bread	£2.50

❏ **SANDWICHES** (Lunchtime Only)

Choice of Granary or White Bread

HOMECOOKED HAM	£2.25
ROAST BEEF	£2.50
TASTY CHEDDAR	£1.75
PRAWNS IN SAUCE	£2.95
PRAWNS & CHEESE	£3.50

❏ **PLOUGHMAN'S LUNCHES**
(Lunchtime Only)

HOMECOOKED HAM	£4.00
STILTON	£4.00
CUMBERLAND SAUSAGE	£4.00
TASTY CHEDDAR	£3.50

❏ **FILLED JACKET POTATO**
(Lunchtime Only)

All served with crispy salad and a choice of two fillings   £3.95

HAM, CHEESE, ONION, TOMATO, COLESLAW, PINEAPPLE & BAKED BEANS (PRAWN & CHEESE IS £1.00 EXTRA)

❏ **MEAT DISHES**

PRIME RUMP STEAK	£7.95
MEGA MIXED GRILL	£8.75
PRIME FILLET STEAK	£8.95
GAMMON STEAK & PINEAPPLE	£6.50

Our Chef will be delighted to serve either Chasseur or Diane Sauce to compliment your Grill. All the above served with a choice of potato, fried onions, mushrooms, grilled tomatoes & crispy salad

CUMBERLAND SAUSAGE Served with French Fries and Baked Beans	£3.75
CHICKEN FILLETS Served with French Fries & Salad	£5.95
HOMEMADE STEAK & KIDNEY PIE with a selection of fresh vegetables	£4.95
HOMEMADE MEAT LASAGNE Served with French Fries & Salad	£4.75

❏ **CHILDREN'S MENU**

CHICKEN NUGGETS & CHIPS	£2.50
SAUSAGE, BEANS & CHIPS	£2.50
SCAMPI & CHIPS	£2.50

☞ *DAILY SPECIALS ALWAYS AVAILABLE*

☞ *PLEASE ASK TO SEE OUR DESSERT MENU!*

Figure 13.2 *Pub restaurant menu*
Source: The Pilot, Eastbourne

licensee or an employee, should not serve persons who are in a state of intoxication. In practice, this judgement is difficult to make and demands training and experience. Additionally, the vigilant licensee must be also be alert for banned substances such as drugs and for under-age persons in the bar areas.

Technical skills

The service of food and drink in licensed premises demands special skills. Cellar skills, for example, are concerned with good practice in the hygienic dispensing of draught beers, minerals and wines as well as the correct storage of both empty and full bottled and draught containers. Similarly, skills in food preparation and service are those usually associated with restaurants which can help towards offering an attractive product which will encourage customers to return.

Business skills

Although public houses are interesting sociable and friendly places in which to work, the licensee must not lose sight of the fact that the business must make a profit in order to survive and grow. Public houses, unlike many other businesses, are prohibited by law to offer credit for the sale of alcohol. This means that pubs are not so much concerned with chasing account customers for payment as with maintaining and improving margins in maximizing profits. Profit margins for 'wet' sales range from 50 per cent to 65 per cent and for food from 55 per cent to 65 per cent.

Marketing skills

Successful public house operations are those which have identified their target market and satisfy its needs, in the same way as alcoholic drinks manufacturers have done to good effect. This strategy demands flexibility and responsiveness from its management and staff which involves a closeness to customers and suppliers. It is important to monitor customers' expectations and perceptions as well as to keep in contact with materials suppliers, so that input prices and quality may be controlled. Larger operations and multiple chains are able to obtain competitive advantage over independent sole traders, in their ability to maximize volume quantity discounts, but all operators are currently aware that their retail prices need to be minimized.

CURRENT ISSUES AND TRENDS

Currently, operators of licensed premises are concerned with emerging trends, which affect the viability of their businesses. These include the following.

Market size

Licensed house retailing has ceased to be recession-proof and has become a part of the wider leisure industry characterized by greater competition for disposable income. Turnover and profits are being adversely affected.

Costs

Economies of scale provide larger organizations with the benefits of buying at advantageous quantity discount terms, but these are not available to smaller traders. The greatest cost for tenants or leaseholders is the rent paid to their landlord that is representing a greater proportion of their turnover. This turnover in the 1990s has been, at best, static, but while many commercial rents have declined since the late 1980s, public house rents have increased. In 2000, annual rentals of approximately £30,000 or more were commonplace.

Consumer trends

Profitability is also being reduced by falling beer volumes and the increasing price sensitivity of consumers seeking value for money. Pubs in rural locations have been particularly affected by drink–driving legislation and have sought to attract customers by offering reasonably-priced food. The expectations of customers continue to rise. Pubs are providing better facilities such as family rooms, better décor and no smoking areas, but such improvements are often beyond the reach of sole-trader tenants or leaseholders whose profits are being eroded.

Investment

The capability to re-invest is linked to profits, especially for sole traders. Licensed retailing is currently regarded as a poor risk by banks and building societies because of the number of recent business failures in this sector. Many publicans have sought to maximize the peripheral income that may be derived from such sources as gaming machines, juke boxes and pool tables. However among the large chains there is considerable investment. For example, Punch Taverns Group spent £90 million on its estate, the company claims that sales have risen by 20 per cent as a direct result of the refurbishing, whilst Yates Wine Lodges invested £104 million in media advertising.

Liberalization of licensing law

Following the success of extended opening hours during the millennium celebrations and responding to public demand, the government is currently considering changing licensing law to allow pubs to open for as long as they wish to – 24 hours a day, 7 days a week if they wish. It is also looking at relaxing the law as it relates to the sale and consumption of alcohol to young people, especially with regard to restaurants.

CONCLUSION

In 1866, Capper wrote:

> There has of late years been a very large falling off in the consumption of the liquors in which he deals, due almost entirely to Parliamentary interference with the trade and to the demands of the National Exchequer. Duties and taxation have been maintained at so high a level during recent years that it has become increasingly difficult for the licensee, faced with rising costs and falling sales, to make a reasonable living. In these adverse circumstances the licensed victualler may well ask himself how he is to keep his head above water.
>
> Capper (1866)

Although this was written over a century ago, it could be applied to the present day. Similarly Capper's suggestions to overcome these concerns are equally relevant:

- Professionalism: apply to the business of keeping a public house the principles that have been tested and proved sound in every other line of business.

- Scope: not to be content merely to sell the beers, wines and spirits which his licence permits, but to seek out profitable side-lines not dependent on the sale of alcoholic liquor – meals for example.

It is clear that the licensed trade sector is experiencing major changes which provide opportunities to review traditional practices in the light of emerging trends. Economic recession has accelerated the rate of change and demanded greater professionalism and business orientation in an increasingly hostile market. Those licensed units which survive will be those who recognize that good-value food provides sales potential if supported by service training and target marketing. These changes may serve to alter the business direction of the British public house. The traditional image of the beerhouse will be replaced by multi-function licensed outlets which resemble a mixture between a continental style brasserie, wine bar or restaurant and which more successfully meet the needs of their customers.

SUMMARY

This sector of the hospitality industry has gone through one of the most turbulent periods of change due to the Beer Orders that required brewers to dispose of many of their tied houses. The sector has also had to respond to changing consumer tastes, through developing branded pubs, creating wine bars, and devising pub-restaurants in which the food offer is a key element. The sector, especially with regard to conventional pubs, is in a slight decline in terms of the number of outlets. Broadly speaking there are three segments of roughly equal size – independents and free houses, pub companies, and brewery owned and operated businesses. But whether a pub is operated by its owner, a lessee, tenant or manager, a range of social, technical, business and marketing skills are needed to run it successfully.

FURTHER STUDY

www.pub-enterprises.co.uk

QUESTIONS

Identify how someone can go about operating a pub. What are the key factors that will influence how they run their business?

CHAPTER 14

Fast food

INTRODUCTION

Fast food has been one of the big success stories in the UK hospitality industry during the past twenty to thirty years. The incoming North American chains, their professional management and modern techniques and approaches, the franchise, the right locations and a number of converging social and market trends have made it so. Today the fast-food industry generates large revenues for its providers and is a valuable contributor to government income, economic growth, the balance of payments and employment. But the success of fast food is not restricted to the UK; it is a worldwide phenomenon with more people than ever consuming fast food both in their home country and abroad. Fast food makes up 32 per cent of the consumer catering market, which is a 23.5 per cent increase in the past ten years (Keynote, 2000d).

With this rapid and dynamic growth, fast food has made an increasingly significant impact upon our diets, our personal spending, our social life and the environment. The fast-food industry has also made a marked impression in the hospitality industry and other industries being the impetus behind numerous modern technological, marketing and managerial developments. The multi-unit chains have spearheaded many of these developments.

WHAT IS FAST FOOD?

Fast food has been defined in a variety of ways with no single definition or interpretation gaining a consensus. Definitions of fast food tend to be product-based, process-based or place of provision-based. Each definition has its own distinct features, application and values. Ball (1992a) reproduces a selection of fast-food definitions and suggests why it has proved difficult to construct a suitable widely-used definition.

The definition of fast food used here is product-based and focuses on the physical composition of the product. It contains four features which must coexist for fast food to be clearly differentiated from other products. These features are:

1. A finished product shelf life of usually minutes (e.g. hot fast food, ice cream) and on occasions hours (e.g. sandwiches). Rapid deterioration occurs beyond these times particularly without holding equipment. This perishability factor is consistent with that of service products generally.

2. Fast product finishing (and in some cases total production) and service times. The range of fast foods, demand levels, production methods and system efficiencies mean that actual times will differ from between 2 to about 15 minutes for products provided to consumers on site to about 30 minutes for those delivered to consumers off site.

3. A hand- or fingers-held product often accompanied with disposable packaging and sometimes disposable cutlery.

4. A low selling price relative to other restaurant products.

Because of its nature fast food can be consumed on the premises or off the premises as a takeaway, or a delivered product.

OPERATIONS IN THE FAST FOOD SECTOR

Fast food is supplied to consumers through a diversity of sources and in both the private and public sectors (e.g. hospitals and schools). Some private sector outlets such as McDonalds' restaurants, KFC outlets or fish and chip shops, specialize in the sale of fast food, selling no or very few other products. In others fast-food sales comprise only a part of the outlet's overall sales. In such cases fast-food sales can be relatively significant (e.g. a Pizza Hut restaurant, or an ethnic cuisine restaurant, such as an Indian or Chinese restaurant, with a takeaway or home delivery service) or minor (e.g. a public house, a garage forecourt shop or a supermarket with a takeaway facility).

Traditional operations

According to Ball (1992a), around the world, the fast-food industry is operating at different stages of development. In Britain fast food, in its traditional form, is a well-established part of the hospitality industry. Fish and chip shops, which sell what is considered by many to be the original fast food, have their origins dating back over a century. Some people claim that the first fish and chip shop was John Lee's in Mossley, Lancashire, which opened in about 1863. Others consider it was Marlin's in the East End of London, which also opened in the 1860s. Ethnic cuisine takeaways also have a long history dating back to earlier in the 20th century. The first Indian restaurant, for example, is believed to have been the Salut-e-Hand in Holborn which opened in 1911 but it was not until the 1950s that both Indian and Chinese takeaways moved into, the mainstream. Keynote (2000c) estimates there to be more than 7500 Indian and 11,000 Chinese restaurants spread across the UK. Traditional operations also embrace other ethnic outlets and sandwich bars. A number of characteristics are common to the majority of these traditional operations. These include them being small single unit, family run, and low capital investment operations. They also tend to rely on rather traditional and fairly labour-intensive on-site food preparation and presentation methods and make little use of sophisticated technology and marketing techniques. Together these traditional operations comprise a large, fragmented and heterogeneous sector.

Modern operations

Since the late 1970s the advance of fast-food chain operations, such as Burger King, McDonalds, KFC and Pizza Hut, has been relentless and widespread throughout Britain and is continuing unabated. The chains have expanded rapidly through franchising, and consequently have polarized the market between themselves and the traditional independent operations. A number of methods of involvement are used by the chains in the fast-food industry including company-owned and managed outlets, franchised operations and joint ventures. These are more fully explained in *Productivity and Productivity Management within Fast Food Chains*, Ball (1993). The chains are strongly branded, largely US-influenced and modern operations with sophisticated technologies. Operations are designed around systems of catering that have been likened to manufacturing production lines, with the design and layout of outlets, the scheduling and procedures of work being carefully and systematically planned to produce consistent and standardized products. Modern operations increasingly offer a combination of eat-on-the-premises, takeaway, drive-through or customer delivery service types.

Convenience stores

A new form of fast food to be developed in the UK is the convenience store. In 1987 there were about 2200 stores catering in Britain, with an estimated sales turnover of £882 million. Only a proportion of this turnover, about 10 per cent, is derived from catering sales, since a convenience store is essentially a typical, old-fashioned, neighbourhood corner shop that also sells food and drinks for consumption as takeaways. But for the retailer, catering sales have the advantage of about a 45 per cent gross profit margin, compared with 15–20 per cent on the other products they sell. About 10 per cent of the store floor area of around 2500 square feet (232 square metres) is devoted to catering food sales, usually located near the entrance. It is presented in a manner very similar to fast-food stores, through the use of illuminated, coloured menu boards, and refrigerated display counters. But there are no staff providing service to the customer. The customers self-select food and drink items off the shelf or from dispensers, heat their food in the available microwave ovens if required, and take their items to a retail-type check-out. It is expected that the average customer spend will be around 95 pence. The range of food and drink items and type of menu on offer varies according to the location of the store. Full-concept units are usually found near office blocks or on major roads. Such units would have the full range of self-service drink dispensers, providing coffee, tea, hot chocolate and fruit juices, along with a range of self-service hot snacks, such as pot noodles, samosas, Cornish pasties and jacket potatoes. The American influence is also present in some chains that offer tortilla-style items, such as 7-Eleven's 'chimichanga'. Smaller units would provide fewer hot food items, concentrating on sandwiches sold over a sandwich/deli counter. One chain is also experimenting with a new concept fast food: high-quality pastry pouches with spicy or sweet fillings, served hot – developed by a major food chain. Another distinctive feature of a convenience store is that it is open from early morning to late at night, seven days a week. The catering potential in this sector is great, since there are many chains operating on this principle, such as Spar, VG and the Co-op, who have as yet not introduced catering food sales into their units. The three major UK chains are Sperrings, 7-Eleven (part of the Guinness organization) and Circle K. The convenience-store concept has also been developed on the forecourts of petrol filling stations. Such forecourt retailing is becoming more sophisticated, although hot takeaway food sales are yet to become widespread. Tesco are trialing mini-supermarkets on Esso sites.

Coffee shops

The late 1990s have seen the emergence of a new style of foodservice operation, namely the coffee shop. It could be argued that these operations are not really 'fast food', but then they are not really restaurants or pubs either. They are included in this chapter because, like most fast-food concepts, they are often franchised operations serving a relatively simple range of products to the mass market in 'high street' locations. By 2003 it is estimated (McCuskey, 2001) there will be 2400 branded chain outlets in the UK. In 2001 Costa Coffee and Starbucks have 50 per cent of this market, with Coffee Republic, Caffe Nero and Aroma also growing rapidly. The past growth rate from 1996 for this industry segment has been at 20 per cent per annum and this is projected to continue until 2005.

The coffee shop concept is based around the idea of serving high-quality fresh coffee in a variety of styles, along with soft drinks and some food provision. The UK chain Prêt a Manger has a high level of food sales, whereas some other chains concentrate on beverage sales. But a key element of the coffee shop concept is the notion of image and style. Starbucks uses the phrase 'a comforting third place' in order to promote itself. This 'third place' is a comforting and welcoming alternative to home and the workplace. A Starbucks outlet is 'an intimate nook where sophisticated people can share coffee … community … camaraderie … connection' (Klein, 2000). Often the décor is specifically designed to match the locale of the outlet. This emphasis on comfort and style enables the operators to sell their products at premium prices, which with take-out sales result in high sales volumes. Another feature of the concept is a high level of repeat business. In the USA the average Starbucks customer visits 18 times in a month and 10 per cent of their clientele visit at least twice a day (McCuskey, 2001). The current trend is for these outlets to copy other operators in the fast food segment by locating their outlets not only on the high street but also in offices, in the suburbs, in healthcare, universities and factory cafeterias.

SIZE AND NATURE OF THE FAST-FOOD SECTOR

In contrast to other industrial sectors in the UK, no government definition or classification of fast food, fast-food operations or the fast-food industry exists. This means that there are no government statistics for the fast-food industry in its entirety. Furthermore the lack of any other universally recognized, accepted and used definition has resulted in different organizations and bodies producing varying figures of the size and value of the UK fast-food market. This means reference to the size data of any one source needs an understanding of the definitions used, the assumptions made and the data collection instruments employed. Any comparisons of size data from different sources must be treated with caution. Table 14.1 shows the relative size of different sectors of the industry in terms of value, as well as the growth or decline in demand for these products.

Table 14.1 *Pattern of change in the takeaway/fast-food industry (£m)*

	1995	1996	1997	1998	1999
Sales turnover fast-food/takeaway market	5,647	5,819	6,192	6,577	6,975
% change year on year	–	3.0	5.9	6.7	6.1
Sales turnover of sandwich market	1,800	1,944	2,092	2,223	2,445
% change year on year	–	8.0	7.6	6.3	10.1
Sales turnover of burger market	1,424	1,339	1,418	1,551	1,628
% change year on year	–	-6.0	5.9	9.4	5.0
Sales turnover of chicken market	325	351	372	392	412
% change year on year	–	8.0	6.0	5.4	5.1
Sales turnover of fish and chips market	715	744	791	825	846
% change year on year	–	4.1	6.3	4.3	2.5

Source: Keynote (2000d)

The strongest and most expanding segment of the market is in sandwiches. This market has seen a great deal of innovation in the variety of products on offer, in terms of both breads and fillings. This has appealed to customers who are concerned about a healthy diet and the time they have to eat lunch. Sandwiches are also sold through a wider variety of outlets than ever before, notably petrol forecourts, convenience stores and specialist chains such as Prêt-a-Manger. Following a decline in 1996 due to the BSE crisis, burger sales have continued to rise. The two major chains McDonalds and Burger King compete greatly on price and run promotions often linked to new movies aimed at kids, such as Monster Inc. They continue to open new outlets, but these tend to be smaller and in non high street locations, such as roadside or suburban drive-thrus, and kiosks in retail parks and MSAs. Chicken fast-food operators face very similar conditions to the burger chains. There is little evidence from this data to show a switch away from red meat to chicken, although this may be happening with respect to household consumption. Finally there was some growth in fish and chips, although somewhat below the rate of growth for the sector as a whole. This actually reverses a major decline in sales experienced during the 1980s. With the exception of Harry Ramsdens, this segment continues to be dominated by independent operators who do not have the branding and marketing expertise of the major chains.

Number of Businesses and Outlets

Most takeaway business is in traditional operations. This is reflected in Table 14.2 which shows that over 48 per cent of all independent takeaway businesses had turnovers of less than £100,000 in 1999 and 84.2 per cent had a turnover less than £250,000. Keynote (2000d) estimated there to be 45,130 restaurants registered for VAT in Great Britain and of this 27,000 were fast-food/takeaway outlets.

Table 14.2 *Analysis of restaurants, takeaway/fast-food businesses by turnover, 1999*

Turnover (£ 000)	Number of outlets	% of the total
1–49	2,805	6.2
50–99	18,665	41.4
100–249	16,500	36.6
250–499	4,540	10.1
500–999	1,600	3.5
1000–4999	905	2.0
5000+	110	0.2
Total	45,125	100

Source: Keynote (2000d)

During the 1980s ownership became increasingly concentrated in the hands of the large companies who have both increased the outlets in their chains and increased their proportion of the total fast-food outlets. Conversely the independents have witnessed a decline in their share of total outlets. It is estimated that over 4000 outlets are chain operated. Table 14.3 details some of the leading chain operators in 2000. Evidence of the rapidly changing situation can be seen regarding McDonalds who have opened over 500 outlets in the UK, as well as Greggs who are a rapidly growing sandwich chain. Market share in each segment largely reflects the number of units. McDonalds have 70 per cent of the burger market and KFC 70 per cent of the chicken market (Keynote, 2000).

Volume of output, meals served and numbers of employees

The fast-food share of total catering sales rose from 29.1 per cent in 1996 to almost 32 per cent in 1999. In 2000 Keynote Publications (2000d) estimated that fast-food sales in Britain were worth £6.9 billion. Hard-hitting promotions and heavy price discounting are hallmarks of the industry. Recent Department of Employment statistics, suggest that fast-food businesses are significant employers. In 1999, 361,000 were employed (excluding self-employed) in restaurants, cafés and snack bars combined with fish and chip shops, etc.

MARKETS SERVED

In spite of the limitations of the many existing definitions of fast food, and the consequent shortcomings of any related size calculations, evidence clearly exists to show that the UK fast-food market is large, significant and growing. The current popularity for fast food is due to a combination of social and other factors. These include:

- Greater average real personal disposable incomes although the recent recession temporarily affected incomes.

- Trading down from relatively more expensive and more formal catering outlets during the recent recession.

Table 14.3 *Major operators of fast-food chains (no. of outlets), 2000*

Operator/trading name	Ownership/franchiser	Number of outlets
Greggs	Greggs PLC	1,084
McDonalds	McDonalds' Corp (USA)	1,016
Burger King	Grand Metropolitan Retailing	608
KFC	Forte/Pepsico	480
Southern Fried Chicken	Fast Food Systems	450
Pizza Hut	Whitbread/Pepsico	430
Wimpy	Wimpy International	283
Perfect Pizza	Scott's Hospitality	206
Dominos Pizza	Domino's Pizza	201
Favourite Fried Chicken	Favourite Fried Chicken plc	91
Prêt-a-Manger	Prêt-a-Manger, (Europe) Ltd	90

Source: Keynote (2000d) and company information

- Less formal eating patterns and more casual eating – 'eating on the run' or 'grazing', as it is sometimes called, has increased.

- An increasing number of women going to work – women have less time at home to prepare meals and are more likely to be able to afford fast food.

- An increase in one-person households.

- Better access to private transport.

- Efforts of the industry to create demand by advertising heavily and offering a quick and efficient service at low prices

- Increased international travel has increased desire for foreign fast foods at home.

- Increased urbanization of population.

Analysis of the fast-food market shows that in 1999 sandwiches had the largest share (see Table 14.4). Sales of hamburger meals were the next largest being responsible for about 23 per cent of total fast-food sales. While there is growth in demand in the fast-food industry generally different parts of the industry have experienced different rates of growth. Market research has shown pizzas and ethnic meals in particular to have had the most rapid growth. The growth of the pizza segment has been helped by its healthy image and its ability to stand up to home delivery.

Growth in demand and consumption of fast foods is not uniform across all types of buyers. Total demand and consumption of fast food can be disaggregated into market segments with distinct buyer characteristics. Buyers vary by income, age, gender, socio-economic group, lifestyle, geographical location and other characteristics. Detailed consideration of these, applied to fast-food customers, is undertaken by West (1992). A profile of visitors to fast-food outlets (Keynote, 2000d) shows that the highest proportion of visitors is in the 15–24-year-old age group. The proportions of visitors to fast-food restaurants steadily decline as age

Table 14.4 *Fast-food market by product sector (total spent in 1999 in £m)*

	Number of outlets	Sales £m	% of total sales
Sandwiches	11,000	2,445	35.1
Burger meals	2,400	1,628	23.3
Fish and chips	8,000	846	12.1
Pizza meals	3,500	720	10.3
Chicken meals	1,100	412	5.9
Others	2,320	924	13.2

Source: Keynote (2000d) and author's estimate

increases. In socio-economic terms, a greater proportion of C1 respondents visit fast-food restaurants. The lowest proportion, by a striking margin, of visitors to fast-food restaurants is in the E group. By region, London and the South East had the highest proportion of visitors to fast-food restaurants which was in contrast to the South West and Yorkshire and Humberside. The regional variations in the proportions of visitors to fast-food restaurants may be due to the geographical distribution and density of fast-food restaurants rather than to any innate regional antipathy to fast-food restaurants.

LOCATION

One of the most important factors in establishing a successful fast-food operation is finding a suitable location. This is because fast food for most consumers is a low-involvement, convenience, often impulse, product for which they are not usually prepared to travel very far. This is unless perhaps the purchase of fast food is linked to other purchases, e.g. cinema tickets or other leisure products. Because, traditionally, fast-food chain operators have relied on relatively high volume sales of low unit cost food and drink items to ensure financial success, locations have been chosen where there are relatively large potential customer flows or concentrations of potential customers in close proximity. This helps to explain why fast-food chain outlets were originally located in prime high street locations but are now to be found in a wide variety of locations with similar customer flows or concentrations. As these locations become exhausted and their associated markets saturated newer locations will be sought.

The purchase, rental and rate costs relating to sites in areas of high customer flow are extremely high and competition for such sites is extremely keen from fast-food competitors and other retailers. Hence it tends to be the large chains who can secure such sites whilst smaller, more traditional operations, e.g. fish and chip shops, ethnic cuisine takeaways and sandwich bars, tend more often to be on secondary sites. These areas do however, still receive reasonable traffic flows.

Newer fast-food locations include shopping centres, either as stand-alone outlets or as part of a food court; most airports; railway stations and motorway service areas, e.g. KFC outlets can be found at certain Welcome Break service areas;

increasingly in educational establishments including universities and large schools; healthcare sites, e.g. McDonalds has an outlet at Guy's Hospital in London; sporting and leisure complexes, e.g. Burger King has outlets at caravan sites, Pizza Hut Express has a 3000 sq ft pizza slice operation in Thorpe Park while a mobile McDonalds fast-food restaurant is frequently seen at major sporting and other venues; defence bases, office and industrial complexes. A recent development has been the tie up of contract caterers with branded fast food. Compass, for instance, has acquired exclusive franchise rights to develop Burger King outlets at all its contracts in the healthcare, education, leisure, travel, business and industry markets. They have also recently acquired the Le Croissant Shop chain and have rights to run kiosk-style Pizza Hut operations, Upper Crust and Dixie's Donuts brands. Demand is therefore the most important influence on the location of fast-food outlets.

The decision about where to locate a fast-food outlet is basically comprised of two separate yet interrelated elements. The first of these is selection of a general trading area. Some of the factors determining the potential of a trading area include:

- population and population density;

- volume of traffic flows;

- income distribution;

- extent of housebuilding;

- nature and extent of competition;

- job security of population;

- health of local businesses;

- presence of advertising media;

- employee availability;

- nearness of supply source.

Second there is the selection of a specific site within the trading area. The key influencing factors on the potential of a site in terms of turnover, cashflow and profit can be categorized as:-

- convenience and approachability factors;

- legal enactments;

- physical conditions;

- occupancy costs.

To find suitable trading areas and sites, to acquire sites and then to administer them, most of the major operators have their own properties division. Property developers, estate agents and others may also approach the operators with sites which they think may be suitable. The major operators use a variety of approaches and computerized databases to evaluate specific sites and identify potential target areas.

PRODUCT OFFERING

Fast-food outlets sell a total consumption package, or what is sometimes called the service package. This defines the offer and consists of a mixture of elements. The food – the burger and fries or the fish and chips – is only one part of this package. Armistead (1985) considers that for a takeaway food outlet the service package consists of physical items or 'tangibles' and service elements or 'intangibles' and that these two elements are about equal in proportion. Table 14.5 details the main features of the total fast-food offering related to a modern operation. It should be noted that these features will vary in their importance to different customer types and will vary between fast-food concepts. The image that a particular fast-food offering has will also vary according to the customer type.

Operators need to pay attention to both sets of elements if they are to succeed – a fast-food operation which sells food which is satisfactory to customers, but which has a slow service in unacceptable conditions will fare no better than one that serves unsatisfactory food quickly in pleasant surroundings. However some elements can be regarded as core, e.g. food, while others might be viewed as peripheral, e.g. newspapers and after transaction services. Once a core element has done its job – met the primary needs – the peripherals of the service package feature next in the customers decision making. Often the core elements offered by fast-food operations are indistinguishable from one another in the eyes of the customer and it is only the peripherals which distinguish the offers of different operations.

The menus of fast-food restaurants/outlets have commonly been regarded as simple, restricted and built around core items such as hamburgers, fried chicken, fried fish, pizza, croissants, etc. This was indeed the case for most modern operations when they were launched in the UK in the 1970s and 80s and in the introductory stage of the product life cycle. Product quality control, standardization, franchising and the internationalization of fast food were all aided by this strategy. Several menu trends however can be observed as the fast-food market has matured in the UK, as markets have become susceptible to customer fatigue and as operators have sought sales growth. These include additions to the product mix. KFC now also sells chicken burgers as well as fried chicken pieces. McDonalds has added sandwiches, salads, baked potatoes, chicken items, pizza and Mexican food in some, if not all, of its outlets. Menu extensions like these have blurred the product sector boundaries and are typical of the industry in its mature stage. Other menu trends in the maturing fast-food market have been the introduction of healthy foods, more desserts, breakfast and children's menus.

ORGANIZATION AND STAFFING

Traditional hot fast-food operations utilize simple low technologies where the equipment is manually controlled and designed more for domestic than industrial use. They have relied heavily upon the social and technical skills: hard work, commitment and the attitude of their personnel (Gabriel, 1988) who in many cases have no qualifications and are self-taught. Outlets are normally small in area and cater for small volumes. Consequently staffing complements are low and are often

Table 14.5 *The main features of the fast-food chain restaurant offer*

Features	Description
Tangible Elements	
Food and drink	Traditionally limited menu
	Consistent controllable quality, precisely specified, equally portioned
	Relatively low prices
Secondary items	Newspapers, children's partyware
Physical environment	Clean, bright, modern, carefully laid out
	Air conditioning, washrooms, functional furniture, staff uniforms, parking
Packaging	Food and drink is distinctively packaged (disposable), easy to handle and for some items temperature retaining
Intangible elements	
Personal contact with staff	Encounter with customers is technology-led and usually very brief. An exception occurs with children's parties
Service delivery	Often a combination of eat-on-the-premises, takeaway, drive through or customer delivery
Promotion	Emphasis is given to value for money, consistent quality and cleanliness. Food/drink items may be distinguished by originality, size, cost competitiveness, fillings, health factors, etc. Promotions are usually bold and colourful to gain attention. Emphasis on children's offers
Outlet atmosphere	Often find bold colours, plants, music and noise. Other customers can be significant in eat-in contexts. Corporate identity prominent
Location	Convenient for the customer whether on foot or in the car and to the customer for delivery, accessible
Emotions felt by customer	Aim to satisfy with the offer
Post transaction service	Little emphasis as yet here. Burger King launched the 'BK Care Line' – a freephone customer information, complaint and enquiry service in 1991

restricted to members of the proprietor's family and, if needed, to two or three hired staff. Where hired staff are used they are normally service staff; family members are usually responsible for production. Complements of more than ten workers would be a rarity. Production and service are both labour intensive and it is usual to find separate workers responsible for each with little overlap of workers into one another's areas.

Modern fast-food units are staffed and organized differently. Those which need high customer volumes and throughput to achieve acceptable returns, e.g. high street operations are labour hungry and need staffing complements to cover long opening hours and probably seven-days-a-week operation. The standardized part-time staff permits greater flexibility. The organization of a fast-food chain must combine strong control with flexibility. Figure 14.1 shows a typical staffing structure for a fast-food chain with likely lines of reporting up to an operations director. The number of regional managers and area operations executives will vary between chains according to such factors as the number of restaurants in the chain and their geographical distribution. Operative staff work closely as a team with each member of staff having a specific task or set of tasks to undertake. Each team is organized and controlled like a finely tuned and well disciplined ship's crew and hence in many fast-food outlets members of staff are referred to as crew members.

Figure 14.1 *Organization chart for a fast-food chain*

OPERATING PROCEDURES

A fast-food outlet is a combination of a production and a retail service outlet. Modern outlets utilize manufacturing-style production methods and techniques similar to those commonly found in factories while simultaneously promoting themselves as food and drink retailers competing with other such retailers. They can thus be considered as both a small factory and a retail shop. Such operations, particularly those operated by the chains, have embraced the industrialization of service called for by Levitt (1976), in that they use mass production techniques, production line principles and systematic approaches in design, planning, organizing and control throughout. These approaches enable customers to be served quickly and facilitate the efficient production of a standardized product of a reliable quality. Operations are driven especially by organized preplanned systems, or soft technology, rather than being reliant upon the discretion, attitude or skill of their workers. Operatives use advanced equipment and carry out simple tasks requiring little skill. Levitt (1976) argues that these technological elements have been key ingredients in the success of McDonalds. Table 14.6 draws on Levitt's work to show the main features and potential benefits of the production line approach in the context of fast-food operations.

Table 14.6 *Features and benefits of production line fast-food operations*

Features	Potential benefits
Limited discretion of personnel	Standardization, order and quality
Substitution of personnel by equipment	Lower labour costs
Division of labour	Specialization of labour skills
	Better control of labour costs
	Simplified training
Standardization of service	Fast service at lower cost

Many modern fast-food outlets are built upon the operational target of closely controlling labour utilization and upon the scientific management principles of work organization, worker selection and training, performance monitoring and the use of scientific methods. These scientific methods can be seen in the way work activities are precisely defined and in the way the total job is broken down into a sequence of tasks, which in turn are broken down into the smallest and simplest of steps. Each of these steps requires the minimum of skill. Figure 14.2 details the steps involved in the task of producing a hamburger in a typical fast-food outlet.

In many of the chain operators, standards and working activities are clearly defined in an operating procedures manual. These are comprehensive documents often comprising hundreds of pages, and cover the whole operation. These manuals, as Ball (1992b) explains, are essentially guidelines for worker behaviour. Staff training is based upon them, work activity is conducted in accordance with them and performance is monitored and controlled according to them. The typical contents of a fast-food operations manual were discussed earlier (see Figure 9.1).

Fast-food operations use a variety of methods to produce food, as shown in Table 14.6. The choice of method is influenced by the ability of the food production area to satisfy the volume of demand and by the shelf life of prepared food. Like food production the service process is systematized in modern fast-food operations. From the initial customer contact with an operation, whether by telephone, fax, computerized message or in person, the service sequence is queue, order, pay, assemble order, service and consume. An exception to this arises with fast-food 'home' delivery service to the customer, where payment occurs after service. The control of food production to reduce spoilage is critical to fast-food operations. Limiting order takers, using a 'bin' person as in McDonalds and using

Time in seconds	Task carried out by crew member			
	1	2	3	4
0	Call out order for six more	Place top half of bun in toaster		
5			Place frozen 1.6oz burger on grill	
20			Sear burger	
50		Remove top half from toaster		Begin dressing top half of bun
60		Begin toasting base of bun	Turn burger	
80				Dressed bun to grill
90		Base of bun to grill		
100			Meat pulled and burger assembled	
110	Wrap-completed burger			

Figure 14.2 *Production of a hamburger using a griddle*
Source: Jones, P. (1988) *Foodservice Operations* (2nd edition). London: Cassell. p. 71.

communication/information systems between the production area back-of-house and the service area front-of-house, as in KFC and Arby's, are all ways used by fast-food operators to achieve this.

Staff training is vital for the production of a consistent product which satisfies customer expectations. The major chains place great emphasis on this whether it be intended for franchisees, managers or operatives. Operatives receive careful training. Just as operatives' tasks are broken down into small steps, so training programmes for operatives are built from small modules of instruction. Once the instruction has been delivered the staff are required to complete a questionnaire to

Table 14.7 *Classification of fast-food production types*

Type of food production method	Description of method	Extent of tie with demand	Application
Batch	Short duration activity	Unlikely to be tied to customer demand	Low-volume outlets or periods
Ongoing	Continuous	Not directly tied to demand but some forecasting	Very high-volume situations, i.e. busy outlet or peak meal periods
To order	Short duration activity	Directly tied	Low volume outlets or periods. For customized menu items

Source: Ball (1992b)

illustrate their grasp of the training. Cost and revenue control are rigorous in modern fast-food operations and, while often time-consuming and costly, are necessary to ensure that the very tight margins within which they operate are not jeopardized. Electronic point-of-sale (EPOS) and other microcomputer-driven management information systems are the norm and provide stock control, sales-mix analysis, staff productivity data, staff scheduling information, etc.

The success of modern fast-food operations greatly depends on their ability to meet the documented standards of operating procedures. In franchised fast-food operations the franchisee is bound by the franchise agreement to operate the business according to the documented procedures and is trained accordingly. Commonly franchised agreements give franchisers the right to audit the franchisee's performance based upon the laid-down operating procedures. The concept of inventory control is frequently used for auditing in both franchised and non-franchised fast-food chains. This is illustrated in Figure 14.3. McDonalds, like many other chains, have area advisors and performance audit teams who regularly visit outlets to check operating performance against standards. In McDonalds' case, they are especially concerned with performance related to QSV and C: Quality, Service, Value and Cleanliness. If a fast-food franchise is found consistently to be failing to meet standards the result can be that a manager is fined or the franchise removed.

CURRENT ISSUES

A number of contemporary issues, including those related to health, the environment and ecological matters, are in the ascendency which fast-food operators will have to confront in the future. Those who ignore them will do so at their peril – if not from a social perspective then certainly from a commercial one. Indeed fast food has been accused of many ills unconnected with foodservice, by George Ritzer (1996) and Eric Schlosser (2000) among others. On the cover to the latter's book, *Fast Food*

Figure 14.3 *Fast-food inventory control sheet*

Source: Jones, P. (1988) *Foodservice Operations* (2nd edition), London: Cassell

Nation, it is claimed that the fast-food industry is 'transforming not only our diet but our landscape, economy, workforce and culture'.

Fast food has received nutritional criticism from many quarters in recent years, which will undoubtedly continue. Some of this has been unjustified, unwarranted and sensational; some has been deserved. Lawson (1992) discusses why some of this criticism may be unjustified, but also, in common with Lobstein (1988) and Silverstone (1993) provides evidence to support the perception that fast food contributes to an unhealthy diet. High saturated fat, salt and sugar levels and low fibre content seem to have come under particular scrutiny. Some operators have responded to the nutritional issues positively and have made serious attempts to shed the unhealthy image of fast food. Nutritional information sheets are provided by the major chains while efforts directed at food include the development of new 'healthy' products, e.g. low-fat burgers by McDonalds and the experimentation of KFC with a Light 'n Crispy product with 20 per cent lower fat content than the original, and the addition of more healthy items to menus. McDonalds in the USA offer 99 per cent fat-free shakes, no-cholestrol muffins, frozen yoghurt, premier ice cream; gourmet versions of existing hot fast-foods and more sophisticated ethnic cuisine dishes are just some developments envisaged. The nutritional profile of fast food will also be enhanced by the continued shift towards the use of unsaturated fats, the development and use of new cooking methods, the continued search for healthy raw materials and the increased promotion and distribution of fast-food nutritional information. Perhaps these kinds of initiatives will result in criticisms being replaced by acclaim!

Green pressures from fast-food consumers, the general public and others, are increasingly being exerted on fast-food operations. These have related to a variety of issues including the types of disposable packaging used, waste disposal, litter and the use of natural resources. Again some companies have responded positively to these issues and have adopted environmentally-friendly policies, appointed environmental managers and taken other initiatives, such as waste reduction measures, litter patrols, the use of recycled materials and energy management. Other ecological issues include the amount of land used for cattle farming compared to cereal farming, the matter of whether rain forests are being cleared for cattle pastureland and the human health consequences, e.g. the possibility of BSE being transmitted to humans, that are associated with intensive animal rearing. Those companies which pay attention to such issues for whatever reason, and their motives could be cynically interpreted as mere tokenism, or as a means of gaining a competitive edge, will increase their appeal to an environmentally and ecologically-conscious public and will improve their image.

FUTURE TRENDS

Future prospects for the fast-food industry both in the UK and worldwide are extremely bright and the industry is expected to continue its charge forward. However, it is estimated that there will be a more moderate growth of 4 or 5 per cent by 2004. The multi-unit branded operations will lead the way for the industry and the future of fast food will be strongly brand related. One trend expected to continue is the increased diversity of fast-food locations. Fast-food outlets will continue to develop in non-traditional contexts and on new sites in the UK. Increasingly, fast food will be available in contract catering sites, pubs, hotels, restaurants, leisure complexes, petrol station forecourts, newsagents, and via in-store concessions and in-house operations in large supermarkets and stores both in urban areas and in out-of-town retailing parks. Some of this development will be aided by the development of franchised small fast-food bar units, requiring lower capital investment: what was identified in Chapter 1 as 'micro-footprinting'.

Opportunities remain for geographical growth by the chain operators in the UK. The more remote parts of the country and the smaller towns and urban suburbs offer particular opportunities. With the dismantling of border controls, the opening of the Channel Tunnel in 1994, which improved the speed and ease of communication between the UK and continental Europe, and with the harmonization of European rules and regulations, opportunities for domestic and foreign fast-food operations are great. Geographical growth is therefore expected by increased internationalization.

Increased numbers of operations using the newer delivery systems, e.g. drive through and home delivery, as well as the development of new systems, e.g. multi-drive-through systems, where outlets have multiple windows designed to cope with high volumes of cars, and customer self-service and self-pay systems, are anticipated. The home delivery market, which is still in its infancy in the UK, will continue to expand and new products which lend themselves to travel more easily than some existing products such as burgers will be developed. Even with burgers, research work is being done to improve their transportability for delivery. The extent to which home delivery will threaten established high street operations is not thought to be great; most of its locations are in neighbourhood areas. As the chains begin to develop in secondary locations in neighbourhood restaurants, they too will need to consider the implications of home delivery. Perhaps another new move will be for smaller street-side hot food carts to get into the lunch-time office delivery market, using mobile telephones to take the orders. The development by the chains of cheaper, fixed or mobile fast-food kiosks, where space is at a premium, e.g. in sports stadia and cinemas, is also predicted.

Further technological advancements are expected within the industry. The chains will be at the forefront of these developments and the major operators will especially continue to invest quite significantly in technological research. These advancements will be required to satisfy the ever changing needs of customers. McDonalds, for example, is testing credit card payment, and Burger King is testing customer-operated ordering terminals. Equipment, and particularly computerized system innovations will increasingly focus on saving time and energy and facilitate productivity and profitability gains. Pressures upon fast-food operators are also likely to come from the 'green' movement who are expected to focus attention on the environmental consequences associated with the methods and equipment used in outlets. As fast-food operations fine tune their activity even closer to particular market segments more sophisticated management information systems and better consumer databases are expected.

Figure 14.4 *Typical fast-food outlet*
Source: Casey Jones

SUMMARY

Although Britain has had fish and chip shops for the last 150 years, the fast-food industry is essentially a relatively recent arrival on these shores, marked by the opening of the first McDonalds in London in 1974. In the USA the term fast food

219

has been replaced by 'quick service'. This neatly summarizes the key operational characteristic of this sector, namely that food, hot or cold, is sold off-the-shelf ready for immediate consumption. However, because this food may be consumed off the foodservice premises, this sector is also associated with takeaways, notably pizza, Chinese and Indian restaurants, which provide hot meals for home consumption. Such restaurants do not operate on a quick-service basis. This neatly illustrates how difficult to it is to obtain clear statistics about the sector, as well as to describe operational characteristics. The sector is generally growing at a rate of over 5 per cent per annum, assisted by extending the location of outlets into all kinds of places and serving the widest variety of consumers. As far as possible, food production in such operations is greatly simplified and automated. Fast-food units sell a large volume of products at very low prices.

FURTHER STUDY

www.macdonalds.co.uk
www.kfc.co.uk
www.pret.com

QUESTIONS

To what extent has the growth of fast-food outlets in the UK slowed down? What factors affect the growth or decline of fast-food market segments (burger, chicken, sandwiches, etc.)?

CHAPTER 15

Employee feeding

INTRODUCTION

Staff restaurants today bear little relationship to those originally set up in the industrial sector as 'staff canteens'. Those facilities, which began to be set up in the 19th century were very much part of an employer's attempt to look after the physical welfare of its employees. Further impetus to expand the sector arose during the Second World War, when the Emergency Powers (Defence) Factories Canteen order 1940 and 1943 made catering provision compulsory for all factories employing more than 250 workers. In the 1970s, governmental pay policy restraint caused many organizations to develop alternative methods to reward their employees. In its simplest form this could be the issue of luncheon vouchers, but in order to give better perceived value to their staff, organizations often offered employee dining facilities. Today staff restaurants are often seen by employers as an important part of the employment package, and are sometimes used as a method of differentiating themselves from their competitors. A survey indicated that the average benefit of a staff catering facility to an employee was circa £300 per annum.

In this sector, catering facilities are ancillary to the main purpose of a business, which may be manufacturing, commerce or retailing. In spite of this, there could be a series of facilities ranging from a simple cafeteria service, perhaps supported by a vended beverage service, to a full range of self service, buffet and table service, and executive dining rooms. Some large organizations have a range of facilities that can be used by employees of different seniority in the hierarchy. The culture of an organization, regarding the relationships between its employees, is often reflected within the dining rooms arrangements. Hence some organizations may have totally unsegregated dining with directors and temporary staff all eating together, while others will have very complex structures for various grades of managerial and administrative personnel. In addition, many commercial organizations have high status dining facilities used for entertaining corporate clients.

The nature of the provision within this sector is changing too, both in response to customer tastes and from the influence of the high street. Several caterers now use the idea of branding of products, which will be discussed in a later section, and the increasing concern over diet and health has been reflected in the provision of salad bars and healthy options within menus. In an attempt to reduce costs and match customer requirements more closely, there has also been an increase in the volume of automatically vended services, and in the provision of snack items.

A major growth of employee feeding has been in the public sector. This has been as a result of government legislation, enacted during the 1980s, requiring local authorities and health authorities to put their catering services out to tender. The Transfer of Undertakings (Protection of Employment) regulations (TUPE) was originally introduced in 1991 to accommodate the so-called 'Acquired Rights Directive' from the European Union and have been the cause of controversy for some time. However the regulations have now been clarified by rulings in the House of Lords, and essentially they mean that at the time of transfer of a business, the contract of employment immediately prior to the transfer will be maintained after the transfer. Hence the transfer of employment of a worker from an in-house catering provider to a contractor or between contractors means that the employment will remain protected. Also the employee will be entitled to terms and conditions of employment no less favourable than those previously enjoyed. The terms relating to occupational pension schemes do not apply, and are subject to agreement by the parties. This has had considerable significance in the public sector contracting, where contractors were previously able to offer staff lower salaries and hence be in a strong position when bidding for contracts brought about by competitive tendering requirements.

SIZE AND STRUCTURE OF THE SECTOR

It is estimated that this sector accounts for 50 per cent of the total number of meals served in the catering industry (Quest, 2001). This sector is worth more than £3 billion per annum, with business and industry representing nearly 50 per cent of this turnover (Keynote, 2000b). The number of outlets and meals served (excluding snacks) in the foodservice management sector for 2001 is illustrated in Table 15.1. The two major methods of operation are self operated (direct management) and contracted.

Table 15.1 *Size and scale of contract foodservice sector in the UK, 2001*

	Outlets	Meals (millions)
Business and industry	8,303	525
Government and agency staff feeding	465	31
Local authorities*	580	44
Ministry of Defence	623	135
Oil rigs	267	17

* includes town halls, police, fire, courts and welfare
Source: Quest (2001)

Foodservice Intelligence suggest that of the 17,893 outlets in the business and industry sector, the contractors operate some 50 per cent of them. Since 1991, the number of outlets in this sector contracted out has grown from 7775 to 8930 a growth of 15 per cent. But the contract foodservice sector as a whole has grown at a rate of 71 per cent over the same period. This is due partly to the very significant growth of contract provision in healthcare and education (discussed in the next chapter), but also in the armed services and catering to the public (which includes department-store catering). Catering in the state education sector has grown by 927 per cent! Of even greater significance is the growth in the number of meals. The contract foodservice operators served 325 million meals in business and industry in 1991, which had grown by 80 per cent to 583 million in 2001. Overall the contracted sector were producing 125 per cent more meals in 2001 than ten years earlier.

Self-operated facilities

In this case the parent organization is totally responsible for the catering provision and usually owns all equipment, has dedicated personnel, and is responsible for the entire operation. This means that a firm involved in commerce or engineering may be responsible for an area of operation outside its own normal field, with the responsibility for the operation often vested in the human resource department. This may present problems for the company, and they may not, for example, be able to benefit from large food purchasing discount arrangements enjoyed by some contractors. However they will be fully in control of their operations. The extent of service provided will be determined by the company's policies. ICI for example, did operate their own facilities as part of their policy to ensure that wherever practicable its employees have access to a good quality meal at a fair price in pleasant surroundings.

Since 1990 there has been a steep decline in firms who operate in this way. In 1990 there were 15,992 self-operated units, by 2000 this had fallen by 44 per cent to just 8963 outlets. Although some of these became contracted outlets, particularly those serving large numbers of employees, overall the number of outlets fell by just over 5000 during this period. At the same time the number of meals served grew slightly. This suggests small firms with small catering outlets no longer offer meals. In 1990, of the 600 million meals served in the business and industry sector, 47 per cent of those were served in self-operated outlets (Quest, 2001). By 2000 the number of meals had grown to 630 million but only 8 per cent of those were served in self-operated outlets.

Contracted services

In this option, the equipment is usually owned by the parent company (client), and the service is provided by the contractor. A contractor, therefore, is usually able to operate with little capital investment in the operation. The 1994 Catering Policies Survey by the Industrial Society suggested that the average life of a contract with a particular contractor is eight years. After this time the client would usually offer the contract to another contractor rather than operate the catering in-house. The survey also looked at the reasons for changing the catering management arrangements, and these, in order of significance were:

1. need for cost reductions;

2. need for improvement in service/quality;

3. company policy change; and

4. need to reduce headcount.

The market is dominated by a number of major contractors: Sodexho, formerly Gardner Merchant the contract catering division of Forte; Compass, originally formed by the amalgamation of Bateman Catering and Midland Catering, and more recently the acquisition of Sutcliffe; and Aramark, which expanded to the UK from the USA in 1972. These large corporations have constantly changing organizational structures, but the current trend is for them to organize themselves into specialist divisions serving particular market segments. In addition to these three large contract catering organizations there are a large number of small- to medium-size operators. These may operate in a number of markets or specialize in particular market segments.

CONTRACTORS AND CATERING CONTRACTS

A management contracting arrangement is defined by Sharma (1984) as:

> an arrangement under which operational control of an enterprise which would otherwise be exercised by the directors and managers appointed or elected by its owners, is vested by contract in a separate enterprise which performs the necessary management functions for a fee.

In the contract catering business, this fee may be made up in several ways. These include a straight fee; one linked to the turnover of the business; one in which purchasing discounts are returned to the client organization to offset against the fee; a combination of the above. It is not uncommon for contractors to gain as much income from purchase discounts obtained, but not passed on to clients, as it is from the fees charged. This will result in local management following a strict policy of using authorized suppliers in order to maximize such discount earnings to the contracting organization.

Contracts are usually one of the following types, or occasionally may be a combination, dependent on the nature of the client's business:

1. cost-plus;

2. fixed price;

3. full cost recovery

4. commercial return;

5. guaranteed performance.

Cost-plus represents a third of all the total number but this number has been declining in the past three years. Under this arrangement the contractor provides the services as required by the client and submits an invoice for all goods and services provided, and thus would include materials, labour and overheads such as disposables and cleaning materials. To this would be added an agreed management fee, hence the term 'cost-plus'. The fee may be fixed in nature or a percentage of the expenditure. The client will have additional costs to pick up such as fuel costs, which are part of a building's overheads, and items such a depreciation on equipment. Clients may also incur heavy and light equipment capital expenditure costs.

Fixed price represents nearly half of the total number, this establishes a total cost within which the caterer will work. The fixed price type of contract was not as popular with the contractor as they had to accurately assess all the catering costs for the period ahead and then bill the client with, for example, one twelfth of the year's projected costs each month. If the contractor underestimated the costs, they have to bear the losses. However if this did occur, the contractor was likely to want to renegotiate, usually on the basis that they had insufficient information on which to make a detailed assessment of costs. This form of contract is becoming increasingly popular with clients, as in this way they can be assured of their catering costs. Public sector organizations, such as local councils requiring a catering provision to the employees at a town hall often use this type of contract. This is often forced on them by the need to put their catering facilities contract out to tender as required by current legislation. By using fixed-price contracts they are able to compare projected tender costs easily.

The full cost recovery contract, which essentially dictates the pricing policy, is adopted where the client does not wish to subsidize the catering operation. If this is acceptable to local employee representatives, the contractor would provide services at commercial prices, and retain all income. The contractor has to operate them rather like any commercial restaurant, and hence runs the risk of making a loss if the management is ineffective. Such contracts may or may not include provision to cover overhead costs such as energy.

Commercial return contracts are a growing trend in catering operations, as contractors increasingly begin to run commercial operations. Again as part of a contract with a local authority there may be some public services in addition to those provided for the employees of the organization. Thus a contractor may offer a fixed sum of money, or a percentage of sales to the client in order to operate that part of the business.

Guaranteed performance contracts can take several forms, but it is quite common for the client to ask that the tariff charged recovers food costs, or food costs plus VAT. In this way such costs are not charged to clients, nor are takings returned to them. It essentially means that the client will only have to subsidize labour and overheads, and that is guaranteed. Such operations usually will involve a 'floating tariff' to customers as commodity prices fluctuate throughout the year. This type of contract has grown from only 4 per cent of the total in 1994 to 12 per cent in 2000 (Quest, 2001).

The BHA Survey, whilst using a slightly different classification of contract types, showed management fee contracts, followed by fixed price contracts as the predominant forms of contract in the UK, as illustrated in Table 15.2.

A contract between a client and a contractor would normally specify the following:

a. A specification of the standards expected with regard to meals and beverages served. Contractors usually have standard portion sizes for catering operations, but will vary these according to individual client requirements.

b. Operating times of the various facilities.

c. Total budget available for the service provision (see contract forms above).

d. Responsibility for cleaning and maintenance of equipment and facilities.

Table 15.2 *Types of catering contract in the UK, 2001*

Catering contract	No. of outlets
Management fee (cost plus)	5791
Contracts with performance guarantees	2250
Fixed price	8502
Partnership	65
Concession (rent)	1222
Total	17830

e. Relationship for VAT purposes, i.e. the contractor acts either as a principal or agent for VAT purposes.

f. Description of responsibilities for insurances and public liabilities.

g. Financial arrangements regarding bill payments and possible client deposits.

An increasing trend is for contractors to offer a range of services in addition to catering, such as office cleaning and grounds maintenance, which will save a client having to deal with several different organizations for different services.

OPERATIONAL ISSUES

For all operators there is the need to provide an adequate service, yet to keep costs under control. For a contractor, there is a constant dilemma for the organization has to meet the needs of both the client and the customer in the various catering outlets. In order to facilitate this there has been a growth in the use of self-clearing systems, self-help systems, takeaways and cashless operations, which result in lower labour costs. Sometimes in an attempt to make facilities more attractive, and in improving the service, the usage of a facility may increase. In a commercial contract this would be good practice, as it would spread the overhead. However, if an operation were run so that each meal provided incurred a subsidy from the organization, then increased customers would mean an increased cash subsidy. Thus normal rules of operation do not always apply in this sector. This may explain the trend of providers to move to a nil subsidy situation with their catering provision.

Alternatively clients could give all employees a pay rise and scrap the meal service. Indeed contractors sometimes have to face this question too at the time of contract renewal. However a number of organizations strongly believe in the need to provide catering facilities, based on a number of factors. First the provision of a catering service reduces the time for beverage and meal breaks. In the manufacturing industry this can make significant differences to productivity, since it shortens the time that machinery is shut down during breaks. In office environments, facilities such as vending machines cut down the amount of time people are away from their desks and can save energy from the use of numerous kettles, boilers and coffee percolators located within a building. Second, at times of low unemployment, the provision of good catering facilities is necessary to attract or keep staff as employee satisfaction may be enhanced by offering opportunities for social interaction and team building. Third, once an organization has committed itself to capital expenditure on its facilities it will want the facilities to be used to provide some return (although not necessarily financial) on its investment. Finally employee representatives may see catering facilities as an integral part of the employment package, and the continued provision of services can be used as a bargaining point for employers during wage negotiations. The Industrial Society 1994 Survey identified six main reasons for providing catering (in order of significance) as general company policy, staff morale, service/perk for staff, tradition/historical, lack of local facilities and keep staff on premises.

Table 15.3 *Breakdown of meal costs*

	Food cost %	Labour cost %	Other costs %
Industrial Society Survey	43	45	12
BHA Survey	40	43	17

The current trend is for organizations to attempt to recover food costs in their tariff structures, and many attempt to add a margin to contribute towards the recovery of other operating costs. A breakdown of food, labour and overhead costs is illustrated in Table 15.3. The average annual subsidy per user of a facility was calculated at £373, or £210 per employee indicating an average take up of 56 per cent.

In this sector, the careful control of food costs is essential to success. As a result most operators have a sophisticated menu planning system which encompasses a mix of commodities in different price bands in addition to the usual menu planning requirements of texture, colour and flavours. Such systems involve standard recipes and presentation standards clearly specified for each operation. Operational management have the task of costing the various menu items and ensuring tariff recovery requirements are met. Food cost plus VAT is currently a common approach being adopted, and this involves the management in carrying out food costings on a regular and frequent basis with menu item prices changing regularly, perhaps daily, especially for vegetables. In sophisticated, high volume locations, such systems are sometimes linked to automatic commodity requisitioning and re-ordering procedures. Further approaches to pricing could involve the banding of menu items with a 'regular' and 'economy dish' being available, with perhaps a 'premium' dish available at key times such as the end of month salary date.

It is also important to control labour costs. The employee feeding sector, like other catering operations employs a large number of part-time employees. However, if we convert part-time staff into full-time equivalents (FTEs), the average number of staff per catering outlet is 7.91. The Industrial Society Survey identified that the average number of meals served per FTE in employee catering outlets is 25 for contractor operated units and 20.6 for self-operated outlets, giving an overall figure of 23.9. Catering management continue to strive to keep operating costs to a minimum, and often resort to technology and mechanization to keep ever increasing labour costs in check. This approach has led to the growing use of automatically vended services, especially for the provision of beverage services.

OPERATIONS

Cafeteria operations

There are three main variations of the cafeteria system: in-line counter; free-flow; and carousel. The 'in-line' cafeteria consists of a single counter along which customers pass to select food and beverage. It is sometimes described as the 'straight-line' cafeteria, but not all such counters are in fact straight, although there are advantages in ensuring the counter is straight – primarily because customers pushing trays along the counter may be distracted enough to push the tray either off the rail where it changes direction away from them or into the counter, thereby spilling items, where it turns towards them. This style of cafeteria can serve between four and eight customers per minute depending upon those factors mentioned above such as speed of the service staff, proficiency of the cashier and the menu display, and also the customer's familiarity with the unit and the order of presentation of items along the counter. Some experts believe that the counter should be arranged logically in the order of the menu so customers select a starter, main course, a sweet and beverage in the 'correct' sequence, while others advocate that all those items served at room temperature or chilled should be at the beginning of the counter, so that hot items are served last and therefore have less time to cool before they are eaten. Whichever method of presentation is adopted, it is important to be consistent so that customers will become familiar with the layout, and will know at which point along the counter they will find particular items.

The length of the cafeteria counter will depend upon the number of menu items, but will be between 6 and 15 metres (20 and 50 feet). The longer the counter, the slower the service is likely to be. This has led to some modifications of the basic idea. The counter may be divided into two, with both halves serving the same selection of items. Customers may start at either end and move towards the cash points located at the midpoint of the counter, or start at the midpoint and move towards either end, as illustrated in Figure 15.1. Alternatively, there may be parallel counters, with the customer flow between the counters on either side. Finally two counters may be placed either side of a central service point running in parallel with each other.

The free-flow system is also known as the 'scramble system' or 'hollow square'. Whereas in-line cafeterias comprise usually one counter in whatever configuration thought suitable, the free-flow system has several counters each serving different meal items, such as hot foods, sandwiches, salads, desserts and beverages. The major advantage of free-flow is that it avoids the necessity to queue, and although short queues may form at periods of high demand, the number of customers that

Figure 15.1 *In-line cafeteria layouts*
Source: Jones (1988)

can be served may be as high as 15 per minute. Customers prefer this layout because the service is quicker, there is less queuing, and the customer who only wants a snack does not have to use the same counter as someone who requires a three-course meal. Additionally, a wider selection of menu items may be offered. In particular, it is possible to operate a call-order counter for grills that in a conventional cafeteria is impracticable. From the caterer's point of view, the free-flow layout has the advantage of flexibility. During periods of slack demand, some counters may be closed, counters may be removed in the event of breakdown and greater use may be made of self-service by customers since the flow of the entire system is not held up by one slow customer.

There are two main types of layout of the free-flow cafeteria. The hollow square has counters placed around three sides of the service area in a U-shape, with the customers entering and leaving via the open side, as illustrated in Figure 15.2. This is used particularly in operations where there is a steady flow of customers throughout the service period, such as in department stores. The echelon design has counters arranged at an angle next to each other. This is used particularly where there is a large number of people to be served, as in the industrial sector. With both layouts it is important that the counters are well signposted so that customers can easily identify the particular counter they wish to use and counters should be arranged so that as little cross-flow takes place as possible.

Figure 15.2 *Typical free-flow servery*
Source: Gardner Merchant

The Carousel was first introduced into Britain some years ago and has been a limited success. It comprises a large rotating arrangement of shelves, approximately two metres in diameter, on which food and drink are presented. Thus customers remain stationary as the carousel revolves once every minute to enable them to select items from it. Only one half of the carousel is in the service area, so that as items are removed, the shelves can be replenished in the serving area behind the unit. Trays, cutlery, napkins and beverages are usually separately available from dispensers so as to avoid congestion at the unit. Cashiers are situated between the carousel and the dining room. As a method of self-service, it has a customer throughput of between eight to ten per minute, which is higher than the traditional in-line counters. It requires less space than many other self-service layouts, particularly in the service area of the operation. However operators must be well trained to re-stock the shelves quickly and efficiently to maintain a steady flow-rate of customers and customers may cause delays waiting for a complete revolution of the unit before making their selection. In this respect, the Carousel is most suited to operations where there is repeat custom on a frequent basis. Use of carousels over a number of years has shown that they are of less use where hot food is being offered as there are problems of maintaining food temperature and quality. They have had greater success in dispensing items such as pre-prepared cold dishes and sweets. Visitors to the Kennedy Space Centre in Florida will no doubt be familiar with the carousel used there.

Automatic vending

The Automatic Vending Association (AVA) recognizes that the development of vending machines in Britain was closely related to the industrial catering sector. 'By the 1950s ... it was clear that the future [of vending] lay in servicing the worker and his [sic] refreshment needs.' The AVA list 82 different types of goods or services that may be vended by machine, but from the caterer's viewpoint, there are four main categories.

- *Beverages – hot or cold* Hot can be further divided into 'instant' which is further divided into dried and frozen products, fresh brew, and capsule vendors which allow customers choice of particular blends of tea of coffee in encapsulated form. Cold drinks too may be dispensed by the machine using concentrates, or alternatively by refrigerated can vendors.

- *Confectionery and snacks* Usually a supply of common branded confectionery goods.

- *Sandwiches* This includes items such as pork pies, Scotch eggs, quiche, etc.

- *Meals – hot or cold* These are offered in refrigerated units, often adopting a carousel type of mechanism to deliver a range products to the customer. Such machines are often sited next to microwave ovens which allow customers to reheat their food. These are used particularly in unmanned facilities, perhaps to provide a service for maintenance or computer staff who have to be on duty throughout the night.

Machines vending such products may be found in cafeterias, offices, factories, refectories, hotel corridors, student common rooms, clubs and pubs, and many other types of location. It has been estimated that there is a vending machine for every 100 people in the UK. The total annual turnover of all types of machine is more than £1000 million. The largest type of vend is from 175,000 beverage machines, which dispense over 3500 million drinks per annum. Another 100,000 dispense confectionery, and 70,000 food and drink. The employee feeding sector is a major user of such machines, with over 76 per cent of all UK companies having beverage vending.

The type of machine will depend upon the product being vended. Those vending pre-packaged goods, such as confectionery, soft drinks and sandwiches need only electricity supplied, whilst cup-vending machines need water supplied also. Machines are temperature controlled and may be ambient, refrigerated or heated. The operating mechanism varies from machine to machine but includes cup, drop-flap, rotating drum, compartment, endless belt, lift, and column and drawer mechanisms.

Vending services can be provided through machines financed by outright purchase, lease and lease purchase, rental or supplier on a commission basis. Purchase requires a large capital outlay as sophisticated machines with many choices, and the capability of delivering freshly brewed products can cost in excess of £5000. Small operators therefore often opt for more simple machines which involve the customer carrying out some mechanical procedures such as placing a cup under the product, pushing a button, and then moving the cup to a water dispenser spout. In addition to the purchase, the operators would have to take out an annual maintenance agreement. Leasing has the advantage that large outlays are not required, and the agreement usually includes a maintenance plan. Rentals are usually for more short-term commitments, and allow a user to change their machines more often, although rentals can be expensive. Many organizations simply contract out their vending operations, and within a catering contract, the vending section may be sub contracted, although the larger operators do have their own vending divisions.

The final option is to consider supplying goods, usually on branded products such as Coca Cola, on a commission basis. Under this type of arrangement, the supplier provides the machine and the operator receives a commission on each can sold on a sliding scale according to sales volumes.

Since the caterer is not expected to be technically capable of maintaining or repairing these machines, the complexities of their mechanisms will not be dealt with here. In those cases where the machines are operated by a vending company on contract to the caterer, all maintenance, cleaning, restocking and control is likely to be carried out by the vending operator's staff. The caterer need only report a machine defect or failure if this should occur. Caterers operating their own vending machines must therefore have well-trained staff responsible for the regular cleaning, replenishing, maintenance and control of the machines. In 1975, 80 per cent of machines were self-operated, but today there is a growing trend towards contract operation, reflecting US practice, where 95 per cent of all machines are on contract.

The advantages of installing vending machines include flexibility, accessibility, control, and labour saving. A vending machine, properly maintained, provides its product 24 hours a day. It allows workers in businesses of all types to take refreshment whenever they wish, according to their individual needs. So long as industry and commerce are prepared to accept their workers having flexible break times, there is no doubt that their performance is improved by providing tea, coffee or other beverages throughout their working day. Machines may be sited in close proximity to the work place, be it factory or office, thus reducing the amount of time required by the user to get to and from the service point. This is particularly important in offices and factories covering several hundred square metres. The machine dispenses an exact measure or amount of the vending commodity for the correct value of coins or tokens, therefore wastage, pilferage and loss are eliminated and exact control is made possible, which was not always possible with trolley service. It is estimated that one machine can be serviced by a member of staff in 20 minutes each day. With the use of disposables, which reduces the need for washing up, this probably involves fewer work hours than a conventional food and drink service would necessitate.

The disadvantages of vending machines have been speed, quality, lack of personal contact and vandalism. A well-trained cafeteria operator can probably dispense teas more quickly than one machine, but even so a machine using instant ingredients takes only 10 seconds to serve one customer. Where speed is particularly important, several machines located around the service area would be needed. Initially there was a great deal of resistance to tea-vending and coffee-vending due to the poor quality of the product, reinforced by its dispensing the drink in a plastic or paper cup. This resistance has been eroded by definite improvements by the manufacturers of vending products and a change in consumer attitude towards the product and disposables. The vending machine has effectively replaced the tea-trolley (see below). It is a factor that vending manufacturers are aware of and have researched in order to design machines that reduce the impact of lack of personal contact. They believe that brightly coloured and well-lit machines can do much to overcome any resistance encountered from the 'impersonal tag'. In addition the public is becoming more used to partly self-help systems, the good customer reaction to the major banks automatic telling machines (ATMs) being a good example. Perhaps because of the above, damage, malicious and otherwise, may be caused by frustrated consumers. No machine is entirely vandal-proof, but modern machines are very robust, despite their increasing sophistication. On contract-operated sites, the contractors have a vested interest in ensuring the security of takings, since they receive a share of them; while a damaged or broken-down machine affects the operators' or caterers' turnovers.

From what has been outlined so far, the catering manager in an operation where vending machines are installed must have three clear priorities. Machines must be sited effectively to maximize their use and provide the best possible service. Staff, if a self-operator, should be well-trained and capable of replenishing, cleaning and regularly maintaining the machines; and if it is a contract operation, the contractor should fulfil these same obligations properly. Finally, clear policies should be established with regard to customer dissatisfaction due to machine malfunction or breakdown. For instance, if a customer complains that the machine accepted money but failed to vend or refund the same, there must be a consistent policy with regard to refunding money or not. In any event, it is in everyone's interest to ensure that the machine is kept in proper working order, so it is advisable to place a notice on each machine that says who should be contacted in the event of any dissatisfaction.

Today payment systems are changing. A number of organizations operate 'free vend' periods for their staff, perhaps for one hour mid morning and one mid afternoon, with the rest of the day being on a tariff basis. Such a system would, of course, require the machine to have a timing mechanism. In order to overcome problems with coin mechanisms, so often the cause of vending machine complaints, many companies in the past adopted a total free vend policy. This proved disastrous with customers taking drinks indiscriminately, with many being left only partially consumed. Interestingly the introduction of any sort of payment, even as small as 5p will cut down consumption to an average of around 3.5 cups per day per person. Increasingly cashless systems are being introduced where employees are either issued with, or buy a 'smart card' which carries an amount of credit which slowly reduces in value as it is used, rather like a telephone card. The Industrial Society Survey identified that of all beverages sold today, 71 per cent are vended, and the average number of beverages consumed per customer per day is 1.63.

Trolley service

Despite the advent of automatic vending, some operators still operate a tea or beverage trolley that tours the factory or offices providing mid-morning and mid-afternoon refreshment. The principal advantage of such a service is that the refreshments go to the employees rather than the employees having to leave their work place to have refreshment. Also, staff representatives have tended to support the person bringing round the tea rather than make him or her redundant through replacement with machines. Like any other form of service, there are essential features that the foodservice manager must be aware of.

One trolley can serve approximately 200 people, if they are not dispersed over too wide an area or on too many floors. It should provide a choice of beverage and snack items, but choice should be kept to an acceptable minimum to simplify administration, control and stock turnover. From experience, a trolley on a regular route will establish a well-defined pattern of sales – so many teas, coffees, glasses of milk, and so on – which enables the operator to stock the trolley sufficiently to satisfy predicted sales without excessive waste. The trolley should be regularly cleaned and maintained so that beverages and food items are served hygienically and presented in an appetizing way. The route of the trolley should be carefully considered and reviewed regularly to take into account the starting, break and finishing times of staff, the distance to be travelled and any obstructions to a smooth schedule, such as lifts. No route will be ideal since it will take about 1½ hours to serve 200 people, for some of whom the trolley will arrive too early, and for others it will be too late. Therefore the caterer should be in close consultation with management and employee representatives to maximize satisfaction with the service. The trolley operator should only serve from designated stops to ensure an efficient service, since experience has shown that it takes longer to serve people when they stop the trolley to purchase than if the trolley stops for a while to serve several people. This also helps to establish a routine so that employees who move around the building know where to find the trolley at any given time.

The control of trolley service is just as demanding as any other food service system. Items may be easily pilfered and cash is particularly vulnerable. Much depends on the security consciousness and honesty of the operator and in some cases, caterers have adopted a procedure whereby stock is 'sold' to the attendant before the service, which he or she then pays for out of receipts, less any returned stock. The attendant is therefore much more likely to guard the stock and cash than otherwise. This system is particularly used outside the employee feeding sector when trolleys are used for refreshment services on trains or at sporting events, such as hot-dog stands at football matches and so on.

Food production systems

Food systems in this sector tend be very traditional, although it is influenced by technological change. Currently, influenced by customer requirements, particularly in relation to 'healthy eating' there has been a return to these traditional approaches. While other sectors may have progressed to decoupled approaches such as cook–chill, sous vide and cook–freeze (see Chapter 16), the employee feeding sector is returning to traditional production, involving the use of batch cooking to help ensure retention of essential nutrients. This is partly a result of the fact that an average size operation serves aproximately 250 meals a day, which does not lend itself to viable high levels of capital expenditure. The idea of centralized production with delivery of food to satellites is only really appropriate in large industrial locations. The influence of the high street has led to food courts being considered in large operations, as opposed to the traditional approach of mass production of a limited number of menu items.

There is still, however, the need for large volume production, and this tends to be reflected in the type of production equipment used. It will be common to see the use of brat pans, pressure steamers and combination ovens in large-scale operations to facilitate batch cooking.

MARKETS AND BRANDING

The customers using in-house facilities are almost exclusively employees of the host organization. Visitors may also use the facilities, and high ranking visitors such as potential customers, financiers and sometimes politicians and foreign dignatories will usually be served in executive dining rooms. The bulk of the clientele, will effectively be in a semi-captive market, and in extreme cases, such as on board an oil rig, will be totally captive. Many industrial sites are in isolated locations, or are far from commercial outlets, and their employees would therefore have little choice other than to bring their own food. Commercial operations often exist with large numbers in a single location, and hence numbers of diners can vary dramatically according to weather conditions. A 10 per cent swing in demand in a location with 3000 employees would cause a variation in meal requirements of 300 in one meal service. This indicates the need for good records of sales trends, and also the ability of the production area to respond quickly to change in demand. This leads to a need for systems and equipment that can be responsive to such changes and hence the use of equipment such as pressure steamers, and steamer/ovens and the use of chilled and frozen items to meet these fluctuations.

Essentially customers in such establishments are generally using the facilities to meet a basic need for food, which is supplied to a good quality at an acceptable price, in the amount of time available. Whereas many public catering outlets such as those in a motorway service area may only change their menu quarterly, menus in this sector usually change daily in order not to cause menu fatigue. As more establishments turn to flexible working methods, and the use of 'flexi time', the opportunity to have a wholesome meal quickly may be seen as a great advantage to an employee. As a result, seat turnover can be quite high and will be determined by the style of the meal provision. Large free-flow serveries in cafeteria style operations will allow customers to get through quickly and return to their work, whereas the executive dining rooms will allow a meal to be enjoyed at a more leisurely pace, perhaps whilst concluding an important business deal. Cafeteria seat turnover may be 2–3 times an hour, and snack bars up to 6, whereas executive rooms may be as low as 0.33 per hour.

Taking a main meal at work may allow employees more time in the evening for social and recreational activities as they may not have the burden of having to prepare an evening meal. Increasingly the staff restaurant is becoming a location for more social meal experiences. This has been reflected in the branding of some staff restaurants outlets, in an attempt to reflect catering outlets in the high street. In 1994 contract caterers had 147 in-house brands and 26 franchises of established brands (BHA, 2001). By 2000 they had developed a staggering 4352 in-house brands and were franchisees of 299 others.

Other trends have been determined by the changing nature of the gender mix of the workforce. The obvious implications of this are the development of menus which reflect a workforce which has an ever increasing mix of different ethnic groups, and the substantial increase in the proportion of the female workforce. This combined with a growing interest by the public in diet and health, has resulted in a trend towards people eating less and towards a more 'healthy diet'. This is given greater emphasis by some employers who feel that they have a responsibility towards their workforce in actually promoting a more healthy diet which is reflected in staff restaurant policy statements, as illustrated in Figure 15.3.

CURRENT ISSUES AND FUTURE TRENDS

Industry concentration

This sector has changed dramatically in the last five years through widespread merger and acquisition activity. Between them, Compass and Sodexho have an estimated market share of 76 per cent. The next largest operator – Aramark – has a 7 per cent share (Keynote, 2000). Compass itself was a contract caterer, but acquired other contractors including Eurest (focusing on business and industry), Bateman (healthcare), Chartwells (education), and Letherby & Christopher (event caterers). The Compass merger with Granada in 2001, also added the contractor Sutcliffes, which has over 2200 UK contracts, as well as medium sized contractors such as Fairfield Catering, Quadrant Catering, Shaw Catering, and so on. Sodexho was an established French contractor who entered the UK market and then took over Gardner Merchant, which had been owned by Forte. They too have acquired other UK contractors, such as Lawson Beaumont Catering.

Investment

It is increasingly the case that foodservice contractors may be asked to invest capital in an outlet in order to win the contract. For instance, 634 contracts in 2000 in the business and industry sector included investment of up to £250,000 (Quest, 2001). Such investment is frequently linked to the redesign or refurbishment of the outlet, often to bring in one of the contractor's branded facilities. Contract

WIGGINS TEAPE WEEKLY MENU

MONDAY	TUESDAY	WEDNESDAY	THURSDAY	FRIDAY
Celery soup	French onion soup	Asparagus soup	Mushroom soup	Tomato soup
Ratatouille Vol-au-vents	Curried eggs with rice	Vegetable lasagne	Mixed pepper quiche	Baked jacket potato, coleslaw and cheese
Sauté beef and vegetables	Lamb stew and dumplings	Corn beef hash	Tandoori chicken	Deep fried cod with lemon poached cod in white wine sauce
Ham 'n' egg	Haddock with prawn sauce	Home-made scotch egg	Grilled lambs liver with onions	Lamb chop lyonnaise
Paella 75p	Chicken Maryland 75p	Roast sirloin of beef 75p and yorkshire pudding	Pork escalopes 75p	Beef carbonnade 75p
Baked beans French beans Cauliflower Chipped potatoes	Sliced courgettes Mixed vegetables New potatoes	Buttered cabbage Sliced carrots Roast potatoes	Sweet corn Sliced green beans Lard potatoes	Tomatoes Garden peas New potatoes
Gammon ham Prawn and pineapple Cheese	Gala pie Scotch eggs Cheese	Cold chicken Egg mayonnaise Cheese	Cold roast beef Tuna and apple Cheese	Assorted meats Cheese
Coffee and walnut sponge and custard	Lemon meringue tartlet and custard	Bread-and-butter pudding and custard	Baked apple and custard	Mixed fruit cobbler and custard
Alpine rice	Sago	Semolina	Tapioca	Creamed rice

ICE CREAM IS AVAILABLE ON REQUEST

SENIOR STAFF DINING ROOM

MONDAY	TUESDAY	WEDNESDAY	THURSDAY	FRIDAY
Celery soup	French onion soup	Asparagus soup	Mushroom soup	Tomato soup
Orange and melon cocktail	Hors-d'oeuvre	Prawn cocktail	Wardorf salad	Stuffed mushroom with garlic
Grilled sirloin steak garni	Chicken Maryland	Roast sirloin of beef and yorkshire pudding	Pork escalopes	Fried cod with lemon
New potatoes Sauté potatoes French beans Grilled tomatoes	New potatoes Jacket potatoes Sweet corn and peppers Cauliflower with butter	Roast potatoes New potatoes Buttered cabbage Baton carrots	Lard potatoes Croquette potatoes Mixed vegetables French beans with almonds	New potatoes French fries Petits pois Sweet corn
Gammon ham Smoked mackerel Cottage cheese with walnuts	Smoked trout Gala pie Roast turkey	Tuna and apple Scotch egg Gammon ham	Roast beef Salmon and cucumber Pork pie	Gammon ham Sardines Smoked chicken

Figure 15.3 *Typical industrial catering menus*
Source: Wiggins Teape

foodservice companies are also becoming involved with the Private Finance Initiative (PFI) whereby in collaboration with other parties, such as builders and civil engineers, buildings are constructed and leased back to the public sector for a specified period, during which the contractor has the foodservice contract. This applies mostly in the healthcare and education sectors.

Contractor diversification

Regarding contractor operations, the 1990s have seen significant changes in the UK foodservice management industry with a number of mergers and acquisitions taking place. The dependence on traditional business and industry of this sector has declined. The trend is increasingly for contractors to develop businesses in providing meal services for the public. The number of contractor-run outlets in state education has risen sharply, partly brought about the introduction of

Compulsory Competitive Tendering (CCT) legislation. Healthcare and the Ministry of Defence have seen significant growth, whilst the number of outlets in business and industry have declined due to current economic conditions. Those offering in-house services seem to be switching to the contractors whose knowledge, expertise and resources are able to better respond to changing customer needs.

Internationalization

In 1993 the overseas turnover of UK registered companies increased from £277 million to £458 million (£293 million EC and $115 million USA). This represented some 23 per cent of the total turnover in the UK (BHA 1994). By 2001 contract foodservice companies were truly global. Sodexho, in 2001, had UK sales of £980 million but this represents only 10 per cent of their total global sales. The company operates 22,200 sites and employs 286,000 people in 70 countries (www.caterer.com). Likewise Compass had an annual turnover of £8.7 billion in 2001, with 300,000 employees in more than 90 countries.

Support services

Once the principle of contracting out is established, some firms also consider the use of contractors for other services. Many contract foodservice companies therefore provide a range of support services. Such services include bar operations, cleaning, housekeeping, property management, laundry, shops and security. In some cases these services are incorporated into the foodservice contract. So for instance in 1995, 635 contracts included cleaning provision, which had grown to 1241 by 2000. Increasingly, contractors have set up separate divisions for the provision of support services, so that separate contracts are increasing.

Supply-chain management

Until the mid-1990s UK hospitality operators were not highly effective in their management of the supply chain. This meant that companies found themselves holding a wide range of stock items and high levels of stock, as well as dealing with a large number of suppliers and processing relatively small orders. For instance, one large UK hotel chain found that it needed 4000 separate food and beverage items to support the range of menus offered in its hotels, which was reduced to just 1000 by simplifying and rationalizing standard recipes and menus. Contract foodservice companies too, have become aware of the need to better manage their inventory and engage in supply-chain management. Since 1995, the number of food suppliers used by contractors has fallen from 5455 to 1904 (Quest, 2001). Clearly they are dealing with fewer but larger suppliers, which reduces administration and increases the likelihood of supplier discounts. Furthermore contractors are working more closely with suppliers in a number of different ways, such as menu and new product development, equipment development, distribution efficiencies, and culinary support.

CONCLUSION

Employee feeding is a very large sector of the UK foodservice industry. In catering for large numbers of people, it uses systems, such as cafeterias and vending. Whilst these systems are not exclusively used in this sector, we have dealt with them here due to their significance. The sector is constantly evolving, and branding has become the emphasis. We can see the likely expansion of this, perhaps with the introduction of 'coffee and pastry' type outlets. It would appear that change seems to be increasingly consumer led, and the sector will have to respond with appropriate changes in production and delivery systems.

SUMMARY

This is another sector of the UK hospitality industry that has changed dramatically in the last twenty years. First, the market has expanded to provide opportunities to cater in the public sector, so that approximately half of contracts are now in hospitals, schools and other public services. Second, the industry has become dominated by two major players, Compass and Sodexho. This chapter identified that there continues to be some in-house provision of employee meals, but self-operated facilities are on the decline. A range of different types of contract exist, with management fee and fixed cost the most popular. Particular forms of service are found in this sector, although they are found in other sectors too, notably cafeterias, trolley service and automatic vending. Increasingly we are seeing the prevalence of branding in this sector.

FURTHER STUDY

www.compass-group.co.uk
www.sodexho.com

QUESTION

Compare and contrast two major contract foodservice companies' approach to branding outlets.

CHAPTER 16

Welfare catering

INTRODUCTION

Definition of the welfare catering sector is not simple. It is an area that was previously known as institutional catering and was closely related to charitable and state social provision in areas such as education, health and the penal system. In these areas profit has not normally been the primary motive and for this reason it is often grouped with employee feeding and identified as cost sector catering. However, with recent developments such as competitive tendering and the resultant move towards a more commercial orientation this distinction has become less clear cut.

Any contemporary definition of the sector is perhaps best guided by application of the general definition, 'the provision of meals for those unable to provide for themselves': inability resulting from age, both the very young and the elderly, illness and any other type of infirmity. Welfare catering is thus generally seen as including food service in education – schools, colleges and universities, healthcare – public and private hospitals, and social care – meals on wheels, day centres, care homes and prisons.

Because of its origins in charity, for many years welfare catering had a rather impoverished image. In recent years however this has changed particularly in response to competition but also as a result of legislation that has led to the building of improved purpose-built facilities and the development of advanced technical food service systems such as cook–chill and sous vide. Concomitant with these developments has been the enhanced status of food-service managers who have a fundamental role in the success of the systems and who must therefore be professionally qualified and technically competent.

The significance of the welfare catering sector is perhaps best illustrated by its size. On the basis of the number of school children, patients, prisoners, attendance at day centres and the number of meals on wheels served, the sector represents over two billion (2000 million) meal opportunities per year, the equivalent of nearly 6 million meals per day (Central Statistical Office, 1995). When compared with the fact that the whole of contract catering industry served just under 1.5 billion meals in 2000 (Quest, 2001) it is clear that welfare catering is one of the major sectors in the food-service industry. Government expenditure on welfare catering has tripled in the past ten years from £108 million to £410 million.

LEGISLATIVE CONTEXT

With its history of state provision the welfare catering sector has been subject to perhaps more legislation and government policy than any other foodservice sector. The provision of meals in schools and hospitals was an integral part of Britain's social policy after the Second World War. In school meals, for example, all education authorities were required to provide midday meals, suitable as the main meal of the day, at all maintained schools and for all pupils who desired them. These services, having been established in the 1940s remained largely unchanged until the 1980s. Change was signalled in 1970 by the White Paper, *New Policies in Public Spending*, which outlined efficiencies expected by the Government in state spending. Despite imposing stringent financial restrictions on government spending during the 1970s the expected efficiencies were not achieved. This led to a number of significant legislative changes in the 1980s.

In school meals the *Education Act 1980* (section 22) removed the requirement that meals should meet minimum nutritional standards and empowered local authorities to determine the nature and extent of the school-meals service they would provide, and to set the charges to be made for them. The only remaining requirements were that meals should be provided for pupils whose parents received supplementary benefit or family income support, and facilities should be provided for those pupils bringing their own lunch-time food to eat at school. The *Social Security Act 1986* replaced family income supplement with family credit and replaced supplementary benefit with income support. Under this legislation free school meals were restricted to children whose parents receive income support whilst those whose parents receive family credit lost their entitlement to free school meals but receive cash compensation instead.

A key development in hospital catering was the circular, *Competitive Tendering in the Provision of Domestic, Catering and Laundry Services 1983 – HC(83)18*, which advised health authorities to invite tenders for the provision of catering and other services. There was, however, a great deal of resistance from the health authorities, the hospitals and the unions with the effect that implementation was slow and in many cases the tender documents so complex and detailed that there were few bids from contractors (Cumming and Hill, 1992). By 1988 over 300 district health authorities had invited tenders but only nine had actually been won by outside contractors (Jones, 1988).

In light of this lack of response the *Local Government Act 1988* was introduced to ensure that it was more likely that catering services would be contracted out. The rationale behind the legislation being that by exposing services to competition and market forces they should evolve into more efficient, financially self-supporting operations. Although the response of outside contractors was still slow – Compass stating that most of the tender specifications were too restrictive and did not allow 'commercial flair to develop the service' (McDermid, 1989) – the years since have seen a steady growth in interest from the commercial sector to the extent that in 1994 welfare catering (particularly education) represented the major growth area for contract caterers accounting for 38 per cent of outlets (BHA, 1995).

During the 1990s the focus moved towards food safety, initially through the *Food Safety Act 1990* and more recently through the *Food Safety (General Food Hygiene) Regulations 1995* which build on previous legislation and contain some new requirements, including the requirement to identify, control and monitor critical food hazard points in the specific food operations employed; the need to ensure that food handlers are supervised and instructed/trained in food hygiene matters 'commensurate with their work activity'; changes in temperature control requirements; and requirements for the transport of food in the course of catering operations. In addition to the requirements of the legislation, a new initiative has been the development of a guide to compliance by caterers published by the Joint Hospitality Industry Congress (1995). This guide gives comprehensive information about the legal requirements as they would be interpreted in catering operations and has the status implied by Regulation 20 of the 1995 Regulations, that is that enforcement officers (Environmental Health Officers) must give 'due consideration' to the guide when assessing compliance with the regulations.

The Citizen's Charter concept has also required welfare caterers to be very much more aware of their provision. For instance, the *Patients' Charter 1995* requires that patients in hospital receive a written explanation of the hospital's 'patient food policy and the catering services and standards they can expect during their stay'. The charter identifies the standards as a choice of dishes, meals suitable for all dietary needs, a choice of portion size, no need to order more than two meals in advance, readily available help to use the catering services and the provision of the catering manager's name.

THE COMPETITIVE ENVIRONMENT

The Local Government Act 1988 had a profound affect on the welfare catering sector. Although interest from commercial companies was slow to develop, largely because of the complex tender documentation and the cost of tendering, the recession in the late 1980s and early 1990s encouraged contract catering companies to look more closely at the opportunities offered by the public sector. By 2000, 38 per cent of the meals served by contractors were in the healthcare and education sectors, as illustrated in Table 16.1. Indeed, throughout the late 1990s, welfare catering and particularly education catering, has represented the major growth area for contract caterers. In 1991, only 41 million meals a year were provided by contractors in the healthcare sector, by 2000 this had grown by nearly 500 per cent to 237 million. Likewise the state education sector saw very similar rates of growth by contractors.

From the above it is clear that the government's desire to see a more competitive commercially orientated environment in welfare catering has to a large extent been achieved. How this develops and how the direct service organizations (DSOs – the original public sector providers) fare in this environment remains to be seen. Whilst established contract caterers are able to withstand the loss of contracts and return to compete in the future, single contract DSOs are unlikely to survive such losses with the result that competition in the future is reduced.

Table 16.1 *Size and scale of contract food service sector in the UK welfare sector, 2001*

	Outlets	Meals (millions)
NHS and Trust hospitals	479	209
Private hospitals and nursing homes	492	28
State schools	4,169	123
Further and higher education	452	95
Independent schools and nurseries	585	92

Source: BHA (2001)

DEMAND FOR WELFARE CATERING

For the purposes of planning services such as welfare catering it is essential to project the future size and demographic nature of the market. With knowledge of birth rates, death rates, net immigration and the current age profile of the population, it is relatively simple to predict the numbers in particular age groups into the future. Table 16.2 shows the age profile of the UK population in 1993 with predictions to 2041. The groups of particular interest to the welfare catering sector are those under 16 and those over 64. These two groups are identified as the dependent population in that they represent that proportion of the population who are supported by those of working age. They are also those who make the greatest demands on the educational, health and care services – nearly 50 per cent of total government expenditure on social protection was spent on the elderly (Central Statistical Office, 2001).

Table 16.2 *UK population by age 1993 to 2041*

Year	%					Total
	<16	16–39	40–64	65–79	>80	(millions)
1993	20.6	34.9	28.8	11.9	3.9	58.2
2001	20.7	32.9	30.6	11.4	4.3	59.8
2011	19.2	30.0	34.1	11.9	4.7	61.3
2021	18.3	29.7	32.7	14.3	5.1	62.2
2031	18.2	28.4	30.5	16.3	6.6	62.2
2041	17.6	27.8	30.1	16.8	7.8	61.2

Source: Central Statistical Office (1995)

The dependency ratio, the number of children and pensioners per 100 people of working age, is a key statistic. The ratio was 63 in 1992 but it is expected to peak in 2036 at 82 when the baby boom generation reaches retirement age and the number of pensioners is projected to be 17 million – by comparison in 1999 there were 9.5 million people over 64 (Central Statistical Office, 2001). This future burden has clear implications for the provision of healthcare services and certainly indicates substantial growth in the demand for catering services within the sector, regardless of whether it is state or commercially based. Another factor that had a substantial effect on the demand for welfare services, such as meals on wheels and day centres, was the 1991 Care Programme Approach which detailed the Government's policy of providing care for as many people as possible in the community. Finally, the proportion of one-person households gives an indication of potential dependency on healthcare services. Whilst in 1961 the proportion of one-person households was 11 per cent it rose to over 30 per cent in 2001 (Central Statistical Office, 2001). This clear upward trend shows the increasing numbers of people who have little or no family to support them in times of illness and who are therefore likely to need healthcare support at various time in their lives.

CONSUMERS AND THEIR NEEDS

The operational characteristics of the welfare catering sector are largely determined by the nature of the consumer groups it serves. The most significant factor being that, as an ancillary service to other activities, (e.g. education, health), welfare catering has to serve a predetermined market created by the primary service with which it is associated. This often leads to extremely varied markets made up of a range of different consumer groups, the best examples being large general hospitals where a whole range of capabilities (physical and mental), age, socio-economic and lifestyle groups will be present. It is these two factors, the predetermined market and the variety of consumer groups, that present the major challenges to the welfare catering sector.

Despite the above, it is nevertheless possible to identify a number of general consumer-need characteristics in the welfare catering sector. These are discussed in the sections below.

Nutrition

More than in any other sector, the nutritional needs of consumers are given particular attention by welfare caterers. The nutritional role of any welfare provision will however be determined by the contribution it is expected to make to the overall diet. With school children, for example, the school meal is only one of a number of feeding opportunities during the day and should therefore be seen within the context of the child's whole diet. Care homes providing 24-hour care, on the other hand, will be providing the resident's whole diet and should therefore plan to meet the appropriate nutritional standards for that type of person and their lifestyle.

Despite the above, the primary role of any meal programme must be a nutritional one and, conscious of this fact, operators within the welfare sector generally try to balance the need to encourage people to eat whilst responding to nutritional guidelines such as the *NACNE Report 1983*, the *COMA Report 1984* and more recent reports such as *The Health of the Nation 1994* and *Nutritional Aspects of Cardiovascular Disease 1994*.

The nutritional role of welfare meals has been most vigorously debated in the school meals' service. Although guidance on nutritional standards had been given prior to the 1944 Education Act, it was not until the Provision of Milk and Meals Regulations of 1945 that specific nutritional requirements were made. These remained largely unchanged until the 1980 Education Act when the government removed the requirement to provide meals of a defined nutritional standard (except for the children of parents who received supplementary benefit or family income supplement). There has been much debate about this policy ever since and there have even been questions asked in the House of Commons. Despite this there are still no minimum nutritional requirements for school meals.

In hospitals, meal programmes often play a significant part in the overall medical care. For this reason special diets play a large role in hospital catering and most hospital kitchens include a special diet bay where meals to meet the particular needs of specific patients can be produced. In addition to diets for conditions such as diabetes and coeliac disease, other more specialist diets such as low potassium diets, reducing diets and renal diets, are also provided. An example of how advanced the provision of special diets has become, is the provision of sterile diets for patients in isolator tents. Patients suffering from severe combined immune deficiency disease or aplastic anemia have to be treated in sterile environments, provided by isolator tents, and any food introduced into the tent must be either aseptic canned foods or irradiated foods.

Social role

The social role of meals in the welfare sector has become increasingly recognized in recent years. The social psychological support provided by meals, particularly in terms of security, is identified by McKenzie (1979) who stated that: 'Food acts as an aid to security. Thus when everything seems to be going wrong we comfort ourselves that things are 'alright really' by turning to established favourite dishes'. As long ago as the 1950s, Dichter (1954) identified that 'The cold cup of coffee ... has deep emotional meaning. To the insecure patient it is a sign. Good hot coffee is symbolic of the home away from home, of being welcome. Bad coffee is the perfect symbol that he is a stranger, that he is receiving what amounts to the orphans negligent care'.

Clearly the role of meals goes beyond the purely nutritional to include wider concepts of care. In health and social care meal times often represent the few fixed points in the day and frequently the only opportunities to socialize. This has also been recognized in the meals on wheels service where in many cases the delivery of meals is one of the few regular forms of contact for the recipient and thus plays a social and monitoring function.

In school meals, the social role is somewhat different. A study in Gloucestershire (Hemmington and Chapman, 1992) established that parents identify the social role of school meals as a key strength of the service. Specifically they identified that they provide one of the few occasions when children can eat together in a fairly formal traditional manner, where children can develop social skills.

Choice and variety

As well as providing nutritionally sound meals it is essential that caterers provide a choice of meals to ensure that all consumers have an alternative that is acceptable to them. Without choice it is likely that some people would find the offered meal unacceptable for reasons of preference, medical condition, religion or beliefs. Without the provision of an alternative some consumers may fail to eat meals and certainly uneaten meals can make no contribution to the diet regardless of their nutritional content.

Variety over time is also important in maintaining interest and enthusiasm for meals. The extent to which variety needs to be offered is largely a function of the frequency with which meals are taken and length of time for which the meals are required. In hospitals, where nationally the average length of stay is 8 days (Central Statistical Office, 1995), two-week cyclical menus are normal. In situations where meals are required more long-term however, such as schools and care homes, more variety is likely and four-week cyclical menus would not be unusual.

Location

Unlike other food-service sectors, welfare caterers have to plan for the fact that because of limited physical or mental capabilities, many of their consumers will not be readily able to feed themselves and that in many cases they will not be able to go to restaurants or other central meal locations. This characteristic of the welfare sector requires that, in these situations (meals on wheels and hospitals for example) the prepared meals have to be transported to the consumers, who are sometimes in remote locations, from central production facilities. A number of systems have been developed to address the problems associated with the transportation of meals and these are discussed later in this chapter.

Consumer orientation

Food service operators have recognized that the key issue has become one of market needs analysis rather than market segmentation. Through analysing the specific needs of their consumers, operators seek to identify the key factors that need to be satisfied with a view to tailoring their product/service to match these needs. In this way it is anticipated that effectiveness and consumer satisfaction can be maximized.

This focus on consumer needs is illustrated by the fact that many hospitals conduct regular surveys of consumer attitudes to the food-service provision. The Gloucester Royal Hospital, for example, conducts regular questionnaire-based surveys which are supplemented by personal discussions with individual patients. Indeed the hospital seeks to meet individual needs by encouraging patients to discuss their requirements with the catering management team.

Similar approaches have been adopted in other parts of the welfare catering sector including school meals and meals on wheels. The school meals service in Gloucestershire, for example, commissioned a major study of consumer attitudes to primary and secondary school meals in the county. As a result of this study it made a number of changes to its operational strategy and devised a marketing plan to address the issues raised (Hemmington and Chapman, 1992). This study is more fully discussed in the section on school meals.

MARKETING

It is often assumed that because welfare catering deals with a captive market there is no need for marketing. This is a commercially dangerous assumption, particularly in light of the current competitive environment as described above.

Recent experience has shown that marketing planning is an essential component in the provision of quality meals services. Whilst market segmentation is not necessarily appropriate, market analysis in terms of needs is essential to the development and provision of a consumer oriented service. Marketing plans in terms of product/service specification, price (where appropriate), location and distribution, and promotion should then be generated in response to the findings of the market needs analysis.

By following market oriented strategies it should be possible to maximize uptake and thereby benefit from economies of scale. Maximizing the uptake of nutritionally balanced meals should also contribute to improved diets in the target consumer group. Apart from these reasons, the fact that contracts are invariably monitored by the client organizations, should persuade contractors that a market oriented approach is appropriate.

OPERATIONAL SYSTEMS

The challenges of catering in the welfare sector, particularly in terms of the large volumes usually involved and the transportation of meals, have led to the development of a number of different systems. Whilst the systems adopted in each of the welfare areas are different, there are a number of general themes common to several of them. These common themes in the operational systems are discussed in this section.

Central production facilities

Perhaps the most fundamental decision in many situations is whether to centralize or decentralize meal production. Decentralization involves the development of multiple production and service units located close to the point of consumption. Centralized systems involve the development of a large-scale central production unit (CPU) which produces the meals in a central location. Meals are then either distributed hot direct to recipients, or in a preserved form (chilled or frozen) to a number of satellite end-kitchens, which are located closer to the point of consumption, where the meals are regenerated and then served locally.

The centralization–decentralization question has been an issue in hospital catering for many years, the debate centring around assumptions of economic efficiencies in centralized systems and quality advantages in decentralized systems. A study by Thompson et al. (1960) helped resolve the debate by making a direct comparison between centralized and decentralized systems operating under similar conditions at the Stamford Hospital, Connecticut. They concluded that although there were no significant differences in customer satisfaction or service temperatures, they calculated that there were possible labour cost savings of

20 per cent with the centralized system. This led to the widespread adoption of centralized systems in both the USA and the UK. More recently a UK study (Woodman *et al.*, 1996) found that a combination of practices in hospital kitchens could significantly improve productivity. They found that hospitals which made little or no use of pre-prepared vegetables, or cook–chill, were the least productive. By introducing pre-prepared vegetables, productivity could be improved by 26 per cent. But by doing this and using cook–chill, productivity was improved by an incredible 196 per cent.

There are nevertheless a number of advantages and disadvantages associated with the use of centralized systems which should be fully considered before their implementation. The advantages include:

- Higher labour productivity as a result of mass production techniques.

- Lower labour costs – reduced by as much as 20 per cent for large units.

- Higher productivity from facilities and machinery which can be utilized for extended periods.

- The need for fewer skilled staff, most of whom are located at the CPU. Skilled staff are not normally required at the satellite kitchens.

- Savings in materials costs through bulk purchasing and closer control at the central unit.

- Improved control over quality and food safety systems – particularly in terms of the ability to demonstrate due diligence.

- Greater standardization leading to improved reliability and consistency of product.

- Lower capital investment per meal produced.

- More social working hours for most of the production staff.

The disadvantages of centralized systems include the following:

- The need for locating, purchasing and obtaining planning consent for an appropriate site for the CPU.

- In the event of contamination the number of consumers affected will be many times that of a single cook–serve location.

- Any breakdown of the system or problems with staff (e.g. labour relations) would have far wider implications.

An alternative to the development of CPUs, and yet one that retains the advantages of centralized production systems, is the purchasing of ready meals in either frozen or chilled form. A number of National Health Service hospitals have adopted this approach, as have several meals on wheels services including the London Borough of Bromley and Oxford County Council who have both opted for frozen meals. By definition, all centralized systems require the support of delivery systems and preservation methods, the nature of which will be determined by the delivery distances and times. The range of eight alternative approaches is shown in Figure 16.1.

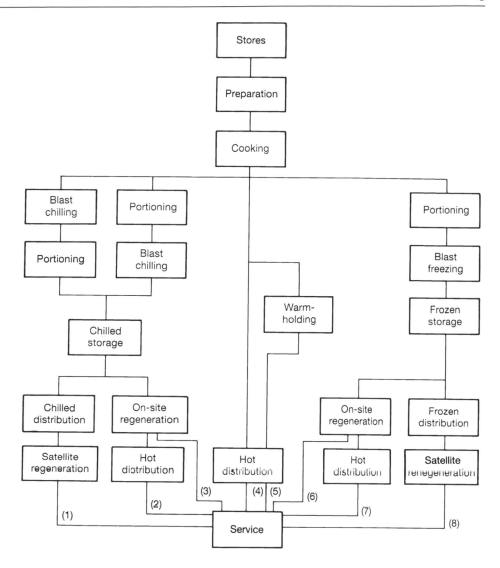

Figure 16.1 *Alternative hospital food-service systems*
Source: Jones (1989)

Meal preservation

Initially, welfare catering systems depended on the warm-holding of foods during delivery. This was usually achieved through the use of various types of insulated or heated containers. Early meals on wheels were delivered using a range of insulation-based methods including wooden hay boxes, wrapping in old blankets and virtually anything else that would retain heat. In hospitals, delivery systems have been based on plates with heat-store elements, electrically heated trolleys and insulated trays.

Warm-holding is most suited to situations where consumption takes place within a short time of production, i.e. where the delivery times are short. This is because with increased warm-holding the palatability, appearance and nutritional value of meals deteriorates rapidly. In terms of food safety the critical factor for these meals is that the food temperature should be maintained at over 63°C from cooking to final service to the consumer. For this reason insulated systems are usually limited to situations where meals can be loaded at a minimum temperature of 80°C and delivered within 30 minutes. Where these requirements cannot be met, heated delivery systems are necessary.

Preservation systems that extend the delivery/storage time are cook–chill, cook–freeze and sous vide. Each of these approaches has a number of advantages and disadvantages in terms of meal production, delivery and quality.

Cook–freeze is based upon preservation through the blast freezing of meals down to below −18°C. Meals preserved in this way can be stored for several weeks which gives much greater flexibility and in their solid state are easily handled and transported. A significant advantage with frozen meals is that with their extended storage times it is possible to deliver several meals in one delivery and therefore reduce the frequency of deliveries. This is a particular advantage for the meals on wheels service where deliveries can be made once a week to those recipients with a freezer.

Regeneration can be either from the frozen state or after thawing. Regeneration from frozen requires that thorough reheating throughout must be ensured whilst defrosting must be achieved in a temperature controlled environment. Another advantage of frozen meals is that evidence of thawing makes it obvious when the system fails.

There are however some drawbacks with cook–freeze:

- Some food items are not suitable for freezing, these include eggs, salads, soft fruits and some sauces.

- Recipes may need modification, some sauces for example may separate and will therefore need modified starch to bind the emulsion.

- The costs of freezing and low temperature storage are greater than for chilling.

Cook–chill systems are based on the rapid chilling of meals down to 3°C (within 90 minutes) and storage at between 0°C and 3°C. Under these conditions meals can be stored for up to 5 days including the day of production and the day of service. The advantages of this system are as follows:

- There is little or no adverse effect on meal presentation, palatability or nutritional value.

- It can be used for all foodstuffs, although there may need to be modifications for some menu items such as sauces.

The disadvantages with cook–chill include the following.

- The whole system needs very close control and monitoring to ensure that health risks are minimized. This is particularly critical in terms of demonstrating due diligence. Hazard analysis and management have become key issues for such systems with the implementation of the Food Hygiene Regulations 1995.

- The critical and narrow range of temperatures involved demands extremely high operational standards. There is also the risk of large-scale loss of meals where temperature requirements are not met.

- Due to adverse publicity in the early years of its implementation, there is some consumer resistance to cook–chill systems.

- There is no easy way to detect breakdowns in the storage system. In the USA temperature sensitive coloured tags are used to detect rises in temperature above 5°C.

Sous vide is the most recent alternative for meal preservation. It is based on the packing of meals in high-barrier plastic bags that look similar to the vacuum packaging used in food retailing. Raw, blanched or semi-cooked foods are placed in the bags and are then either back flushed with an inert gas such as nitrogen, or are vacuum packed. The foods are then cooked, chilled and stored in the bags. The advantages of this process are that it:

- extends the storage time of the meals to up to 21 days;

- minimizes food deterioration (particularly that due to dehydration);

- reduces cooking loss;

- reduces nutrient loss;

- protects food from contamination.

Despite these advantages, sous vide has not been seen as applicable to the welfare catering sector largely because of costs. The capital costs associated with establishing the system are significant and there are also revenue costs associated with the packaging which make meals expensive.

Distribution systems

The transportation requirements of meals will be largely determined by the type of preservation adopted. As previously discussed, where hot meals are being transported they will either have to be insulated or placed in heated containers to ensure maintenance of the meals above the minimum temperature of 63°C. With storage time critical to the quality of meals in these systems, distribution networks must be designed to minimize delivery times.

Chilled meals present a similar problem of temperature control during distribution. Indeed the problem is accentuated by the very narrow band of permissible temperatures (0°C to 8°C) which are unlikely to be maintained by merely insulating the meals. For this reason it is essential that chilled meals are distributed in refrigerated transport with temperature monitoring equipment. It should be noted that although the legal maximum storage temperature is 8°C, good practice would be storage at 0°C to 3°C.

Frozen meals should also be distributed at their storage temperature, i.e. frozen. It might be tempting to allow these meals to thaw during delivery but thawing without temperature control is an unacceptable hazard. Delivery in a chilled environment, (i.e. 0°C to 5°C) would also create potential problems since such meals would have to be regenerated and consumed on the day of delivery thereby reducing flexibility at the local level. There is also the risk that they may be re-frozen or stored at the satellite location.

Regeneration

One of the advantages of hot meal delivery is that it requires no regeneration and therefore no heating equipment at the point of consumption. Systems that employ preservation techniques, however, inevitably require some form of regeneration at the local level. Suitable technologies for the regeneration of meals include infra-red ovens, convection ovens and combination steam ovens. Microwave ovens are only suitable for the regeneration of individual meals, meals on wheels for example, and therefore have limited use in volume feeding situations such as hospitals, schools and luncheon clubs.

The regeneration of frozen meals from the frozen state requires particular care in terms of ensuring that the whole food mass is thoroughly heated to an acceptable temperature, that is above 63°C. Frozen meals present particular problems for microwave ovens which can tend to leave ice pockets whilst heating the rest of the food mass. The solution is to heat the food slowly allowing conduction to stabilize the heat distribution through the food and therefore thaw any ice pockets.

Information systems

The evolution of computer-based information systems has led to the development of sophisticated real-time information systems in parts of the food service industry, particularly the fast-food sector. The welfare sector has been slow to realize the benefits such systems can bring to its large volume, logistically complicated, situations.

This looks set to change, however, with contract caterers introducing their information systems to welfare contracts, DSOs will have to follow suit to remain competitive. Indeed Highland Catering Services (DSO) have already introduced a system in their school meals service which provides half hourly reports from all schools on the numbers of items sold, sales volume, number of customers by age group, the mix of paid and free meals and the average spend per customer. The system provides managers with comparative information which can then be used to monitor performance at each unit relative to other units.

SCHOOLS

Although the provision of school meals was encouraged by the Education (Provision of Meals) Act 1906, no statutory requirement to provide school meals was made until after the Second World War when the Education Act 1944, implemented by the Provision of Milk and Meals Regulations 1945, required all education authorities to provide meals at all maintained schools for all children who desired them. This legislation provided the basis of the national school meals service that was to prevail in the same basic form until 1980.

As discussed earlier, the Education Act 1980 empowered local authorities to determine the nature and extent of the school meals service they would provide and to set the prices for them (although they were still required to provide free school meals for those eligible for them). This legislation has had a radical affect on the nature of the school meals service in the years since 1980. In 2001, the duty to provide free meals to eligible pupils, paid lunches where parents request them, and to comply with nutritional standards, rests either with the Local Education Authority or with schools who have a delegated budget for this purpose. Schools must also provide free facilities for pupils eating meals they have brought to school with them. Free school meals and free milk (if milk is provided in the school) are provided to children whose parents receive Income Support, Income-based Job Seekers' Allowance, or support under the Immigration and Asylum Act 1999. New regulations governing the compulsory minimum nutritional standards came into effect on 1 April 2001. These are now food-based rather than nutrient based making them easier for everyone to understand (www.dfes.gov.uk/schoollunches). All secondary schools, and those primary and special schools that have opted to, have delegated funding for school meals from April 2000. This means they may choose continue to use the LEA's catering service or contract it out to another provider if they so wish. The legal duty of provision rests with the school however, and they must ensure caterers comply with health and food safety regulations

Within the context of government requirements to reduce expenditure, individual local authorities exercised their autonomy in a variety of ways. Some reduced their provision to the statutory minimum, Buckinghamshire, Dorset and Lincolnshire, for example, others such as Merton and Croydon, contracted the service out to commercial operators. Many authorities however chose to maintain the service through reducing costs, charging prices that would cover costs and providing foods that children would buy. These policies led to a major change in style of service where traditional set meal arrangements were replaced by cash cafeteria systems which were defined by the Inner London Education Authority as:

> a service where items on the tariff are separately priced, the charge being related to the standard meal charge, and where pupils have the freedom to buy as much or as little as they wish. In each cash cafeteria it is possible for children to buy items equivalent to a full school meal ...

The cash cafeteria is now the dominant style of food service system in the school meals service and whilst it brings a number of benefits in terms of cost/revenue and in encouraging pupils to eat, there are also concerns particularly in terms of the effect such systems have on children's diets.

Size of the school meals market

Table 16.3 shows the number of school pupils in the United Kingdom from 1970/1 to 1998/9. The total number of schoolchildren in the UK reached a peak in 1977 when there were 11.3 million pupils. Since then the number fell to 9.2 million in 1990, rising again in 1992/3 to 9.5 million. Regardless of these variations the potential school meals market is clearly very significant and it is this potential volume of business in a captive environment that has been attracting commercial operators to the sector in recent years.

Despite the large potential market discussed above, only 45 per cent of children had school meals in 1993. In fact the proportion of children taking school meals had declined from 64 per cent in 1979 to a low of 43 per cent in 1989/90. In the

Table 16.3 *School pupils in the UK by type of school (thousands)*

	1970/1	1980/1	1990/1	1992/3	1998/9
Public sector schools					
Nursery	50	89	105	111	109
Primary	5,902	5,171	4,955	5,077	5,376
Secondary	3,555	4,606	3,473	3,606	3,791
Non-maintained schools	621	619	613	607	616
Special schools	103	148	114	117	115
Total	10,231	10,633	9,260	9,518	10,007

Source: Central Statistical Office (2000)

light of discussions on schoolchildren's diets (see below) it is interesting to note that 'other arrangements' such as chip shops and cafés accounted for just under a quarter of all lunch time meals in 1993. A survey of all pupils in Scotland in 2000 found that 47 per cent were taking school meals, the same proportion as four years earlier. This suggests that meal provision in schools has stabilized, after its significant decline in the 1980s. This may be due to some of the factors considered below.

Nutrition and healthy eating

With the publication of the *NACNE* (National Advisory Committee on Nutritional Education) *Report 1983* and the *COMA* (Committee on Medical Aspects of Food Policy) *Report 1984* concern focused on the nutritional aspects of school meals. The policy of allowing choice had led to concern about the effects it would have on the diets of children. The issue was referred to the Sub-committee on Nutritional Surveillance of COMA which carried out a study examining the contribution of school meals to the overall diets of school children. The study concluded that there were 'no significant differences between the average energy or nutrient intakes of children taking school meals from outlets offering a free choice cafeteria style service and those obtaining a fixed price school meal' (Committee on Medical Aspects of Food Policy, 1989).

Despite these findings, nutrition education had already been identified as a key factor in improving the eating behaviour of children (British Dietetic Association, 1980). In response many local authorities developed their operational and marketing plans around the theme of healthy eating. East Sussex Education Authority produced a promotional campaign to promote school meals and raise children's awareness of the nutritional implications of food choice, in Durham a 'Right Bite' theme was developed offering wholefood, low-fat and low-sugar menu items. Group 90, the school contract caterers on the Isle of Wight, introduced a healthy eating system based on a traffic light theme where children are advised to choose only one red coded meal item, up to two amber items and as many green items as they like.

Following these local initiatives, the Education (Nutritional Standards for School Lunches) Regulations 2000 laid down agreed minimum standards. The government is also encouraging schools to adopt a 'whole school approach to food' which relates to how food and nutrition is taught in the curriculum, the stocking of tuck shops with healthy products, policy on eating in the classroom, and so on. The DfES website identifies Wolsey School in Croydon, Torquay Boys' Grammar School and Alnwick Middle School in Northumbria as outstanding examples of schools that have adopted such an approach. A National School Fruit Scheme is currently being piloted in 2002, with the intention to roll it out nationally in 2004. This will entitle every school pupil to free fruit every day.

What do consumers want?

A key factor in the provision of quality services is an understanding of consumer needs. Gloucestershire County Council commissioned studies of consumer attitudes to school meals in primary and secondary schools (Hemmington and Chapman, 1992). Whilst in secondary schools pupil attitudes were investigated, for the primary school study the attitudes of parents were investigated. The findings of these studies provide an interesting perspective on what school meals consumers want.

The parents of primary school children identified the following key issues. Healthy eating was by far the most significant issue for parents who specifically identified the need for less convenience food, chips to be offered less frequently, more whole foods, no tuck shops or ice cream vans and more guidance for children on food choice. The social role of school meals was a significant issue, parents identifying that school meals provide one of the few opportunities for children to eat together in a fairly formal, traditional manner. They were also of the opinion that social skills should be taught and that the dining environment should be kept quiet and peaceful. Other issues identified by parents were value for money, the impracticality of going home and the extra work associated with making sandwiches.

The study of secondary school pupils, on the other hand, revealed another set of issues. The dining environment is a major determining factor in pupils' perceptions of school meals. Where dining rooms are perceived to be boring, cramped and oppressive pupils prefer to spend their lunch time elsewhere. With regards to quality of meals, many pupils said that they would pay more for meals outside school, or even save their money, rather than have school meals. Choice and variety of foods was the third most important issue. Traditional meals service was perceived to offer limited choice while cash cafeterias were seen as a positive improvement.

The school meals service's response to these findings was to develop both operational and marketing plans to address the issues raised. These included the development of a *Healthier Eating Manual* to advise catering supervisors, the introduction of a new pre-formed plastic tray based service and a marketing and promotional campaign. The result of these strategies was that uptake rose from 27 per cent to 32 per cent despite a price increase during the period.

HOSPITALS

The modern hospital catering service was created as a result of concerns about patient diets during the Second World War. The Briscoe Committee 1943 identified extreme nutritional inadequacy in the diets of patients in London hospitals and recommended that specialist catering departments be set up within hospitals. This recommendation was implemented as part of the National Health Service Act 1946 along with the appointment of professional full-time catering officers who introduced meal choice and the use of recognized recipes and methods of food preparation.

Although significant improvements were made in the service up to the 1970s, the provision remained below the expected catering standards of the time and a number of critical reports, including the Egon Ronay Organisation and the Consumer Association, were published during the 1970s and 1980s. This and the government's demands for efficiencies in public spending led to legislation requiring competitive tendering as discussed in section 3 of this chapter.

Size of the market

In 2001, there were approximately 3000 National Health Service Trusts managing 1200 hospitals throughout the UK. The NHS spends a total of £500 million a year on food, serving over 300 million meals.

Operational systems

All the issues discussed above–centralization, preservation, distribution and regeneration – apply to hospital catering systems. Centralization brought with it the problems associated with the transportation of meals, particularly the maintenance of food temperatures. Early delivery systems were based on bulk delivery using electrically heated trolleys. Continuing problems with the quality of food delivered in this way led to the development of highly specialized systems specifically designed for hospitals.

Tray-service systems

In particular, the development of tray-service systems has perhaps been the most radical development leading to a number of variations on the basic tray theme. The first of these tray systems was the Ganymede system which was based on plates with heated metal pellets that release heat into the plate over the period of delivery. A number of other similar heat store systems have been developed including the Grundy Finessa and the Heatrex system. These systems have been successful in keeping meals hot, but have tended to suffer from the problem of drying foods out.

Another approach to tray delivery has been the use of heated trolleys as opposed to heated plates or plate bases. Southmead Hospital in Bristol uses the 'Traymeal System' for the delivery of 750–800 meals per day with maximum delivery times of 20 minutes. This system is based on trolleys which have hot and ambient compartments for different meal components. The hot compartment is heated by a heat store which is electrically charged for 40 minutes before delivery.

A third approach to tray delivery is based upon insulation rather than additional heat. These systems are based on insulated moulded plastic trays which contain two to four bays for meal items. Because there is insulation between the different bays it is possible to place hot and cold foods adjacent to each other in the same tray and they will both be insulated and therefore remain hot or cold as originally loaded. Temprite, which is probably the leading system of this kind, has been installed in both the Gloucester Royal NHS Trust Hospital and the Cheltenham General Hospital. Experience indicates that these systems are suitable for deliveries of up to 30 minutes where loading temperatures of at least 80°C can be achieved.

All the above tray systems depend upon the same logistical support system. Menus are sent to wards in advance to allow patients to make their choice of meals – examples of lunch and supper menus are shown in Figures 16.2 and 16.3. These menus are then returned to the catering department and used as the basis for subsequent meal production. Food is then portioned and plated on trays using a conveyor belt system (see Figure 16.3). As trays are completed and reach the end of the conveyor they are placed into trolleys and immediately conveyed to the ward.

The logistics of this system are critical and precise timings have to be met to ensure that meals are delivered in time and in an acceptable form. Normally the meal service will be staggered over a period of one to two hours with each ward being processed over a specific time slot. On arrival at the ward, the meal trays should be immediately distributed to patients to ensure receipt in an acceptable condition.

Cook–chill systems

Cook–chill systems have been discussed earlier. Meals can be chilled in either individual portions or in bulk multiple portions depending on the desired food service style. At Frenchay Hospital in Bristol, for example, bulk chilled meals are produced at the hospital's CPU which are then loaded into insulated trolleys and are then regenerated at ward level in convection ovens. The reason for bulk meals in this situation is primarily in order to facilitate family-style service at central tables in the ward. Whilst this is acceptable for the majority of patients, for some it is not possible and for these patients meals are plated from the original bulk supplies.

Individual chilled meals can be portioned either before chilling, which increases storage space requirements, or after chilling, which creates problems of temperature control during the portioning process. The regeneration of pre-portioned meals can also create problems in terms of the variable rates at which different foods heat up.

Ready meal systems

A number of hospitals are now adopting a ready meal system based on either frozen or chilled meals. This approach removes the need for a CPU and the associated problems of food manufacturing and allows the hospital to concentrate on regeneration and service. The use of specialized food manufacturing companies enables hospitals to benefit from highly advanced technical facilities that they would be unlikely to be able to provide or operate themselves. The choice of appropriate suppliers could also be beneficial in terms of demonstrating due diligence.

Day 1 Monday	Day 2 Tuesday	Day 3 Wednesday	Day 4 Thursday	Day 5 Friday	Day 6 Saturday
Vegetable Lasagne	Vegetable Pizza	Roast Lamb	Chicken Sweetcorn Pie	Fried Fillet of Fish	Minced Beef Lasagne
Grilled Ham Steak & Pineapple	Beef Casserole	Spinach Potato Bake	Vegetable Hot Pot	Poached Fish	Cheese & Tomato Flan
Shepherd's Pie	Poached Fish	Minced Chicken	Grilled Sausages	Vegetable Curry	BBQ Spare Rib Chop
Gravy	Parsley Sauce	Mint Sauce	Parsley Potatoes	Sweet & Sour Pork	BBQ Sauce
Sautéd Potatoes	New Potatoes	Gravy	Creamed Potatoes	Rice	Minced Beef
Creamed Potatoes	Creamed Potatoes	Roast Potatoes	Sliced Green Beans	Chipped Potatoes	Jacket Wedges
Sliced Green Beans	Carrots	Creamed Potatoes	Baked Beans	Creamed Potatoes	Creamed Potatoes
Sweetcorn	Peas	Cauliflower		Peas	Sweetcorn
		Mixed Vegetables		Carrots	Courgettes
Eve's Pudding	Lemon Meringue Pie	Apple Pie	Apricot Crumble	Fruit Flan	Fresh Fruit Salad
Custard	Low Fat Yoghurt	Fresh Fruit	Custard	Milk Pudding	Cream
Fresh Fruit	Fresh Fruit	Fresh Fruit	Apricots in juice	Fruit Cocktail	Milk Pudding

Day 7 Sunday	Day 8 Monday	Day 9 Tuesday	Day 10 Wednesday	Day 11 Thursday	Day 12 Friday
Roast Chicken	Chicken Fricassé	Steak & Kidney Pie	Roast Turkey	Lamb & Vegetable Casserole	Fried Fillet of Fish
Seasoning	Vegetable Sauce with Pasta	Chilli Bean Casserole	Vegetable Milanaise	Cheese & Broccoli Flan	Poached Fillet of Fish
		Honey Roast Ham	Poached Fish with Cheese Sauce	Minced Beef Lasagne	Cheesy Ratatouille
				Gravy	Beef Curry
					Tartare Sauce

Day 13 Saturday

Shepherd's Pie
Cheese & Tomato Pizza
Sausages
Gravy
Mashed Creamed Potato
Chipped Potatoes
Mixed Vegetables
Baked Beans
Fresh Fruit
Pineapple Upside-down
 Sponge
Custard
Milk Pudding

Custard
Milk Pudding
Fresh Fruit

Milk Pudding
Low Fat Yogurt

Milk Pudding
Yogurt

Milk Pudding

Day 14 Sunday

Roast Beef
Cauliflower Cheese
Savoury Minced Beef
Gravy
Yorkshire Pudding
Roast Potatoes
Creamed Potatoes
Carrots
Green Vegetables
Trifle
Fresh Fruit
Milk Pudding

Figure 16.2 *Hospital lunch menu cycle*
Source: Gloucester Royal NHS Trust Hospital

Schedule of equipment
1. Conveyor belt
2. Dispenser for cutlery
3. Dispenser for trays
4. Pellet ovens – four tube
5. Dispenser for bases
6. Dispenser for plates
7. Rackmasters for bowls
8. Bain-marie for pudding
9. Bain-marie for meat
10. Bain-marie for gravy
11. Bain-marie for potatoes
12. Bain-marie for soup
13. Bain-marie for vegetables
14. Dispenser for bowl lids
15. Dispenser for lids
16. Reject trolley
17. Tray trolleys

Figure 16.3 *Tray-service production line*
Source: Jones (1988)

This system also allows for the preparation, regeneration and service of meals at ward level. Catering staff on each ward order chilled or frozen meals the day before they are needed according to a menu cycle. This allows patients to pre-order on the same day (as opposed to the day before) or in some cases to select what they want from a heated trolley of prepared meals.

The NHS Plan and Better Hospital Food Programme

The current Labour government, as part of their 1999 election manifesto, committed themselves to improving the NHS. Following extensive consultation, a NHS Plan has been established as 'a long-term strategy for modernising and improving health services around the needs and expectations of patients'. In 2001 an Audit Commission report identified the NHS wasted £18 million a year on hospital food, largely by overproducing meals or having high rates of plate waste. The report identified one third of hospitals as needing to improve their standards. Patients' nutritional needs were not always met due to limited menu choice, poor timeliness of meals or lack of assistance in choosing or eating meals. According to this report 40 per cent of adults admitted were malnourished on admittance to hospital or became so during their stay!

It is therefore timely that as part of the NHS Plan, a £40 million Better Hospital Food Programme has been implemented. Patient research in the NHS had shown concern about poor menu descriptions, complicated ordering of meals, time delays between ordering and delivery, poor presentation of food, wrong food temperatures, portion size, and an onerous complaints procedure. Specific research into food and meal preferences was also conducted through a survey of 612 patients in three hospitals and trials of new dishes were conducted in 11 hospitals in all parts of England.

The Programme seeks to improve standards in a number of ways.

- There will be a new NHS menu covering breakfast, drinks and snacks, a light lunch time meal and improved two-course evening dinner. This pattern of meal service has been changed to reflect modern eating habits.

- Dishes on this menu have been specially designed by the NHS Menu Group comprising leading chefs from outside the NHS (such as Loyd Grossman and Shaun Hill), NHS caterers, dietetic professionals, nurses and advised by a Patient's Food Group, with representatives from the Patients' Association, the Patients' Forum, and other bodies such as the Multiple Sclerosis Society. Recipe information for 500 dishes was initially made available through a CD-ROM and on a website (www.betterhospitalfood.com). Trusts are also being invited to submit their own recipes for possible inclusion in a 'National Dish List'. Patients will be informed about dishes through a booklet made available to them all. This will list dishes in a number of categories – main menu, children, soft diets, vegetarian, special diets, cultural and religious, and 'all hours'.

- The NHS is also working with prepared meal producers who supply the NHS such as Delta Dailyfood and Brake Brothers so that they too can supply dishes from the new range.

- There will be a 24-hour NHS catering service which will allow in-patients to have a light alternative outside of regular meal times. Where possible this should be extended to other groups such as long-stay attendees in Accident & Emergency, out-patients, and day patients. There are three elements to this provision. The Snack Box has been specifically designed for use throughout the NHS although Trusts are free to determine for themselves the precise contents, which will include 6 snack items such as sandwiches, yoghurt, packets of biscuits, fruit, and cold drinks. Each Trust must have three alternative Snack Boxes, one of which must be suitable for children. The second element is a Ward Kitchen which will provide hot and cold drinks and light refreshments such as toast, biscuits, cake and fruit to support the 24-hour service. The third element is the 'Light Bite', which is designed to be an extension of the Snack Box service to include a range of hot plated meals, probably microwaveable.

- By 2004 at least half of all hospitals will have ward housekeepers, whose role will be to serve meals and drinks, monitor the quality, assist patients, deliver 24-hour service, monitor plate waste and obtain customer feedback. Such housekeepers will be the main way in which the three elements identified above will be delivered.

- There will be systematic evaluation by dieticians of the nutritional value of hospital meals.

- There will be unannounced inspections of hospital catering.

- Patients views will be systematically collected and included in the Performance Assessment Framework designed to monitor the NHS Plan.

CARE HOMES

Demographic trends in the UK population have been discussed. In particular the dependency ratio was identified as 63 in 1992 and is expected to rise to 82 by 2036 when the number of pensioners is expected to reach 17 million, accounting for approximately 23 per cent of the population (Central Statistical Office, 1995). This growth in the elderly dependent population has led to a growing need for long-term care in residential homes of which there are now over 21,000 in the UK.

In Gloucestershire for instance there are 124 registered care homes with an average occupancy of 23 people. Given that the average amount of money spent on food is £17 per person, per week, the total market is worth around £345 million per year in raw materials alone (Jordan, 1992). With the sector being so fragmented in terms of the proportion of small units averaging around 25 residents and with no dominant players and virtually no structure in terms of associations, it is not an area of any great interest to commercial catering organizations.

In virtually all establishments, lunch is the main meal of the day and most offer a choice of meals at lunch time. It is normal for homes to have at least one designated cook, who has primary responsibility for the menu. It is however usual for residents to have an input into menu planning either through informal expressions of meal preferences, through more formal meetings and, in some cases, suggestion boxes. The most common food production system in this sector is cook–serve, where meals are prepared ready for serving between 5 and 30 minutes before service.

MEALS ON WHEELS

The meals on wheels service was started in the 1930s by the Invalid Kitchens of London. It was further developed during the Second World War by the National Old People's Welfare Committee (NOPWC) and the Women's Royal Voluntary Service (WRVS), largely in response to the inability of the elderly, sick and frail to attend communal feeding centres of that time. After the war, the NOPWC largely concentrated on the development of meals on wheels. By the 1960s a national network of meals on wheels schemes had been developed. This was helped by the National Assistance Act 1962 which had permitted local authorities to provide meals for old people in their homes and to help voluntary organizations by allowing the use of local authority premises and equipment. Over time, local authorities generally assumed control over meals provision, with the WRVS largely concerned with delivering the meals.

Market size and demand

Consistent with the demographic trends already discussed, the demand for meals on wheels has steadily risen. The number of meals rose from 13 million in 1969 to

38 million in 1993. The number of meals served elsewhere to the elderly and physically disabled, such as in luncheon clubs, in 1993 was 15 million (Gledhill, 1993).

In terms of what users of this service expect, a number of studies have examined the attitudes of the elderly to meals on wheels. Typical of these was a study in Leicester (Tilston *et al.*, 1992), which found that:

- Most recipients (86 per cent) were either satisfied or very satisfied with the service. This could however be the result of fear that criticism would lead to withdrawal of meals.

- The key determinant of the perceived quality of meals was the quality of the protein element (usually meat or fish). Sausages and beefburgers were considered inferior substitutes for meat.

- The 'easy to cook' meal, delivered weekly or monthly, was not a popular alternative. Such meals require suitable storage and cooking facilities in the home. Other studies have suggested that, frequently, users do not store or reheat such meals correctly, increasing the potential for food-borne illness.

- The most acceptable delivery time was midday to 12.30 pm, with most complaints from those who received meals before 11.30 am and after 1.30 pm.

- Evening meals were not popular. Most elderly people see lunch time as the principal meal time of the day, and probably have some concerns about opening their doors on dark evenings.

- Mashed and croquette potatoes were particularly disliked. In view of the fact that the potato is an important source of ascorbic acid in the diet, meals on wheels menu planners need to think of other ways in which this nutritional element may be provided, for instance by offering cabbage as a vegetable, or orange juice.

Research also shows that the service achieves far more than just feeding people. The daily visit to deliver the meal also enables a check to be made on the well-being of the recipients and also fulfils a social role in terms of enabling people living on their own to meet and talk with someone, however, briefly, every day.

Nutritional aspects of meals on wheels

Until the DHSS circular 'Organisation of meals of wheels' in 1970, nutritional objectives in this sector had not been very clear. With the involvement of local authorities however, a concern for diet and nutrition became evident. The 1970 circular noted that meals on wheels would only make a significant contribution to nutrition if at least five hot meals were served each week. The importance of protein was emphasized and the role that dried milk as a supplement could play in this was identified. It was advised that fats and carbohydrates in excess should be avoided and fruit should be offered once a week. Since there is loss of vitamins if food is warm held, providers were urged to avoid delay in delivering meals.

Despite this, a number of studies identified ongoing problems with this service. Many recipients of meals on wheels also received some meals from friends, neighbours and family as well. Overall their diet, especially that of the house-bound elderly, was low in vitamin D and ascorbic acid. Although the meals on wheels service provides adequate portion sizes, with sufficient energy values and protein content, the effectiveness of this was reduced if there was too long a delay in serving the meal or the recipient did not eat it. Plate waste was rarely monitored. In 1992, the Advisory Body for Social Service Catering recommended quality standards, including nutritional guidelines, designed to address these issues in their publication *A Recommended Standard for Community Meals*.

Another feature of this service is the need to recognize and serve the needs of people with a range of dietary needs. Some of these needs relate to medical conditions which may require salt-free or low-sugar content. Other dietary needs relate to ethnic origin and may necessitate the provision of halal or kosher dishes. For instance, in the 1990s, 10 per cent of meals served by Westminster Meals Service were kosher.

Operational systems

The meals on wheels service has traditionally focused on the delivery of hot meals. The actual transportation of meals was originally on foot, with the first 'wheels' being those of bicycles and prams! Maintaining meals at an acceptable temperature was a problem and a number of improvised insulation methods were adopted, including the use of hay boxes, old blankets, Canadian Red Cross dinner pails, and virtually anything else that would retain heat. After the war, these methods were replaced by either heated systems, such as Food Conveyor's 'Hotlock' which maintained heat through the combustion of charcoal, or by insulated containers. In the 1980s, the traditional Hotlocks were phased out and replaced by electric alternatives such as Corsair or Exelarc.

Despite this widespread common approach to delivery, there has always been concern about hot meal delivery, for three main reasons. First, meal quality in terms of acceptability may be low. Second, the warm holding reduces nutritional value. And third, warm-holding increases the growth of pathogens if contaminated. A number of studies of meals on wheels found food at temperature between 30°C and 62°C, rather than the prescribed – and safer – 63°C. It is therefore not surprising that alternative systems have been trialed. These include a study (Armstrong *et al.*, 1980) that compared the delivery of partially prepared meals that were frozen, pouch sterilized or packed as raw ingredients, which were temporarily stored and then regenerated in the recipients homes. Although in some cases food quality and nutrition was increased, users did not find in-home regeneration acceptable. The same study also investigated a delivery system based on the regeneration of frozen meals in a specially adapted delivery vehicle, but it was found to be 40 per cent more expensive than the conventional system. The delivery of chilled meals has also been studied, but the relatively low margins of food safety with this system have largely prevented its widespread adoption.

PRISON CATERING

There is little published information on prison catering. There are 135 prisons in England and Wales, housing 65,000 prisoners. As in other sectors, catering provision may be in-house or contracted out. The average food-cost allocation per prisoner in 2000 was £1.44 a day (www.caterer.com). Many prisons operate cafeterias as described in Chapter 15, although this will vary according to the prison type. Open prisons allow inmates a fair degree of freedom within the confines of the boundary wall, whereas high security wings or prisons have much closer control over prisoners. However there are some features unique to this sector. Food and meal quality is seen to play a role in rehabilitation, just as in the other welfare sectors it is recognized to have a social as well as nutritional role. 'Hot food served at regular times helps keep prisoners calm and potentially riot free' (Webster, 1995). Another distinctive feature in this sector is that prisoners may often play a role in food preparation and production. Prisoners may perform such tasks as pot washing, vegetable preparation, bakery, butchery and kitchen portering. In many cases this is tied into enabling prisoners to gain qualifications such as NVQs as part of their rehabilitation. Likewise, in some prisons, the foodstuffs used are actually grown on prison farms and market gardens. As with most cafeteria systems in the welfare sector, most prison caterers operate to a menu plan over a five- or six-week cycle, with limited choice each day.

CURRENT ISSUES AND FUTURE TRENDS

Between 1945 and the late 1970s, the welfare catering sector as a whole was relatively stable. Even the introduction of new technologies such as tray serve systems, free-flow cafeterias and central production seemed to have little impact on the nature of the customer experience or meal product offered. However, during the 1980s legislative changes had a major impact on catering provision in all parts of the sector. During this period the major drive was to maintain standards of provision whilst significantly improving productivity and efficiency. The main way this was to be achieved was through opening up public service provision to competition. This would enable contract foodservice companies to apply commercial principles and expertise thereby reducing costs. In practice, this was very slow in developing. Commercial firms found that local authorities, hospital trusts, and other public service organizations devised tender documents that were so detailed and so complex that bidding was too time consuming. Furthermore, this sector operates on very low margins so that the financial return was not great. So in 1991 contract foodservice companies only had 450 contracts for outlets in state education and 337 in healthcare. By 1995 this had changed dramatically with significant growth in both these sectors due to changes in the legislative framework and tendering process, the opportunity presented by the end of five-year contracts awarded in the 1980s, and the growing expertise of commercial firms in this sector.

Although provision is less standard nationally than in some other sectors of the foodservice industry, parts of the welfare sector are now very similar to commercial operations. Familiar high-street brands or contractor's in-house brands may be found in schools, colleges and hospitals. Menus and dishes match more closely the meal offer of restaurant and pub chains, reflecting a much wider range of ethnic food and styles of cookery. Some of the most significant change has occurred back-of-house, whereby welfare caterers now have much more sophisticated information systems and manage their supply chain more effectively.

Information systems are essential in any high-volume operation that seeks to provide customers with variety over a long period of time. This is the case in fast food, and equally true in this sector. Operators now have systems that enable them to monitor frequently, or even in real time, all aspects of the operation – number of items sold, sales mix, rate of purchase, average spend and even market segmentation. This enables operators to manage their inventory more effectively, plan menus appropriately and compare performance between units to monitor wastage and unexpected losses.

The development of central production facilities in this sector has partly been overtaken by developments in food manufacturing, food wholesaling and contract foodservice. Large scale manufacturers such as Findus and Birdseye now produce high quality products aimed at the catering industry. In nearly every case they are able to supply meals at a much lower cost than those prepared in a hospital or local authority CPU. As hospitals and schools already have regeneration kitchens and assembly serve layouts, switching from in-house meal production to outsourcing has been relatively straightforward. One major food supplier specifically set up prepared meals distribution centres in Plymouth, Aylesbury and Kettering dedicated to serving hospitals

Clearly the major current trend is less a focus on costs and efficiency but on service and quality. Taxpayers' expectations are that food served in the welfare context should be as good as can be found anywhere else it is purchased. The role that food and meal times play in helping patients to get better, old people to have social contact, and prisoners to be rehabilitated is being emphasized. The new initiatives identified in this chapter are all designed to be a 'public service ethos' in this sector that potentially was lost through privatization and commercialization. A clear feature of this is much greater involvement of users in decisions about their meal choice and delivery, as illustrated by the NHS Patients' Food Group.

SUMMARY

This chapter has looked at foodservice in hospitals, care homes, schools and prisons. It is a sector that has been affected by the contracting out of foodservice as discussed in the previous chapter. A feature of the sector is the special needs that client groups, such as hospital patients, the elderly and school children may have, especially with regard to their health and diet. Meals may also play a social role in this sector. To keep costs down and produce meals in large volume, this sector was one of the first to adopt central production facilities and cook–chill methods. In hospitals, which require tray service for patients confined to bed, this has also involved the development of specific systems for plating and keeping food hot. This is also the case with respect to meals on wheels. The major issue currently facing the sector is the raising of standards, which in the National Health Service has involved patient groups, industry professionals, health workers and celebrity chefs working on a better hospital food plan.

FURTHER STUDY

www.betterhospitalfood.com

QUESTIONS

To what extent are customer needs different between schools, care homes, hospitals and prisons?

CHAPTER 17

Travel catering

INTRODUCTION

Travel catering is a relatively well defined sector of the foodservice industry, which has shown modest growth in the last few years. Although rail, airline and ship catering differ in terms of the types of food they offer and the systems they use to provide the service, they have many factors in common. In particular, passengers who are travelling long distances cannot make the same choices about where to eat or drink that are open to people travelling by private car. Organizations also have the operational constraints of providing staff and raw materials to a unit that moves from one location to another. This requires a sophisticated logistic planning system for the allocation of staff and distribution of materials. In this chapter each sector of travel catering will be looked at in turn – airline, rail, ferry, cruise ship and terminus catering.

AIRLINE CATERING

One of the unique aspects of airline catering is that the cost of the catering service is usually included in the price of the airline ticket. The nature of in-flight catering is fundamentally related to the airline, flight type and class of ticket. There are a number of different dimensions to this. These include the duration of flight – either long haul or short haul; the type of route – domestic or international; the type of flight – charter or scheduled; and class of service – budget/economy/tourist, club/business/executive, or first. Foodservice varies from a sold beverage and a pack of nuts or crackers on a short domestic flight, to two or three meals served on china and accompanied by wines and liqueurs, as is found on a first class long-haul flight. One of the main determinants of the nature of the cabin service provided is related to the duration of the flight. For example, a domestic flight from London to Manchester takes less then 1 hour, whereas a long-haul non-stop flight from London to Los Angeles or Hong Kong takes around 13 hours.

Size and nature of in-flight catering

The market for in-flight meals is obviously closely related to the growth in the number of people travelling by air. In spite of the increased competition from road and rail, particularly for short-haul flights, and despite changes in methods of conducting business because of electronic mail and teleconferencing, the number of air flights has increased by 5 per cent per year. Despite the short-term impact of 11 September on air travel, it is expected this growth will continue for the next decade.

Throughout the 1990s the nature of in-flight catering was changing because of marketing and financial and operational pressures on airlines. Particularly in the case of short-haul flights, where there is competition, not only with other airlines but also with rail, airlines have responded to this pressure in different ways. Some airlines, such as EasyJet and Ryanair have chosen to compete on the basis of low costs and the fact that passengers need a simple and efficient journey from airport to airport. To this end, some airlines have reduced the cabin service to a simple cold snack or a trolley buffet service during the flight. On such 'no-frills' airlines, passengers pay for any food and beverage items they select.

With regard to full service carriers, there are two clear schools of thought in the airline catering industry, most clearly illustrated by the differences between the Asian and North American approaches. In Asia, many airlines have maintained direct control over on-board provision and operate their own in-flight meals kitchens. For example, since 1980, Singapore Airline's catering operation (SATS) has continued to expand and renew their in-flight kitchens to meet the demand for finer meal service for their thousands of passengers. In the USA, the birth of in-flight meal service is usually traced to the 1930s when J. Willard Marriott decided to sell boxed meals from one of his Hot Shoppes to passengers queued up for flights out of an adjacent airport (Romano, 1993). That side operation grew up to become Caterair, but in the decades that followed, the multi-billion-dollar market was largely left to contract operations that had the high-volume production techniques to provide in-flight meals for the few dollars that the airline allotted (Romano, 1994). In Europe many airlines did operate their own kitchens, especially at hub airports. Some have now divested themselves of these, notably British Airways and KLM, whereas others have deliberately grown their catering divisions, notably Lufthansa with LSG SkyChef and Swissair with Gate Gourmet.

LSG SkyChef and Gate Gourmet both grew through merger and acquisition during the 1990s. Of just over 600 flight kitchens world-wide, LSG operate around 200 and Gate Gourmet around 150. The growth of these two global caterers has intensified competition for catering contracts, and over a five-year period prices have been forced down some 15–20 per cent (Pilling, 2001). Through outsourcing, the industry has pushed down the costs of in-flight catering to about 4 per cent of overall airline operating costs in the USA and around 6 per cent in Europe (Gill, 1999). Consolidation is not over in this business, because although 50–60 per cent of the market is in the hands of the two big players, the rest is very fragmented. The smaller caterers are competing by forming alliances with each other. One such alliance includes Servair, Alpha flight service, Abela Catering, Flying Food Group, Eurest Inflight Services, Singapore Air Terminal Service (SATS), and two airline caterers in Italy.

Location

The location of in-flight operations is clearly driven by the need to service airlines and therefore facilities will develop in line with the distribution of international travel routes and destinations. Airlines may, in some circumstances, supply aircraft with enough supplies for both the outward and return leg of a flight ('back-catering'), but it is more common for aircraft to carry supplies for a single journey. Most national and international airports have a least one in-flight production kitchen. Often there is spare capacity, as airlines over the years have cut back on their level of on-board service. Kitchens vary is size depending on whether they cater specifically for one airline or they have contracts to supply many. At London's Heathrow, there are eight units, two Gate Gourmet kitchens, one supplying British Airways short haul, the other serving long-haul routes; two smaller units, one serving Japanese and Korean airlines, the other serving El Al; and four other kitchens of various sizes serving the remainder of airlines operating out of the airport. The number of meals they produce ranges from around 5000 up to 25,000 per week.

Caterers prefer to have their kitchens built literally on the boundary of the airport, so that they have a 'land-side' to which goods are delivered by road, and an 'air-side', from which the caterer's lorries deliver trollies for loading onto the aircraft. In the UK most units are not in this location, but are outside the airport boundary, normally on an adjacent industrial estate

Product offering

The service of food and drinks to passengers on an aircraft has become a standard feature for many airlines, even on short-haul flights of less than two hours duration. There is a case to be made for all airline passengers to be served a non-alcoholic beverage because of the dehydrating effect of flying. But many services are considerably in excess of the level of provision needed to satisfy basic physiological needs of passengers for food and drink. Another of the original functions may have been to entertain and distract passengers from what could be a tedious or frightening experience, but this function has now to a considerable extent, been superseded by in-flight entertainment systems. However, the function of food and beverage service on aircraft has become a way of defining a unique characteristic of an airline – it is a means of product differentiation in what is otherwise a fairly standard way of covering long distances in a short period of time. Particularly where there is competition on a route, airlines may use the cabin service as a means of marketing their product.

Both the taste of food and drink and the appetite of passengers change when flying at altitude. This affects the nature of food offered and the time of service. For example, the flavour of foods become less distinct and the aroma of wines is reduced. At high altitude, many people react more strongly to alcohol and caffeine. A further effect of long-haul flights is that the body becomes dehydrated and therefore passengers are encouraged to drink non-alcoholic beverages and water at regular intervals. Because passengers are restricted in the amount of movement and exercise they can take, heavy foods and those which are difficult to digest are avoided. Many airlines, in their business and first-class service, offer a choice of light and easy-to-digest meals for those passengers who react adversely to more substantial meals whilst in the air. For example British Airways have a 'Well-being' menu choice on many flights. The cabin service can play a large part in countering jet lag. The timing and nature of meals served is designed in relation to the time of arrival at the destination so that the flight finishes with a meal that is appropriate to the time of day at the destination.

Menu planning plays an important part in the process of providing airline meals.

There are severe limitations on the service (tray size etc), on the technology (selecting foods and recipes which are tolerant of the time/temperature process involved) and on the needs of captive and sedentary customers. Planned menus are converted to standard recipes which are used as the basis of the in-house or contract specification to control quantities, quality and cost. Photographs are often used to communicate precise information about both the meal and tray layout. Because of the importance of meal service as a means of breaking up the monotony of a long flight journey, particular emphasis must be placed on the appearance of the meal. Attention also needs to be paid to satisfying the requirements of specific groups such as vegetarian and vegan customers and those with particular ethnic requirements. For example, in order to satisfy international customers, it may be necessary to provide kosher and halal meals.

Organization and staffing

Flight kitchens are now being developed which have capacities in excess of 40,000 meals per day and service flights for up to 40 different airlines – for example the facility provided by KLM at Schiphol airport. These modern in-flight kitchens are designed for year-round, 24 hours per day operation (17 to 18 hours for production, four to five for cleaning and maintenance) and therefore employ up to 1000 staff. The production units are divided into a number of departments, such as goods reception, central warehouse, preparation kitchens (meat, fish, vegetables), hot kitchen, cold kitchen, pastry/bakery, packing, tray assembly, trolley assembly, dispatch and waste disposal. In addition to these production areas, a number of ancillary areas are required, such as offices, changing rooms, product development kitchens and quality control laboratories.

   In all in-flight catering systems, hygiene plays an important part because of the use of high-risk products, such as meat, fish and dairy products, which are stored at chilled temperatures for long periods of time. Strict quality control is required, based on the principles of risk assessment, precise time temperature control, microbiological testing of products and hygiene audits of all storage and production areas. In-flight production kitchens either have their own laboratory or send materials to a commercial laboratory for testing. This testing includes the quality of all raw materials and finished dishes and the hygiene standards of all production areas. Samples of all meals produced are kept until one week after the flight has ended in case there have been any food related illnesses or complaints reported.

Standard operating procedures

Operating procedures can be divided into a number of activities: those which take place in the production unit; the transportation to the airport; the loading of materials onto the aircraft; the service of food and beverages to customers and crew; and the transfer of waste and materials for washing back to the production unit. Typically, the service provided is much more than just the food and beverage requirements of the flight but also includes duty-free sales, blankets, pillows, linen, toiletries, newspapers, magazines, children's games, baby food, first aid kits and printed menu cards.

   Whether the service is provided by a subsidiary of the airline company or by a contractor, the basis of the service will be a detailed specification for each flight. Initial production planning is done one to two weeks before the flight, when an estimate is made of material requirements for each flight, to allow the ordering of materials. Four days before departure, production plans are prepared for each department. Final adjustments are made on the day of the flight, when the detailed planning sequence is commenced. For each flight, there is a planned sequence of preparation of meals, assembly of materials and printing of labels for trolleys and containers. This includes all the special meal requirements, such as vegetarian, special diets and one of requirements for first class and VIP customers. An inventory list of all items required on the flight is printed out to allow inspectors to check for the correct assembly of items for each flight. A full load for a 747–400 consists of 6.5 tonnes of materials, including over 800 laid-up meal trays. Checking is essential to ensure that all of the requirements are present.

A computer system is used to link the production facility with information from reservations and check-in. Food items are produced to a schedule based on the estimated time of departure of the flight and on the projected number of passengers in each class. The majority of items are provided using a sophisticated cook–chill system. All foods, whether to be served hot or cold, are prepared in advance and chilled to below 5°C and held in chilled storage until they are ready for service. During transportation, dry ice is used to maintain the temperature of food items. Not all foods are produced in this way. For some flights, hot meals may be packed in insulated trays whilst still hot and kept above 60°C until they are served to the passenger. This system may be used on short-haul flights where the meal must be served as soon as the aircraft is in the air.

The majority of hot food items are cooked in bulk, using large-scale equipment such as convection ovens, combination ovens, pressure cookers and continuous fryers. The cooked dishes are then portioned into bulk containers and rapidly chilled. Following this, they are then held in chilled storage until required by the assembly department. In a similar way, all baked items such as breads and desserts are prepared in advance and chilled.

A few hours before the flight is due to depart, the process of packing, assembly and loading begins. Meals which are to be served hot are taken from chilled storage and packed into oven-proof containers, which may be foil, plastic or china. The foods are portioned into oven containers in accordance with the flight specification, which will lay down the weights of each component of the meal and the appearance of the meal. The oven containers are then loaded into oven racks and kept in chilled storage until they are required for assembly. Food assembly areas require control of temperature if hazardous foods remain in this area for any length of time out of refrigeration. Temperatures of 10°C or less are recommended.

The next stage is referred to as 'tray setting', which consists of assembling all of the items needed on a meal tray. For large operations a conveyor belt may be used to carry the trays past a series of assembly points. At the end of the conveyor, assembled trays are then placed into trolleys. There are several different sizes of trolleys used by the airlines and it is important that the correct trolleys are used to suit the type of aircraft used on a specific flight. Labels are placed on the outside of the trolley, indicating the flight number, the contents of the trolley and its location on the aircraft.

Two to three hours before a flight, all of the trolleys and containers are assembled in the dispatch bay. At this stage checks are made to ensure that all requirements are complete. These materials are then loaded into special delivery vehicles. The vehicles are designed to have pneumatic elevators to raise the height of the platform of the truck to that of the loading door on the aircraft – this is 9 metres above ground level in the case of a 747. At the last minute ice and newspapers are added to the load. The complete load for a long-haul Boeing 747-400 aircraft is made up of over 40,000 items which must be supplied by the catering company. This load occupies over 60 square metres of space.

The journey of the trucks is planned to coincide with the requirements of the airline. Communications links are vital. Flight times are subject to delays and cancellations and there is often less than two hours to unload, clean and reload an aircraft. Before loading can begin, the used trolleys and containers must be removed from the aircraft into an empty truck and returned to the in-flight catering unit. To cope with last minute needs, the catering company will have a fleet of small vans which can be used to facilitate last minute changes which arise after the trucks have started their journey.

After they have been loaded onto the aircraft, materials and equipment are stowed in the galley areas. Small aircraft may have two galleys, whereas a 747-400 may have six galleys. The precise configuration will be specified by the airline. All trolleys and containers must be stowed in the correct location in each of the galleys on the aircraft, so that cabin crew do not have to search through a number of trolleys before finding what they want. To this end, catering staff liaise with the cabin staff to check that all materials are on-board and that materials are located in their correct storage areas. All equipment and supplies must be securely fastened ready for take-off.

Figure 17.1 *Hi-Lift truck*
Source: Gate Gourmet

At this stage, cabin crews have more to think about than just food and drink, since they need to ensure that all passengers are correctly seated, their cabin luggage securely stowed and that safety instructions are completed. However, even with all of these other activities taking place, cabin service may have started with the service of a complimentary drink to first and business class passengers while the aircraft is still on the ground. Also, the first meal to be served may be loaded into the on-board convection ovens, if the meal is to be served as soon as the flight is in the air.

The planned service of food and drink starts as soon as the plane is in the air. The exact sequence depends on the time and duration of the flight. A short domestic flight may have a full hot breakfast or dinner service in the short time that the aircraft is in the air. A charter flight may have only a beverage and chilled snack service. A long-haul flight may serve two or three hot meals during the flight together with frequent drinks, to reduce the effects of dehydration and jet-lag.

Whatever the nature of the flight, the sequence of service is similar. The pattern of service will be largely dictated by the configuration of the aircraft, taking into account factors such as the number of aisles and the number of seats in each section. Oven racks with pre-loaded hot meal containers are placed in the ovens 15 to 20 minutes before they are required for service. Cabin crew then start service according to a planned sequence, which will vary from one airline to another. For a given meal there may be one trolley for meal trays and hot meals and a second for beverage service. In addition to this, items such as bread rolls and hot beverages may be required. At the end of the meal, trays are returned to the trolleys which in turn are relocated in the appropriate galley storage area and made safe for landing.

When the aircraft has landed, used trolleys and containers are transported to the local in-flight unit for sorting and cleaning. Conveyor belts are used to allow staff to separate glasses, china and cutlery from all of the waste material. There are now many initiatives to reduce the volume of waste and to maximize recycling of materials. In some operations, this activity has been automated, with magnets used to remove cutlery and powerful water sprays to rinse off waste food, plastic materials and napkins. Large flight dishwashing machines are used to wash all of the glasses, china and trays. These are then returned to store until needed for the next flight. In order to service an aircraft, three sets of all equipment are required, one set on the aircraft, one at the start of the flight and the other at the destination.

RAILWAY CATERING

The provision of food and beverages on the railways has undergone dramatic changes in the last few years, not least due to the restructuring of the railways in line with recent government policy and the provisions of the Railways Act (November 1993). The institution that was once British Rail is now no longer, although the name lives on. Names such as British Transport Hotels, Travellers Fare and more recently InterCity On Board Services have all disappeared, although some still operate under a new mantle. On 1 April 1994, Railtrack was set up as a separate government-owned company and the then existing passenger businesses (Network South East, InterCity and Regional Railways) were replaced by 25 passenger train operating units which were to be franchised.

Prior to privatization rail catering was the responsibility of InterCity On Board Services (ICOBS) on all InterCity and Network South East trains. Catering on other routes was open to tender from other catering operators. Since privatization each of the train operators is responsible for its own on-train catering, but the majority of catering is contracted out to Rail Gourmet, recently acquired from Swissair by the Compass Group. As in contract foodservice, contracts vary from a fixed amount per meals sold to a percentage of the profits. In 1997, Rail Gourmet had 95 per cent of the market, with 15 contracts to supply 1000 trains a day with food and drink (on trollies) and to cater on 350 of them. In 2001, Sodexho entered the rail market by setting up a new division – Sodexho Travel – and winning the contract to cater for First Great Western. This contract is estimated to be £5 million per year. It sees a switch back from microwaved hot buffet items to freshly cooked food with chefs on board each train.

The market

The single most important issue in contemporary rail travel was the opening of the Channel Tunnel. This had a significant impact on both the airlines and ferry companies which operate on the short-haul continental routes and, once the rail services were operating at full capacity, the competition for business on the London/Paris/Brussels routes became even more fierce.

Eurotunnel's 'Le Shuttle' train carries drivers and their vehicles between Folkestone and Calais in 35 minutes. These specially designed trains transport both private and commercial vehicles but there are not catering facilities provided on board. Passengers are free to move between carriages, but the only seating accommodation available is in their vehicles. Food and drink may be purchased at the terminal prior to the departure of the train, and commercial vehicles have the additional facility of a 'truck stop' at Ashford in Kent. This catering outlet, owned by Eurotunnel, provides HGV drivers with a wide range of facilities including accommodation (for those prohibited from driving at the weekends) and can issue tickets for the tunnel journey.

For foot passengers there is the Eurostar train to Paris and Brussels. Whilst in the tunnel, these high-speed trains share the tracks with 'Le Shuttle', however dedicated tracks will eventually be made available on both sides of the tunnel enabling Eurostar to travel the distance between Waterloo International, Paris Nord and Bruxelles Midi in approximately two hours. The on-board services on Eurostar are provided by Rail Gourmet. Eurostar's main competitors are the airlines and it is to airline standards of catering and on-board services which Rail Gourmet operate. There are two standards of catering provided dependent upon the type of ticket purchased. First class passengers, whose meal is included in the ticket price, are catered for in a similar style to an airline's club class, with a full range of meal occasions catered for dependent upon the time of day. The food on board Eurostar first class will be cook–chill rather than freshly prepared, reflecting both the airline-style image and the company's pursuit of consistency of product. Staff regenerate the food on board, with the production of this food taking place in central production kitchens similar to those operated in airline catering. The menus reflect a mix of French, Belgian and British tastes. For services other than first class the catering facilities are a buffet car offering a restricted range of simple items and a trolley service of snacks and beverages are available for those who wish to remain at their seat.

Product offering

The type of catering facility a passenger may expect when travelling by rail may be viewed from two perspectives: in-terminal catering and on-board catering. With regard to the latter, this is dependent upon the duration of the journey, the class of ticket purchased and the time of day. On-board catering can range from a beverage served from a trolley to a silver-served three- or four-course meal in the Pullman car. Certain types of service will only be operated on the longer journeys and only passengers in possession of specific classes of ticket are eligible to use the clearly designated catering facilities. Certain service are only available at specific periods of the day, although it is now perceived as necessary to provide some form of catering facility at all times on longer journeys, for example in the buffet bars, in an attempt to provide a good customer service.

The types of service offered on-board are as follows:

- *Trolley service* This is an at-seat service offering hot and cold beverages, sandwiches and snacks from a trolley pushed through the carriages and stopping at the customer's request. This form of service is generally not available at weekends.

- *Buffet bar* The buffet bar service offers, in addition to hot and cold beverages and snack items, a limited range of hot food such as burgers, pizzas, lasagne and stews. These are reheated in the galley behind the buffet and the customer takes them to his/her seat for consumption. This service also includes a Breakfast Tray and an Afternoon Tea Pack.

- *At-seat service* GNER serve first class and standard plus passengers in their seats hot and cold snacks and drinks during breakfast, lunch and dinner service times.

- *Restaurant car* These services operate a traditional meal for both lunch and dinner. Depending on the rail company this may be relatively formal silver service, or less formal, plated 'bistro-style' service.

- *Sleeper service* Operating only on designated night services, mainly from the south of England to Scotland, this is an 'at berth' service of refreshments at the end of the journey. Additionally, first class passengers may choose from fruit juice and croissant or a cooked breakfast.

Staffing

Staffing on board will vary in accordance with the type of services being offered. On services operating a buffet service only, one member of catering staff would be required. Where both buffet and trolley service are in operation, a minimum of two staff members would be required, with up to 7–8 members required for the provision of the above plus full restaurant services. The Chief Steward is responsible for the catering services on board.

Generally staff work approximately 39 hours per week over 7 days, although on the Glasgow/Edinburgh to London routes they may work a set of four 10 hour shifts, making the return journey in each case. Catering staff are not normally expected to rest overnight away from their base station except in the event of

Figure 17.2 *First-class restaurant car*
Source: Travellers Fare

unforeseen circumstances. Each InterCity route has an appointed Trains Manager who is responsible for the whole operation, helped by a number of Assistant Managers and clerical support staff.

Operational procedures

Prior to any catering services being provided there is a complex system of ordering food items to be done. Passenger loads for specific journeys are calculated, often based on previous sales data and the Trains Manager places the orders a week in advance with suppliers for each train. Based on past sales figures, the required amount of food stock is delivered to the respective trains. Staff are then issued with this stock, for which they are responsible and any shortages at the end of the journey must be accounted for. Should extra supplies of certain foodstuffs be required en route due to excess demand, staff can phone ahead to the next pick-up point and supplies are collected there upon arrival. This additional stock must also be reckoned for in the closing inventory. On the Edinburgh to Kings Cross route, for example, these pick-up points would be Newcastle, Doncaster and York.

On most InterCity routes the main catering vehicles used are of the Mark IV type. The kitchens on board are of a modular design, allowing pieces of equipment to be removed as required, for example allowing ambient sections to be replaced by chilled units. Electricity is the type of energy used in these modern galleys, although refrigeration is still a problem with the kitchen moving at speeds of up to 125mph.

Considerable investment is now taking place and during 2002 and thereafter, much of this rolling stock will be replaced.

In the Restaurant Car, most menu items will be prepared using conventional cooking methods as far as possible with food being brought on board in its raw state. Steaks, for example will be purchased in vacuum packs and cooked to order, but items such as roast beef would be delivered in a pre-prepared state. Likewise with some of the hot dishes served in the Buffet Bar.

A high degree of control is maintained in the provision of food and beverage, irrespective of the route operated. All commodities are logged out to trains and the catering staff are responsible for this. Issues to the staff are recorded at the beginning of the journey and a closing stock taken at the end. The staff member must then submit the relevant cash sum for the stock consumed. This system applies to all types of service. Due to the nature of the food items, the trolley services and Buffet Bar are 100 per cent controllable. Here most items are prepacked (even tea and coffee come in sealed containers) and stock easily reconcilable. Control over fresh produce does pose more of a problem, but accurate forecasting and strict production and portion control are implemented.

There are a number of problems which are inherent in the provision of food and beverage on trains aside from the fact that the kitchen is moving at high speed. Water, electricity and refrigeration supplies are expensive and revenue losses can be costly if they fail. In order to achieve the high standards of service, staffing levels must also be high. While breakfasts and evening meals are profitable, there is less uptake in the restaurant cars at midday, when staffing levels have to be as high as for the more profitable periods. Additionally, timetabling has to be accurate so staff are not away from their home depot overnight, yet providing enough staff to deal with a busy breakfast service could leave the train top-heavy with staff on other journeys.

MARINE TRAVEL CATERING – SHORT SEA ROUTES

The classification of commercial catering within marine travel encompasses two distinct sectors – passengers on short sea routes and clientele on board cruise ships for an extended duration of five days or more. Each of these sectors presents different demands on the foodservice operator as the customer expectations across these sectors will vary; indeed within one sector there may be a broad range of expectations and needs which the caterer must address. This may range from the basic physiological need for a substantial filling meal, in the case of a commercial vehicle driver, to providing corporate entertainment in a silver service restaurant at the other end of the spectrum. This is highly evident in the provision of catering on the short sea routes operated in the English Channel and the Irish Sea.

It is in the short sea route sector of marine catering that the most significant advances have been made in the last few years, spurred on by the opening of the Channel Tunnel. Today competition between ferry operators in this sector is fierce with a number of types of transport available to carry passengers on the relatively short crossings in the Channel and the Irish and North Sea to continental Europe. These include roll-on/roll-off ferries, hydrofoils and, more recently, high-speed catamarans. The type of catering facilities offered is limited by the size of vessel in which it is being offered and the duration of the crossing. Thus, on certain routes the facility may range from a kiosk offering hot and cold beverages, sandwiches and snacks to a full à la carte, waiter service restaurant, or a combination of these and other facilities.

Size and scale of sector

There are relatively few operators in the short sea sector of the market. The market is dominated by P & O Stena Line, formed in 1998 with the merger of P & O and Stena Sealink, each with approximately 30 per cent share of the market. Other operators with a significant impact include Brittany Ferries (French owned with approximately 10 per cent of the market), Sea Containers' subsidiary, Hoverspeed (5 per cent of the market) and Sally Line (4 per cent of the market). Within the short sea sector there are a number of markets served by these operators. The short sea sector had over 19 million ferry passengers in 2000, with 15 million of those travelling between Dover and Calais. Analysis of these markets shows three distinct types. There are holiday makers or clientele travelling by sea for pleasure purposes; commercial vehicle drivers; and the business community.

Each type of market will present the caterer with their own specific needs. Recognition and fulfilling their needs, as in any catering operations, is the key to success. Some operators provide concessionary restaurants for commercial vehicle drivers, recognizing that their particular needs are quite different from those of the pleasure traveller or the business executive. Most operators offer a business or club class package, with waiter service of complimentary tea and coffee in clearly designated lounges, designed specifically to meet the needs of the busy executive, with facilities on some of the multi-purpose 'superferries' extending to on-board conference rooms and associated services.

The period spent on board a ferry can be viewed as a pause in the journey which is totally under the passengers' control. Increasingly it is being marketed by operators as being 'part of the holiday experience' and importantly a time of relaxation for the passenger, be it as a holiday maker or commercial vehicle driver. Passengers therefore must be provided with catering facilities commensurate with their needs. Indeed, P & O established in a survey, that the provision of catering facilities is the third most important service as requested by their passengers. Moreover, often two ferry companies will operate on the same route at a similar fare structure so the standard of on-board catering can be a deciding factor in their choice of operator.

All of the major operators in the short sea sector are located at the main seaports of the South East of England (Southampton, Dover, Newhaven among others) as well as Fishguard in Wales and Stranraer in Scotland. A number of other services operate from the north-east of England and from the north of Scotland. The location of quayside facilities to service the catering operations on board ship is a key feature of most of the major operators. The logistics of supply of food commodities to a variety of locations, timings and so forth is complex, with the larger companies operating a system of central purchasing of all food items with a distribution to all ports on a daily basis.

Product offering

The number and types of catering facilities on board ferries varies according to the physical constraints of the vessel, the number and type of passengers it carries and, importantly, the duration of the journey. Many modern ferries are more akin to floating hotels, with a range of services available to make the trip relaxing and entertaining. Food and beverages are provided in outlets ranging from kiosks, for simple snacks, to self-service style restaurants seating up to several hundred people on the new 'superferries'. Silver service restaurants still feature on many vessels, especially those offering a premium class service although this style of food service system tends not to be found on the very short sea crossings due to constrictions of time. On average, there tend to be between 3–5 various food and beverage outlets on most ferries, obviously dependent upon size, not including staff feeding facilities. Some of these are well known high street brands, on franchise agreement. Others are in-house brands developed by the operator. The immediate potential market, while captive for the period of the journey, is not totally dependent upon the on-board catering facilities (unlike airline catering they are free to bring their own refreshments), with an average passenger uptake of the catering facilities ranging from 32–60 per cent, dependent upon the time of day.

Organization and staffing

Staffing on board ferries will vary according to the time of day, the facilities offered and the type of vessel. It is difficult to generalize about staffing structure, as not all operators will manage their vessels in the same fashion. Generally each vessel will have a purser, who is responsible for the provision and service of all 'hotel facilities' and to whom the staff report. Other key members of catering staff on board are the assistant purser and the senior chief cook. On a ferry with a complement of 100 staff, up to 60 of them may be primarily involved in catering but they may also be called upon to perform other duties. At the less senior levels, staff may work a variety of shifts, for example two weeks continuously day on, day off, followed by one week of night shift followed by six days off.

Standard operating procedures

Computerized central purchasing is common practice given the scale of some of the operations. At P & O, for example, the food requirements for the short sea fleet are handled through Dover, with designated large-scale suppliers of meat, vegetables and frozen produce being used. Individual food items are sourced by management and their supply to the company's dockside warehouses is dealt with by one of these designated suppliers (who will purchase the item from the manufacturer and negotiate prices with P & O). Each vessel must carry sufficient supplies for the return journey as victualling of vessels takes place only in the home port. However, specialist items such as patisserie, may be delivered to the ship in France.

In keeping with consumer demand, there is a greater emphasis now placed on the use of fresh produce, with many of the dishes being prepared on board. To facilitate this, cook–chill production systems are also used, with regeneration of dishes on board ship, while other food items, especially fast food products are prepared in much the same fashion as they are in their shore based counterparts.

With regard to service of food, this is similar to restaurant operations based on shore, incorporating self service, buffet, waiter service, silver service and kiosk styles of service. The supply of food and beverages to passengers usually takes place port to port in order to maximize sales and provide efficient customer service. Meal provision is therefore less restricted than it may be in other forms of travel catering.

CRUISE SHIP CATERING

After a period of decline in the 1970s, the world cruise market is growing at a tremendous rate. Estimates show that the market is due to double by the year 2005 with a worldwide increase from 5.3 million passengers to 11.5 million passengers. Several of the large companies are investing heavily in new cruise ships with this growth in mind. P & O took delivery of the Oriana (67,000 gross tonnes) in 1995, the Sun Princess (77,000 gross tonnes) in 1996 and two further superliners in 1997. In addition to liners such as the Canberra and the Sea Princess, P & O will be in a strong position to capture this increase in both the UK and the worldwide cruise markets.

Product offering

The logistics of provisioning a cruise ship are rather more complex than those of a cross-Channel ferry. In addition to the vast amount of equipment required, the liner may be at sea for an extended period of time and will often have to restock in foreign ports. However it must have, at all times, sufficient supplies to maintain a full catering service to high paying, often demanding passengers.

Irrespective of the category of the ship, or the ticket price, it is often the quality of the food which determines the success of a voyage. The price of the food, (and, in some classes, often the beverages) is included in the ticket price and for this reason a variety of restaurants are operated. Thus the facilities may range from one (or several) full silver service fine dining rooms, through to self-service restaurants and coffee shops. In many respects the facilities offered on board resemble those in a large luxury hotel with a full array of leisure and shopping facilities, staffed and managed in very much the same manner.

Staffing

Generally, the passenger–crew ratio on most ships is very high, with an average of one crew member to every two passengers. However, on the most luxurious ships this ratio can almost be 1:1. As in a luxury hotel, all grades of staff are employed; however working hours are long, with up to 14 hours a day not being unusual. Coupled with working seven days a week, often for several months, shared accommodation with work colleagues and living at sea, make working in this sector of marine catering rather arduous. The financial rewards are high, often with tax-free wages and substantial tips and the opportunity to travel the world, making this a particularly interesting field in which to work.

TERMINUS CATERING

In addition to the provision of a food and beverage service during the journey, the availability of restaurants, coffee shops and bars is a common feature of the airport, railway station and port terminal buildings. These facilities are most fully developed at airports, where airport operating companies are well aware of the importance of income from catering and other retailing concessions to the financial performance of the airport. The service has been expanded from the provision of food and beverages, to include large retailing operations, largely through the leasing of space to concessionaries.

Retailing has been most fully developed at airports, where very large numbers of people visit major international airports and are often there for long periods of time waiting for flights or waiting to meet friends and relatives. For example, Heathrow Airport receives over 40 million visitors and passengers each year, which represents a large potential market. In a modern airport, great care is taken over the location of catering and retailing concessions and integrating them with seating areas, check-in desks and transit lounges. Refreshments are required both on the land-side (before security checks/emigration control) and air-side (after security checks/emigration control and for passengers in transit).

The recognition of the importance of retailing activities has resulted in the development of large retailing areas in airports. A large international airport may receive 50 per cent of its revenue from retailing concessions. Concession income is much more significant for airports with a large proportion of international travellers, as compared with commuter airports. The trend is towards the provision of a large number of small units rather than a few large concessions. Also, we have seen the introduction of familiar high-street brands into these retailing areas. A good example of this is in The Village at Gatwick.

CURRENT ISSUES AND FUTURE TRENDS

Because of the effect of the recession on business travel, a number of airlines have had to rethink the nature of what they offer to customers. This is based on quantitative and qualitative market research. In particular, there has been pressure on first class service during the recent recession. A number of airlines have eliminated their first class service and upgraded the business class. There is a move towards simple fresh food, with an emphasis on service.

As was described earlier, there have been a number of approaches developed to control the cost of in-flight meals, but this is proving quite difficult in practice. One way of controlling cost is to reduce the amount of labour required. This can be done, for example, by buying in ready prepared food items which will reduce the number of catering staff required. Purchase of ready to assemble food products can include: ready portioned meats; ready prepared sauces; and cook–freeze/cook–chill products. In addition to catering staff, a large number of people are required to pack and assemble meals, trays and trolleys. The use of robotics is being introduced in order to reduce the cost of some of these activities.

There are other issues which have had an impact upon travel catering in a marine environment. The provision of a new type of high-speed ship (HSS) by Stena Sealink, meant a change from the current concept – due to the speed at which these vessels can travel the journey times on HSS routes was significantly reduced, with greater emphasis placed on quick dining outlets such as fast food.

SUMMARY

This chapter has considered catering for aircraft, trains, ferries, cruise ships and in transport termini. Many of the systems that are used in these segments are also found in other sectors. In-flight catering is based around cook–chill and tray lay-up systems, similar to those used in hospitals. Rail catering operates back-bar production kitchens and table service restaurant cars, as well as a trolley service. Ferries and termini are likely to have facilities very similar to those found on motorway service areas. It is very difficult to obtain statistics for the size and scale of this sector, as it is not usually considered separately. However it is clear that a very large number of people are served meals in these forms of transport.

FURTHER STUDY

www.gner.co.uk

www.ifca.co.uk

QUESTIONS

In what ways are catering on board aircraft, trains and ships different to each other? What are the reasons for this?

CHAPTER 18

Outside catering

INTRODUCTION

This specialized sector of the food service industry is probably one of the most difficult to operate successfully and one of the most speculative. Unfortunately it is extremely difficult to estimate the size and turnover of this sector, since by the very nature of things outside catering is not a permanent operation. The kind of events vary from garden parties for just a few people, up to a few thousand at royal garden parties; fêtes and other fund-raising events; exhibitions – either on permanent sites such as the National Exhibition Centre or Olympia, or on a much smaller scale at other temporary events; agricultural and county shows; air shows – such as Farnborough and Biggin Hill; sporting events of all kinds – the British Grand Prix, the Grand National, and so on; private functions – such as wedding receptions, clan gatherings, anniversary parties and other social occasions.

There are few statistics on the size and nature of this sector due to the temporary nature of these events and the type of operator involved in the business. Much of the Standard Industrial Classification is based on information relating to licensed premises, VAT registration or other sources. In this sector, no license is required to operate as an ouside caterer, there are no premises exept possibly a base store and kitchen, and there are many small operators who may not be registered for VAT. Broadly speaking there are three or four major outside caterers who operate throughout the UK – firms such as Searcy, Payne & Gunter, and Ring & Brymer; a number of medium-sized firms with a regional base; and a very large number of small operators.

CUSTOMER DEMAND AND TYPES OF OUTSIDE CATERING

Outside catering can be broadly divided into two main types of function as discussed below.

Contracted functions

In this case, the operator agrees to cater for a specified and guaranteed number of customers. In this respect it is very similar to banqueting, except that instead of providing food and refreshment in a banqueting suite, the setting is likely to be a semi-permanent chalet, as in the case of many of the agricultural and county shows, or a marquee on the lawn for 'one-off' events, such as wedding receptions or garden parties.

Speculative functions

Figure 18.1 *Outdoor catering chalets at Wimbledon tennis tournament*
Source: Hunting Aerofilms Ltd.

The outside caterer in this instance is not assured of any custom, but contracts to provide refreshment on a site for members of the general public attending the event, as in the case of many sporting events. If the attendance at such meetings is high, then the rewards are great, for the caterer can achieve a very high turnover in a very short space of time. But the risks are high too, for attendance is often subject to the vagaries of the weather, to the extent that many outside caterers will insure themselves against losses due to adverse weather conditions affecting business. The relationship, though, is not always adverse. For instance, during tennis matches at Wimbledon, as shown in Figure 18.1, breaks due to rain or bad light increase food and drink sales.

A major source of demand is known as 'corporate hospitality'. Many companies invite their stakeholders to events as part of their marketing effort. In the case of customers such hospitality is effective promotion and public relations; for employees it may be part of an incentive package; for suppliers it is largely public relations; and so on. Until recently most corporate hospitality was at spectator events. The firm would hire a box or marquee at a major sporting event and provide meals and drinks before, during and after the event. For instance, the National Westminster Bank, sponsors of the one-day cricket competition, have a large marquee for invited guests when the final is held at Lord's Cricket ground. In 1993, the cost of attending the British Grand Prix or a five nations rugby match at Cardiff Arms Park was nearly £400 per person per day. Increasingly, firms are devising participative events in which the invited guests are able to take an active part. Such events may include rally driving, parachuting, paintballing or golf. For instance, Viceroys, based in Kent, offer 'action experiences' which include clay pigeon shooting, quad bikes, dune buggies, and war games.

Such is the size and scale of these activities, in 1988 the Corporate Hospitality Association was formed in the UK. Members of the association are of three different types. First, there are principal suppliers, who are often outside catering firms, or the venue at which an event is taking place, such as Wembley Stadium or Alton Towers. They sell corporate hospitality packages which might include parking, meals, drinks and entrance tickets for an all-inclusive price. Second, there are agents who buy hospitality from such suppliers and sell it to their customers, sometimes having added value to the package by including guest speakers, celebrity guests, flowers, and other ancillaries. Such agents may be able to negotiate discounts with suppliers due to their 'bulk' purchase of hospitality. Third, there are brokers who are hired by clients to find suitable hospitality packages. They purchase these, often on a commission basis, from suppliers or agents. Some operators may be both supplier and agent, or agent and broker. In 1990, the principal firms in the corporate hospitality business were Keith Prowse, Cavendish, and Mike Burton (agents/brokers); and Payne & Gunter and Ring & Brymer (suppliers/agents), with an estimated annual turnover of £500 million.

During the 1980s, corporate hospitality had a 'bad press'. For instance, an article in *Management Today* refers to 'send-it-to-Ascot-and-bugger-the-expense mode of most British corporate entertainers'. This and the recession of the early 1990s and the Gulf War caused purchasers to modify their demands and select alternatives to spectator-based events. The BMSL Survey of 1990 had predicted strong growth in the market which did not materialize. In 1991 business was down by about 30 per cent. Keith Prowse who had been the market leader with £10 million turnover, nearly twice that of its nearest competitor, collapsed due to cash flow problems.

OUTSIDE CATERING OPERATORS

Just as there are two main types of catering in this sector, so there are also two types of caterer engaged in this business.

Professional outside catering firms

These range from sole traders with their mobile ice-cream vans or hot-dog stall up to very large firms. The larger firms are very much specialists, with a great deal of experience. Such firms do not only cater for the functions noted above, but also undertake catering for firms and organizations on the clients' premises, providing food and refreshment at meetings, seminars and conferences. This type of catering helps to even out the somewhat seasonal nature of their business, as true outside catering is obviously only undertaken in the summer months in most cases. Such specialist outside caterers operate very much like any other type of caterer. They have a management team in charge of sales, operations, personnel and administration, which forms a nucleus of permanent staff, fully trained and familiar with the operating standards and organization of the firm. In addition they employ as many part-time staff as they require for a particular function, since it is not economic to employ waiting staff permanently due to the fluctuating nature of the business. None the less, the part-time staff, more often than not, have regularly worked for the firm at the same annual events year after year. It is usual for full-time employees to fill the key personnel roles such as control clerks, chalet managers, chefs and storekeepers, while the part-time staff work under their supervision.

But there are also a very large number of small operators. One study (Cappell, 1993) has looked at small businesses in this sector in Sussex. Eighty-three caterers were identified, with nearly every town of a significant size having at least one operator. Nearly three quarters of these were sole traders and one-fifth were partnerships, and over 90 per cent employed less than ten full-time staff. Among this sample, over 40 per cent had no catering qualifications and a further 20 per cent had only gained such qualifications after setting up the business. Many of these businesses are operated from home and the most significant market served was wedding receptions.

Non-specialist outside caterers

Outside catering is often undertaken by hoteliers, restaurateurs and others who are not regularly in the business of catering outdoors. In some cases they are very successful, but there are pitfalls awaiting the unwary. Such caterers are usually prompted to take on outside functions for two reasons. First, they are aware that the rewards for success are high; and second, because regular clients of their hotel or restaurant specially request them to 'do' the local fête or a daughter's wedding reception. The pitfalls are twofold. In attempting to cater elsewhere, the regular business is deprived of key personnel and equipment which results in a lowering of the hotel or restaurant's standards to the dissatisfaction of customers. Likewise, due to a lack of trained staff, inexperience in outdoor catering, shortages of equipment, and so on, the quality, presentation and service of the food is not up to the standards expected by the client, who expects the restaurateur to be as successful on the back lawn as in his or her own restaurant.

OPERATIONAL ISSUES IN OUTSIDE CATERING

There are problems associated with outside catering that are specific to this particular sector of the industry. On permanent or semi-permanent sites some or all of the *essential services* are plumbed in, i.e. sanitation, running hot and cold water, electricity and gas. But more often than not, cooking has to be done on Calor-gas stoves, water transported from a distance and lighting provided by gas or paraffin lamps (although the light is not such a serious problem as most outdoor functions are held in the longer summer evenings).

In view of the above and the sometimes primitive accommodation, it is extremely difficult for the outside caterer to meet the *hygiene* regulations. In addition, many semi-permanent sites are subject to regulations, conditions and specific requirements laid down by the local health authority's sanitary department. The outside caterer must ensure that the storage of foodstuffs, cleaning and washing of kitchen and service equipment, practices and activities of staff are all of the highest standard; not just because at all special events (like the Farnborough Air Show or Royal Ascot week) health inspectors visit all the catering units on site, but because the good name and reputation of the firm depends upon the quality of the food and service that it provides.

Security is a major headache for the outside caterer. Foodstuffs, cellar stocks and equipment all have to be stored often in only canvas marquees or tents that are extremely difficult to make secure. At the same time, it is necessary to hold relatively high stocks of everything as the caterer is usually miles from base and would not have the time or opportunity to leave the site to replenish stocks or to provide for some unforeseen eventuality. Thus theft and pilferage are not unknown. The public attends the larger events in its thousands, so that inevitably there are dishonest elements who will take advantage of the crowds and circumstances to remove anything that is not secure. At the same time, in order to staff the event, caterers have no option but to employ part-time and casual staff about whom they know very little. Such staff may not physically steal items from the site, but they many consume food and drink while at work or break equipment due to malpractice, both of which will affect caterers' profits.

Apart from the security problem, two aspects of *staffing* are problematic. First, it may be extremely difficult to obtain the required numbers of staff and second, staff may require some training. At an event like the Farnborough Air Show, several thousand staff are required for a period of nine days. Usually, firms have well-established links with casual staff and they can find enough staff from such contacts, but for the larger events they employ housewives and students, particularly those studying hotel and catering subjects. This may necessitate bringing the staff in on the day before the event or some hours before it starts to brief them fully on the style of the operation and train them up to the required level of service.

Finally, acts of God, a term borrowed from the insurance companies, adequately describes the unforeseen and unpleasant thing that can befall the outside caterer. The most obvious factor is the weather. In the UK one tends to think of torrential rain, but very hot weather can have as much impact, placing an enormous strain on coolers and portable refrigerators and making it very difficult to serve the type of food demanded by the consumer, namely crisp salads, ice cream and cool drinks. There is also the problem of insects, particularly in the summer months. Flies and wasps not only increase the risk of contamination by cross-infection, but also are extremely unsightly around beautifully presented foodstuffs or circling the heads of hot, thirsty customers and may also upset staff trying to prepare or serve food.

OPERATIONAL ASPECTS

Generally speaking, the prices of food and refreshments at outside catering functions are higher than those usually charged in regular outlets such as public houses and restaurants.

The reason for this higher pricing policy is the need to cover the additional costs of catering outdoors. Such costs include the following.

- *Marquees* Although some catering firms may own their own tentage, usually it has to be hired from firms specializing in this area. The cost of this may be borne directly by the client or it may have to be passed on to the customer through prices.

- *Transportation* All foodstuffs, beverages and equipment have to be transported to the site either in the firm's own vans or in hired transportation so there are the running costs of petrol, drivers' wages and hire charges and the possible capital costs of depreciation, insurance, and so on, to take into account.

- *Fuel* Where the caterer has to provide his or her own fuel for the operation, particularly for cooking, the costs of this may prove to be more expensive than usual.

- *Equipment* The caterer must take great care to ensure the safe transportation of equipment, particularly crockery and glassware, that may have a value of several hundred pounds even for a relatively small function. This may require the use of special packing cases and boxes designed for such purposes which add to the cost. But in addition, whatever the equipment is packed in, staff are involved in the considerable task of packing and unpacking on site and in stocktaking to assess losses and breakages.

- *Insurance* Many outside caterers have the additional cost of insurance against unforeseen events, in addition to the normal insurance costs related to equipment and employees' protection. It is likely that the premiums are higher for outside caterers than for those who operate under normal circumstances.

- *Depreciation* Large sums of money are tied up by the large stocks of equipment needed for peak-season business.

- *Losses* Finally, caterers will probably find that despite all the care they have taken, they will still have relatively high losses of equipment due to breakages, misuse and pilferage; certainly far more than on a secure site. Such losses, of course, have to be passed on to the customer.

Due to the very wide range of catering events that may be undertaken and the wide variety of firms engaged in the business, no detailed analysis of operating procedures can be given.

In many respects an outside catering function is no different from a 'banquet' function. Full details of the client's requirements should be taken and in addition the caterer should visit the site to establish means of getting to and from the site and how close transport can get to the unit before, during and after the event; services available on site and requirements with regard to power supplies, portable generators and gas bottles; size of floor area and storage space in both preparation and service areas in order to plan the siting of cooking equipment, tables and chairs, buffet tables and service points; availability of premises before the event for the setting up of equipment and mise-en-place, and after the event to close down and remove equipment; levels of stock that will be required and can be stored securely on site, and the provision of security personnel should they need to be left overnight; and other security arrangements concerning the admission of catering staff and personnel to the site during the event.

During the function itself the preparation and provision of food at outside catering events may be carried out in three basic ways. All food can be centrally prepared and sent out to be re-heated and dressed on flats or plates on site; all food can be prepared and served on site; or a combination of the two. There is no doubt that there are sound reasons for using a central kitchen or commissary. Standards of food are maintained since the cooking of food is either carried out or monitored by the firm's permanent staff. Wastage may be reduced due to bulk production. Centrally prepared dishes may be more impressive than it may be possible to prepare on site. Stricter control of foodstuffs is made possible. Storage of raw materials is eliminated on site. Less equipment is required on site. Staffing levels on site can be reduced and fewer skilled personnel are required there.

The disadvantages of a central kitchen are the degree of organization required to ensure that all the outside units receive the food that they require; difficulties associated with transporting prepared foods safely; problems of re-heating or re-constituting dishes on site, with all the possible dangers of contamination; staff on site may not have the experience or know-how to cope with any of the problems that may arise; there is little or no chance of food being returned if too much is allocated, despite strict supervision. Thus, there can be no doubt that it requires a great deal of skill and expertise to organize an outdoor catering event successfully and achieve a profit.

A typical example of a large-scale outside catering event is the Farnborough Air Show, which is held every two years. It is a multi-million pound venture attended by all the major aerospace manufacturers and aviation firms, who exhibit their hardware in the exhibition halls. They also entertain their clients and personnel in chalets arranged in rows overlooking the runway to give the best possible view of the air show itself. These chalets are semi-permanent in that supply roads, concrete bases and essential services, such as sanitation and water are in situ. But the chalets themselves are only erected for the show and are essentially marquees and tenting fixed to scaffold poles, although the client firms renting them go to considerable trouble to make their interiors as plush and comfortable as possible as illustrated in Figure 18.2. A large catering firm at the show may be catering for over 40 different companies, ranging from one chalet unit up to the largest of the show, comprising seven chalet units joined together, from a central compound on site. For purposes of administration and control, chalets would be divided into zones of approximately equal size, with a zone manager acting as trouble-shooter for the five or six chalets under his control. Likewise, vans and drivers would be allocated to carry all stores and provisions for each zone from a central compound. Both zone managers and drivers could be equipped with short-wave radios to keep in constant touch with each other and the compound as telephone lines were limited and always busy. The compound, built primarily for security purposes, contains all administrative offices, the stores, cellar, linen 'room' and staff canteen. It is likely to be staffed 24 hours a day for the entire eight days of the show by full-time employees of the company and provides back-up services in all areas such as staffing, training, hygiene, public relations, and so on. Each chalet has its own manager in charge of the unit. Each manager is fully briefed before the show and given a dossier containing all the information he or she may require, including names and telephone numbers of key personnel at the compound, notes on administrative procedures, stock control and staffing, security procedures, general hints on staff training, Calor-gas safety instructions, copy of the occasional licence granted for the sale of intoxicating liquor in the chalet, function sheet and menus, and so on. In most cases menus have been determined in advance in consultation with the client, so food would be issued each day according to the specification. Some items could be blast-frozen at a central commissary off-site, others prepared in the compound, but it is left to the chefs in each chalet to put the finishing touches to the dishes and to present them attractively. Liquor stores have likewise been predetermined for the chalet's bar, with enough stock to last three or four days to minimize the movement and requisitioning of new stock. Most clients dispense their refreshments free of charge (although they are careful to control access to the chalet so that only bona fide guests are entertained) so that bar stocks are provided on a sale or return basis. Equipment is delivered to each chalet on the day before the show opens and checked against a stock sheet. It is returned on the last day, again after a stock check, so that breakages and losses can be calculated. Staffing for a typical chalet serving 100 customers a day, for morning coffee, lunch and afternoon tea, might comprise one chalet manager, two chefs, two bar stewards, six waiting staff and two kitchen porters.

During the course of the show, the large outside catering firm could be responsible for the service of tens of thousands of meals and employ many hundreds of staff, most of whom are working for them on a part-time basis and travelling up to 60 miles (96 kilometres) each day to get there. Every member of staff has to be provided with a uniform and passes to get into the show, and they have to be directed to a particular chalet and eventually paid at the end of it all. Chalet managers ae responsible for the standards and performance of staff and are given guidelines concerning this.

CURRENT AND FUTURE TRENDS

The 2000 Millennium celebrations did not attract as much attention as originally expected, as clients believed the period would be too busy or too expensive. Keynote suggests that an increase in marketing promotion should be undertaken to reassure clients. Demands from clients have also increased resulting in only the largest companies being able to meet all demands. The future (Keynote, 2000a) could see a higher level of concentration in the industry as the less competitive firms will be forced out of the market.

Market growth is expected as major venues are increasing their corporate hospitality capacities. However it is estimated that prices for high profile sports events will dramatically increase. Keynote estimates events such as Wimbledon Tennis Championships are subject to a 35 per cent price increase per year between 1997 and 2000.

Figure 18.2 *Chalet interior at major event*
Source: Ferranti plc at Farnborough Air Show)

CONCLUSION

Outside catering is a specialized sector of the food service industry covering a wide range of functions and events. Although the Farnborough example highlights an event much larger than most outside catering events, it illustrates the essential point – it is a risky business that requires a great deal of forethought and planning, down to the last detail with regard to all aspects of the operation. And once the function is under way, it is essential to control very closely the movement of stocks and performance of staff, for without strict control the potential profit from an outside catering function may not be realized. In many respects this type of catering provides a real challenge to the professional caterer and a great deal of his job satisfaction is to be gained from the diversity of operations and difficulties surmounted.

SUMMARY

This sector of the hospitality industry is unusual in that it typically takes place in marquees or temporary structures at a wide variety of events, such as trade shows, sports events, social gathering and family celebrations. This creates some special challenges for managers who provide foodservice in this context. Although there are some large operators, such as Letherby & Christopher (part of the Compass Group) who contract to provide foodservice at major events, there are also many small and local operators.

QUESTIONS

What role can central production units and cook–chill play in the provision of outdoor catering? What are the problems with the use of this system?

REFERENCES

Acheson, D. and Wicking, N. (1992) 'Fast-food Franchising and Finance', in S. Ball (ed.) *Fast Food Operations and their Management*, Cheltenham: Stanley Thornes.

Angelo, R. M. and Vladimir, A. N. (1994) *Hospitality Today, An Introduction*, Chicago: Educational Institute of the American Hotel and Hotel Association, p. 125.

Armistead, C. (1985) 'Introduction to Service Operations', in C. A. Voss *et al.* (eds) *Operations Management in Service Industries and the Public Sector*, Chichester: John Wiley.

Armstrong, J., O'Sulivan, K. and Turner, M. (1980) *The Housebound Elderly – Technical Innovations in Foodservice*, Huddersfield: Huddersfield Polytechnic.

Audit Commission, (2000) *The Way to go Home: Rehabilitation and Remedial Services for Older People*, London: The Stationery Office.

Automobile Association (2000) AA Guide.

Baker, J. (1994) 'Expanding Budgets', *Hospitality*, December, 17–19.

Ball, S. D. (1992a) 'Understanding Fast-food Operations', in S. Ball (ed.) *Fast Food Operations and their Management'*, Cheltenham: Stanley Thornes.

Ball, S. D. (1992b) 'Fast-food Technology and Systems of Operation', in S. Ball (ed.) *Fast Food Operations and their Management,* Cheltenham: Stanley Thornes.

Ball, S. D. (1993) Productivity and Productivity Management within Fast Food Chains – A Case Study of Wimpy International, MPhil Thesis, Huddersfield University.

Ball, S., Jones, P. Kirk, D. and Lockwood, A. (2002) *Hospitality Operating Systems*, London: Continuum.

BMRB International (1992) *Target Group Index*, London: BMRB.

Boer, A. (1992) 'The Banking Sector and Small Firm Failure in the UK Hotel and Catering Industry', International Journal of Contemporary Hospitality Management, 4:2, 13–16.

Brewers' Society (1999a) *The Public's Attitudes Towards Pubs*, MORI, The Brewers' Society, November.

Brewers' Society (1999b) *Pubs the 'Best of British'*, The Brewers' Society.

British Dietetic Association (1980) 'School Meals, Policy Statement', *Journal of Human Nutrition*, 34, 316–18.

British Hospitality Association (BHA) (1994) *Contract Catering Services*, London: Market-power.

British Hospitality Association (BHA) (1995) *Contract Catering Survey*, London: British Hospitality Association.

British Hospitality Association (BHA) (2000) *British Hospitality: Trends and Statistics 2000*, London: British Hospitality Association.

British Hospitality Association (BHA) (2001) *Contract Catering Survey*, London: BHA.

Burkart, A. and Medlik, S. (1981) *Tourism Past, Present and Future*, London: Heinemann.

Butler, D. (1992) 'Picking the Spot', *Management Today*, January, 61–2.

Campbell-Smith, G. (1967) *Marketing the Meal Experience*, Guildford: University of Surrey.

Cannon, T. (1980) *Basic Marketing*, Eastbourne: Hold, Rinehart & Winston.

Cappell, J. (1993) *Outside Catering in Sussex*, unpublished dissertation, University of Brighton.

Capper, W. B. (ed.) (1866) *Licensed Houses and their Management*, London: Caxton Publishing.

Central Statistical Office (1995) *Social Trends 25*, London: Government Statistical Service, HMSO.

Chartered Institute of Public Finance and Accountancy (1986) *Education Statistics*, London: CIPFA.

Chase, R. R. (1981) 'The Customer Contact Approach to Services: Theoretical Bases and Practical Extensions', *Operations Research*, 29:4.

Committee on Medical Aspects of Food Policy (1989) *Sub-committee on Nutritional Surveillance: The Diets of British Schoolchildren*, London: HMSO.

Cousins, J. and Lillicrap, D. (1999) *Food and Beverage Service*, London: Edward Arnold.

Craymer, J. (1994) 'Computer Commuters', *Business Travel World*, 20–2.

Cumming, M. and Hill, B. (1992) 'Competitive Tendering for National Health Service Domestic Service', in R. Teare (ed.) *Managing Projects in Hospitality Organisations*, London: Cassell.

D'Ambrosio, R. (1993) 'Key Upgrade by Mount Charlotte Thistle', *Business Travel News*, 5 April, p. 43.

Davis, S. and Meyer, C. (1988) *BLUR the Speed of Change in the Connected Economy*, Oxford: Capstone Publishing.

Day, C. (1992) 'More Guests Stay in Budget'; *Estates Gazette*, 23 May.

Department of Education and Science (1979) *Annual Report*, London: HMSO.

Department of Health (1994) *Nutritional Aspects of Cardiovascular Disease*, London: HMSO.

Dichter, E. (1954) '*A Psychological Study of the Hospital–Patient Relationship*', The Modern Hospital, 83: November.

Economist Intelligence Unit (1991) *Competitive Strategies for the International Hotel Industry Report No. 1180*, March, London: Economist Intelligence Unit

Edwards, M. (1993) 'Playing the Name Game', *Caterer & Hotelkeeper*, 4 February, 36–8.

Foodservice Intelligence (2000).

Gabriel, Y. (1988) *Working Lives in Catering*, London: Routledge & Kegan Paul.

Gill, T. (1999) 'Food for Thought', *Airline Business*, 75–6.

Gledhill, R. (1993) 'The NHS Carve-up', *Caterer & Hotelkeeper*, 19 August, 30–3.

Go, F. and Welch, P. (1991) *Competitive Strategies for the International Hotel Industry*, London: Economic Intelligence Unit.

Goldman, K. (1993) 'Concept Selection for Independent Restaurants', *Cornell HRA Quarterly*, 34:6 (December), 59–72.

Goodall, B. (1991) 'Understanding Holiday Choice', in Cooper, C. P. (ed.) Tourism, Recreation and Hospitality Management, Vol. 3, London: Belhaven Press.

Harrison, L. and Johnson, K. (1992) *UK Hotels Group Directory, Hotel and Catering Research Centre, University of Huddersfield*, London: Cassell.

Hegarty, C. (1993) *European Golfer Spending*, Golf Research Group.

Hemmington, N. R. and Chapman, F. (1992) 'Planning in a Regional School Meals Service', in R. Teare (ed.) *Managing Projects in Hospitality Organisations*, London: Cassell.

Hempels (1979) *Caterer & Hotelkeeper*, 8 February.

Herne, S. (1994) 'Catering for Institutionalised Elderly People: The Care Home's Dilemma', *British Food Journal*, 96:9, 3–8.

Heskett, J. L. (1986) *Managing in the Service Economy*, Harvard Business School Press.

Heskett, J. L. (1990) *Service Breakthroughs: Changing the Rules of the Game*, New York: Free Press.

H M Government (2000) *The NHS Plan: A Plan for Investment. A Plan for Reform*, London: Stationery Office.

HtF (1999) *Research Report*, London: HtF.

Industrial Society, The and Touche Ross (1994) *A Survey of Catering Policies, Costs and Performance*, London: Industrial Society.

International Hotel & Restaurant Association (IH&RA) (2000) *Leading Hospitality in the Age of Excellence 1995–2005*, IH&RA.

JHIC (2000) *Leisure in the New Millennium*, London: Joint Hospitality Industry Congress.

Johnson, R. (1988) 'A Framework for Developing a Quality Strategy in a Customer Processing Operation', *International Journal of Quality and Reliability Management*, 4.

Joint Hospitality Industry Congress (1995) *Catering Guide to Compliance with the Food Safety (General Food Hygiene) Regulations 1995*, JHIC.

Jones, P. (1988) 'The Impact of Trends in Service Operations on Foodservice Delivery Systems', *International Journal of Operations and Production Management*, 8:7, 23–30.

Jones, P. (1988) *Foodservice Operations*, London: Cassell.

Jones, P. (1989) *Food Service Operations*, 2nd Edn, London: Cassell.

Jones, P. (1996) 'Operational Issues and Trends in the Hospitality Industry', *International Journal of Hospitality Management*, 18:4, 427–42.

Jones, P. (2001) 'Critical Success Factors in Small Hospitality Businesses', *Hospitality in Focus*, 3, 8–12.

Jones, P. and Huselin, A. (1980) 'Thinking About Catering Systems', *International Journal of Operations and Production Management* 10:8. 42–52.

Jordan, F. (1992) *A Research Project Investigating the Relationship Between Contract Catering and the Residential Care Homes Sector*, Cheltenham: Cheltenham & Gloucester College of Higher Education.

Keynote Report (1994) *The Restaurant Industry*, London: Keynote Publications.

Keynote Report (2000a) *A Market Sector Overview: Hotels*, 15th Edn, Hampton: Keynote Publications.

Keynote Report (2000b) *UK Catering Market*, London: Keynote Publications.

Keynote Report (2000c) *The Restaurant Industry*, London: Keynote Publications.

Keynote Report (2000d) Fast Food and Take Away Outlets, London: Keynote Publications.

Kirk, D. (1995) 'Hard and Soft Systems: A Common Paradigm for Operations Management?', *International Journal of Contemporary Hospitality Management*, 7:5, 13–16.

Kleinwort Benson Securities (1991) *Quoted Hotel Companies: The World Markets 5th Annual Review*, London: Kleinwort Benson Securities.

Lang, S. (1994) 'The Pub and Social Trends', The Pub in 2000 Conference, November, London.

Lawson, J. (1992) 'Nutritional and Environmental Issues Confronting Fast-food Operations', in S. Ball (ed.) *Fast Food Operations and their Management*, Cheltenham: Stanley Thornes.

Levitt, T. (1972) 'Production Line Approach to Service', *Harvard Business Review*, September/October.

Levitt, T. (1976) 'The Industrialisation of Service', *Harvard Business Review*, September/October.

Lillicrap, D. (1971) *Food and Beverage Service*, London: Edward Arnold.

Lobstein, T. (1988) *Fast Food Facts*, London: Camden Press.

McDermid, K. (1989) 'In-house Bids Win Contracts', *Caterer and Hotelkeeper*, 18 May, 14.

McKenzie, J. (1979) The Eating Environment, in G. Glew (ed.) *Advances in Catering Technology*, Applied Science Publishers.

Medlik, R. (1978) *Profile of the Hotel and Catering Industry*, London: Heinemann.

Medlik, R. (1981) *Profile of the Hotel and Catering Industry*, 2nd edn, London: Heinemann.

Medlik, S. (1994) *The Business of Hotels*, Oxford: Butterworth Heinemann.

Melaniphy, J. C. (1992) *Restaurant and Fast Food Site Selection*, New York: John Wiley.

Milne, T. and Thomson, M. (1988) *Patterns of Successful Business Start Up*, Sterling: University of Sterling.

Mintel Marketing Intelligence (1992a) 'Britain Eating Out', *Mintel Drink Intelligence Report*, London: Mintel Publications.

Mintel Marketing Intelligence (1992b) 'Roadside Catering' in *Leisure Intelligence Report*, Vol. 2, London: Mintel Publications.

Mintel Marketing Intelligence (1994) 'British on Holiday at Home' in *Leisure Intelligence Report*, Vol. 1, pp. 1–26. Mintel Publications.

Mintel Marketing Intelligence (1998) *Pub Catering*, London: Mintel Publications.

Moncrieff, M. (1947) *The Small Hotel*, London: Blandford Press.

Muller, C. C. and Woods, R. H. (1994) 'An Expanded Restaurant Typology', *Cornell HRA Quarterly*, June, 33–45.

Newell, M. (1965) *Mood and Atmosphere in Restaurants*, London: Barrie & Rockcliff.

NHS Estates (2001) *National Standards of Cleanliness for the NHS*, London: NHS Estates.

O'Connor, J. (1993) 'A Review of Dining Out Patterns', *International Journal of Contemporary Hospitality Management*, 5:5, 3–9.

Pickworth, J. R. (1988) 'Service Delivery Systems in the Foodservice Industry', *International Journal of Hospitality Management*, 7:1, 43–62.

Pilling, M. (2001) 'Food for Thought', *Airline Business*, 48–50.

Powers, T. F. (1985) 'A Restaurant Typology', *Cornell HRA Quarterly*, June, 33–45.

Projection 2000 (1991) *Budget Hotels*.

Quest, M. (ed.) (1999) *British Hospitality: Trends and Statistics*, London: British Hospitality Association.

Quest, M. (ed.) (2001) *British Hospitality: Trends and Statistics*, London: British Hospitality Association.

Ritzer, G. (1996) *The McDonaldization of Society*, Thousand Oaks CA: Pine Ridge Press.

Romano, M. (1993) 'Airline Food: Sky High', *Restaurant Business* 92.15, 66, 69.

Romano, M. (1994) 'Who's Feeding Them Now?' Restaurant Business 93.12, 62, 64, 69.

Roper, A. and Carmouche, R. (1989) 'Budget Hotels – A Case of Mistaken Identity?', *International Journal of Contemporary Hospitality Management*, 1:1, 25–31.

Schlosser, S. E. (2000) *Fast Food Nation*, London: Penguin Books.

Schmennen, R. and Swink (1988) 'On Theory in Operations Management', *Journal of Operations Management*, 17, 97–113.

Sharma, D. D. (1984) 'Management Contracts and International Marketing in Industrial Goods, in E. Mayhack (ed.) *International Marketing Management*, New York: Praeger.

Silverstone, R. (1993) 'Whiter Fast Food?', *International Journal of Contemporary Hospitality Management*, 5:1, 1–3.

Tarpey, D. (1993a) 'Looking Back at 1943', *Caterer & Hotelkeeper*, 4 March, 40–4.

Tarpey, D. (1993b) 'Looking Back at 1968', *Caterer & Hotelkeeper*, 4 February, 30–4.

Tarpey, D. (1994) 'Food in the Fast Lane', *Caterer & Hotelkeeper*, 3 November, 68–9.

Tarpey, D. and Walsh, D. (1993) 'Quality, Service and Rising Costs', *Caterer & Hotelkeeper*, 12 August, pp. 6–8.

Taylor, D (1977) *Fortune, Fame and Folly*, London: IPC Business Press.

Taylor, D. and Bush, D. (1974) *The Golden Age of British Hotels*, London: Northwood.

Thompson, D. (ed.) (1993) *The Oxford Dictionary of Current English*, Oxford: Oxford University Press.

Thompson, R. (1994) '*Fast Food's Chain Reaction*', Independent on Sunday, 1 May, p.3.

Thompson, J. D., Hartman, J. and Pelletier, R. J. (1960) 'Two Types of Tray Service Studied Side by Side in Hospitals', *JAHA*, 34: 1 February, 82–88.

Tilston, C. H., Gregson, K., Neale, R. J. and Tyne, C. (1992) 'Meals-on-wheels Service in Leicester: A Marketing Study', *British Food Journal*, 94:2, 29–36.

TRI Hospitality Consulting (2000) *UK Hotel Industry 2000*, London: TRI.

Webster, J. (1994) 'Truckers Take a Break', *Caterer & Hotelkeeper*, 29 September, 60–1.

Webster, J. (1995) 'An Inside Job', *Caterer & Hotelkeeper*, 9 February, 70–1.

Weinstock, J. (1994) 'New Hotel Strategy: Offer More for Less', *Restaurants & Institutions*, 15 July, pp. 68–72.

West, A. (1992) 'Fast-food Marketing', in S. Ball (ed.) *Fast-Food Operations and their Management*, Cheltenham: Stanley Thornes.

Whitehall (1981) in P. Jones (ed.) *Foodservice Operations*, Eastbourne: Holt, Rinehart & Winston.

Woodman, J., Clark, J. and Rimmington, M. (1996) 'Productivity in Hospital Kitchens', *The Service Industries Journal*, 16:3, 368–78.

INDEX

accommodation experience   25, 30–1, 41–3, 45

accommodation operations   13–14, 31–2,   37–9, 69, 84, 98–9

Accor   2, 28, 34, 77

acoustics   137

airline catering   19, 141, 143, 268–74

air conditioning   136

air travel   85

airport hotels   48, 53–5

all-suite hotels   57

assets   40

average spend   50, 92, 153, 182, 227, 265

banqueting   52, 165, 166, 167, 289

Bass   2, 34, 152

bed spaces   30, 36, 89, 103, 107, 119

Beefeater   149, 153

Better Hospital Food Initiative   260–2

billing   39

'blur'   13–14, 139, 149

boutique hotel   41–3

branding   44, 54, 82, 169, 188, 235

breakfast   57, 171

Brewers Society   11, 190

British Airways   269

British Hospitality Association (BHA)   1, 11, 36, 225

British Tourist Authority (BTA)   225

budget hotels   50, 52, 74–6

buffet service   176

Burger King   2, 203, 204

business travellers   27–9, 47, 49, 54, 78, 84

cafeterias   130, 133, 150, 228, 253

Campanile   48, 79, 83

care homes   240, 262

carvery   152, 168

Center Parcs   60, 61

central production kitchens   247–9, 271, 290

central reservation systems   40, 43, 50, 55, 81, 84, 85

cleanliness   110–11, 113, 134

coffee shops   204, 205

community care   107

Compass   2, 72, 79, 153

competition   2, 83, 242

compulsory competitive tendering   103, 240, 241

computerised reservation systems   35, 40, 50, 55

conference facilities   48, 52, 54, 57

conference market   51–3, 57

consortia   40, 50

consumer choice   130

consumer demand   25, 50, 92, 103

consumer spending   36, 49, 131, 152, 156, 158

convenience stores   203–4

cook-chill   176, 240, 250, 257, 272

cook-freeze   142, 250

corporate hospitality   285–6

country-house hotels   49, 60

country resort hotels   60–5, 71

cruise ship catering   281

décor   54, 135

decoupling   142

demographic trends   28, 32–4, 243

design   41–3

De Vere hotels   2

diamond hotel rating scheme   88

diet   6, 19–20, 145, 216

disintermediation   40–1

disposables   233

drive-through   147

employment   7–8, 37–8, 91, 140, 157, 192, 206

environment   43, 93

ethnic restaurants   152, 153, 162, 202

Eurostar   275

family restaurants

family service   142, 161, 175

fast food   134, 143, 147, 201–5

ferry catering

Fish!   157

fish and chip shops   133, 147, 202

flight catering   141

food production systems   235

food service operations   13, 14, 134, 139, 141, 147, 166, 176

Forte   2, 76, 79

franchising   85, 152, 203

furnishings   27, 105, 136

fusion cuisine   164

299